BAGEHOT ON SPONSORSHIP, MERCHANDISING AND ENDORSEMENT
Edited and updated by Hayley Stallard

AUSTRALIA
LBC Information Services
Sydney

CANADA and USA
Carswell
Toronto ● Ontario

NEW ZEALAND
Brooker's
Auckland

SINGAPORE and MALAYSIA
Thomson Information (S.E. Asia)
Singapore

BAGEHOT ON SPONSORSHIP, MERCHANDISING AND ENDORSEMENT
Edited and updated by Hayley Stallard

HAYLEY STALLARD (Ed.)

LONDON
SWEET & MAXWELL
1998

Published in 1998 by
Sweet & Maxwell of
100 Avenue Road, Swiss Cottage, London NW3 3PF
(http://www.smlawpub.co.uk)
Typeset by LBJ Typesetting Ltd of Kingsclere
Printed and bound by MPG Books Ltd, Bodmin, Cornwall

No natural forests were destroyed to make this product;
only farmed timber was used and replanted

British Library Cataloguing in Publication Data

A CIP catalogue record for this book
is available from the British Library

ISBN 0421–616–504

PREFACE

I am not aware of another book on the market which provides such a practical guide to the "ins and outs" of sponsorship as Richard Bagehot's. His invaluable experience and grasp of the issues that can impact on a sponsorship campaign give the reader a head-start in negotiation of the contract. The pitfalls are highlighted with an explanation of the options and likely consequences of "losing" on any particular point.

Since the first edition was published in 1989, significant changes have taken place, both in growth of the global sponsorship industry and in the law. Personalities are now able to command huge sums of money and are more aware of their rights. This second edition takes into account the changes following the introduction of the Trade Marks Act 1994; recent cases on personality rights; the demise of the IBA; the Sponsorship Codes of the ITC; the new rules of the ABSA and Sportsmatch; and new tax rules. In the future we are also likely to see greater harmonisation of the rules across the European Union following its Green Paper on Commercial Communications and the impact of the Tobacco Advertising Directive.

The complexities of sponsorship demand specialist advice from practitioners with relevant working knowledge. This book takes a "broad brush" view to illustrate principles which are important. Whilst certain aspects of sponsorship follow a familiar pattern, there are no regulatory requirements or industry-wide standards governing what can and cannot be done. The intention is to give the reader a greater understanding of how sponsorship works, rather than putting forward views in the form of a master plan.

My thanks go to Karen Earl of Karen Earl Limited, and Mark Abell of Field Fisher Waterhouse, for their valued contributions.

Hayley Stallard
August 1998

CONTENTS

CHAPTER 1

HOW SPONSORSHIP WORKS

CHAPTER 2

SPONSORSHIP CONTRACT NEGOTIATION

CHAPTER 3

SPONSOR'S RIGHTS

CHAPTER 4

SPONSOR'S OBLIGATIONS

CHAPTER 5

OBLIGATIONS OF SPONSORED PARTY

CHAPTER 6

MERCHANDISING

CHAPTER 7

ENDORSEMENT

CHAPTER 8

SPONSORSHIP TAXATION

Tax Table

CHAPTER 9

BASIC CONTRACT POINTS

How Sponsorship Works

1. Introduction

1–01 Sponsorship is a form of marketing whereby the sponsor contributes to, or underwrites, the cost of staging an event, or the cost of a participant in a prestigious event, or the cost of an individual competitor or a team under a periodic agreement, in return for the grant of marketing and promotion rights by the sponsored party. These rights entitle the sponsor to promote the image and products of the sponsor in connection with the event or individual(s) concerned. The primary purpose of sponsorship is to provide financial assistance to a wide range of beneficiaries involved in the worlds of sport, leisure, entertainment and the arts. The commercial spin-off is to enable the sponsor to benefit from the marketing opportunities to be created from its association with the event or individual which it sponsors.

Not all events have a commercial opportunity, such as where a company is supporting a charitable cause with no expectation of any clear promotional benefits in return, or where its support is by way of patronage of the arts.

1–02 Sponsorship possibilities are almost limitless, as there is an almost inexhaustible supply of good causes which need funds to start, to stay in existence, or to develop their potential. Their needs are diverse, as are their capacity to provide their sponsors with a commensurate marketing opportunity. For many sponsors their return is not only calculated in financial terms, but an element of satisfaction is also achieved in helping worthy causes.

Whatever the event or subject being sponsored, the major areas of commercial, legal and financial considerations will still need to be examined, to see if they are applicable for the benefit and protection of both parties. This book refers mostly to limited popular attractions to sponsorship, but some of the details of their structure and operation, in some way, will apply to most other sponsorship deals.

2. Extent of sponsorship

1–03 Sponsorship is very big business, and has expanded into an industry in its own right. It is normally thought of in the context of sport, leisure and the arts, but it extends to charitable, educational and other activities. They cannot all be dealt with in detail, so for illustrative purposes this book refers mainly to sporting events (such as athletics, motor racing or football clubs) and to cultural events (such as opera productions). Between them they will encompass all the normal rights and obligations of sponsorship, and specific examples based on each of them can be applied, or modified to apply, to most other circumstances.

3. Forms of sponsorship

1–04 There is a distinction between sponsorship purely for commercial promotion, and sponsorship intended to assist worthy causes but where the promotional value is reduced. Sponsoring a cultural event, such as the cost of mounting a one-month run of an opera, will have limited promotional opportunities. Helping to defray the ordinary annual cost of running an opera house or other artistic or cultural institution by "buying" individual seated boxes, or paying for other individual prestigious benefits at a premium, is another form of sponsorship. The money is equally useful to the recipient, but the event is not a platform for media advertising. A prominent reference in every production programme as a patron or sponsor, and possibly free advertising in the programme, may be the only public acknowledgment available from the sponsored party for that contribution by the sponsor.

Sponsorship of charitable entities, or promotions to raise money for charitable purposes, such as for education or to help disabled people, may be of a local nature with a limited promotional value, or they may extend nationally, such as to "Comic Relief". This kind of sponsorship is not entered into for purely commercial reasons, in the sense of primarily benefiting the sponsor. If commerciality of the event will boost the sponsored party's income, then any suitable method will be examined.

1–05 Within the academic world, one means of sponsorship is to endow a "Chair" at a college or university for the study of a specific subject. For example, a sponsor may create and endow a new department at a university to research and expound upon a particular theory. The contribution of the sponsor is the provision of the endowment fund, which will have to be adequate for the salary and other research costs of the person appointed to that post, for a reasonable period of time. The college or university will be reluctant to accept such a fund if it is considered to be inadequate, because its continuation may need substantial support from the university's annual budget. The prestige value acquired by the sponsor will be that the Chair will be called, for example, "the [Sponsor] Chair of . . .". That would be good for the image of a sponsor whose products or services are related to that area of research.

Sponsorship includes circumstances where the sponsor is not supporting an independent third party, but is using part of its marketing budget on an unusual expense. An example is where a commercial company buys and runs a race horse, calling it "Product Nag". If the horse is successful, the product name gets wide publicity in areas which would not have otherwise been canvassed by ordinary media exposure or sales promotion campaigns. Running the horse also gives the company an additional reason to entertain people at race meetings. This would be similar to the hospitality facilities which would be available to the sponsor of an established horse race, but would happen more frequently and wherever the company's horse happens to be running.

1–06 Another example is where the company, being interested in a particular sporting or leisure area, creates and funds a new event called the "Company Event". This could be a major exercise, and may be undertaken to highlight and develop the sponsor's market profile, corporate substance and image. Part of the cost may be the creation of a team of experts and providers of facilities and services to design and manage the event. It may well be that in due course the team or venue becomes an essential part of the event, to the extent that they are indispensable, and without which the event could not be staged. At that point the balance of power and decision-making shifts from the company and, to all intents and purposes, the team or venue owner and the company become joint proprietors of the event. It is important for the company, in those circumstances, to have from the outset an agreement with the team clearly setting out the ground rules on what is to happen to the event at the end of the sponsorship period.

The sponsor may provide money, goods or services, or a combination of them, depending on the requirements of the sponsored party. The purpose of sponsorship is twofold. It is a means of promoting the image, reputation and profile of the sponsor, or of its products. It also enables the sponsored party to finance the event, activity or whatever is being sponsored, in a manner which is tax efficient and which is an economical and justifiable use of part of the sponsor's marketing budget.

4. Commercial value of sponsorship

1–07 Sponsorship is not a legal concept, it is purely a commercial marketing route which has the following advantages.

(a) For a sole sponsor there is an exclusivity to the sponsor for the benefit of being associated with the sponsored party and the event. Primary and secondary sponsors get their own levels of exclusivity, as does an official supplier of products. The differences are of only consequential marketable value.

(b) High audience or media exposure events are more marketable than those with a limited public interest or profile, because there is a prestige and public awareness connected with them which is not otherwise available.

(c) The potential marketing exposure for the sponsor, the cost of sponsorship, and the target audience can be more accurately defined and controlled than through ordinary blanket media advertising. The audience may be more limited, being only those who are interested in the event or whose businesses are related to the event activity. But, as they will be paying attention to the event, the sponsorship awareness will be significant.

(d) If the sponsor manufactures a product or provides a service which is connected mainly with sport or the arts, sponsorship of the right nature provides a valuable consumer awareness by associating the event with the product or service. There are major sponsors, such as insurance companies and banks, which get involved in those events, such as football leagues and operas. This gets their names associated with non-partisan events, as every member of the public is a potential customer in some way.

(e) If the business of the sponsor is wholly within sport, such as a tennis racket manufacturer, it will be concentrating its budget and effort where it counts most. That sponsor may be only a division of a larger group of companies, also related to sport, so the whole group benefits.

1–08 There are also potential disadvantages or limitations in the commercial value of sponsorship which must be taken into account, such as:

(a) Even an international status event will not be of interest to every section of the public. This is an important consideration where the sponsor's product or service is of a general nature, such as a major bank.

(b) The sponsored event may be a failure, which would be something outside the control of the sponsor. For example, a football club which was successful last season may not win any games in the sponsored season, and may be relegated to a lower division. No sponsor wants to be associated with a failure. Where the sponsored party is backed for the potential of winning, as opposed to simply happening (such as an opera), the risks (and price) are assessed accordingly.

5. Sponsorship is not investment

1–09   The relationship between a sponsor and the sponsored party is not one of an investor, and it is not a joint venture. These distinctions are important, because of the different legal consequences of being involved in a commercial enterprise. For example:

(a) There are strict rules regulating the ability of any party to advertise publicly for investment funds, which would be wholly impractical for a party looking for sponsorship. Some considerations are:

(i) An event suitable for sponsorship is not a profit-making business in a commercial context. Football clubs make or lose money, but that is for the benefit of developing the club, not for enriching its share-holders. Similarly, athletics events may make a profit, to be used for the sport as a whole. The concept of raising money is not to be confused with the intention of making a gain. Investment is only relevant to a commercial enterprise for the prime purpose of financial gain for the proprietors. Nevertheless, official suppliers of products may recoup, through their franchise on site sales, more than it cost them in sponsorship charges.

(ii) A sponsor provides funds which do not entitle it to any proprietary rights in the event. An investor, on the other hand, intends to acquire a portion of an asset with a value commensurate with the amount invested.

(iii) A sponsor gets no financial return directly from its sponsorship: its return is the benefit of promotional opportunities for as long as it is a sponsor. An investor looks for a financial return out of the prof-itability of the venture. However, there are circumstances in which the sponsor can obtain a financial return on its sponsorship, and perhaps a profit. The sponsor of the making of a television pro-gramme can negotiate the entitlement to a percentage of programme sales income. It is also possible for a sponsor to negotiate the entitlement to a percentage of ticket sales receipts for a major event, such as an outdoor rock concert.

(iv) When a sponsorship agreement ends, so does the interest of the sponsor. An investor's interest in a venture only ends when it disposes of its investment in it.

(b) No sponsor wants to be related to or liable for any aspect of the business or other activities of the sponsored party in connection with running the event.

(c) The sponsored party does not necessarily need the money, and may simply be in the market for the highest bidder that is anxious to associate itself with the event for promotional purposes, and has placed a significant value on that marketing strategy.

1–10   The sponsorship agreement must make the parties' relationship clear, and the means of producing the funding must be consistent with it. The sponsor is not looking for any return on its funding other than the marketing opportunities it makes from it. How the funding is calculated, paid and controlled is dealt with in chapter four.

6. Sponsorship is not a recommendation

1–11   Sponsorship is not to be confused with merchandising or endorsement, but there is a connection which should be considered by a potential sponsor, particularly if it is the sole sponsor or a primary sponsor. Merchandising may be applied as a secondary means of enhancing the sponsor's funding, such as by using the event logo or name on T-shirts or other usual merchandise often used to promote the sponsored party, and to produce an income. Endorsement of a service or product is by an individual who, in consideration of receiving substantial payments, personally recommends and promotes the relevant goods or services, by granting the right to use his name and image to do so. A sponsor does not normally intend to be represented as endorsing or recommending the sponsored party as an active development of its sponsorship.

On the other hand, there is an implicit approval by the sponsor of what the sponsored party stands for and what it is doing that needs funding, otherwise it would not be a sponsor. This might be relevant where the sponsored event is controversial to some people. For example, sponsorship of the U.K. course fishing championships would be against the principles of those who are against such sports, for whatever reason. There may also be organisations in need of sponsorship which would refuse to accept it from a tobacco company, as they are opposed to smoking.

1–12   In sponsorship the payment is made by the sponsor so that its name will be associated with the sponsored party or the event. If the sponsor is a subsidiary sponsor, the primary sponsor has the limelight of publicity and association with the sponsored party, so inevitably any subsidiary sponsor is seen to be aligned with the primary sponsor. There is no form of recommendation, but any conflict of image may reflect adversely on the subsidiary sponsor. Preliminary research into how the subsidiary sponsor can benefit most from its deal, together with a sensible choice of event to sponsor where there is no natural business connection, should make this potential problem academic.

7. Sponsored party's objectives

1–13   The objectives of the sponsored party are to raise funds for the support of its event, and/or to procure the provision of products or services which are needed by the event. If the event is one of a larger scale of similar events, such as one athletics meeting out of those set for the season, the sponsorship may be sought by the governing body of athletics as a continuing effort to keep the body funded.

Achieving the goal of sponsorship attraction, and the funding required, can be difficult for even a well-known prestigious event; nothing is guaranteed. Therefore, so far as it is reasonably possible, the sponsored party has to make the promotional value of the event attractive to the type of sponsor being sought. Even major institutions have limits to their sponsorship budgets, and they consider very carefully how to use them. They exercise a balanced judgment of what is good for the institution, and what should be supported more by way of public service.

1–14   If the event is an established annual event, where traditionally the name of the event contains the brand name of a product of the sponsor, the sponsored party would be more interested in establishing a long-term viable and harmonious commitment by a sponsor, rather than concentrating on maximising one year's support from whatever source on a year-by-year basis.

The objectives of the sponsor and the sponsored party are different, except where the sponsored party is looking for a sponsor which will promote its participation with the event through television and other media advertising, and by other forms of publicity. This gives the sponsored event or party a status and reputation reflected by that of the sponsor.

1–15 The objectives of a sponsored party will depend upon who or what is to be sponsored, but among them will be:

(a) To find a sponsor with the right image and status to project the event accordingly. This will depend on what kind of event it is, and whether it would be preferable to find a sponsor whose business or products are related to the event activity.

(b) To ensure that the sponsor is well capable of funding and supporting the event for at least the initial period of the sponsorship agreement. There are two areas for discussion with the potential sponsor. The first is to ensure that it is fully aware of the whole potential direct and indirect cost in each year of the event. Many sponsors enter into sponsorship projects without having prepared realistic cash-flow and costing requirements, and later discover that the true cost exceeds that which they could afford to pay. The second is to ensure that the sponsor looks at the sponsorship on a reasonably long-term basis, in the absence of any dramatic intervening event.

(c) To ensure that the sponsor is compatible with the context of the event. There are some products which do have, or may in the future have, restrictions placed upon them in respect of TV advertising. This may extend to indirect advertising, such as being prominently displayed on a racing car, athletes' vests or on football arena boards. The sponsored party will have to choose new sponsors carefully for these reasons. A sponsor which is inhibited in any way from making full promotional use of the event may not be the right choice.

(d) To ensure that the basic commitment of the sponsor to the concept of sponsorship is serious, especially where the sponsored party is looking for a long-term supportive relationship. The sponsored party's main obligation is to the benefit and development of the event. Frequent changes of sponsor will not be good for its image, will be disruptive to the event management, and will create confusion where the name of the event contains the sponsor's product name. It may also undeservedly cause potential sponsors to keep clear, as a constant turnover of sponsors creates the impression of conflict or unreliability for the sponsored party.

8. Sponsor's objectives

1–16 In the absence of purely philanthropic motives, such as for an arts event which has no real commercial spin-off, any sponsorship project should be considered by the sponsor as an extension of its overall marketing strategy. What should a potential sponsor be looking for in a sponsorship deal, and how should it decide what to sponsor? Any proposal must be analysed and assessed to see if it fits the sponsor's image, if it can be built upon in lateral advertising, and whether the annual marketing budget will cover it. Essentially the commercial question is whether the sponsorship proposal is perceived as good value for money. Sponsorship is used, for example, to enhance the sponsor as follows:

(a) As a means of launching new products, and keeping up public interest in them during the sponsorship period. If the event is an annual, long-standing one, and if the sponsor's product has been linked with the event for a long time (such as being part of its name), there is created an incalculable added value for the sponsor simply by reason of the long association. If it is a famous sporting event, it becomes part of sporting history, to the point where the sponsor cannot afford to be outbid for the event when its agreement comes up for renewal.

(b) By publicising the fact that the company is the sponsor, and therefore making it known that it has interests outside those of being purely a profit-seeking commercial concern. This creates a different kind of public acceptability not directly related to product purchase, although that is the ultimate objective.

(c) By promoting the sponsor's corporate image in general terms, such as by having its logo identified with the sector of the sponsored activity.

(d) Depending on the event, by obtaining television and press media exposure for its product which it would not be able to purchase elsewhere, or for the same cost. The prime medium is television, and a comparison of the cost of regular TV advertising with the sponsorship cost, which generates the less concentrated but equally effective TV exposure, shows that constant sponsorship reference gets the message home effectively and economically.

9. Preliminary research by sponsor

1–17 A potential sponsor, particularly if it has not previously been involved in sponsorship, should ask itself the following basic questions before proceeding to investigate any deal.

Potential benefit

1–18 Would the sponsor or the sponsor's product benefit from sponsorship, i.e. what are the promotional objectives? The kind of sponsorship chosen will determine whether the benefits have to be achieved in a short period, or whether it allows for long-term planning. For example, if the sponsorship is of a single event, the marketing opportunities are limited. Sales promotion campaigns and advertising based upon the event have a short lifespan, which may not be long enough to make a serious impression. There is then nothing left to build on, as the event rapidly ceases to be newsworthy. The fundamental question is whether the expense of such a concentrated effort for a short life-span event will have worthwhile results.

Some events, such as the Olympic Games and World Cup Football, have a significant period of public interest. They are capable of sustaining a prolonged marketing campaign by the official sponsors during the run-up to the event, and for some time afterwards.

1–19 If the sponsorship is of a football club over a football season, or is for the next three annual stagings of a prestige arts event, in the process of establishing the identity of the sponsor in association with the event, consumer awareness can be developed and product market share can be planned and maintained over a period of time. The overall level of advertising of any product must be maintained, and increased according to market demands, if market share is to be kept in the face of competition. The benefit of sponsorship is that it is another means of advertising.

Choice of sponsorship area

1–20 What would be the best sponsorship area for the product to be identified with, to maximise its promotion potential? If the company's products are related to or used in an area which is familiar with sponsorship, that would be the choice. Obvious examples are sports or leisure-related products. Are there any other relevant factors the sponsor should consider, such as are the products already being endorsed by a well-known personality and is he or she well known in any particular field or does he or she portray any particular image? The following factors may be relevant for consideration when making the decision.

(a) If the chosen sport or cultural activity is already well serviced by major sponsors, then the impact of the sponsor's entry into the arena will be more difficult to make newsworthy. Furthermore, the sponsorship cost may be higher, and those looking for sponsorship may be less marketable. Sponsorship may not reach saturation point, but in marketing terms the value of the proposal needs to be related to the relative significance of the sponsored party.

(b) If the sponsor is trying sponsorship for the first time, it may consider looking for an established sponsored party where its existing sponsor's agreement has expired, or where it is in an open market option position on renewal (see chapter two). The sponsor should ask for an explanation of why the existing sponsor is retiring. Is it because there is a personality clash, is the sponsored party being too greedy on terms, or is there any other reason a new sponsor should be aware of? A prospective sponsor should get the permission of the sponsored party to talk with the previous or continuing sponsor, to see whether any operating problems or personality differences have created an atmosphere within which the prospective sponsor feels the relationship could not work. If the circumstances which made the previous sponsor decide to terminate the sponsorship might apply also to a prospective sponsor, it should find out before being committed, so that it can decide whether or not to proceed.

1–21 The potential snags are that a following sponsor may find it hard to shake off the ghost of its predecessor from the public recognition of the event. Major sponsors can become synonymous with the sport they have sponsored, and it is not difficult for such a company to maintain its public image acquired through major sponsorship long after it has terminated. In addition, in such a case the sponsored party will be aware of its market value, and will make demands accordingly.

Identifying a party to sponsor

1–22 Having chosen to pursue sponsorship, a potential sponsor with a reasonable image and significant funds ready to pay to the right beneficiary will not normally have any difficulty in finding one to sponsor. To sort out the genuine potential candidates, the sponsor may decide to use a sponsorship consultant, as described in chapter two (paragraph 2–13).

10. Seeking relevant information

1–23 Having found a suitable candidate for sponsorship, what information should the prospective sponsor seek from the sponsored party?

Sponsorship costs

1–24 What are the overall sponsorship costs likely to be? This will not be limited to a cheque to the sponsored party under the sponsorship agreement. There will also be the costs of hospitality facilities used for entertaining the sponsor's customers; the cost of banners, placards and arena boards, and anything else that can be done to make the most use of the event premises. The sponsor will also have, for example, the unseen internal cost of the marketing department dealing with its participation in collaborating with the sponsored party; devising and executing marketing and promotional activities to cash in on the sponsorship; and there will be a host of lesser knock-on costs. These may all be worth the expenditure but they must be budgeted for.

Potential benefits

1–25 What are the potential benefits, by way of marketing rights and event "perks", to be gained from the sponsorship? These should be identified whether or not the sponsor can immediately see how it will make use of them all. They will differ in some respects depending upon what the event is. There will be a "core" of benefits which will be common to most types of event. Some of the possibilities are discussed in chapter two. It is up to the sponsor, in a planned strategy, to make the most of opportunities presented.

Potential disadvantages

1–26 Are there any potential disadvantages of the sponsorship deal to the sponsor, other than those inherent in some sporting activities? If the overall costs have been realistically anticipated, the only likely disadvantages will be where for some reason the sponsor is prevented, or inhibited, from exercising its marketing rights. A recognisable and assessable disadvantage is not the same as a risk inherent in the sponsorship subject. Such risks include the sponsored opera which may not happen because the theatre is damaged by fire; the sponsored football team which does not win any games and is relegated to a lower division; or the racing driver who fails to finish any race he enters. The potential of any disadvantage or lack of marketing opportunity is then based upon the fact that the sponsored event or party is a high risk in itself. Recognition of that factor should be taken into account in the calculation of the sponsorship fee.

Other commitments of sponsor

1–27 The sponsor must make sure that it knows of all of the other sponsorship commitments expected from it, apart from the fee. Sponsorship is intended to create a mutual benefit to both parties, so any additional needs of the sponsored party which can be provided by the sponsor and which are acceptable to it should be agreed, whether they are provided free or at a discounted cost. To be realistic, all non-cash provisions to the sponsored party should be costed by the sponsor, so that its marketing budget can accurately reflect the financial impact of the sponsorship upon the sponsor.

Sponsored party's obligations

1–28 The obligations of the sponsored party are dealt with in chapter five, but they should be clearly identified as part of the initial assessment and decision-making process by the sponsor. To some extent these will mirror the rights of the sponsor set out in chapter three. In this context the sponsor should establish the positive actions to be taken by the sponsored party, most of which may relate to the event itself. The sponsor is using the event as the basis of part of its product marketing strategy, which will be helped by what the sponsored party does to develop the event and make it successful.

11. Commercial assessment by sponsor

1–29 Depending on whether the sponsorship proposal relates to a single event, such as an athletics meeting, or to a season's events of, for instance, a football club, or to a motor racing team or driver, the initial assessment to be undertaken by the sponsor should also cover the following points:

(a) Is the proposed project of a sufficiently high profile, or is it of sufficient public interest, to give the sponsor value for money when comparing the sponsorship fees with the perceived value in promotional terms? To be taken into account can be the experience of other sponsors of similar activities, and to what extent the proposal is complementary to the company's existing marketing plans, or whether it will be experimental.

(b) The level of commitment of the sponsor both in financial terms and in time. Is the sponsorship fee a fixed amount, or can it fluctuate depending on results, or upon any other factor not within the sponsor's control? If so, for the protection of the sponsor, there should be a limit on any potential increase in the fee. A projected budget and cash-flow chart should be prepared for all the costs of the sponsor connected with sponsorship, to see whether they fit within the sponsor's annual budget, or whether it needs to be modified.

(c) In what circumstances can the sponsor terminate the sponsorship prematurely if the event or the sponsored party is a disaster? This would only apply where the sponsorship is a long-term commitment, over several years. If one year is a disaster, however that may be defined, that may be due to unusual adverse circumstances. If the sponsor wants such a termination right, it would have to be clearly stated, both as to the circumstances in which the right can be exercised, and the formalities of doing so which have to be complied with.

(d) In what circumstances can the sponsor extend its period of sponsorship where the project is successful, and upon what terms? The extent of the sponsorship, and the identity of the sponsor, may have been the material factors behind the success of the event, and the sponsor should not be a hostage to fortune on the renewal. Few may be prepared to sponsor an unknown quantity, but many will be prepared to sponsor a success. Either the sponsor should have the right to extend the sponsorship agreement on payment of an increased fee according to an escalating formula, or it should have a matching option if the sponsorship rights to the event are put on the open market for offers.

12. Types of sponsorship

1–30 The differences between a sole sponsor, a primary sponsor and a secondary sponsor are as follows.

(a) A sole sponsor will be the exclusive source of funding for the event, and the only sponsor connected with the sponsored party, with the exclusive right to be publicly known as supporting the event. It is able therefore to control absolutely how the promotion rights granted under the sponsorship agreement are marketed for the benefit of the sponsor and its brand product which is associated with the name of the event. The sponsor's name and logo is used in conjunction with that of the sponsored party and/or the event, with no dilution of the promotional impact which would otherwise be due to the presence of other sponsors. This would not be the case for a cultural sponsorship such as of an opera, but the sponsor would then be identified by referring to the production as "being in association with" the sponsor, or in a similar way making it known that the production would not exist but for the sponsor's support.

1–31
(b) A primary sponsor has a similar status to that of a sole sponsor to the extent of being associated with the name of the event, but it shares the overall sponsorship cost of the event with one or more subsidiary sponsors, and they each have different levels of marketing rights. This will normally happen where the cost of sponsoring the event is too great for only one sponsor, or where a variety of non-competitive (and probably complementary) minor sponsors enhance the whole project, while not reducing the value of it to the primary sponsor. The most common example is the sponsorship of a motor racing team. Nescafé Blend 37, Winfield, Benson & Hedges and Red Bull are the primary sponsors of the teams they support, and for their contribution they have the team named after them and have the racing cars painted in their distinctive colour schemes by which their products are identified. Such a colour scheme, or packaging "get up", is in itself a form of trademark with substantial value and goodwill, as (for example) smokers recognise the packets of cigarettes on a shelf instantly by those colours, without having to see the manufacturer's name. The mental association is asserted when spectators see the racing cars with the same colour scheme.

(c) A secondary sponsor, which is no less vital to the support and success of the sponsored party, tends to provide specialised goods or services as its sponsorship contribution, although it can be a lower-level provider of a cash fee. The most common is the "official supplier" status of product manufacturers. For a motor racing team, examples would be the manufacturers of tyres, oil and other items without which the motor racing team could not function at all. The terms on which these are provided are negotiable, but the charisma of supplying these specialised products to a winning team provides an invaluable platform for promoting the standard equipment in an enormous but highly competitive retail market. It is also a means by which the product manufacturer is able to test its products to their limit in real circumstances. Artificial testing in simulated conditions is not the same, and through the years most of the significant motor vehicle developments of safety and structure have come about as a direct result of experimentation in the course of motor racing.

The advantages and disadvantages of each type of sponsorship will now be examined in more detail

13. Sole sponsorship

1–32   A sole sponsor has the following advantages:

(a) The event may include the name of the sponsor or its product in the event title, and any trophy will be known as the "sponsor" trophy.

(b) The sponsor has promotional exclusivity over the event, its arena boards and banners at the event venue have prime locations, and there are no other sponsors' requirements to consider.

(c) The promotional value in media terms, especially if the event is televised, is unique, and the prestige of being the sole sponsor gives any product promotion related to it additional impact.

1–33   Disadvantages of being a sole sponsor include:

(a) The sponsor has to cover the whole of the required funding for the event. As the sponsor is the only commercially publicised supporter of the event, it may also have to provide any additional manpower or other sponsor-related contribution to the running of the event. Any shortcomings in the preparation of the budget for the event will be seen closer to the date of the event. The accumulated cost of many minor ordinary requirements can become significant, or the contingency element of the sponsorship fee may be found to be inadequate to cover unexpected costs. If that happens then either the sponsor will have to increase its contribution accordingly, or the sponsored party will have to obtain the additional necessary funding from official suppliers or any other source whilst not granting those parties any sponsorship rights conflicting with those of the sole sponsor.

(b) The event may be a disaster for any reason, or the administrator of the event may fail to organise it properly so that it is a shambles. As a consequence the sponsor will be associated with the event in adverse circumstances, and it will not derive the anticipated commercial and promotional benefit from it. No sponsorship agreement gives the sponsor the right to claim compensation for projected failure to do business, or for damage to the sponsor's image. The sponsor may be able to terminate the agreement, or to reduce the following year's fees to an agreed extent, but the decision on what to do should be at the sponsor's discretion and the sponsorship agreement would have to cover the point clearly.

14. Primary sponsorship

1–34   Primary and secondary sponsors exist where an event or entity has appointed co-sponsors to varying degrees. The reason for having multiple sponsors of a motor racing team is the sheer cost of putting it on the track and keeping it there. The glamour of, and the public attraction to, motor sports is such that if a team is known to participate competitively with a reasonable chance of being within the top six in any race, that is enough to justify substantial sponsorship. Justifying sponsorship and getting it are not the same thing: motor racing is big-league money, and the sponsor is looking only at its cost-effectiveness. It is one of the few forms of sponsorship which is purely commercial—there is no room for sentiment at that level of cost.

1–35   Major sponsorship budgets, such as for motor racing, may be decentralised by the sponsor in order to be able to afford it. This can be done by spreading the cost over a group of companies, each contributing a proportion relative to its acquired benefit, or as otherwise agreed internally.

It may also be possible for each local sponsor group company to pick up the cost of sponsoring the motor race being held in its country, where that cost is a calculated contribution to the overall cost during the year. The contracting sponsor may have other means of spreading the cost. A point to watch in the sponsorship agreement is the extent to which any contributor to the sponsorship fee can actively obtain a benefit from having made a contribution to the sponsor's budget. Any limit on this extension of participation and benefit should be stated.

1–36   Because all the "Murphy's Law" possibilities exist, there is no guarantee that a particular combination of driver and vehicle will win any race, or the championship. However, sufficient development and support funds will enhance the chances of a competitive team being successful, and it is probably true to say that without sufficient funds a team is unlikely to be competitive. In a specialised event such as motor racing, the sponsors will mainly come from companies which have connected products or services. The major exception is the tobacco companies, which have dominated motor-sport sponsorship as the only way to get television coverage for their products, and in an effort to distract attention from the depressing effect of government health warnings upon their image.

1–37   A primary sponsor has the following advantages:

(a)   The team is known as the sponsor's team, the identity of the manufacturer or promoter of the team taking joint status (see paragraph 1–30(b)). It will also have the prime visual sites on the car and the driver's helmet and overalls for its company or product name decals although where there are secondary sponsors, there must be left for them enough high profile decal or name space to justify their participation. Many primary sponsors are not connected with the activity being sponsored, so there is only a commercial exposure deal to be done in return for supporting the team. There would otherwise be a limiting factor on the choice of available primary sponsors.

(b)   The sponsor has become the primary sponsor because it has put up the level of sponsorship funds which were set by the sponsored party as being the criteria for that status. One advantage the primary sponsor has over a sole sponsor is that it does not have the whole funding risk. Its participation will generally be conditional upon being satisfied that the sponsored party will be capable of generating by way of secondary sponsorship, or by the appointment of official suppliers, additional funding or product supply which may be required in excess of the budget and projections seen originally by the primary sponsor.

(c) The promotional value of being the primary sponsor is probably proportionately in excess of the value of being a secondary sponsor, comparing the relative kudos with the relative fundings. There is no means of attributing different levels of value among several sponsors. There can only be one primary sponsor, and there can be any number of secondary sponsors.

(d) Except for the dilution of the sponsorship kudos and effectiveness where many secondary sponsors are brought in, there are no real disadvantages to being a primary sponsor if the deal is right, other than those applicable to a sole sponsor, as set out in paragraph 1–33.

15. Secondary sponsorship

1–38   A secondary sponsor can be relatively modest all the way through to being substantial, depending on its financial contribution to the budget of the sponsored party. The advantages of being a secondary sponsor are:

(a) While there will be a minimum contribution required from any sponsor, a secondary sponsor can choose its level of funding and negotiate appropriate recognition accordingly. Taking the motor-racing example, if a secondary sponsor is not connected with the motor trade, given the right deal it can find a home for its cash support on a non-partisan basis. If the secondary sponsor is a motor-trade product manufacturer, the racing team will not accept its sponsorship if it in fact uses competitive products, and the sponsor would not make an offer of sponsorship. The secondary sponsors tend to be those companies whose products are used by the team, *i.e.* there are ready-made sponsorship opportunities without opposition.

(b) If it is new to the world of sponsorship, a secondary sponsor can take a limited risk and use the experience to assess the value of sponsorship to its organisation. It can get first hand experience of what can be expected of big league sponsorship, both as to a sponsor's contribution, and as to what is possible by way of return. This can apply to any event where there are multi-sponsors, but the sponsor would first research the project fully.

(c) If a secondary sponsor pulls out from a sponsorship deal after the expiry of its minimum period of commitment, that is not a significant factor in adjusting its marketing strategy, it is not a point of criticism, and it does not cause concern amongst its customers as a sign of possible retrenchment.

(d) If their team wins, they can all put out promotional material or media advertising congratulating the team on its win, and reminding the world that it has done so using that sponsor's product. For major secondary sponsors, such as oil and tyre companies, it is possible that several teams were using their products, which increases their chances of being able to congratulate somebody.

1–39   The disadvantages of secondary sponsorship are:

(a) If there are many of them (such as for a motor-racing team), then the impact of a decal on the side of a car, on overalls or on a helmet, is reduced, irrespective of the relative financial contributions of other subsidiary sponsors.

(b) If the secondary sponsor can only afford participation at a relatively low level of contribution, top teams may not want to get involved. This is because advertising space has a high premium, and arranging sponsorship and dealing with all sponsors during the season can be time consuming. If these restraints do not exist, lower level sponsorship may be welcomed. For example, if for a lower level sponsorship fee all the sponsor wants is for the team's star, such as Nigel Mansell, to make personal appearances at important promotional events of the sponsor, that might be acceptable. The number of appearances would be specified, they would have to fit in with his schedule of business and private engagements, and any expenses incurred in doing so would have to be covered. The choice of team and star driver would also depend on any endorsement agreements entered into by the driver not being competitive with the sponsor or its products.

(c) Lesser teams, which may be prepared to accept any reasonable sponsorship offer, may never win or get a placing which justifies press advertising such as "X Company congratulates the Y Team on . . .", in which case there is little value in the deal to the sponsor. However, if the lesser team should produce miraculous results, that would be newsworthy and the promotional possibilities would be significant.

1–40   A sole sponsor negotiates the sponsorship agreement in detail with the sponsored party without having to consider outside interests or influences. Where there are multiple sponsors, each is negotiating the best deal it can get. There is normally no collusion or consultation between them to establish an acceptable package which only differs in grading by, *e.g.* the level of contribution and the access to high level rights. The sponsored party may set out a predetermined range of benefits packaged to reflect the differences between greater and lesser sponsors. Packages can then be selected according to contribution of costs and participation in rights, with each secondary sponsor being aware of the basic promotional rights of all others.

Different events or participants in different sports or other activities have different requirements. For each of them there will be a range of rights and obligations of a common nature, which are discussed in chapters three and four. The needs of the sponsored party determine which kind of sponsorship is sought, and the sponsored activity determines the kinds of benefit which can be offered to a sponsor in return for its financial contribution. Set out in Appendix II are examples of sponsorship agreements with different parties or events, and broadly what they need by way of support, and how they might appeal to a potential sponsor.

16. Official supplier sponsors

1–41   There are many events, such as the Olympic Games, or the World Cup Football Competition (plus intermediate championships), where there are several major international product manufacturers which provide very significant sponsor-ship funds between them for the event such as under the IOC's TOP worldwide sponsorship programme. The title of the event is not available to a sole or primary sponsor, and the sponsors are subject to the same contractual conditions, except (in some cases) for the fee. The sponsors tend to be major manufacturers, such as Kodak, Visa and Coca-Cola. Their marketing value is to have the exclusive right to the title of "Official Supplier" of their respective products or services. This is equivalent to being a sole sponsor in the appropriate product category, and the more prestigious the event, the greater will be the attributed commercial value. The key value is in the fact that these events are televised world-wide. The public interest generated and maintained by the organisers for their own benefit enables the sponsors to maintain promotional activities on an international basis for a long time.

1–42   A major feature of official supplier status is exclusivity within the relevant product category. International events also provide an element of exclusivity, in that there is only one Olympic Games or World Cup Football Competition. There are a greater number of international tennis tournaments or motor-racing events. To an international company which has a high level of sponsorship commitment as part of its worldwide marketing strategy, to be the official supplier at unique international events of that nature can be essential for its image.

Part of the cost and benefit of being the official supplier is that the event has to be supplied with the product by the sponsor on an agreed basis, and the media and the semi-endorsement usage when properly presented has a high influence on the consumer.

The television exposure is carefully maximised, depending on the product, by a wide variety of means. Except for the Olympic Games, banners and stadium boards are standard rights, and siting them within the best or potentially most frequent or likely TV camera shot is an art born of experience and research on site. The plums are "on screen" credits, such as those which will be available for the official timer of athletics events, when a finishing line electronic timer board also gets consistent television screen time.

17. Attracting sponsors

1–43   Potential sponsors usually have little difficulty in finding a suitable worthy cause to accept their funds, unless the funds offered are inadequate, or the terms and conditions demanded by the sponsor are excessive for the contribution, or are otherwise not acceptable to any reasonable sponsored party. The more usual difficulty is for the party which is looking for sponsorship.

Whatever activity the sponsored party is connected with, it has to be able to convince a potential sponsor that the project is worth considering. While different activities have different needs, a party looking for sponsorship has to be impressive, set out its case clearly, and sell itself as being an attractive sponsorship proposition. Among the required features of a properly presented package to potential sponsors are the following.

(a) Structure of events

1–44
  (i) An explanation of the structure and status of the party looking for sponsorship, and of the event or activity it wants sponsorship for, and

why sponsorship is justified. The justification should be explained in the context of why and how a sponsor would benefit; the needs of the sponsored party will be evident. The prominent promotion rights should be listed, and any other information which would be of general interest to a potential sponsor should be given. There should also be a detailed, well-constructed and realistic explanation of the track record of the event, its current status, and the projected plans for the future development of the event. It may not be capable of development other than by better facilities, such as for a horse race meeting.

(ii) Before approaching any specific proposed sponsor, the sponsored party should take into account the likely philosophical compatibility of that party with the identity of the sponsored party, and the event for which it is seeking sponsorship. Sponsors want their sponsorship to reflect their image and reputation favourably, because it will be used for marketing their name and their products. The manufacturer of an upmarket exclusive product which is also expensive is not likely to sponsor a darts competition, as the televised coverage image does not fit the manufacturer's marketing strategy. It is quite possible that what is perceived to be a down-market product will be prepared to sponsor an upmarket project such as a series of international cricket test matches, because that would enhance and benefit that product's own market image. Whether such an offer of sponsorship would be accepted is another matter, and the above comments would apply.

(b) Current sponsorship status

1–45

(i) If the event or activity has previously been sponsored, but the sponsorship has been terminated, there should be a brief explanation of the sponsorship history and the reason for termination, without breaching any confidentiality restriction. For cultural or charitable events, where there is no competition for sponsorship (all sponsors are welcome), the question will not normally be necessary.

(ii) If there is existing sponsorship which will be continuing, so that this is secondary sponsorship which is being sought, there should be an explanation of the level of additional sponsorship required, and how it fits in with the existing sponsor.

(c) Calculating sponsorship requirements

1–46

(i) If the sponsored party wants to cover all the costs of the event with a little excess, but is not out purely to make a profit (such as for a charitable fund), it should prepare a reasonably detailed profit and loss account of last year's event, and a budget for this year. For an existing event or activity there must have been some sources of income, such as entry ticket sales, even if there has been no previous sponsor, otherwise the event would not exist. The budget should have a sufficient contingency reserve to avoid a cash-flow problem arising before any further sponsorship payments are due.

(ii) Where the sponsorship agreement is to cover several years, the fee will be increased on an annual basis. This is because the event costs go up, the value of the sponsorship increases, and perhaps the sponsored party should create a reserve for development costs. The increases can be reasonably well calculated over a three year period, but after that there may need to be a re-examination of the fee level in the light of the circumstances appertaining at that time. In this context the comments set out in (d) (i), (ii) and (iii) below are relevant.

(d) Financial viability assessment

1–47 With all the information available under (a), (b) and (c) above, the sponsor can then examine the factors which are important to it, such as:

(i) Is the event cost effective, and are any management charges or similar payments made to any party connected with running the event, whether or not the party is associated with ownership or management of the event? If there are, to whom are they paid, are they necessary, and are they reasonable for the input of that party? No sponsor wants to subsidise any payments made to event proprietors or associated parties, unless they can be shown to the sponsor's reasonable satisfaction to be for good commercial reasons at the appropriate going rate, and calculated on an arm's-length basis.

(ii) The above is only relevant where the sponsorship fee is to be calculated as the shortfall between income from all sources and the total costs of running the event. If the sponsorship fee is a sum of money negotiated without reference to the costs and other income of the event, such as in respect of a secondary sponsor, the sponsor may be curious to check that the event is sufficiently funded, but would have no right to inspect its books.

(iii) Is the budget for the year reasonably based, so can the shortfall to be covered by sponsorship be both identifiable and containable? Inadequate budgeting can have two unintended effects on the sponsor. If the fee is fixed in accordance with what turns out to have been an exceptionally gloomy budget, the sponsored party will end up with an unexpected profit. However, if the budget is badly prepared or deliberately seeks to show a much more sound financial position than will be the case, the agreed sponsorship funding will be inadequate. This will put the sponsor in the position, possibly, of having to provide considerable further funding or not having a sponsored event at all. Any budget should be checked carefully for realism.

(iv) What will be the likely increase in the shortfall in the next three years, or for whatever further period the sponsor may want to continue its sponsorship? The same budgeting and forecasting comments apply as under (iii) above.

(v) If the event is already established and sponsorship is simply a means of obtaining additional income, rather than to cover a financial shortfall, accounts will not be necessary in the calculation of an agreed fee, but the sponsor will want to be satisfied by accounts that the project is financially viable in any event.

(e) Ascertain sponsorship benefits

1–48 The sponsored party should prepare a list of benefits which it is prepared to provide, or which it considers the sponsor will obtain, as being directly attributable to the event. These will include lesser considerations such as free tickets, hospitality facilities, and access to restricted parts of the event venue. These facilities will have a value to any sponsor which is a commercial company, as being the kind of facility which cannot otherwise be acquired, and which would be used to entertain prospective customers. They project a prestigious image for the company, which is part of the reason for sponsorship.

(f) Evaluation of corporate benefit

1–49

(i) The sponsor should assess the potential value of the event in corporate promotion terms, including the promotion of the product related to the name of the event. The sponsor should also compare it with what can be achieved for the same expense in media advertising or by any other promotional campaign. To some extent this is subjective guesswork, as it is difficult to relate the sponsorship to any specific upturn in trade. There are many sources of comparative information which will be useful to the sponsor, such as the TV ratings, and the research information which is constantly being compiled for the evaluation of TV related programmes. These will include sponsored events which have TV coverage, so that viewing figures can give a reasonably accurate indication of public awareness and interest.

(ii) Sponsorship of the event creates a different consumer awareness which is intended to benefit the broad corporate image of the sponsor. If the event's title contains a brand product name, such as the "Widget Tennis Tournament", promotions are directly related to that product, and will be more attention-catching than ordinary media advertising. However, such promotions tend to have significant promotional value only during the period within which the event is also of public interest.

(g) Tax effectiveness of sponsorship fee

1–50 The sponsor will want to be satisfied that the expense incurred in the sponsorship will be fully tax deductible in its accounts as being a justifiable trading expense. If this is not the case, the expenditure by the sponsor will have to be compared with other known tax-deductible promotional projects, to establish a true comparison of ultimate cost, and therefore of value for money. The tax and accounting factors are dealt with in chapter eight. If a significant sponsorship cost is not tax deductible, that may modify the sponsor's marketing budget in real terms.

1–51 The extent to which a potential sponsor will examine all of the above considerations in depth will depend upon how significant the proposed expenditure is in the sponsor's overall available budget for marketing, and its desire to get involved whatever the cost. The explanatory package as set out in paragraphs 1–44—1–50 will generally only be needed either if the event is new and is short of funds, or if the event is long-standing but up to now has not needed sponsorship. The public awareness and commercial potential of an established event will be self-evident. The level of sponsorship support required even for an established event will depend on the extent to which the event is self-financing.

Armed with a complete explanatory and promotional package to show why the event is well worth sponsoring, how does the party wanting sponsorship find an appropriate and willing sponsor? It depends greatly upon the public profile of the event, what constitutes the event, and how much funding is needed. The constitution of the event will have a direct influence on whether it is a televisable event, or whether it is a minority interest event with limited spectator appeal.

1–52   The party wanting sponsorship, and its advisers and marketing consultants, will need to examine its requirements in the light of other activities of a similar nature, so as to identify the most likely sources of sponsorship. There are many organisations which are experienced in advising on sponsorship opportunities, both for those looking for sponsorship, and those potential sponsors which are looking for a suitable event or sponsored party to approach. Some of these organisations are listed in Appendix IV. There are also many specialised agencies which provide sponsorship advice and assistance, but these will be on a commercial basis. As well as approaching these organisations, the sponsored party can be doing its own research, for example:

(a) An examination of the "competition" is necessary, *i.e.* which companies are currently sponsors of similar events. That may eliminate as potential candidates any major company which is already sponsoring a significant event within the same field of activity, but that is not necessarily the case. For example, Whitbread is a major sponsor through its different brand products, such as Stella Artois for the tennis championship, and Heineken for rugby. If a new recognised major circuit tennis championship were to be created, Stella Artois may be interested in sponsoring it. Insurance companies, such as Cornhill, seem to favour cricket sponsorship, but whether it would be prepared to sponsor two major cricket events in a year may be doubtful. Coca-Cola sponsors the Football Association League, but would it be prepared also to sponsor a regional minor league? These are the questions which need to be researched. Major commercial companies may be prepared to sponsor many events each year, so they are always worth approaching.

(b) Try to find which companies, products or services are identifiable with the relevant activity, so that there is a common-ground reason for approaching them for sponsorship.

(c) If the event is within the cultural arts, or if it is an acceptable commercial manner of promoting a charitable entity, it may appeal to a broad cross-section of companies, irrespective of what they do.

(d) The potential commercial targets, and the approach to them, will be different where the sponsored event is to be a one-off event, rather than a seasonal or annual event which would need a much deeper corporate commitment of a long-term nature.

(e) If the sponsored event's requirements are not necessarily cash, but the provision of goods or services, the potential market for a sponsor is limited to those companies which provide those services or produce those goods.

18. Creating a sponsorship property

1–53   A distinctive title, emblem, device or logo is commonly devised as a means of giving an instant identity to a sponsored event which, when sufficiently promoted, comes to be recognised as that event's visual graphic representation. In marketing terms such recognition is valuable, as its isolated use is associated with the event, so that its name becomes widely promoted. Consistent and frequent use of the title or logo ultimately creates a permanent association with the event, at which point it becomes a trade mark.

One of the rights granted to a sponsor will be the right to use the sponsored party's trade mark in connection with advertising the sponsor's association with the event, or to promote the sponsor's brand product which is the subject of the sponsorship. See chapter six for a more detailed reference to trade mark registration in connection with the protection of merchandising rights.

1–54 When a sponsored party is looking for a trade mark to distinguish its event, the following points should be considered:

(a) The logo must not be an unauthorised copy, modification or derivation of any other logo created and used by anybody else. There are practical limitations to that broad statement. The conflicting similarity will be only within the United Kingdom for national events. There is also a difference between concept and design. For example, if the emblem is the British bulldog (or some other unoriginal device), that will not prevent the sponsored party from using a bulldog, providing it does not look like the one already in use. However, if a bulldog is a registered trade mark within the same class of activity, advice should be obtained on the possibility of infringement before the sponsored party starts to use it. The logo should not be used in any manner which may reasonably be considered either to cause confusion between the two logos, or to create an assumption that the two organisations which use the logos are associated, due to the similarity of the logos.

(b) If the logo is not an original made-up word or device, but is a commonplace word or representation, any proprietary rights or exclusivity of use will be strictly limited to association with the sponsored event. It does not give the sponsored party absolute rights against all others in connection with third-party use of something similar in an unrelated field of activity.

(c) If the logo is a wholly original device which is distinctive in its own right, it may be entitled to copyright protection if it is an artistic device, and any unauthorised use may be prevented under the common law action of "passing off". The rules of passing off are strict, and not all apparently infringing uses will come within those rules (see paragraph 1–57 below).

19. Trade mark protection

1–55 Once the sponsored party has created its trade mark it needs to consider how best to protect it. A sensible sponsor will want to be satisfied that the event's trade marks are protected across a sufficiently wide range of goods and services to cover the sponsor's proposed activities. Trade marks are distinguished only by whether they are registered trade marks or unregistered trade marks. The distinction relates to the form of legal protection given to each, and the means of effecting that protection. These are described below.

1–56

(a) While any well-established name, emblem or logo is known as a trade mark, for trade mark registration purposes it has to be connected with either goods or services. An application for registration is made within the class for which the event is relevant, taking into account potential merchandising rights, for example those relating to toys, clothing and paper material, if the logo is to be merchandised. It may also come within the service marks class for education and entertainment. The sponsor will also want to protect the use of the logo in connection with its own business and goods (which may be a class not applicable to the sponsored party), and may be authorised by the sponsored party to apply for registration accordingly. This would be under a written agreement with the sponsored party to ensure that the beneficial interest in the logo remained the property of the sponsored party.

(b) United Kingdom registration will take around 12 months from the date of application to the date of registration if all goes well. Therefore registration may only be practical for a long-term or ongoing event sponsorship, or where the event to be sponsored is not due to happen until well into the future, so that registration will be in place by that time.

(c) Certain words, such as geographical names or personal names, or words not being distinctive of the goods or services to which they are attached, are not eligible for registration (see further chapter six, paragraph 6–42). If there is any doubt, or if the connection between the word and an obscure geographical name is considered tenuous, it is possible to challenge an application by applying for a hearing, when the subject can be discussed fully so that the views of the sponsored party can be explained in context.

(d) Even if a trade mark is registrable, it is not invalidated if registration is not applied for. The legal and practical differences between a registered trade mark and a common law trade mark relate to the level of difficulty with which they are protectable. A registered trade mark is protected through its registration, and a clear breach can be restrained simply by proving the breach. If damage or loss has been incurred by the registered proprietor as a result of that breach, a claim is more easily made, although damage or loss is not necessary to enable a claim to be made.

1–57 The protection of an unregistered trade mark can only be effected within the rules of "passing off". This is a common law concept, which is based upon the need to prove the existence of deliberate confusion and damage, and the misappropriation of goodwill, by whoever is using the similar logo. Despite the similarity of the two logos or names, infringement is only confirmed if a passing-off action is successful. For a passing-off action to succeed, the following circumstances must exist:

(a) the plaintiff must have acquired a reputation or goodwill in his trade, goods or mark in question;

(b) the offending actions must contain a misrepresentation which leads to confusion or deception in the minds of the consumer; and

(c) the misrepresentation must cause damage to the business or goodwill of the trader by whom the action is brought. This is the crucial difference between a registered and an unregistered trade mark. If, in the case of an infringing use of an unregistered trade mark, there is no confusion or no likelihood of damage suffered by the complainant, then there is no actionable infringement. To sue for breach of an identical registered trade mark, confusion and damage do not have to be alleged or proved.

20. Sponsoring the arts

1–58   The public image of sponsorship generally relates to sporting and competitive events, such as football, motor racing or snooker, because they have a wide public interest at the top level, and they are capable of attracting national television and press coverage. The televised broadcast of these events is usually in prime time, and the press coverage extends to many pages at the back of all daily newspapers. That is the reason why the sponsors are prepared to pay large sums of money for that sponsorship. The publicity and promotional value for the sponsor and its product is well worth the cost.

The poor relation in the sponsorship stakes has been the arts, as cultural events do not generally get televised. Their press coverage is limited to paid advertising and to critical comments in the arts section of newspapers, and which are tucked away so as not to interfere with the news of the day, be it politics or sport. While arts events receive varying degrees of public exposure, the limitation of numbers is the seating capacity for the number of performances of the event; or the number of walking viewers who go to see a static exhibition of ancient Egyptian artifacts. With the possible exception of an exhibition which is open for a few weeks, these audiences are modest when compared with a sporting event, even if it is not televised. The commercial exposure a sponsor gets from an arts event is minimal in comparative terms. On the other hand, it is possible to spend much smaller sums of money effectively. Depending on the arts event, between £5,000 and £50,000 may be all that is required to ensure the happening or the survival of the event. In serious sports sponsorship that kind of money may not even be enough to make the sponsor an eligible contributor to the overall funding of the event so as to warrant sponsor status, even at a lowly level of recognition.

1–59   The arts covers a wide range of activities, including exhibitions, operas, concerts, and other events of a public interest or benefit nature (not being commercial events), which are organised by or under the auspices of the recognised arts organisations. For the purpose of this section these will be organisations which are recognised for funding purposes by the Department for Culture, Media and Sport although there are many smaller arts-related exhibitions and events which may not come within its remit. This recognition does not depend upon the sheer size or prominence of the organisation; its constitution and operational bona fides are the basic criteria.

Arts organisations are commercial in the sense that they have to raise money to pay for the events they organise, such as by seat ticket sales, selling advertising space in programmes and by running money-raising activities. They are not commercial in the sense that they are not intended to produce profit for private gain. Certain events may be profitable, but that profit only goes towards the cost of the next event, or into the organiser's general purposes fund for similar events. Any significant arts organisation also has to have an administrative structure which means having the cost of staff, and inevitable office running costs, all of which have to be paid for. The cost of mounting any important and impressive exhibition or stage event is considerable. Despite all efforts, most of the major arts-related organisations are perpetually short of money.

1–60   That is why the concept of sponsorship is so vital as a means of an arts organisation receiving a known amount of additional income, without having to spend money to try to generate it. The expenditure by the sponsor can be from the modest to the generous, depending on its balance of social conscience against the need to obtain reasonable value in promotional terms from the sponsorship payments. Realistically the sponsor will only get from the arts organisation public recognition for its contribution by credits in media advertising, on the event programme cover ("presented by . . .", or "in association with . . .") and possibly with promotional material for the sponsor and its products being displayed in the foyer of a concert hall, or in an exhibition hall. The sponsor can, of course, use its own advertising and promotional material to refer to the sponsorship, which also has the effect of publicising the sponsored event.

1–61   To give companies an incentive to sponsor the arts, there is an important organisation called the Association for Business Sponsorship of the Arts (ABSA), the contact offices of which are set out in Appendix IV. The association administers the Pairing Scheme, a government scheme, on behalf of the Department for Culture, Media and Sport. The scheme has developed since its inception in 1984, and the Rules were amended in 1998. The basic concept of the scheme is that:

(a) when a business sponsors the arts for the first time the scheme may match the amount of sponsorship by 25 per cent or £500, whichever is the greater;

(b) the minumum eligible sponsorship is £1,000;

(c) the maximum eligible sponsorship in kind is £5,000;

(d) first-time sponsors who sponsor a project offering exceptional access to the arts will be eligible to a match of 50 per cent of the sponsorship;

(e) where a first-time sponsor commits to the same arts organisation for three consecutive years, the sponsorship may be matched on a 100 per cent basis in the first year;

(f) at least 50 per cent of the award money must be used by the arts organisation to supply additional benefits which would not otherwise be available to the sponsor or the arts organisation;

(g) the maximum single award is £25,000 and the maximum aggregate award to a single arts organisation within a financial year is £50,000;

(h) for established sponsors (as defined in the Rules) financial awards have been replaced by recognition in the form of a certificate and attendance at a Pairing Scheme reception.

1–62   The Rules of the scheme are set out in Appendix V. The eligibility for payments from the scheme is not automatic: each application is considered on its merits and not all applications are successful. By not being successful, there is no implied criticism of the application; there are limited funds and there have to be priorities.

Only commercial sponsorship is eligible. The criteria are very realistic, the objective of the scheme is to boost sponsorship money coming in to help the arts, and to encourage that new or increased sponsorship by ensuring that the arts organisation receiving a grant from the scheme actively does something for the promotion of the sponsor. Therefore the sponsored party and the sponsor must each receive a positive benefit from participating in the scheme.

21. Sportsmatch

1–63 Launched in 1992, Sportsmatch is another government incentive scheme to encourage the sponsorship of amateur grass-roots sport and physical recreation events in Great Britain. Funded by the Department of Culture, Media and Sport it is administered by the Institute of Sports Sponsorship in England, and by the Scottish and Welsh Sports Councils in those respective countries. The basic concept of the scheme is that:

(a) when a business sponsors grass-roots sports for the fist time, or increases its amount of sponsorship, Sportsmatch may match the amount of sponsorship £1 for £1 for the first year;

(b) the minimum eligible sponsorship is £1,000 and the maximum that will be matched for any one event or activity is £50,000;

(c) where a sponsor has committed up-front sponsorship for a further two or three years, Sportsmatch may agree a further award for those years (up to 50 per cent in year two, and up to 25 per cent in year three).

1–64 Evidence will be required that the event or activity would not have taken place without Sportsmatch. This is quite the opposite of the rule under ABSA's "Pairing Scheme". Like the Pairing Scheme, however, the sponsorship must be commercial and mutually beneficial to the parties.

The Scheme is discretionary and certain sponsors are ineligible. These currently include alcohol and tobacco sponsors of under-18 activities, and alcohol sponsorship of motor-sports events, although these rules will need to be amended when the E.U. Tobacco Advertising Directive is implemented by Member States. Charities are also ineligible sponsors. Full details of the scheme and its rules are set out in Appendix V.

22. Competition Law implications

1–65 Provided the sponsorship does not discriminate or take advantage of a monopolistic position, and is organised in a fair manner, there will not generally be any grounds for intervention under domestic and E.U. competition laws. However, certain aspects of sponsorship can cause problems and parties therefore need to be alert to these issues when drafting their agreements.

The granting of exclusive rights is usually an essential element of any sponsorship deal and should not generally be regarded as objectional. However, the Commission may scrutinise individual arrangements which have the effect of partitioning the European Market or inhibiting competition. Exclusive arrangements must always be objectively justifiable by reference to their scope and duration.

1–66 The grant of "Official Supplier" status has been the subject of particular examination by the European Commission in recent times, in a case concerning the Danish Tennis Federation's (DTF) agreement with the tennis-ball manufacturers, Slazenger, Tretorn and Penn, whereby the DFT designated those brands as "official" and forbade the use of other brands at official tournaments. As a result of the use of "official" stickers attached to their packaging by exclusive distributors, parallel imported balls were effectively prevented from being used in tournaments. The Commission took the view that the agreement infringed both Article 85 and Article 86 of the Treaty (being both a restrictive trade practice and an abuse of a dominant position) and the DTF was forced to amend its practices. The duration of the sponsorship agreement was reduced from three to one year, and the stickers had to be amended to remove the references to "DTF official balls" and to "selected" or "approved" by the DTF. This was because the word "official" implied that the marked balls were of a higher quality when this was not the case.

Parties to a sponsorship agreement should therefore be aware that such designations will only be acceptable where it is clear from the strap-line that there is a relationship of sponsorship, or it can be justified on technical grounds. In other cases it may be misleading to consumers and anti-competitive.

CHAPTER 2

Sponsorship Contract Negotiation

1. Preliminary concerns

2–01 As a point of strategy, it is important for any party looking for sponsorship to make every reasonable effort to ensure that a company which has offered sponsorship genuinely wants to do so, and has fully understood the extent of the commitments it will have to make. If a company does not fully investigate both the potential benefits and the costs and obligations of entering into the sponsorship deal, but does so only because the marketing manager "has to do something this month", the consequences for both parties can be disastrous, but the sponsored party comes off worst by far. The scenario may be along the following lines:

(a) The sponsor and the sponsored party are put in contact with each other. The sponsored party makes its presentation, and the sponsor is impressed. Having considered the project, the sponsor confirms that it is delighted to oblige and, not with the greatest of care, negotiates an agreement with the sponsored party, which is signed and becomes effective.

(b) In reliance on the sponsor's contractual commitments, the sponsored party proceeds with the finalising of all things necessary for the staging of the event. This includes the sponsored party entering into commercial commitments, including the associated expense, covering all third parties who are under contract to play their part in the event, or to provide facilities, products or services to it.

(c) At a crucial stage in the run-up to the event the sponsor's marketing manager is fired. His replacement looks at the sponsorship agreement in dismay, considers it was a silly decision, and decides to pull out now rather than go through with it.

(d) The sponsored party finds itself without funds (except for what may have been paid by the sponsor up to that date), with an ex-sponsor, with legal proceedings being issued (at expense) against the ex-sponsor for damages, compensation, and possibly specific enforcement, and with no time to find a new sponsor prior to the event.

2–02 The above example is a bit drastic, but without putting off a potential sponsor, the sponsored party should ensure, for its own protection, that the sponsorship decision has been made at the proper level, and that during the negotiation of the agreement, all the important matters are fully discussed. If disaster strikes because the sponsor has gone bust at a very early stage in the sponsorship agreement, while that may be a "no fault" situation, it reflects upon the choice of sponsor. A major company should not go bust. But if sponsorship is being considered from a small company, in reliance on which the sponsored party will undertake commitments of its own, it should research the sponsor thoroughly for its financial and business standing, with (if thought necessary) appropriate bank references. However, if all of this is seriously thought necessary, then a long-term sponsorship deal with that company may not be worth the risk of later problems.

2. Negotiation case study

2–03   As a case study, set out below are the actions and strategy which may be adopted in a typical major sponsorship proposal by a potential sponsor. The reactions of the sponsored party will be reflected by the inquiries made by the sponsor, and its requirements under the deal. The details of the proposed rights and obligations of both the sponsor and the sponsored party are set out in the following chapters.

2–04   The preliminary stages will be:

(a) The sponsor will first consider whether it wants to be a sponsor, and if it does, then it will ask for the kind of information about the sponsored party referred to in chapter one, paragraphs 1–43—1–50, and will make the internal analysis referred to in chapter one, paragraph 1–29.

(b) The next stage will be the submission to the sponsor of the basic contractual and practical requirements of the sponsored party. These will then be subject to detailed negotiation on any point with which either side is not fully satisfied as the general negotiations continue.

(c) If the sponsor is to be the primary sponsor, apart from its own rights and obligations, it will want to ensure that the sponsored party is committed to a mutually agreed formula for bringing in subsidiary sponsors. The main points will relate to the comparative funding as between the primary sponsor and any subsidiary sponsor; the level of exposure and other benefits a subsidiary sponsor can expect for its money; and that no subsidiary sponsor will be a competitor of the primary sponsor.

3. Contract holding position

2–05   Neither party should sign anything unless they intend to proceed with the agreement, but due to speed being of the essence, or due to a holding position being required, the following are possible means of dealing with the intended commitments. A brief description of certain legal aspects of contract law are set out in chapter nine, to give an indication to a non-legal reader of those practical things which need to be dealt with, or looked out for, in connection with legally binding documents.

Letter of intent

2–06   The parties may sign a letter of intent, to demonstrate that, subject to a firm commitment, there is a serious interest in sponsoring the event. The letter will be in general terms, indicating that there is an intention to proceed if the contractual terms can be agreed. It is essential to state that this letter is not to be considered a legal commitment by the sponsor, although if it is in very general terms, although encouraging in its tone, it would not be adequate as a legally binding document, even if it had been intended to be so. It would be a serious misapprehension if either of the parties genuinely considered that a letter of intent would in fact be legally binding. Neither, of course, will the sponsored party be bound to conclude a deal with the sponsor for so long as there is no legally binding agreement between them. A letter of intent is only a preliminary confirmation of good faith prior to serious negotiations.

Grant of first option

2–07

(a) The sponsored party may grant a first option to the sponsor. Unlike a letter of intent, an option is intended to be a legally binding document, and so must comply with the conditions necessary to make it effective and enforceable. An option is a firm contract, but conditional upon being exercised in accordance with its terms. A badly drafted option may be defective, and the sponsor may find that it has no enforceable rights after all the negotiations it has gone through.

(b) (i) A first option may be granted where the sponsored party has established a final non-negotiable financial and commercial framework for the deal, and the sponsor is being given exclusivity for a period of time within which to decide whether or not to accept the deal. The option will be open for, say, 30 days, and must be exercised by the sponsor in writing within that time. During that option period the sponsored party should be contractually prevented from making any deal on any terms with anyone but the sponsor, or even from entering into any preliminary discussions with a third party.

(ii) There are two schools of thought on this position. One says that if the sponsor is likely to exercise the option, third-party discussions direct the sponsored party's attention and energy unnecessarily. The other says that, as the sponsor cannot be guaranteed to exercise the option, the sponsored party should prudently provide itself with an already discussed alternative sponsor, otherwise the option period will be wasted time. The question is really whether the sponsored party should be disadvantaged if the sponsor spins out the option period and then does not exercise it. Should the sponsor be concerned about the sponsored party's back-up safeguard if the sponsor knows it will exercise the option?

2–08

(c) If the option is exercised, the sponsor and the sponsored party become bound by the sponsorship agreement terms, and legally enforceable obligations have come into existence between them. The sponsor is not entitled to exercise the option correctly, and a few days later change its mind, and try to revoke the option. Once exercised, the option is irrevocably effective. The sponsored party may release the sponsor on the basis that it will be of no use to have an unwilling sponsor, but it may require some compensation for the expense and inconvenience caused, including taking care of commitments entered into on the strength of the option exercise, and having to look for another sponsor.

(d) If the option is not exercised, neither party has any commitment to the other, and the sponsored party can do any other deal it wants with any other party. An option exercise is not valid if it purports to accept certain terms of the deal, and to reject or modify other terms. That only represents a counter offer to the sponsored party. If the sponsored party accepts such a counteroffer, then a modified agreement will have been concluded between them. If it does not accept the counteroffer and the option period expires, the option will have lapsed.

Matching offer rights

2–09

(a) (i) When a sponsor's agreement has expired, but it still wants to continue the sponsorship, the sponsored party may be anxious to establish the market value of the event for the negotiation of an appropriate sponsorship fee. In that case, if there are several interested sponsors, the sponsored party may grant the existing sponsor a matching offer option. This can get for each party what it is ultimately prepared to settle for. The mechanism is that the existing sponsor is granted an option to "match" the highest offer obtained by the sponsored party from any other bona fide interested sponsor.

(ii) The third-party offer must be a genuine firm offer capable of being legally accepted by the sponsored party, to avoid it putting in a sham offer just to encourage the sponsor to pay more. The advantage of a matching offer option to the sponsor is that it has the right to get the deal if it wants it at that cost. The benefit to the sponsored party is that it gets the best deal available, *i.e.* either from the sponsor or from the third party which has made the offer to be matched.

2–10

(b) One disadvantage to the sponsored party is that, in all fairness, it should notify all interested parties of the existence of the sponsor's matching offer option right. They then know their proposals are being used as a benchmark by the existing sponsor, but ultimately the party prepared to pay the most will get the deal. In this context the sponsored party should look at the proposed sponsors on an all-round basis. The fee is only a part of the package, although it is the most important element to most events.

(c) A matching offer right should if possible be negotiated and written into a sponsorship contract at the outset for the protection of the sponsor, rather than negotiating the option when the sponsorship agreement is about to expire (see chapter three, paragraph 3–27).

Conditional agreement

2–11

(a) (i) The parties may consider entering into a conditional agreement. The condition may be, for example in the case of an athletics meeting, that within a stated period after the agreement is signed, the sponsored party gets written confirmation that specific athletes will be appearing, or that the event will be televised. The sponsor should be notified in writing that the condition has been fulfilled.

(ii) The conditions precedent would be those which the sponsor sees as being of the essence of its commitment to the sponsorship of the event. If the condition is met in the time, the agreement is confirmed as mutually binding, and if the condition is not met then the agreement lapses and the sponsor has no commitment to the sponsored party. The sponsor can then review its position, and decide whether or not to proceed on the status of the event known at that time.

(b) If, in the above example, the condition is that two named athletes will appear, the condition clause must deal with what happens if only one of them confirms his attendance. Once the whole of the condition is satisfied, and the sponsorship agreement is final, what happens if both or one of the two athletes subsequently fail to appear, due to injury or for compelling personal reasons? What also happens if the athletes subsequently simply change their minds? The legal position as between the sponsored party and the athletes will depend on whether they signed a legal agreement, or whether they simply voluntarily confirmed in a letter that they would appear.

2–12

(c) (i) If the sponsored party has (unwisely) guaranteed their appearance, to the sponsor, on which representation the sponsor entered into a binding sponsorship agreement, it may be able to terminate the agreement for fundamental breach, or it may choose to continue, but claim against the sponsored party for damages, represented by a reduced fee.

(ii) If the agreement is silent on the point, the legal position will depend on the wording of the clause setting out the condition. For example, if the condition is only that the sponsored party will obtain written confirmation of the athlete's attendance, receipt of such confirmation will satisfy the condition, and subsequent non-appearance does not affect the sponsor's legal commitment. If the condition is in two stages, *i.e.* first, that such written confirmation is received (which confirms the agreement and triggers the first sponsorship payment) and, secondly, that he will actually appear on the day and race, then non-appearance will be a breach of the second part of the condition.

(iii) The sponsor's protection may be holding back a part of the sponsorship fee which is agreed as being attributed to the perceived value of the appearance of the nominated athletes. At that point it is too late to withdraw the sponsorship, but it could enable the sponsor not to pay the second instalment of the fee, which has been attributed to the value of that athlete's appearance.

(d) This vitally different effect between the two condition clause wordings at (c)(ii) above demonstrates how carefully the sponsorship agreement should be drafted, for the benefit of both parties. Within the "boiler plate" clauses (*i.e.* those common to most agreements and which are not dependent on the nature of the agreement), a sponsorship agreement should always have a *force majeure* clause, which should be wide enough to cover this kind of situation , but not so as to nullify the terms of the condition.

4. Sponsorship agents and consultants

2–13 Sponsorship is a major sector of business in its own right, and is no longer an amateur's world. Because it is spread over most sporting, cultural and educational activities, both potential sponsors and those who seek sponsorship may be unaware of the availability of suitable matching partners. They will probably not have the experience to undertake an assessment of compatibility, and to negotiate all of the terms and conditions which may be appropriate to their individual requirements. The sponsor may be looking at specific areas from which it would benefit, and may be undecided as to whether to do a one-off test, or to have a medium-term commitment. The party looking for sponsorship may not care where the money comes from and its immediate need for forward planning may depend on how much sponsorship it can obtain. Uncertainty in planning a campaign for consideration by both parties can result in a hasty and unwise decision being made.

Either party in those circumstances would benefit from obtaining the assistance and advice of an established reputable sponsorship agent who has experience and contacts within the scope of putting together potential partners in a sponsorship venture. There are several such agencies, and while the larger ones may be able to assist any inquirer, there are some which specialise in, *e.g.* athletics, or culture and the arts, or international events such as yacht racing.

Distinction between agents and consultants

2–14 In the field of sponsorship, agencies usually represent rights-holders and work on a commission basis. A sponsor who is dealing with the same agency needs to be alert to the fact that the agency is interested in maximising the level of the sponsorship fee. The sponsor should contract with the rights-holder directly, not the agency, unless the sponsor enters into an ongoing relationship with the agency to help it exploit its sponsorship package. In that situation the sponsor needs to anticipate a conflict of interest between the sponsor, the rights-holder, and possibly other sponsors of the same event for whom the agency is working, and set out clear objectives in the sponsorship agency agreement that the agency must meet.

A sponsorship consultancy, on the other hand, works for the sponsor to exploit the sponsorship rights. It will work on a fee basis and will have nothing to gain from the price paid for the rights and no direct relationship with the rights holder. In fact a sponsorship consultancy will be battling against the sponsorship agency to bring the price down. A sample sponsorship consultancy agreement is available to ISBA members.

Before appointing any sponsorship agency to act as its adviser, the sponsored party must discuss with the agency and get written confirmation of at least the following information:

(a) Fee for preliminary discussions

2–15 What fee (if any) will be payable if, after discussions with the agency, it is not appointed? There should be no fee, except that if the agency at the request of the sponsored party has undertaken some preliminary work during the period of discussion, it may be due some payment based on the value of the work done. Before any such work is requested, the possibility of cost should be clarified.

(b) Fee for unsuccessful efforts

2–16 Upon appointment, what fee will be due to the agent as remuneration for the work that it does? For example:

(i) Will the agent be paid a retainer? If, notwithstanding all reasonable efforts, there is no success in finding adequate sponsorship money from an acceptable sponsor within an agreed period, resulting in termination of the agency agreement, will there be a fee for the time spent by the agency, as well as repayment of any expense it has incurred?

(ii) If the agency is successful in obtaining firm offers from willing and suitable sponsors, none of which are accepted by the party seeking sponsorship, is there a fee for the agent's wasted effort? This scenario is not likely because sponsorship money is hard to find at the best of times, but the consequences should be considered. A fee may be payable at the rate the agency would have received for the event, or during the first year of a periodic sponsorship, if the sponsorship deal had been concluded.

(iii) A party seeking sponsorship is not obliged to accept any sponsor put forward by the agency, but if there is no valid reason for rejecting a proposed sponsor, the agency will have done what it was asked to do (*i.e.* find a suitable sponsor), and it will be entitled to be paid. The agency agreement may say that no suitable sponsorship should be unreasonably rejected, at least for the purpose of crystallising when the agency fee becomes payable. This clause in the sponsorship agency agreement should be checked very carefully, to make sure that the agent's entitlement in those circumstances is fairly set out and is absolutely clear.

(iv) The fee will also be payable if the party seeking sponsorship rejects a sponsor put forward by the agent, but some time later (even after discussions with other potential sponsors) goes back to that previously rejected sponsor and then accepts it and enters into a sponsorship agreement with it. The agent may not have negotiated the deal, but it did originally introduce the sponsor to the sponsored party.

(c) Fee on finding a sponsor

2–17 (i) What will the fee be if the agency finds a suitable sponsor, and an agreement is signed with the party seeking sponsorship? It will be a percentage of the sponsorship funds, normally between twenty per cent and one third, depending on all of the circumstances, plus expenses. The commission will be payable on all funding under the sponsorship agreement in cash, for so long as the agreement with that sponsor continues, whether that is under the initial agreement or any renewal of it.

(ii) If the sponsor also provides goods or services as part of the sponsorship fee under the contractual commitment, the agency may also want to have its commission calculated on the value of those goods or services. If it does, the basis of valuation of the goods or services must be agreed, *i.e.* at the cheapest rate that would have been charged to the sponsored party if the supplier was not a sponsor. Then the sponsored party must also ensure that it has the necessary cash from somewhere with which to pay that commission calculated on such goods or services.

(iii) Depending on the extent of the obligations of the agency to actively participate in the running of the sponsored event, such as being available for advice, or to attend special functions, there may be continuing expenses of the agency to be reimbursed. The kinds of expense for which the agency can claim reimbursement must be set out by category, and should exclude any ordinary business expense. Any expense in excess of a given figure should be first approved by the sponsored party, to ensure that its budgeting is not exceeded.

5. Agency agreement terms

2–18 There will be two agreements to be negotiated by the party seeking sponsorship: the agreement with the agency to represent that party in procuring sponsorship and negotiating with sponsors, and the agreement between that party and the sponsor. Once the agency agreement is signed the efforts of the agency will be concentrated on the business of getting sponsorship deals. The following practical factors should be borne in mind when negotiating the agreement with the agency:

(a) While the agency will have its standard form of agency representation agreement ready, the party seeking sponsorship should be advised by its legal advisers upon the meaning, reasonableness and consequences of the standard terms, and upon whether they should be modified or added to. "Standard" relates to that particular agency's terms and conditions. There are no industry-wide standard terms; each agency has its own style of agreement.

(b) Standard terms are designed to cover normal circumstances as perceived by the agency, which may or may not all be appropriate for each client of the agency. Then there will be other additional clauses which are needed to give effect to all of the other individual terms which may be negotiated and agreed between the parties. Standard terms should be considered to be there for initial guidance only.

2–19

(c) If the agency is not prepared to modify or extend its standard terms to accommodate the reasonable requirements of the party seeking sponsorship, then it should seriously consider not appointing that agency. On the other hand, if a reputable well-established agency with major clients considers that the demands of the potential client are unreasonable, it will decline to continue with the negotiations. What is "reasonable" depends entirely on the circumstances of the proposal being negotiated.

(d) Will the agency in consultation with the sponsored party (its client) negotiate the sponsorship agreement between each prospective sponsor and the sponsored party, or will that be done by the sponsored party's own legal advisers in consultation with the agency? If it is the former, will the whole cost of negotiation come within the agency fee, and if it uses its own solicitors will their charges be payable by the sponsored party?

(e) The agency is being appointed because of its experience and expertise, which will include advising upon what terms can best be obtained for the sponsored party, and advising upon the form of sponsorship agreement to submit to the proposed sponsor's legal advisers. If the sponsored party wants to double-check the proposed deal's terms and the draft documentation through its own solicitors, assuming that they are experts on sponsorship, it may do so at its own cost, and provided that does not unreasonably hold up or interfere with the progress being made by the agency.

2–20 Will the sponsorship money be paid directly to the sponsored party, which will then pay the agency, or will the agency receive the payments, deduct its commission and agreed expenses, and pass the balance onto the sponsored party? That will depend upon how organised the sponsored party is, how much is involved, when it is due to be paid, and whether there are several sponsors involved. If the agency is well established, and provided that the sponsored party does not lose out on interest on deposited funds, it may authorise the agency to receive all sponsorship fees paid for specific purposes, and to account to the sponsored party accordingly.

2–21 During the sponsorship period, what will the agency be doing for the sponsored party to justify the total commission payable? The four areas which need to be addressed are:

(a) to procure sponsors, and to negotiate and conclude the agreements for the benefit of the sponsored party;

(b) actively to advise and consult with the sponsored party during the planning of the event, during the event itself, and tidying up the loose ends afterwards;

(c) the management of the sponsor's activities in connection with the event, during the sponsorship period; and

(d) licensing of and managing any other form of promotion rights, such as by merchandising.

6. Capacity of the parties

2–22 Most organisations which obtain sponsorship are not commercial companies or organisations, so for the safety of both the sponsor and the sponsored party, the following simple precautions should be taken to ensure that there is no fundamental unintended flaw in the validity of the sponsorship agreement.

Sponsor

2–23 The sponsor, which is likely to be a commercial company, should check its memorandum of association to satisfy itself that it has the corporate power to enter into sponsorship arrangements, particularly those which might not be obviously to the direct marketing benefit of any of the sponsor's specific products. The articles of association should be checked to see whether a sponsorship agreement can be signed by an authorised executive, or whether it needs the authority of the board of directors.

It may depend on the level of sponsorship being considered. A £50,000 deal may be accepted as being within the level of marketing expenditure which is allowed for in the company's annual budget, and which can be committed by the marketing director without higher authority being obtained. If the sponsorship is, for example, either a level of £500,000, or a long-term commitment which can reach that level of cost overall, it might not be considered as something undertaken within the ordinary course of the company's business, and therefore it will require the prior approval of the board of directors.

2–24 A marketing director sometimes exceeds his internal authority, and signs a sponsorship deal for which he should have obtained the approval of the board of directors. If, on discovery of that deal, the board confirms that it would not have approved the deal had it been consulted, the question then is whether the company is bound by the sponsorship agreement signed by the marketing director on its behalf. If the marketing director showed every sign of having the ostensible authority to make the deal, and the sponsored party had no reason to doubt that was the case, the company will be bound by the agreement.

If the sponsored party had reason to question the marketing director's authority, such as where the deal is far higher than any previously entered into by the company, or if for major points the marketing director says he needs to consult his colleagues, the sponsored party should ask for written confirmation of that authority. If a major deal is being negotiated by a marketing manager, the sponsored party should realise that he may not have an absolute authority to commit the company. The answer is to ask for a copy of the resolution of the board of directors authorising the signing of the sponsorship agreement by the marketing manager.

Sponsored party

2–25 If the sponsored party is a limited company then the same comments will apply to it within the context of receiving sponsorship funds in consideration of granting to the sponsor the rights set out in the sponsorship agreement. The sponsored party may not be a limited company, but may be a partnership, or an unincorporated club, or an association which is the governing body of the activity being sponsored, or an entity established by a charter. Because none of these are normally established for a commercial enterprise, the committee, council or other governing body should check whether the constitution of the sponsored party covers the right to seek and receive such funding, and the right to grant rights for the commercial exploitation of the event.

2–26 The constitution of the sponsored party will also indicate how it is able to enter into legal contracts, which contain enforceable commitments and liabilities to a greater or lesser degree. For example:

(a) A limited company as an independent legal entity will itself enter into the agreement through its authorised signatories, who have no personal obligations or liabilities although they signed the contract. They signed it as the company's authorised representatives.

(b) An unincorporated members' club has no legal identity separate from the members, who may empower the club's committee to commit the club contractually. In this case the members of the committee, and probably the club members (depending on its constitution), will remain personally liable for any commitment entered into by them on behalf of the club. Whatever the form of the sponsored party, its means of committing itself legally has to be established and reflected in the description of the sponsored party at the beginning of the sponsorship agreement.

(c) An association may simply be a central organising body established as a matter of convenience for the administration of a number of related clubs, and with no fixed constitution in its own right, and with no independent recognised legal identity. Such a loose association has no capacity in itself to enter into any legal contract, and if it is not properly constituted, it may well not have any authority to do so on behalf of its associated clubs. If the clubs intend to be legally bound by the sponsorship agreement all together, a duly authorised representative of them all could sign it, possibly the association's general secretary. The decisions and signatory authorities should all be confirmed properly in writing by those who are empowered to exercise those responsibilities.

2–27   If the purported party to the sponsorship agreement has no legal identity, *i.e.* it does not exist in its own right to sue or to be sued, then whichever individuals signed the sponsorship agreement as representing that sponsored party may well be personally liable to the sponsor for all of the sponsored party's obligations. In the absence of being able to prove that they have acted in good faith only as the authorised agent or representative of an independent legally constituted entity which accepts the role of principal and that it is the contracting party, the individual signatories will themselves be deemed to have acted as principals. This problem should not occur in an organised environment, but it might happen where a small or inexperienced unincorporated body is taking on a commercial venture for the first time.

7. Identity of sponsored party

2–28   It may sound self-evident, but the sponsor should require the sponsored party to satisfy the sponsor that the sponsored party is the correct party to contract with for the sponsorship support. The sponsored party has to be legally entitled to grant the rights contained in the sponsorship agreement, and has to be the liable party if the sponsor is entitled to make a claim against it. This precaution is as much for the protection of the sponsored party as it is for the sponsor.

Within the event activity, those sponsorship rights may belong to an association or governing body, which has delegated the administration of the event to the local active branch. There may not be a clear ownership of the event in the proprietary sense—it may be happening because a group of different concerns have pooled their efforts and expertise to create one unified effective working party to stage the event. In these circumstances, who should be responsible as the sponsored party, and who should receive the sponsorship funds, must be established.

For a new event, or an existing one which is new to sponsorship, the identity of the sponsored party should be researched and agreed, if it is not clear from the start. If the "owner" is a representative of a number of interested parties, they will decide between themselves how any sponsorship funding is to be allocated and spent. The sponsor will not be responsible for what happens to the funding after it has been paid to the party which contracts as the "sponsored party" with the correct authority.

8. Dispute Resolution

2–29 The importance of a clause dealing with dispute resolution is often underestimated and parties consistently fail to address the risk of a breakdown in relations or communication. A swift and effective method of resolving differences between the parties is the key to a successful sponsorship. Court action is not necessarily the best option, and delays, bureaucracy and the expense of court litigation have led to the development of alternative means of dispute resolution, often referred to as ADR.

ADR is to be distinguished from arbitration, which is governed by the Arbitration Acts and organised under the arbitration rules of bodies such as the International Chamber of Commerce, the Chartered Institute of Arbitrators and the London Court of International Arbitrators. Arbitration can be more informal than court proceedings and is generally, but not always, quicker and less costly.

ADR includes conciliation and mediation procedures such as those set out in the Centre for Dispute Resolution (CEDR) Model Mediation Procedures. A mediator will act as an expert, not an arbitrator, in the settlement of disputes and, for example, could involve the appointment of an expert by a sports' governing body to deal with technical disputes.

The Court of Arbitration for Sport

2–30 CAS was created in 1983 to offer parties a means of settling disputes adapted to the specific needs of the sports world. Based in Lausanne, Switzerland (with two decentralised courts also available in Sydney and Denver), CAS is competent to hear any dispute directly or indirectly linked to sport, including disputes over sponsorship contracts, and is suitable for both domestic and international sports related disputes. For a dispute to be submitted to arbitration by CAS, the parties must agree to this in writing.

CHAPTER 3

Sponsor's Rights

1. Introduction

3–01 The most important thing for a sponsor is to determine exactly which rights it is granted under the sponsorship agreement. The rights represent the value in return for the sponsorship fee. The sponsor's rights will depend on what the event is, different kinds of events have different attributes and activities which generate rights appropriate only to themselves. There are rights which will apply to most events whatever they are, because they all have common factors. The rights acquired will also depend on whether the sponsor is the sole sponsor, a primary sponsor, a secondary sponsor, or an official supplier. The sponsorship responsibilities of each are different, and so will be the returns by way of promotional opportunities. This chapter describes the normal rights which can be acquired, and will also refer to specialised rights in the more familiar types of individualised sponsorship. This will not be a complete list—it is up to each sponsor to ask for and negotiate whatever rights it would like, assuming they are appropriate to that kind of deal and that the sponsored party is free to grant them.

2. Exclusivity

3–02 Because the association of the sponsor with the sponsored party, and the marketing and promotion opportunities created by the sponsored event, are the main reasons for a sponsor entering into any sponsorship agreement, the more exclusive the sponsorship, the greater the value to the sponsor. Marketing is, by its nature, a competitive activity, the purpose of which is to persuade consumers to buy one company's products as opposed to those of another. Sponsorship is a different means of attracting attention to the sponsor and its products, and if several sponsors (even if not competitive) publicise their support for and association with the same event, it does not always have the same impact as that which can be obtained through having exclusivity.

It will depend upon the event. For example, a motor-racing team is expected to have many sponsors, and that does not affect the impact for each individual sponsor. If the event is an opera being staged at Wembley Arena, that show is a one-off production, although it may last for a week. Depending on the cost of staging it, one large corporate sponsor would be usual, but two major institutional sponsors can benefit equally. The impact of a number of small sponsors would be much reduced, to the possible extent that any individual sponsor's contribution may not be noticeable.

3–03 A sole sponsor has exclusivity of sponsor-related promotional activities, and has the sole responsibility of undertaking all of the sponsor's obligations. This would be normal where the event name contains the brand name of the sponsor's product.

A primary sponsor, to all intents and purposes, has exclusivity, although it does not have it contractually. Winfield and Benson & Hedges are the primary sponsors of their Formula One Teams, which are named after them and which become synonymous with them. If that team is referred to in the press, or on television, or as a general topic of conversation, automatically there is reference to or recognition of the primary sponsor. For promotional purposes this is as good as having exclusivity. Primary sponsors get the lion's share of the public recognition, but they also put up the lion's share of the sponsorship cost.

3–04   Secondary sponsors, such as oil, tyre and spark plug companies, within their own product category have exclusivity of sponsorship, and have the same promotional capacity from being involved in a winning car. In motor-sport it is likely that such secondary sponsors will have their products used by a number of competitors, and so have spread their exposure accordingly. The difference for motor-sport secondary sponsors are that:

(a) They may not put money into the teams, but they will make their products available to them free or at a significant discount. They will also provide teams with technical assistance on and off the track, which may be crucial when it comes to engine and chassis tuning.

(b) A product-related secondary sponsor is chosen by the team (see (c), below). Therefore, irrespective of whether the secondary sponsor wishes to provide products to a given team, that team may already be contracted to use only the products of a rival manufacturer.

(c) Because motor racing is one of the most competitive sports, and because success depends largely on the faultless performance of components under the greatest possible stress, teams will choose only those products they believe will give them the greatest reliability.

3–05   Even if a sporting competitor is not sponsored by, for example, the makers of his running shoes, or the tennis racket or golf clubs he uses, and assuming also that the competitor is not endorsing those products for the manufacturers, is it possible for the manufacturer of that product to make marketing use of that fact? The inference of most advertising which associates an individual with a brand of product is that the athlete or competitor endorses or recommends the product. Any promotional use of that nature might be preventable by the athlete or competitor, by injunction if necessary, if he has not approved of it (see chapter seven, paragraph 7–11 *et seq.* on personality rights).

Official suppliers have exclusivity within their authorised product range, which will be those products supplied to and used by the sponsored party for the event. Official suppliers are in a similar position to that of secondary sponsors which provide products. The practical difference is that, for example, a motor-racing secondary sponsor's products will be crucial to the team, whereas many official suppliers' products have no direct connection with, or essential use for, the event for which they are appointed. The official timekeeper to an athletics event is a crucial exclusive category; the official supplier of soft drinks is exclusive but not essential.

The competition law aspects of any exclusive arrangements must be carefully considered. See further chapter one, paragraphs 1–65 and 1–66.

3. Title of event

3–06   The most prestigious form of exclusivity is to be able to establish the title of the sponsored event as being "the Widget Event". Apart from any promotion or advertising done by the sponsor to publicise its relationship with the event, whenever the event is referred to by the media news, or in media reports (such as televised events, or the televised announcements of event results), or by any other means at no cost to the sponsor, its name is getting exposure which could not be bought.

There are certain limits to this exposure which may be set by the BBC or ITC, such as excessive "in camera" views of the sponsor's boards at snooker matches which cannot be justified by the editorial needs of the programme itself. The placing of these boards has to be agreed so as to give reasonable exposure to the name of the sponsor and not to inhibit camera views, as snooker players remain static on camera for so long at any one time. They are either sitting down just underneath such a board, or they stand in front of a backdrop and take time to cue for a shot. Whilst the BBC will seek to credit the sponsor of an event fairly, it will not necessarily use the sponsor's name in the title of the television or radio coverage of the event. Visual credits in results information will be given but event sponsor's logos will not be used. The ITC Codes are designed to maintain a reasonable limit on commercialism which does not constitute the ordinary style of directly paid for advertising. It is also recognised that without adequate television coverage sponsorship would be reduced, and certain events which rely on sponsorship may cease.

3–07   The sponsor title value of a one-off event which will not be repeated will depend on many factors, and advertising and promotions centred on it must be planned with enough lead time to make an impact. This also gives the event a considerable benefit, as its own advertising budget may have been modest. The same considerable indirect benefit also applies, for example, to Formula One racing cars, where the name and reputation of the car's designer and manufacturer gets an equal amount of value from the constant joint reference with the name of the primary sponsor.

The same prestige and value apply where the event is a single event which is held annually, such as a tennis championship or a horse race, or where there is a seasonal series of events, such as a football league. The sponsorship agreement will be for a minimum period of time, so the promotional possibilities can be planned accordingly. Those examples are of non-partisan sponsorship, where the identity of who wins is not material, except for short-term public interest at that time. If the sponsor is connected with a partisan element, such as a notorious football team, it may receive an adverse backlash from those who (on an emotional basis) consider that particular football team as "the enemy".

3–08   Seasonal sponsorship can be of, say, a football club first division team. In that case the sponsor is backing its judgment on performance, but the football club will not change its name to include that of its sponsor, or its sponsor's related product. Therefore the sponsor will not have the benefit of a "sponsor title". But the club will publicise the name of its sponsor whenever possible, and the team shirts will have the name, and possibly the distinctive colour scheme, of the sponsor upon them as prominently as the rules will allow.

A sponsor title can be attached to a participant, rather than to the event as a whole. For example, in the major horse show jumping competitions, some of the horses will be called "Sponsor Nag", where the sponsor's name is part of the horse's credited name. All announcements and on-screen identity flashes refer to the full name of the horse, thus providing some of the value being purchased by the sponsor.

The event being sponsored may be a cultural event, such as an opera production, musical concert, ballet tour by a foreign ballet corps, or an exhibition of Chinese art or Tibetan historical artefacts. Because these kinds of events are more restrained in their public presentation, they are not likely to be advertised as "The X Insurance Company Egyptian Exhibition", but there will be a reference to the sponsor wherever reasonably possible in a manner suited to the event.

4. Title of sponsor

3–09   A sole or primary sponsor is closely related to the event through being part of its name. Secondary sponsors may have no specific title, and may simply provide cash or products, such as in motor-racing sponsorship. On the other hand, whatever the title is of the event, certain categories of sponsor may have titles of their own, even though they do not have any direct connection with the management or direct support of the event. Whether or not the title of the event is primary sponsor related or not, the suppliers of goods or services in exclusive categories are known as "the official supplier of . . . ." to the event.

As the choice of the official suppliers ensures that the goods are non-competitive, it does not matter how many such subsidiary sponsors there are, provided they are relevant. Official suppliers of timing devices, drinks and camera equipment are examples of products or manufacturers having their own individual title. Official suppliers also pay sponsorship fees for the privilege of being appointed within their product category. As an example of the marketing use of the title, advertisements may state that X Company is the "Official Supplier of Y Products to the Z Event".

5. Sponsorship agreement period

3–10   The period of the sponsorship agreement will depend on what kind of event it is, or (for the sponsorship of a participant) what kind of sport it is. The period may be influenced by which products are being provided by the sponsor, or whether it is only providing cash. For an individual who is sponsored it will also depend on whether the event being competed in is a commercially orientated one, or whether the participant has to retain an amateur status for international or Olympic eligibility. To retain the artificiality of amateur status, athletes cannot receive remuneration for what they do. However, the equivalent payments can be made to a trust fund which is established in accordance with the relevant rules. Amateur trust fund arrangements are referred to in chapter eight (tax aspects). Examples of how contract periods are generally calculated are set out below.

If the event is a strictly one-off event, such as a charity concert which is unlikely to be repeated, the agreement will simply cover the event, including any postponement of it. The period will effectively be from the date of signing the agreement, through to the completion of the event, and for a period thereafter during which the sponsor can complete its promotional campaigns based upon its association with the event.

3–11   If the event is a regular annual event, such as the Oxford and Cambridge Boat Race, or a famous horse race, the agreement will be for a minimum initial period of an agreed number of years, and thereafter on an agreed basis subject to recalculation of the level of the sponsorship fees. There is no norm for such a period—it depends on the relative long-term commitments of each party. If the event is a horse race which has become a regular feature in the racing calendar as the "Sponsor Handicap", which traditionally is always held at the same race meeting and may be the star attraction, the race organisers would find it most inconvenient to have to change the race title on a change of sponsors every two or three years. Subject to agreement on the sponsorship fee, the sponsor of an established race with a sponsor or product-related title will want to ensure indefinite continuity to protect what will have become a valuable investment in goodwill. A contract cannot have an indefinite period and, if it does, it may well be terminated by reasonable notice given at any time. Therefore there must be a definite means whereby the sponsor can reasonably ensure continuity. The normal problem is the level of the fees, so a fair means of renegotiating them periodically is put into the sponsorship agreement.

3–12 Sponsorship of high-profile, high-cost events is looked at on an annual basis, because there are far more potential events looking for substantial sponsorship than there are serious available sponsors. A non-aligned sponsor, such as a manufacturer of products universally used in the motor trade, or an unrelated product, such as from the tobacco industry, needs to limit potential exposure to sponsorship costs for specific projects in case circumstances arise which make continued sponsorship of that project a bad decision. Motor-racing publicity tends to focus on the participants, both the drivers and the cars, more than on the identity of the events. The same applies to, for example, professional football leagues, where the sponsor of the league has a sponsor-related title, *e.g.* the "X Football League". All football fans may recognise the league title, but how many of them are influenced by it next time they want to buy a camera, or start up a bank account? At that level, sponsorship will only be available to major sponsors for a minimum period, and it has a significant exposure in cost and commitment terms.

Annual competitions over a period of time, such as snooker championships, will normally come within paragraph 3–11 as regular individual events. However, they may also be part of a wider championship or tournament "circus", and so the period of sponsorship of such an event may be related to a series of events. The contract period will still be on an annual basis, but again for minimum periods.

3–13 There are events which are periodic but not on an annual basis, such as the Football World Cup, the Olympics and the Round the World Yacht Race. For the first two examples there are no sole or primary sponsors, apart from the host countries in which the events take place. On each occasion the sponsorship arrangements are separately negotiated by the relevant governing bodies, or their authorised representatives. The Football World Cup is also treated for sponsorship purposes as part of a series of European competitions, so the period of sponsorship may have to cover the whole period in between World Cup events.

For the sponsorship of individual participants, the period of sponsorship may not be calculated on a time basis: it may relate to a series of events in which the participant competes. Where individual sponsorship is also related to the sponsor's product, it becomes part of an endorsement package, and will last for as long as the individual uses that product.

3–14 As the sponsor is paying significant money for the sponsorship rights granted to it, it should have a reasonable period within which to make use of the marketing opportunities. For example:

(a) For a one-off event, the agreement may not state a period for the sponsorship, assuming that the date of holding the event is the effective end of the agreement. That is so in the sense of the sponsor's obligations, but it should be entitled to make what marketing use it can of its association with the event for so long as it considers it has a referrable value.

(b) For an annual event, such as a horse race or tennis tournament, the sponsor will have its rights until some specified time after the event if that is the last of the events being sponsored. Otherwise the rights continue uninterrupted until the sponsorship agreement terminates, even though in the mid period of each contract year public interest in the last event has died down, and there is not yet any advance publicity for the next event. The same applies to other types of event which occur seasonally or occasionally. It is necessary to put an end date on the agreement, so that if the sponsor does not renew the agreement, the sponsored party knows when it is free to seek another sponsor.

6. Sponsorship termination

3–15 Like all commercial contracts, sponsorship agreements will be terminable:

(a) Upon a specified date set out in the agreement.

(b) (i) Upon the party being able to terminate an otherwise ongoing agreement by an agreed period of notice in writing. For example, the agreement may be for a minimum period of five years, and thereafter it may be terminable on either party giving to the other not less than three months' written notice by a given date. If neither party gives notice, the agreement will continue, so it becomes an annual term. The three-month notice would need to be given on or before a specified date reasonably soon after the end of the current sponsored event or season. Alternatively either party may be entitled after the initial period to give not less than 12 months' written notice to terminate the agreement, expiring on an anniversary date of the agreement.

    (ii) The period within which notice may be given should be long enough to enable the sponsor to evaluate both the advantages and the downside of proceeding into the next sponsorship period, which may be another three or five-year commitment. The notice period should also be long enough so that if the sponsor decides not to proceed into the next sponsorship period, the sponsored party has plenty of time in which to find a substitute sponsor.

3–16

(c) Upon failure by one of the parties to remedy a material breach of the agreement in time in accordance with a breach notice in writing. A breach notice should specify the breach and require its remedy within, say, 21 days.

(d) Upon the bankruptcy, liquidation or cessation of business of one of the parties. If the sponsored party enters into administration the administrators may have a continuing obligation to fulfill the contract terms. If a liquidator is appointed the sponsor will rank as an ordinary creditor unless it has taken some security over the assets or made it clear that any fees paid do not become the sponsored party's property until it has performed the related activity.

(e) Upon failure of the event to be held at all, whether or not that is due to a *force majeure* cause. For a single event there is nothing to terminate, but there may be an adjustment of the fee depending on what commitments were undertaken up to the cancellation date. For an annual event, the sponsor will assess whether the failure affects its enthusiasm. For a season of motor races or football matches, one failure within the season may not create a problem, except for fee calculation.

3–17   Because of the nature of sponsorship, the sponsor may also want the right to terminate its contract if, for example:

(a) Where the sponsorship money was to be spent on specific items or for specific purposes, and it has been spent on other things or applied generally to the event costs. If that only happened because event commitments and sponsorship payments dates changed, and no overall damage has been done, a reasonable explanation should suffice. However, if that unauthorised allocation of the sponsorship fees means that more money needs to be found to pay for what the fees should have been used for, there will be a problem.

(b) Where the sponsored event or the sponsored party so changes its image, management or primary purpose that it is inimicable to the sponsor, the sponsor's reputation and image, and the fundamental reason why it undertook the sponsorship in the first place. This would not happen with established sponsored events. It may happen where the event is a one-off event to raise money for deprived children, but changes its aims and intends to contribute all profits to build a sauna for the local tennis club. The sponsorship agreement should state the purpose for which the funds will be used, if that is not already clear.

(c) Where conditions placed in the agreement as being "of the essence" of the sponsorship commitment have not been complied with. These might be guaranteeing certain competitors appearing at an athletics meeting, or the obtaining of other sponsorship to cover a known shortfall where the sponsor is putting in a limited amount. This could happen where the sponsor may be a primary sponsor, but the event will not proceed unless further sponsorship to a specified minimum sum is obtained. This problem is common in motor racing, whether for a team of cars or for an individual competitor.

3–18

(d) If the event is not staged within a stated period. This would come under (c), and may occur where the sponsor agrees to be committed, providing the sponsored party organises the event by a given date. This may be because the sponsor has an occasion on a given date which could profitably be linked with the holding of the event to be sponsored. If that event is to be later, then the sponsor is not interested in it. The sponsored party may approach sponsors on the basis that if the funding is in place it can stage the event. It is a chicken and egg position, and willing sponsors do not wish to have an open-ended commitment.

(e) In the event of regulatory change that might make it impractical or even illegal for the sponsor to continue with its sponsorship. For example, the E.U. Directive on Tobacco Advertising, as well as threats to ban alcohol sponsorship, should be addressed in any long-term sponsorship contract by such a company, and should allow for termination, assignment and/or brand substitution rights to sponsors in sensitive product categories. The sponsor will then have greater flexibility than simply relying on the *force majeure* clause.

3–19 The sponsorship agreement should set out those circumstances in which the sponsor can:

(a) Cancel its sponsorship commitment by termination of the agreement. This would release the sponsor from any continuing obligation to pay further sponsorship fees.

(b) Where relevant, demand repayment of any sums which may have already been paid to the sponsored party, or for its benefit. This right need not be dependent on the sponsor terminating the agreement to make the right come into effect. The individual circumstances will depend upon the kind of activity being sponsored, but they will usually relate to a complete failure of the event, or the failure of the sponsored party to fulfil the essential pre-conditions on which the offer of sponsorship was based.

3–20 The sponsorship agreement would have to be very clear on the issues or events which would entitle the sponsor to terminate the agreement under the matters referred to in this paragraph, with no "grey areas" of ambiguity or doubt. They should be specifically set out, if they are to be identified separately from the usual contractual reasons upon which either party should be able to terminate the agreement. All such conditions which have been agreed as being fundamental to the sponsorship agreement should be stated to be "of the essence" of the agreement, as not all breaches of agreement entitle the injured party to terminate it. It must also state whether the termination right is absolute on the breach or event, or whether the sponsored party is entitled to have the opportunity to remedy the breach in order to avoid termination. The clause is intended to protect the sponsor, and should therefore be worded for its benefit.

3–21 Upon termination and subject to the terms of the sponsorship agreement, repayment may be required of all or part of the sponsorship fee paid to the sponsored party since the signing of the agreement (for a one-off event) or referable to the current contract year (for an annual event under a long-term agreement). Following the example set out in chapter four, paragraph 4–24, the sponsorship agreement would have to set out the circumstances in which any repayment or rebate of the sponsorship fee can be exercised by the sponsor. The right is normally related to non-performance, and how that is assessed depends upon the style of activity to which the sponsorship relates.

Unless there are exceptional circumstances, the sponsor should never make any payment to the sponsored party before an agreement is signed. The repayment clause should also refer to what is to happen if, notwithstanding the lawful demand of the sponsor for repayment of the whole sponsorship fee, the sponsored party has properly spent a proportion of the fee received, such as in accordance with a budget known to the sponsor. Whether the whole of what has been paid to the sponsored party so far should be repaid, or only the balance remaining, should depend on the cause of termination.

7. Postponement of event and extension of contract period

Single event

3–22 If the sponsorship agreement has a fixed period to cover a single event, with the holding of the event scheduled to be well within that period, what happens if for any reason the event is cancelled, or if it is postponed to a date outside the contract's fixed period? The possibilities are as follows:

3–23 **(a) Cancellation**

(i) Cancellation implies that the event will not take place at all, *i.e.* there is no possibility of reinstating it. This might happen if it is to be performed by persons who subsequently find that they are not available, or that there are contractual prohibitions which had not previously been spotted. Depending upon the wording of the sponsorship agreement, cancellation may be a breach or may be a "no fault" circumstance. Either way the agreement has ended, and will not be resurrected.

(ii) The event will not have happened, and if the sponsor has been promoting a product already in connection with the event, that promotion will have to be wound down. Depending on the wording of the sponsorship agreement, the sponsor may have a claim against the sponsored party to recover that wasted expense. The clause would have to be reasonable.

(iii) The sponsor will also want the return of any fees already paid to the sponsored party. Its rights will depend on the wording of the sponsorship agreement. The sponsor may already have had some value from the initial fees paid by it. The proportion of the fee paid on signing the agreement may have been specified as being non-returnable, but that would not be expected to benefit the sponsored party if it did not hold the event. Even so, if the sponsored party is in breach of its own commitments, such as to hold the event, a claim may still be made against it on both counts. Whether sponsorship money already paid by the sponsored party on proper expenses will be recoverable, nevertheless should be referred to in the agreement.

3–24 **(b) Postponement**

(i) Circumstances may have arisen which have forced the sponsored party to postpone the event, or which have made it advantageous to the sponsored party for that to be done. If postponement will take the staging of the event outside the specified period of the agreement, the agreement should be extended for the time needed to cover the event itself, and such a period afterwards as would have been originally available to the sponsor

47

for post-event promotion. If the sponsorship agreement states a date upon which the event is to take place, a voluntary postponement is itself a breach of contract. A postponement to a date which is still within the contract period should be acceptable to the sponsor unless the specified date was of the essence of the agreement to provide sponsorship.

(ii) If the postponement means that material contract terms will be modified, the sponsor should be given the opportunity to review its position, and decide within a reasonable time whether it still wants to sponsor the event. For example, additional unacceptable cost may be involved, or the date or place of staging the event may be inconvenient. A major consideration would be where the original date and venue would have had TV coverage, but the new date and venue means that there will be no TV coverage.

Annual event

3–25

(a) If the sponsorship agreement is for five years to cover five annual events, and in the third year the timing of the event is wholly different from its established date, providing it is staged within that year there is no need to extend the contract period. If the event to be held in the fifth year has to be postponed into what would be the sixth year, an agreement extension should be granted, so that the sponsor gets five events, as intended within its sponsorship agreement. It could equally well be argued that the fifth year event was simply cancelled, so the sponsor only gets four events within its sponsorship contract period.

(b) Whether the sponsor would be entitled to claim an extension to cover the next event, so making it five in six years, will depend on whether the agreement refers only to a time period, or to a specified number of events. Where a cancelled event is not covered by an extension of the agreement, then the sponsor should not make any payments to the sponsored party for the year in which cancellation takes place. Any related fee already paid in advance will be repayable by the sponsored party.

Negotiated extension

3–26 Due to the increasing commercial value of an event which is held annually, it may be a part of the sponsorship agreement that the sponsor's rights will terminate at the end of the minimum period commitment. This would enable the sponsored party to put the sponsorship rights on the open market for the attention of all potential sponsors, to establish their then current value. The following points should be considered by the sponsor when negotiating such a clause:

(a) The sponsor may wish to be able to exert some moral pressure on the sponsored party, with which it may have an excellent relationship. An example is where the sponsor initially took the risk of sponsoring the event (perhaps when others would not), and then built it into the prestigious event it is today with consistent effort and funding. In these circumstances the sponsor would want to have some "edge" over prospective new sponsors when the rights become openly available (see (d), below).

(b) Alternatively, if the current sponsor "bought in" after the retirement of the previous sponsors, when the event was already established, it may only have maintained the event at its original level, and may not have developed it. In this case there is no good reason to give any advantage to the sponsor, which may only be doing an acceptable minimum of work and promotion based upon the event. The difficulty when drafting the agreement is that what has actually been done by the sponsor can only be measured at the end of the period of the agreement. If the event is such that a benchmark can be established as a test of (for example) whether (c), below, should operate, it should go in the agreement.

3–27

(c) When negotiating the original agreement, it may be sensible of the sponsor to offer a pre-determined attractive uplift of fees in future years, to secure a longer minimum period before the sponsored party feels compelled to seek a market valuation of the rights. This can be done either by stating the amount of fee to be paid in each year, or by establishing a formula whereby the uplift in each year is calculated. When the minimum period expires, naturally the sponsor and the sponsored party will discuss the subject of renewal fees. The sponsor might agree to whatever the sponsored party considers to be the current value, or they may find a mutually acceptable compromise to cover the next few years.

(d) (i) In anticipation of the time when the event will be put on the open market to establish the current commercial level of fees for the next period of sponsorship rights, the sponsor should include in the agreement a means of giving it an edge over offers which come from other potential sponsors. The sponsored party should be willing to grant the sponsor a "matching offer option" in respect of the sponsorship renewal. This would give the sponsor the right to match the highest offer the sponsored party gets from all parties interested in the sponsorship deal. Because the event has been developed over the years, the "deal" terms to be considered by potential sponsors may be a fee plus ancillary commitments for products or services. The highest offer will have to take all of these items into account.

(ii) The mechanism is that the sponsored party gives the existing sponsor in writing the details of the highest offer received by the sponsored party. This must be a bona fide arm's-length offer capable of being accepted by the sponsored party. The sponsor then has, say, 14 days within which to respond in writing upon whether or not it wishes to continue with the sponsorship on those highest offer terms. If so, then the sponsored party is obliged to grant the rights to the sponsor on those revised terms, and the new sponsorship agreement is drafted accordingly. If not, that is the end of the sponsor's rights, and the sponsored party is entitled to grant the rights to the party making that highest offer. A matching offer clause must be well drafted to cater (for example) for the situation where the sponsor declines to match the "highest offer", and the sponsored party then proposes to grant the rights at a lower level, or varied rights which would have been acceptable to the sponsor had it been made aware of it.

8. Consequences of postponement, extension and termination

3–28 Postponement of an event should be avoided unless it is absolutely necessary, such as if the stadium burns down. If the event is a small local event the only problem may be getting another suitable venue at a later date. For any significant event, the kind of venue required is fully booked for a long time ahead. The event may be a major tennis or golf tournament, or a qualifying event in the motor-racing calendar, and very difficult to reinstate in that competitive season. Participants or competitors also have schedules to maintain. It would depend to a great extent on how early in the season the postponed event occurs.

For an event where the date is not crucial, whether or not postponement is possible will depend on how close to the date of the event the decision to postpone it is taken. The consequences will depend on what has to be unscrambled and repaid, and whether there are non-cancellable third-party commitments relating to the original date.

3–29 If the period of the agreement is extended due to the postponement of the event, the following may need to be considered by the sponsored party:

(a) Third-party agreements, such as the venue (if hired), caterers and security. These will either have to be renegotiated if already signed, or terminated with any cancellation compensation being paid, depending on how close the event date is. Each of these may have cancellation charges built into their own agreements or terms and conditions of business. If sufficient prior notice is given, they may be able to re-book that date, and so reduce their loss, and possibly the cancellation charge. If they are not being re-booked for the postponed date (such as where a different venue is used), they may not be co-operative on reduced cancellation charges. All of the competitors, participants and subsidiary sponsors will have to be notified, and any other parties who are involved in the event. Claims for compensation, or for a contribution to expenses already incurred, may be made against the sponsored party, especially if the event is cancelled at the last moment.

3–30

(b) An assessment of costs: for example, will the postponement have caused expense to be incurred which is not recoverable, and which will need to be incurred again when the event is reinstated? If so, that will affect the amount of financial support required by the sponsored party when a new date is fixed for the event. That may increase its sponsorship requirements. If the sponsor is a sole sponsor with a fixed commitment to the sponsored party, then the sponsored party will have to find additional funding from elsewhere if the sponsor does not agree to increase its payments. In this case it could not be done by granting additional sponsorship rights.

(c) What commitments need to be made in order to secure the holding of the event upon its revised date? This will probably be a complete re-run of whatever was done in respect of the event prior to its original date.

3–31 For a once-only event, cancellation of the event and termination of the sponsorship agreement have the same practical effect, although the legal consequences may be different. Cancellation of the event by the sponsored party will be a fundamental breach of contract. The cancellation may be accepted by the sponsor in the light of the prevailing circumstances, subject to whatever terminal financial arrangements are agreed. If termination is in accordance with the terms of the agreement, it will normally be by the expiry of time after the completion of the sponsored event in the last year of the agreement, or termination by one party because of the breach by the other party of an important matter in the agreement. Termination which is unauthorised, and which is therefore a breach of contract, may leave the following matters to be dealt with.

3–32   If unauthorised termination is by the sponsor, the sponsored party will:

(a) Be entitled to prevent the sponsor from continuing to publicise and promote its connection with the sponsored party and the event.

(b) Have the right to find an alternative sponsor for the event immediately on terms which the new sponsor will accept.

(c) Have a claim against the terminating sponsor for damages and compensation. The compensation will be to cover:

    (i) any shortfall by the sponsor of its contractual payments.

    (ii) the cost of the sponsored party getting from elsewhere any facilities or services the sponsor was to provide or pay for separately from the sponsorship fee;

    (iii) Any other expense incurred by the sponsored party as a reasonably direct consequence of the termination, and which would not otherwise have been incurred. Any damages awarded would be of a punitive nature as general compensation.

(d) Be entitled to retain all monies already paid by the sponsor pending the calculation of compensation, even though that may have been in advance for the future exercise of sponsorship rights.

3–33   As a general legal principle, the sponsored party will be under an obligation to do whatever it reasonably can to mitigate any loss which it incurs through the sponsor's breach. If, for example, it is able to find a sponsor which pays a higher fee, and which provides greater product related assistance, the claim by the sponsored party for compensation on those grounds may be reduced or eliminated. If, despite reasonable efforts by the sponsored party, it can only find a new sponsor which is not prepared to pay the same fees as the breaching sponsor, the shortfall over the original sponsorship period may be claimed as a part of paragraph 3–22(c)(i), above. The sponsored party may still have a claim for general damages for breach of contract, whatever new sponsorship agreement it is able to obtain.

3–34   It would be unusual for a sponsored party to cut short a sponsorship agreement unless it had received a significantly better offer from a rival sponsor, and is prepared to risk the consequences and breach the first sponsor's contract to get it. If unauthorised termination of the sponsorship agreement is by the sponsored party, the following points may be relevant, particularly if at least one event has already been completed, and with several years still to run on the minimum sponsorship agreement period.

(a) If the sponsor has paid any money for the forthcoming year, then it should all be refundable, even if some of it has been spent by the sponsored party in accordance with its budget. The sponsor will not have had its value for money and a refund would be part of a legal claim. If the termination is relatively close to the commencement of the sponsorship agreement, and if the sponsor had paid a significant "start up" amount as a one-off payment, all or most of that should also be refunded to the sponsor.

3-35

(b) The sponsor may have entered into third-party commitments for the purpose of undertaking its obligations under the sponsorship agreement, or it may have other continuing obligations to third parties under annual agreements. If these cannot be unscrambled at no cost, any cost in doing so may be claimed against the sponsored party. An example may be that the sponsor has agreed to pay the annual venue hire costs as a direct commitment to the venue management. The sponsor may have undertaken to purchase products, or to pay for services, all of which are for the benefit of the sponsored party. Either the sponsored party or the new sponsor should take over these commitments, or the sponsor may claim an indemnity from the sponsored party for the liabilities it has, even though it is not now the sponsor of the event.

(c) The sponsor will have a claim for damages to take into account the loss of marketing and product promotion rights in connection with the sponsored event. This will be aggravated if the title of the event is "sponsor event" or "product event". As sales promotion and media commitments and planning have a long lead time, the sponsor may already have committed expenditure (such as media advertising and printing costs) which cannot be cancelled without paying a cancellation fee, or which cannot be switched to any other use or benefit to the sponsor. Any such inevitable cost will be included in the claim against the sponsored party.

3-36 If the sponsored party wrongfully terminates the agreement, depending on when that happens, and what the event is, the sponsor should first consider its legal position. The choice is to accept the termination and to go through the matters set out in paragraph 3-34 or to contest the termination and to endeavour to get an injunction to prevent the sponsored party from appointing another sponsor, and to get an order for specific performance. The court would probably consider that monetary compensation would be adequate, in which case it would not grant these orders. The main reason is that it is impractical to force the parties to work together by a court order: the sponsor's business is not fundamentally dependent on the sponsorship continuing, and on a balance of convenience proper financial compensation would be the appropriate remedy.

9. Promotion and advertising

3-37 Both the sponsor and the sponsored party will be advertising the event, to ensure that it achieves a capacity crowd or audience, and that the participants are the top people in the relevant activity. The event may be an open event where the participants or finalists have survived qualifying rounds, or it may be an invitation event, where the participants are invited to attend. This would not apply to an event which comes within the arts or non-competitive leisure.

The event name

3–38 The sponsor will be entitled to use the event name, and its association with it as its sponsor, to promote its own image and products. This will be by way of:

(a) Media advertising, such as press advertising and in television advertising. Some products are also suitable for posters and billboards, and other forms of passive advertising.

(b) Sales promotions campaigns. This is an extremely competitive sector, and while standard attractions such as "10% free" are universally used, a promotion based upon sponsorship which is appropriate for the legal restraints governing promotions can be very attractive and beneficial. These are generally "on pack" promotions, but may be product-orientated competitions.

The programme

3–39 The programme for the sponsored event has limited possibilities, but the participants, officials and audience will take a close interest in it. The front cover and whatever other page is considered to be the most effective for advertising should be available free to a sole or primary sponsor, and it can take out as much other paid advertising as is reasonable. The front cover will present the event title and other relevant information with a bold reference to the sponsorship by the sponsor. The back cover can be an advertisement by the sponsor. The centre pages will usually set out the details of the event, be they horse races, athletics events, or the cast and production credits of an opera or musical concert. The event title will be at the top, and somewhere prominent, but in keeping with the style of the event, will be the sponsorship credit. Inside the front cover there may be a potted history of the relationship between the sponsor and the event.

Banners and boards

3–40 Whether the event is held at the Albert Hall, at a major race course, or at an athletics or sports stadium, a feature of the atmosphere will be the banners, placards, arena boards and flags. What is used and where they are placed will be set out in the sponsorship agreement, but they will differ depending upon the type of event. The agreement will also deal with the number of signs permitted, their size and, in some cases, anything which should appear on them. Examples are:

(a) For a football match which is televised, the sponsor may be limited to two arena boards, to be placed, together with all of the other boards, around the perimeter of the spectator security fence. A primary sponsor may be able to choose its arena board placings, and so may secondary and official supplier sponsors, but in an order of priority. The key to successful arena board placing is to establish on an arena or stadium plan exactly where the TV camera positions are. The expertise is then in assessing perimeter places which will, on balance, get as much background on-screen time as possible. Three obvious spots are across the stadium on the centre line of the pitch, and correctly angled boards to the pitch side of each goal as seen from the camera position. The boards should be placed to be visible when corners are taken, or when there is a mêlée around the goal mouth. There are determined sizes for arena boards, and they generally consist wholly of the name of the sponsor, or a product, so as to be catchy, simple, and legible from a distance.

3–41

(b) For a horse race, to have a suitable board at the winning post and a banner at the start line will catch the TV camera for the most static on-screen shots. Then comes the warm blanket which is put over the horse as it is led into the winner's enclosure, plus possibly a banner somewhere around the parade ring.

(c) Much the same applies to an athletics meeting. An example of where a secondary sponsor can obtain excellent exposure is the "official timer" of the event. The whole event depends on the efficient and accurate functioning of the timing system. The exposure areas include an on-screen flash such as "Timed by X", and electronic time boards for the benefit of competitors and spectators placed strategically about the track, at the winning post, and possibly on a giant screen system. Most of these will be in TV camera view in the case of a televised event.

Photographs

3–42   The sponsor may wish to be entitled to use photographs of the event in, for example, product promotion campaigns, general media advertising, or even in its glossy annual report to illustrate some of the innovative marketing strategy it is adopting. If the event is an opera or other event related to the arts, the sponsor may want to publicise in its annual report that it is supporting that event, and is thus making a useful contribution to society as well as making a healthy profit. The arbitrary use of photographs can cause problems, so the right to use them must be researched. The following are among the points to consider:

(a) The right to publish and use photographs should be contained in the sponsorship agreement. The granting of that right only means that the sponsor may use photographs provided that any third-party consent which may ordinarily be required for the commercial use or publication of photographs has been obtained. The contract right will cover photos of the venue taken by the sponsor without further consents being required.

3–43

(b) (i) If the sponsor commissioned an independent photographer to take the photos, the copyright in those photos will only belong to the sponsor if the photographer assigns the copyright to it in writing. A natural and common misconception is that if photographs are commissioned and taken in consideration of an agreed fee, the copyright in the photographs is automatically assigned to the commissioner, without any formality or reference.

(ii) This matter is best dealt with in the agreement for the photographic commission, which will normally be an exchange of letters confirming the terms of date, fee, expenses and anything else. There must be a clear reference in writing to the copyright being assigned by the photographer to the sponsor, and a copy of the letter or agreement should be countersigned by the photographer. In the absence of all that, the sponsor will only have a licence to use the photos for the original purpose for which they were taken. There may have been no specific reference to the use of the photographs in the commission letter, so it only becomes a problem when the photographer challenges the sponsor's use of the photos. For example, if a photograph is specifically commissioned for use as a concert programme front page, it may not be used as a large poster to be separately merchandised by licence through a third party. When in doubt, the photographer should be consulted on the rights granted.

3–44

(c) If the photo is of a crowd scene at the event, such as a mass of spectators, or athletes, or if it is a wide angle shot of a stage full of performers in general terms, individual personal consents to the use of the photograph containing their image will not be necessary. Another common misconception is that a "crowd" is three or more people so that a photographic image of a famous or key individual featured in that "crowd" may be used in the sponsor's promotional campaign without that individuals consent. The true position will depend on a number of factors which are explained in chapter seven, paragraph 7–11 *et seq.* on personality rights, but it has little to do with the number of people portrayed in the "crowd" scene where the particular individual can easily be identified and has not simply been "incidentally included". If appropriate, the agreement between the sponsored party and each featured or key person attending the event should clearly establish that the sponsored party may grant photograph rights to the sponsor in connection with the event and the participation of that person in it including photographs featuring that person in that context. The same will apply whether it is a major rock concert at Wembley, or an opera at Covent Garden.

3–45

(d) If the photo features wholly any individual athlete or performer, their consent should be obtained, unless (as referred to in (c), above) the sponsor has absolute rights, and the individual has given unconditional consent, under or through the operation of the sponsorship agreement. In the absence of clear rights, the following should be checked by the sponsor, although it may be the sponsored party's obligation to do so.

   (i) Obtain the written consent of that person to the use of either any photographs taken at the event, or only agreed photographs. In this case the person's consent should not be unreasonably withheld or delayed. The negotiations may be conducted through the person's agent or manager. Their concern is to ensure that the photo is top quality and shows the performer in his best light, consistent with his projected image and general publicity. To get it absolutely right, for non-competitive events the photos may be arranged to be taken in stage-managed and posed circumstances.

   (ii) What, if any, are the limitations placed on the sponsor in the use and publication of the photos? Their use should only be in the context of the event, and promoting the sponsor and its products in connection with it. To avoid any dispute in the future, it would be better to expressly set out in writing what use can be made of photographs.

(iii) The sponsor would have to be careful that the use of the photos, when connected with the sponsor's product promotion, does not become any express or implied endorsement of that product by that individual. The British Codes of Advertising and Sales Promotion state that an advertiser who promotes its products by connecting them with an individual should first obtain his consent and should not claim or imply an endorsement where none exists.

(iv) If the individual has a lucrative business being marketed as a personality, or as endorsing products for fees, that individual may charge a fee to the sponsor for the commercial use of that individual's image in connection with the "Product Sponsor Event". The sponsor's rights under the sponsorship agreement should make clear that it is the sponsored party's obligation to ensure that all such rights are unconditional.

10. Television exposure

3-46   For major sponsorship deals the most important element is television exposure, as that is the means of reaching a large audience, which concentrates on the TV screen to a greater extent than when it reads any media which contains advertising. Television programming is designed to entertain the public, and there is great pressure on all TV channels to put on what the public wants to see. For commercial TV channels that is the most important aspect, as the viewing figures for individual programmes influence the charge which can be made for advertising during them. The events which are most likely to be sponsored, such as sport, the arts and leisure, compete for viewing time in accordance with public taste. Those events, such as football, which are recognised as being the most popular on a national level, get priority.

Then there is horse racing and athletics, down to snooker and darts. A few years ago snooker was not considered to be anything but a very limited participation leisure club level event, which would not hold sufficient viewing attention to warrant the expense of televising, and taking up valuable scheduled programme slots. The emergence of snooker as a major recognised competitive and leisure activity industry came about through the commercial efforts of a few entrepreneurs, such as Barry Hearn, who took the risk of promoting rising youngsters, and who have succeeded in making them wealthy and skilful personalities. Without television, snooker would probably still be in the shadows.

3-47   For an event within the arts, such as an opera, the television exposure would be by way of having a performance of the opera filmed, and then broadcast. Whether such a performance would be included as part of a regular opera season of TV broadcasts, or whether the opera would be specifically staged for the television production, would depend upon the availability of the right stars, the technical difficulties in directing and presenting it for studio filming, and the cost. The cost of either style of production would be the basis of the sponsorship required. An important factor for a filmed production is that the final programme is a valuable asset, which will be marketable worldwide as a TV programme and possibly a video recording. The potential income in the end should well exceed the total production costs, although that money would not come in for a considerable time. The production would normally be funded by a consortium of TV companies if it is a major cost. If there is already set up a sponsored opera performance, and subsequently the TV rights were sold, would the sponsor be entitled to participate in this windfall? Not unless its sponsorship agreement with those putting on the opera covered the point specifically. Whether it ought to participate depends on whether the sponsorship fee was to cover an income shortfall, and the destination of commercial proceeds.

3–48 If the televising of the event is a fundamental aspect of the sponsorship deal, and which affects certainly the amount of the fee payable by the sponsor, and possibly whether the sponsor would be interested in the first place, the following items should be dealt with when negotiating the sponsorship agreement:

(a) What are the contractual terms?

    (i) The contract must stipulate that TV exposure is of the essence of the agreement, and that a specified portion of the fee is attributable to the TV coverage, based upon a stated minimum anticipated number of hours broadcast. That period of broadcast will be based upon previous experience of the event having been televised, or upon the likelihood of getting it broadcast as a newsworthy event as well as a popular sporting attraction.

   (ii) For an established event with a history of being televised, there should be in place an agreement with a TV company. This may need renewing at the start of the sponsorship period. If the event has never been televised, the sponsored party should approach a TV company to see whether they would be interested. There is little point in the sponsorship agreement referring to the adjustments to the fee, for TV coverage of it is extremely unlikely to be obtained, except to cover the future possibility.

3–49

  (iii) What is the position if for any reason there is no TV coverage at all? This assumes that a TV coverage agreement exists, but it is possible for the filming to be cancelled, or the film taken not to be shown at all. There is also a distinction between live coverage and the later transmission of edited highlights, although both may happen for an important sporting or other competitive event. By the time it is discovered that there was no TV coverage the event will have happened, so there is no point in having a cancellation clause for that failure, unless the fact of no coverage becomes known to the sponsor sufficiently in advance of the date of the event. This would have to be a matter of months, to be fair to the sponsored party. If the loss of television appears to be a permanent one, and TV coverage is of the essence of the sponsorship being provided, the sponsor should be entitled to terminate the balance of the sponsorship contract period. If the sponsored party is told well before the event that there would be no TV coverage this year, it would have to tell the sponsor, to enable it to decide what to do.

  (iv) If for an event there is less than the anticipated level of TV exposure in hours which is stated in the sponsorship agreement as a target, the sponsorship agreement can set out a formula so that the TV attributed portion of the fee for that event can be reduced to take account of the shortfall. This might be by way of a reduction in next year's fee, unless the event is within the last year of the sponsor's contract period, in which case a cash refund may be needed.

3–50

(b) (i) The event may be one which should be of interest to any TV company, and the sponsored party may be able to get one of them to commit to televising the event and broadcasting not less than a specified portion of it. The sponsor should ask for a sight of that contract, whether or not it is completed before the sponsorship deal is negotiated, particularly if a significant portion of the sponsorship fee is based upon TV coverage.

(ii) The agreement will effectively give the exclusive rights of televising the event to that TV company, but there will normally be no absolute commitment by the TV company to broadcast the event. That may depend on whether the intention is to broadcast the event live, or whether it will be filmed for later transmission. In the latter case the transmission scheduling is easier. For a live transmission there are many factors which, on the day, may curtail it or make it either inconvenient or impossible to do.

3–51

(c) The siting of arena boards, electronic timers or advertising banners will then be agreed with the sponsor when the TV camera sites are established.

(d) Whatever the event, the presentation of the trophies or prizes is an important emphasis for the sponsor, as the announcer will mention the sponsor, and will probably introduce the managing director of the sponsor as the person by whom the prizes are to be presented. This will take place in front of a back drop consisting of the event name, which may be a sponsor product title.

(e) Where necessary, depending on the product to be highlighted by the sponsor in connection with the event, the sponsor and the sponsored party should check the BBC and ITC rules on the coverage of sponsored events and what can and cannot be done or presented in deliberate camera view. In particular, BBC rules require that the sponsored events which it broadcasts are free standing and have not been created by a sponsor merely to attract broadcast coverage. Additionally, close-ups of sponsors' branding on the clothing of participants is avoided.

3–52   The event may be a sponsored expedition, such as the climbing of a difficult route up Mount Everest. A permanent record of the event can be produced, and TV coverage hoped for, by making the event the subject of a documentary TV film, from the earliest preparations through to the dispersal of the team after the event has been concluded. The production of filming a documentary is not the responsibility of the sponsored party: normally, the filming rights and obligations would be taken up by an experienced production company. This would ensure that, upon completion of editing the film to documentary length, it would be attractive to TV channels for subsequent broadcast.

Because of the cost, and to obtain the expertise needed, and to create a better opportunity for future broadcast, the filming may be the result of a joint venture between the sponsor and a TV channel. The latter puts in the equipment, personnel and expertise, and the sponsor provides the funds. Some consideration will be given to whether the climb was going to happen anyway, with the filming side being a development of the project; or whether the climb is only being organised for the primary purpose of putting a film together. The contractual arrangements would be slightly different in each case. For example, in the first case the sponsor may not be responsible for certain costs which are being incurred by the expedition, and which are not related to the filming element.

11. Broadcast sponsorship

3–53   Only the commercial channels are permitted to receive funds for broadcasting sponsored programmes (although outside funding for BBC publications associated with programmes may be agreed, provided no on-air credits are given). One of the main concerns of an event sponsor is to ensure that it is not ambushed by a competitor sponsoring the broadcast of the event. For this reason the Institute of Sports Sponsorship Code of Conduct advises members to refrain from undertaking programme sponsorship unless it has first been offered to the event sponsor by the television contractor.

The ITC and the Radio Authority have devised codes on programme sponsorship which are set out in the appendices to this book. In this context, sponsorship is treated quite differently from advertising although there is nothing to prevent sponsors buying advertising slots in and around the broadcast they sponsor, subject to meeting the criteria set out in the Codes.

3–54   Broadcast sponsors must take the usual steps to protect their positions in their contracts with broadcasters. Many of the issues concerning event sponsors will also affect broadcast sponsors particularly regarding TV exposure times. In particular it will be important for the sponsor to ensure that the broadcaster has the rights to broadcast the events, and if the broadcast sponsor is also the event sponsor, all the agreements should be cross-referenced.

Where the event will be broadcast in other countries, it will also be essential to ensure that the respective countries' laws and applicable codes are complied with at both the event and broadcast sponsorship levels.

"Virtual" Advertising

3–55   One major technological development, which will greatly improve the value that event sponsors receive when their events are broadcast, is electronic imaging systems, such as EPSIS or Imadgine, which can alter the received broadcast to suit different markets. This enables one sponsor of an international event to target different markets with different brands, and sponsored events to sell the same advertising board several times over to different sponsors in different territories. The ITC has developed guidelines to ensure that viewers are protected.

12. Obligations relating to participants

3–56   Most events have some kind of participant, but normally sporting events are those in which the participant or competitor can also be used to promote the name, image and product of the sponsor. For this purpose, the sponsor would have to be the sole or primary sponsor of the participants or the event, entitled over all others to make use of the competitors in this way. Motor racing may be the major exception, where the car and driver are plastered with logos, names and emblems of different sizes, and in different visually important (*i.e.* valuable) areas.

3–57 Examples of the rights which can be granted to a sponsor in respect of participants in the event are as follows:

(a) (i) The participants may be asked to wear a vest (for athletes) or a shirt (for football players) which is either in the distinctive colours used by the sponsor in its get up or logo, or which has on it the name or logo of the sponsor's product. This will be subject to the ITC rules on size, position and prominence of such advertising. A football club deal will have taken this requirement into account, but for an athletics meeting, or bowls competition, that may not always be possible.

(ii) For example, if the athletics event were to be sponsored by a well-known athletics footwear company, an athlete who is personally sponsored by a competitive brand of footwear may not be prepared to be personally associated visibly and publicly with the event sponsor's product, and his personal sponsorship contract would probably prohibit him from doing so. If he wins the event, and photos or film of him doing so wearing the wrong product's vest are publicised, his personal sponsor would be most upset. It follows that no competitor will be entitled to wear on his clothing the logo or name of any other company product, whether or not it is a sponsor of that individual, during the event. This is enforced under the rules of the International Amateur Athletic Federation, whereby the national federations are required to insert suitable provisions in their contracts with individual athletes, teams or clubs to cover IAAF competitions.

3–58

(b) (i) In certain limited circumstances the event or the competitor may be required to use the sponsor's products. If the sponsor is a drinks company, the event premises may be required to sell the sponsor's product, and no competing product, in its public bars during the period when the event is held. This could only apply where it would be appropriate for the sponsor's goods to be used, *i.e.* where they would normally be used as a category of goods, or where they are specialist goods which would be beneficial.

(ii) For example, if a bank sponsors an event it would not require anyone to commence using its services as a condition of sponsorship. If a timepiece manufacturer is a secondary long-term official supplier sponsor, such as for athletics and other time-related events or competitions, it might require the event venue to replace its public clocks with those of the sponsor, at the sponsor's cost. The sponsor would naturally provide all of the timepieces and timing equipment needed for the event, and it would be obligatory for them to be used.

(iii) Whether the products are retained by the sponsored party after the event or at the end of the sponsorship agreement depends upon their value, and the official supplier's agreement with the sponsored party. Presentation watches and clocks may be retained, the time-keeping equipment will not. Electronic timing displays would only be available during the event. They are sophisticated developed systems which can be hired from the relevant specialists. The manufacturer of the running shoes used by an athlete may sponsor him providing he continues to use them; and the same applies to a tennis racket manufacturer with a tennis player. Both of these examples would only normally apply to an international or world-class performer. The sponsorship may also be related to an endorsement deal, to complete the publicity exposure.

3–59 In any activity which attracts sponsors there are individuals who are the "stars", and who bring a greater dimension to promotional possibilities. The stars are those who are currently, or who have notably been in the past, the winners, the champions of their sport, or celebrated personalities within the arts. The sponsorship of an individual is undertaken for the same reason. A potential benefit to a sponsor is to be able to call upon an individual who is sponsored, or who is a member of a sponsored team, to make personal appearances for the promotion of the sponsor or its product. One example is the availability for interviews relating to the event, which has a dual purpose of promoting the event as well as the sponsor or its products. Another example is the sponsor being able to call upon the individual to make himself available purely for the promotion of the sponsor, such as to be the celebrity to open a new store of the sponsor.

3–60 Apart from the case of a sponsored individual, these activities will not be part of the normal obligations of, say, a football team member when his whole team or club is the sponsored party. Therefore any such plans will have to be dealt with in the sponsorship agreement, or negotiated at some time during the sponsorship period. The football team member would expect to be paid a separate fee for the promotional appearance, plus any expenses incurred by him in doing so.

The football team sponsorship fee may be calculated on the basis that the sponsor will have free of additional charge the right to call upon the team on no more than (say) five occasions to supply a nominated player to do a personal appearance for the sponsor. Who it is, and when would be convenient, will depend on personal and team commitments. Expenses would still be paid to the team member who is appearing.

If any photographs taken at the appearance will be used for promotional purposes they will come under the rules referred to in paragraphs 3–42—3–45.

13. Event facilities available to sponsor

3–61 Within reason, the sponsor should be able to make practical use of the event to promote itself, and that is usually done by way of hospitality. Event hospitality can be a pleasant and unusual forum within which to do business. Part of the "perks" of being a valued customer or potential customer of the sponsor is to be wined and dined in an impressive manner. Sponsors grade the level of hospitality they give to their executives according to how important they rate the recognition of their achievements. It is also used to return lavish hospitality previously received from other people.

3–62 Sponsored events are ideal opportunities to provide hospitality in unusual surroundings, or to provide entertainment in a manner not available to anybody else. Examples of the kinds of hospitality provided are as follows:

(a) (i) Reserved seating. Because the sponsor has the inside track on internal arrangements for the event, the sponsorship agreement will entitle the sponsor to an allocation of top-price seats, with specifically reserved blocks of seating as agreed. A number of the seats will be provided free as part of the benefits of sponsorship, and some of them will be available at a reduced cost, or at full cost but with a priority purchase right. The priority purchase seats will have to be taken up by the sponsor, and paid for, no later than a specified period before the event. Any such seats not taken up by that date will be put into the pool of publicly available seats. The limited number of free seats will be taken by the sponsor for executives, favoured customers and whoever else it chooses.

(ii) If, for any reason, the sponsor does not wish to give out all of its free seat allocation for business or promotional purposes, the sponsorship agreement should state whether they should be returned to the sponsored party for release to the public, or whether the sponsor will be entitled to dispose of them privately. In practice a sponsor will never find itself wondering what to do with good tickets for a popular event. It is not uncommon for a sponsor to put together a sales promotion campaign for the sponsor product, which has as prizes so many double tickets to the event. The sponsor would need to reserve these from its free or purchased allocation. If the event is not a reserved seating event, the sponsor will get so many free entry passes to distribute as it pleases.

3–63

(b) (i) On the basis that watching any event is thirsty work, the most popular perk is the provision by the sponsored party of impressive hospitality facilities exclusive to the sponsor, with a bar, waiters and adequate space in which the lucky chosen ones can relax, have a drink and a chat, and get themselves together for the event. Depending on the event, hospitality may be provided before, during and after the event. If the event is a day out at the races, all-day hospitality will be appreciated, provided (for some) it is not indulged in too liberally.

(ii) The refreshment hospitality facilities may be a marquee set up in a part of the venue premises which is only available to holders of invitations, or it may be access to the members-only bar and lounge on the permanent venue premises. The facilities to be provided should be set out in reasonable detail. It may be that the reserved seats are also for those provided with hospitality, in which case the numbers of people invited is limited accordingly. If it is not necessarily a seated event, such as a horse race meeting, the numbers of people on the hospitality invitation list will need to be limited. This is because the catering and bar facilities may only be sufficient for a certain number, and the sponsor cannot expect to be able to admit an endless stream of people, who are also spectators. There should be a guest list, and the sponsor must resist all temptation to invite for hospitality anyone not on it.

(iii) The hospitality facility should have adequate security by way of strictly controlled access—for instance, only to those who can produce their printed invitation. Gate-crashing is a challenging pastime which is a feature of any event where it is known that free food, drink and shelter (if it is a rainy day) can be had if you are bold enough to bluff your way past the door attendant. "I'm terribly sorry, I seem to have mislaid my invitation" should be met with polite but firm rejection, should there be any doubt as to the eligibility of the applicant for refreshment.

(iv) If the sponsor is a drinks company, then the hospitality facilities and the public bars at the event will be providing or selling only the sponsor's drink in its category during the period of the event. If it is a brewer, then only its beer and lager will be available. One argument against the condition imposed by the sponsor is that it deprives the dedicated drinker of one particular beer during the event if the sponsor is another brewer. As with any drinks promotion, the hope is that those who are encouraged to drink their beer will be so impressed with it that they will be converted and will continue to drink it. It is not an unreasonable discrimination in those circumstances, and deprivation of a competitive brew for one day will not injure their constitution.

3–64

(c) The event may be one where it would be suitable for the sponsor to have a prominent display of its products, with the possibility (where the product is appropriate) of those attending the event being able to purchase the products, perhaps at a discount price. The products may also be available for demonstration purposes. An example may be where an off-road four wheel drive car manufacturer sponsors a country fair. If it is held over a wet weekend there will be plenty of real situation demonstrations and those squires who are sufficiently impressed can order a vehicle on the spot, with or without free green wellies.

14. Merchandising rights to event title and logo

3–65 Sponsorship of an event, even over many years, only becomes marketable as being of public interest for a period shortly prior to, and during, the event. When the event is over, all the fracas dies down, and public attention is directed elsewhere. Therefore the sponsor has to concentrate its promotion campaigns, competitions, media advertising, revised product packaging and all other means of generating business using the goodwill of the event, over a relatively short period of time.

Some events have a longer promotional lead time than others, usually directly related to the importance of the event and its financial and commercial possibilities. For example, sponsoring a U.K. national athletics meeting has one useful time-span for promotion, but being an official supplier or other sponsor to the Olympic Games has a much longer promotional run-up. For the Olympic Games the sponsorship deals will have been put together well in advance, and the cost to sponsors will be so great that, whatever the perceived added value to their business, they are paying a heavy sponsorship cost just to enable them to be a recognised sponsor. That fact alone is a valuable public image factor. Therefore the sponsors maximise the lead time on product promotion referring to the event, and use the benefits of success for as long afterwards as possible.

3–66 One method of getting promotional use out of what might otherwise be dead time, such as between the staging of annual events, is to set up merchandising agreements. Merchandising is not sponsorship. It is a commercial exercise of its own, whereby a merchandising company is granted the exclusive right to make and sell specified categories of product which display the title or logo of the event. A sponsor which has a product, such as a clothing manufacturer, on which the event name or logo could be used to create a separate line, should require as part of the benefits of its sponsorship package the exclusive merchandising rights in the clothing category.

Merchandising will not be suitable for all sponsors and, even if it is, the grant of those rights, where they are appropriate, may be an influence on the sponsorship fee. Alternatively, instead of receiving a fee from the sponsor for the rights, a sponsored party may be better off granting the rights directly to merchandising companies in consideration for a royalty on the sale of each item of the merchandiser's product which contains the event name or logo, for example, "T-shirts, mugs and other consumer goods, as a means of raising additional revenue.

3–67 Any merchandiser which is not connected with the sponsor (such as being its wholly owned merchandising subsidiary) should be prohibited from using any reference to the sponsor or its logo. The categories of goods for which the merchandising licence is valid may be limited to those approved by the sponsor, if it is the sole or the primary sponsor of the event.

The sponsor may not approve the concept of third-party merchandisers being appointed: it may require the exclusive merchandising rights for the event for itself. That will normally depend upon the sponsor being the sole or primary sponsor, and also upon it being the manufacturer of goods which would benefit from being merchandised or promoted with the sponsored party's logo. Merchandising is an enormous industry in its own right, and may possibly be of no interest to the sponsor except on a limited non-commercial scale. In this case the sponsored party should be entitled to grant the merchandising rights for the event to another party, such as a professional merchandiser. Merchandising is dealt with in detail in chapter six.

15. Official appointment to event management

3–68 The sponsor may want to appoint one of its executives to sit on the management committee of the event, or the sponsored party may ask the sponsor to provide such a person. This might apply where the sponsorship is of the event itself, such as a charity gala event. There may be several possible reasons for doing so. For example, the sponsor's chairman may become the management committee chairman to enhance its status; the sponsor's finance director may be brought in to assist with the accounting structure with special reference to cashflow forecasts and income needs; or the sponsor may just want to keep an eye on things. This will not normally arise where the event is a major commercially sponsored event.

If a representative of the sponsor is appointed to the management of the event, his personal responsibilities and obligations will depend on whether, for example, he becomes a director of the company which runs the event, or whether he is simply an outside unconnected but available consultant for use when the board of directors feel the need. If the event is not owned or run by a company, but is organised by an association (such as for athletics), any sponsor's representative is likely to be a consultant. Whatever the status of the event, the position of that person will normally be an honorary one, *i.e.* no remuneration will be payable and he will only be involved with event business which concerns him. His advice does not have to be taken and he does not give it in any capacity (even if he is a solicitor or accountant) whereby the question of professional negligence should arise. To make the position clear, there should be a letter of consultancy which sets out all these points.

3–69 Can the sponsor's representative have any liability to a third party which has a valid claim for compensation or damages or otherwise against the event directors or committee? The committee may have issued a defamatory statement about someone, or the event itself may have breached or wrongfully terminated a legal agreement with a third party, possibly another sponsor at a secondary level. The question of liability will depend, for example, upon whether:

(a) the representative (notwithstanding his honorary consultancy capacity) could be made equally liable as having, in practice, been active in directorial or management decision making and policy making to the same extent as all of the others, and whether he was customarily put forward as having that level of authority and responsibility;

(b) he had any direct connection with the matter causing the potential claim.

If the representative's capacity is purely as a consultant, the letter setting out his terms of reference—such as how much time and effort he is prepared to make available—should also contain an indemnity from the company or committee for any such liability.

16. Indemnity

3–70 Particularly where the sponsor has no managerial or administrative role in connection with the event, the sponsored party should indemnify the sponsor from any third-party claims arising out of the event, directly or indirectly and back this up with adequate insurance. There is no joint venture agreement or partnership between the sponsor and the sponsored party, and the sponsored party must not hold itself out to third parties as having any authority in this matter, make any statement, or enter into any commitment on behalf of the sponsor. (see further chapter five, paragraph 5–34).

17. Sponsor's other activities

3–71 If the sponsor is a major company, or is a group of companies each of which may have different products or services, it should make sure that in its sponsorship agreement it does not restrict itself, or its associated companies, from sponsoring other activities of a nature which do not compete with the sponsored event. That may need to be expanded in certain areas of sponsorship: for example, an insurance company may have several cultural events to sponsor each year; they may be in the same category, but are not necessarily competitive.

CHAPTER 4

Sponsor's Obligations

1. Introduction

4–01 In return for the rights granted by the sponsored party, the sponsor has obligations to the sponsored party. These are primarily the payment of money or the supply of goods or services to the sponsored party, but may extend to other kinds of assistance for the benefit of the event. These obligations represent the sponsored party's expectations of the sponsorship deal. They are negotiated by the sponsored party to whatever level the status of the event will justify, and they will be a reflection of the commercial value of the event to the sponsor. If the event is well established and the sponsor has just taken over the event sponsorship, the obligations of the previous sponsor should already be well defined, although the level of payments may be negotiated to bring the deal up to date. The sponsored party may also have found some inadequacy in the sponsorship terms from the experience of the previous years, in which case these can be dealt with in the new sponsorship agreement. The event may be a new one, in which case the sponsored party will have to examine its needs from the sponsor, based on the experience of others who stage similar events, and with the benefit of expert advice.

4–02 If the sponsored party has appointed an agency to look after its affairs, and to manage the event and procure and negotiate sponsorship contracts, it will be guided accordingly. Its future requirements should not be underestimated, particularly where the sponsorship fee is required to wholly or partially finance the staging of the event. Where sponsorship is not a financial necessity, but a useful contribution to general funds, the sponsored party can accept whatever deal it likes, without having to put the money as its first priority. An example may be where a race course already holds races, or an athletics association or club already runs an event, and only needs additional funding to help promote or develop the event.

2. To promote the event

4–03 The sponsor should be committed to promoting the event, although it is not always practical to specify minimum levels, or any specific means of doing so. For the sponsor, the primary objective of being committed to sponsorship is to promote itself or its products, not to promote the event as such. But if the event is not publicised, and remains obscure, there is little to which the sponsor can harness its promotional campaign associating it with the event. Publicity for the event will occur when the sponsor promotes its own image or product in connection with the event; the relative emphasis between the sponsor's interests and the event will depend on the style of promotion. Promoting the event will also be promoting the sponsor, so wherever possible it should combine the two.

If the event has a sponsor product brand title, there are many ways of linking the event and the product in promotional activities, but it will only be done when the sponsor's marketing department feels that the public interest in the event is high enough to warrant the expenditure on special stylised packaging or media advertising. For an annual or a one-off event there will be an optimum period for promotion immediately before and after the event. The period available before the event is longer than the period after the event, and will depend on the building-up interest which can be generated. It will also depend on the event itself.

4–04   The London Marathon is a one-day event but the pre-event interest and planning covers a considerable period prior to the event, and the event gets full TV coverage on the day. The Grand National has a high level of public interest for a shorter period prior to the event, and it is also fully televised. Furthermore, both those examples generate national interest for what is a local event. But, from a public point of view, there are other one-day events which have a high focus of interest only on or about that day.

Passive promotion of the event will occur whenever the sponsor refers to the event, if the event title contains the name of the sponsor or of one of the sponsor's products. As the sponsor advertises the product in relation to the event, or when a sales promotion campaign is run linking the two, the event is being publicised. The sponsor can also advertise in the vicinity of the venue to support the event, and where appropriate, to help sell all of the available spectator tickets. The sponsored party and the sponsor may undertake joint promotions of the event in other ways, such as if the proceeds of the event are intended to go to a nominated charity. This could extend to some publicity for the charity, which may have other means of collecting funds which need a boost.

4–05   When the sponsor and the sponsored party initiate discussions on the deal, they should map out, in practical terms, what they each consider would be suitable promotional activities for the event. These would be separate from whatever the sponsor wants to do with its own marketing plans for the event-related product. The sponsor should clarify whether any such specific event-related promotional costs are to be borne as part of its sponsorship fee commitment.

The sponsor should not commit itself to any specific expense or activity to promote the event outside its own budgeted advertising or sales promotion campaign, unless the extent of the additional commitment is limited and clear. If the sponsor is a secondary sponsor, or an official supplier, the event title will not be related to it, and it will not get any benefit from promoting the event independently of its own product promotional activities.

4–06   The secondary sponsors will be able to benefit from the reflected value of the major sponsor's promotion or advertising of the event itself. As public awareness of the event is created and enhanced, their own sponsorship level and limited promotion activities are more closely identified as being connected with the event. If an event has the kind of status that warrants secondary sponsorship or official suppliers then it is a major event. World Cup football and motor racing are two good examples. At that level the cost of acquiring the rights are so great that only major manufacturers or suppliers can bid for them. They do so in the knowledge that the projected support promotion costs will be very high in money terms; but their initial assessment will have been that the overall cost is essential and/or good value.

If some event-orientated advertising or promotion obligation is imposed in the sponsorship agreement, however general it may be, all sponsors with similar rights should ensure that they have the same obligations; unless, possibly, the levels of participation and fee paid are significantly different. For example, secondary sponsors are all in one general class, but different sponsors (depending on their product) may be more deeply involved, or may have a higher profile in relation to the event. Co-sponsors of an event, such as an operatic week at Wembley, will usually have equal billing if they put up cash in equal amounts. If one provides cash and the other provides facilities, it may not be possible to equate on value, but unless there was a substantial disparity in their contributions, they would still probably get equal billing as it may be impractical to differentiate between them on advertising posters.

3. Calculating the sponsorship fee

4–07 The principal obligation of the sponsor is to pay a cash fee to the sponsored party in consideration of all the sponsorship rights granted to it. The fee will be agreed between the parties, and may either represent the anticipated shortfall of income related to the expense of running the event, or it may simply be as much as the sponsor is prepared to pay for the privilege of being a sponsor. The sponsored party will set the amount that it is prepared to accept, and the sponsor has to assess whether it represents reasonable value for money to promote the sponsor or its product. In the first case the event is not intended to be profit-making, but needs cash support to enable it to be staged. In the second case it is likely that a surplus of cash is wanted after the event, either (for example) to pay to a charity, or to go into general support funds. The tax aspects of both paying the fee by the sponsor, and receiving the fee by the sponsored party, are dealt with in chapter eight. There are also further references to problems connected with the sponsorship fee on termination in paragraphs 3–19—3–21, above.

Fee based on shortfall of income

4–08 If the fee is agreed as being an amount required to cover the balance of the cost of the event, where that shortfall (if any) will not be known until after the event when its accounts are drawn up, the following points should be considered. The primary purpose of sponsorship is financial support, and it may not be possible to calculate accurately the likely cost of staging the event. The potential income may be calculable, such as by assessing a "full house" on ticket seat prices, but the unknown factor is what proportion of the available tickets for a full capacity of spectators will be purchased by the time the event starts. There may be other income to be taken into account, such as stall franchises and on-site merchandising licences, which also may not be known until after the event.

The sponsor should have a maximum liability for the income shortfall provisions, whatever the circumstances, which must be stated in the sponsorship contract. The sponsored party would have to accept that if that maximum liability is less than the "loss" on the event accounting, the sponsored party will be wholly liable and responsible for the outstanding balance. The sponsor should be wary of that possibility arising, if the result is that third parties end up by being owed money for services rendered for the event, and not paid. The event may be promoted as "The Widget Event", so the association of the widget manufacturer with the event raises the manufacturer's profile. This may have been seen as an unintended silent assurance by the suppliers, which might otherwise have asked for payment up front, or for a guarantee of payment. If they are not paid, or if they have to sue the sponsored party to be paid, that reflects badly on the widget manufacturer, especially if the failure to pay by the sponsored party creates significant adverse publicity.

4–09 No sponsor will write an open-ended cheque for any sponsored party, as this could be viewed as an invitation to a disorganised sponsored party to incur excessive or unnecessary expenses that might not otherwise have been contemplated. There may be all sorts of unexpected genuine expenses, or increases in known categories of costs. These may not have been allowed for, because the sponsored party did not prepare the cost projections and cashflow budget carefully, or did not allow a generous contingency to cover such eventualities.

The sponsored party may not be run by a businessman who is used to the art of preparing budgets and forecasts, and who is able to anticipate problem areas where costs have not been absolutely settled. The total deficit could amount to far in excess of what the sponsor wants to pay, or can afford to pay. That is why the sponsorship agreement must set an absolute limit of liability of contribution by the sponsor.

4–10 There is also a point at which the sponsorship fee could exceed the value the sponsor would attribute to it in terms of the promotional benefit of the event. Where the sponsorship fee is not a fixed amount, but there is a cap on the sponsor's total liability, the sponsored party has flexibility in how it manages the finances for the event (see paragraph 4–11, below, in connection with suggested limitations on the sponsored party's ability to indulge in creative accounting).

The sponsor's obligations would also have to refer to the situation where all other income for the event being taken into account, in fact there is no shortfall at all. In the absence of anything to the contrary, in this style of sponsorship fee calculation, if there is no overall income shortfall, no fee is payable. For example, would there be a minimum fee in any event to pay for the fact that the sponsor was granted promotional rights in respect of the event, even though it did take a risk on the potential amount it would have to pay?

4–11 Where a "contribution to cost" sponsorship payment is to be made, the agreement must set out how the "cost" is to be calculated. This is not the same as the sponsor contributing to an overall loss, as in paragraph 4–08, above. The intention is for the liability of the sponsor by way of its fee to be identified with an agreed item of cost, which it may pay directly, or for which it may pay the sponsored party for onward transmission (see paragraphs 4–13—4–15). The sponsor's liability would be the whole payment of, or a contribution towards a specific cost, such as the cost of the hire of a hall or equipment, which would be a known amount. Alternatively, the contribution could be a fixed amount towards a pool of prize money, when the amount to be paid out may not be known at the time the sponsorship commitment needs to be made.

Under both paragraphs 4–08 and 4–11, above, the sponsor's normal intention and expectation would be to help towards genuine running costs, and not to contribute towards the profit of a third party which is not an unrelated arm's-length provider of services, goods or facilities needed by the sponsored party in the staging of the event. Hence the attribution of the sponsorship fee towards a loss with a limit, or to a nominated category of cost. For example, if the sponsored party just happens to own the equipment hire company, which itself makes a profit on hiring the equipment to the event, the sponsor may want that cost to be excluded in calculating the profit shortfall or as a valid "contribution to cost" figure.

4–12 The sponsored party should be obliged in the sponsorship agreement to provide the sponsor with a reasonably detailed budget analysis of the costs to which the sponsor is expected to contribute. The sponsorship agreement should also set out those categories of cost which will be accepted by the sponsor as coming within the definition of "cost". Fixed item costs can easily be obtained. But if, for example, the cost in question is stipulated to be the provision of all music-related expenses incurred in staging the event, what is that intended to mean? Depending on the kind of event, it could mean just background music cost or, for a major football cup final, it could mean the cost of hiring the Pipes and Drums band of the Coldstream Guards for the interval. Where the sponsored party appears to have an absolute discretion in incurring the cost, if the sponsor has an absolute liability, the sponsorship agreement must set out some reasonable means of limiting its agreed financial exposure.

Direct payment for goods or services

4–13   Instead of paying a fee in cash, the sponsor may agree to pay directly for the cost of providing goods or services, again to a specified amount. In the first case the sponsored party would have to make sure that the supplier's account is paid promptly and fully by the sponsor. A direct contract between the sponsor and the supplier may not be a usual form of financial support, but could be of use where the cost of the item is subject to VAT, and the sponsored party is not registered for VAT, but the sponsor is. On the other hand, it may be more convenient for tax purposes (for the sponsor) if the cost is paid in cash to the sponsored party, which can then make its own arrangements with such suppliers, particularly if the sponsored party is a charity.

4–14   (a) If the sponsor agrees to contract directly with the supplier, but for all practical purposes the supplier deals entirely with the sponsored party, the sponsor should look carefully at the supplier's terms and conditions of doing business. For example, where the goods are hired from the supplier, its terms and conditions of hire may state that if the goods are damaged or stolen, the "customer" shall be wholly liable for the repair cost or the cost of replacement of the goods, or for the excess payable by the supplier when it claims on its insurance.

(b) The sponsor considers that, in accordance with the sponsorship terms, it should only be responsible for the hiring fee of the goods, and that any of the loss or repair liability should be the direct responsibility of the sponsored party. As the sponsor is contractually the "customer", and as the supplier has no contract with the sponsored party, all such additional costs or liabilities would have to be paid by the sponsor.

(c) It should then have a right of indemnity from the sponsored party set out clearly in the sponsorship agreement, so that it can claim for reimbursement against the sponsored party. A formal claim would only have to be made if the sponsored party refuses or fails to reimburse those costs to the sponsor, or to pay them direct to the supplier. Should that be the case, it could be evident that the relationship between the sponsor and the sponsored party has failed, possibly permanently. The sponsor should therefore research the matter very carefully before agreeing to accept direct liabilities of this nature.

4–15   (d) If the sponsored party contracts directly with the supplier, and the sponsor agrees to pay the supplier's invoice, for the same reasons as in (a), above, the sponsorship agreement must make it clear that the only liability of the sponsor is the original hire fee, not any further or consequential amounts due to the supplier from the sponsored party. In this context the sponsor should also look carefully at the terms and conditions of the supplier.

(e) If, for example, the "hire fee" is an amount per day from collection (or delivery) to the day of collection (or return), the defined hire fee can mount on a daily basis for a long time if the sponsored party absconds with the goods supplied, or if they are stolen. The definition of hire fee may be "any and all monies due from the customer to the supplier under this Agreement and howsoever arising". In that case the hire fee would include all loss and damage claims, and excess hire fee and any interest payable on it. Therefore the sponsor fee commitment in respect of that specific supply of goods should be specified to be "X days normal hire fee", with specific reference to no responsibility over and above that amount. To be safe, a stated fixed amount should be put as the outside limit on the hire fee liability. The hire fee may be payable in advance, but the same principles apply to the wording of the sponsorship agreement relating to this liability.

(f) The individual expense may be the public address system, or the hire of premises in which to hold the event, or anything else of a reasonably substantial nature. This is more likely to apply to a secondary sponsor, as a primary or a sole sponsor will always have to provide the bulk of all of the cash required for the staging of the event. This kind of sponsorship is not the same as the official supplier status sponsor providing its own products.

An agreed fixed fee

4–16 The sponsorship fee may be an agreed substantial sum, not related or limited to any event income shortfall, or to any specific cost allocation. If the sponsor is to be the sole or primary sponsor, the sponsored party will have to calculate carefully all the costs of staging the event, plus a liberal contingency before quoting an overall fee. If the sponsor has experience in sponsoring similar events, it may be able to judge whether the quoted fee is reasonable within the context of the proposed event. If it does not have the experience, it should seek expert advice, to avoid the problem referred to in paragraph 4–08. What the sponsored party thinks it needs, and what a sponsor is prepared to pay, may not be compatible. If that remains the position, then there is no sponsorship deal.

If the sponsor agrees to pay a fixed sum, it is not relevant whether or not the sponsored party makes a profit on the event. If the sponsored party is, for example, an athletics association or other body governing a full-time leisure activity or sport, the excess of sponsorship money received by it over the costs of staging the event is not a "profit" in the normal sense. It is additional income from that source to be put into the general kitty for the benefit of that association's sport as a whole.

The sponsor will be concerned to be satisfied that, if it is a sole or primary sponsor, the sponsorship fee will in fact be sufficient for the event to be undertaken. There is no point, and every disadvantage, in the sponsored party quoting a lower than required fee for fear of losing the sponsor, but at the same time realising it may not be enough to enable the event to proceed. Inevitably there will come a time when the money runs out, and to save the event, and to prevent it from being commercially embarrassed, the sponsor will have to top up the deficit. Alternatively, but only if the sole or primary sponsor approves, the sponsored party can try to find additional sponsorship, but time will be short and new sponsors may be put off by the sponsored party's current problems.

4. Payment of sponsorship fee

4–17 How the fee is paid depends on several factors, such as the cashflow needs of the sponsored party, the dates by which specified proportions of the fee are agreed to be paid to the sponsored party, and subject to any safeguards in the sponsorship agreement for the sponsor against overpayment. There may be conditions imposed by the sponsor which determine the final amount payable for the event, or during a sponsorship year. For example, the sponsorship fee may be reduced if TV coverage is not obtained for the event. Whether that is done by a refund, or whether the sponsor retains that element until after the event, should be set out in the sponsorship agreement.

There may also be a formula by which the basic sponsorship fee is increased, should specified events happen. Different kinds of event will have different needs, and in this context only sole or primary sponsors are likely to be affected. Secondary sponsors, with lesser commitments, would normally be expected to pay their fees in one lump at some specified time prior to the event.

4–18 For a one-off event, such as a concert, a substantial part of the cost of staging it will be incurred well before its date, so payment of the sponsorship fee should be scheduled accordingly. Depending on how far in advance the sponsorship deal is set up, a proportion of the fee may be paid on signing the sponsorship agreement, with the balance to be paid by a stated date. For an operatic event or a serious music concert, the organisation will need a considerable lead time, because the right "stars" are engaged for many months ahead, and the right kind of venue has to be booked on a date which suits the key performers.

The sponsored party, to be safe, may decide to ensure that what it considers to be adequate sponsorship is safely secured by a signed agreement committing the sponsor to the event and all that is needed to stage it. If the sponsored party sets up the event without prior sponsorship in place, and then finds that it has inadequate funds and that the anticipated sponsorship cannot be found, it would be embarrassing and damaging to the reputation of the sponsored organiser.

4–19 Where the sponsored party is going to organise the event, but wants to ensure that if it does so, sponsorship will be in place, the sponsor may be committed to the sponsorship fee conditional upon the sponsored party getting satisfactory agreements with the stars and a suitable venue within a specified time. At that point the sponsored party cannot guarantee that the event will happen at all, but it will have the confidence of contingent funding backing it up. If the event cannot be arranged as proposed, the sponsor loses nothing but any non-returnable research funding it may have granted to the sponsored party, as referred to below. Sponsors are not investors or risk-takers so they would not normally be prepared to fund an event which is not already set up, or the planning for which has yet to be started. An exception may be the setting up of a charity event, where it is likely that all concerned will help on a friendly basis, rather than being a little cynical, and very business-like.

The sponsor, on signing the sponsorship agreement, may pay the sponsored party an advance on account of the sponsorship fee to enable it to undertake the preliminary research for the event, and the negotiations to obtain the necessary contracts for the venue, the stars, and all else required for the event. The sponsor will have to agree whether that advance will be written off, or partly or wholly repaid, if the sponsored party fails to get the event set up. That may depend upon the sponsor being satisfied that the sponsored party has used all reasonable endeavours to get it all together. The sponsor should make it clear that if the sponsored party incurs any cost or liability in trying to set up the event, and if it fails to do so, there will be no comeback on the sponsor.

4–20 The sponsor should also think carefully before allowing the sponsored party to try to get the event together on the statement that " 'X' Company will be sponsoring the event", or words like " 'X' company is backing me". On the other hand, it is essential to make people aware that the required sponsorship is available to the sponsored party, as that is its credibility. Frequently suppliers, artistes, competitors and the like will say they will be interested in being involved, provided the basic funding is available and so the sponsored party must have some means of confirming that fact.

For a sponsorship contract with several years to run, and with a single annual event which is being sponsored, the payments can be made on a regular pattern during each contract year to suit both parties, based upon their experience of the needs of the sponsored party leading up to, and during, the event.

4–21 The sponsorship may be on an annual basis where during each year there is a series of events covered by the annual sponsorship fee. The payment of the fee will usually be in agreed tranches, which themselves may each be subject to pre-conditions being fulfilled, usually relating to performance. For example, if the sponsored party is an individual racing-car driver, the following will be relevant factors to be examined by the sponsor prior to being committed to sponsor that individual. It is assumed that the sponsor is satisfied that the racing driver is capable and experienced enough to be worth sponsoring in the first place.

The sponsor will want to ensure that the driver's sponsorship budget is realistic, especially if the sponsor is his sole or primary sponsor. Motor racing is a very expensive sport if it is carried out properly with a first-rate car, equipment and back-up. There is no point in trying to do it on the ridiculously cheap, which is not to be confused with careful control of cash resources. The budget must not be too optimistic for the cosmetic purpose of not discouraging a prospective sponsor.

4–22 For a season's worth of racing, to what extent is the sponsorship fee supporting an existing car, team of mechanics and other crew, spare parts, race transportation, etc., or is it paying for the cost of acquiring all of these from scratch? The factors affected will be the start-up time between signing the sponsorship agreement and being ready to race; the proportion of the budget used up in this period, and the ability to retain cash reserves to replace items in due course, and to cover all costs during the racing season.

Based upon an assessment of the above, the sponsor can establish how front-end loaded the actual expenditure is, and how much is needed after that to support each race in the relevant formula's season. The more front-loaded is the need for cash, the greater the exposure of the sponsor if the project is a disaster at an early stage. In the sponsorship of motor racing it is possible to spend a lot of money on a driver, without achieving the success which ultimately justifies the expense in marketing terms. Most other forms of sponsorship do not carry that kind of risk.

4–23 To minimise the risk on payments, the sponsorship fee can be separated into different elements. There can be a basic fee for the privilege of being the driver's sponsor, and then the balance can be split into equal portions dependent upon the driver starting each race. A pre-condition of each race-day tranche payment will be the appearance of the driver and car on the starting grid; no race, no pay. By itself that might operate harshly against the driver where, with the greatest enthusiasm he and his backing team turned up in time for all pre-race preparation, did all the practice required to the best of his ability, except that he came off the track on the last practice lap, and found that the barrier is stronger than the car. That's life in the racing business, but the result is that he does not appear on the starting grid for the race.

Should he be penalised by non-payment of that race instalment, or should non-payment only apply if he does not turn up at the race meeting at all, for any reason? Psychologically, if the driver knows that his sponsorship money depends on him getting onto the starting grid, he is not going to go all out for a good grid place in case he does have such an accident on his practice laps. Motor racing is such a competitive sport that a half-hearted effort will be useless. The sponsor should accept the risk as part of the assessment of the viability of its sponsorship plans. The drafting of any specialised sponsorship agreement must take into account the quirks of that activity. The sponsor can reserve the right to penalise the driver, for crashing on practice, or it may decide not to, if the sponsor is pleased upon how the driver is performing on an overall basis.

4-24   There are other circumstances in which the sponsorship fee may be adjusted, either up or down, examples of which are as follows:

(a) (i)   If the sponsorship is of an event, such as an athletics meeting or a horse race, where a major attraction for the sponsor was the promise of TV coverage, that should be set out in the agreement as being "of the essence" of the sponsorship deal. In that case the sponsor should make it clear whether it is expecting regional or national coverage. That would depend on where the event is taking place, and whether it warrants only local interest.

(ii)   A proportion of the fee will be attributed to the value agreed between the parties to the TV exposure. That proportion, therefore, will be rebatable according to an agreed formula. For example, while no TV cover can be guaranteed, it is usual to have, say, a minimum total of one hour non-continuous coverage for an international status athletics meeting. If the sponsorship is of an important horse racing meeting, the TV coverage should be of a minimum number of races. Apart from TV programme scheduling, organising all the equipment and facilities to enable TV filming to be undertaken can be a major exercise, which is expensive to arrange. Therefore, TV coverage will not be made available without very good reason.

(iii)   It might be agreed that the proportion of the fee attributed to TV coverage will be rebated by 15 per cent for each 10 minutes short of an hour's transmission time, if an hour is all that can reasonably be expected. For a two-week tennis tournament the coverage will be expected to be considerably greater than one hour, but the same rebate principle applies. That would leave a modest balance of that attributed portion in favour of the sponsored party in the event of absolute disaster, with no TV coverage at all.

4-25

(b) (i)   If the sponsorship is of a football team, there may be a basic level of fee for the season as a minimum support to the club, with the possibility of the team earning bonuses which would increase the whole year's fee according to a plan. This could include bonuses for league table placing, major competition wins, and any other hallmark of a successful season.

The sponsor must have a maximum liability for the year. The logic behind such a scheme is that such an incentive can benefit both parties. If the team is successful it earns more in sponsorship, so recognising the increased sponsorship value of a successful season. The sponsor benefits by being associated with a successful team.

(ii) For this to work, the team to sponsor will have to be chosen carefully. If the sponsor takes an already successful team from last year's season, such as if it has been promoted to a higher division in the league, or if it won a major championship last year, the level of basic sponsorship fee required by the team or club for the new football season will already take its previous success into account. The team may have difficulty in maintaining that level of success in this season, especially if it was wholly unexpected on the basis of the team's previous mediocre history. Any team may have one fairy tale season, but the sponsor should look for a team with an acceptable history of effort and relative (even if not spectacular) success.

4–26

(iii) The sponsor should not take on a team which is hovering above the point of relegation to a lower division, and which does not appear to have a realistic chance this season to improve significantly. Whilst the sponsorship fee for such a club may be lower, it may not do well enough to earn any bonuses, and will become disillusioned. Any circumstances in which the sponsor may be reluctant to publicise its sponsorship of the club remove the purpose and value of sponsorship. It could have a negative value if the image of the sponsor suffers as a result of being seen to be the sponsor of an embarrassing failure, despite the efforts of the sponsored team. If, against all the odds, the team staged a miraculous recovery over the season, the promotional value of the team to its sponsor would be high, due to the additional publicity it would get for having done so.

(iv) This is an example of where sponsorship would be needed by an unsuccessful team for support and to boost morale far more than for an already successful team. The sponsor's decision to undertake the sponsorship despite the risks would be influenced more by the broader concept of assessing the potential of the team than by the commercial need to choose a safe project to ensure a marketing success for the sponsor and its products.

5. Supply of sponsor's products

4–27   The sponsor's obligations may not be limited to the payment of cash. It might have agreed to provide the sponsored party with a selection of its products, if those are of any use to the sponsored party or to the event. For example, if the sponsor is the manufacturer of sound and electronic equipment, it may be providing an outdoor concert with a public address system or specialised lighting. At a different level, the sponsor may be the manufacturer of office equipment, and the administrative section of a permanent governing body or association of the sponsored event may have its offices equipped accordingly. The possibilities are endless: it is a matter of matching the sponsor's product with the needs of the sponsored party. The terms of the product delivery deal will depend, to some extent, on whether:

(a) the sponsorship is only of a one-off event or of a long-term nature;

(b) the products are only needed for the event itself (such as a competition timing system, or a sound system), or whether they would be retained and be useful over a period of time (such as office equipment).

4–28   In respect of sponsor's products which are provided to the sponsored party, the following points should be considered.

(a) It should be stated whether the products are being provided free or only at a reduced or nominal cost.

(b) Will the products be retained by the sponsored party after the sponsorship agreement has ended, or will they be returned to the sponsor? It may be agreed that, after termination of the sponsorship agreement, the products can be purchased by the sponsored party on terms set out in the agreement. This will depend on whether the products are gifts or on loan.

(c) The sponsor may contract to supply the products, but that may be done directly by the sponsor, or through a sponsor's distributor which is local to the sponsored party. What maintenance commitment will the sponsor undertake for the products, where relevant? For example, if the supply of products originated through the local distributor of the sponsor, presumably the equipment will be new, so there will be the manufacturer's normal warranty against a defect or malfunction. If the sponsored party is not paying for subsequent maintenance and repair of the products during the sponsorship period, that should be referred to in the agreement. Maintenance for any product is essential, otherwise the manufacturer's warranty may not apply should there be any defect or malfunction of the product.

6. Sponsor to provide trophy

4–29   In respect of any trophy provided by the sponsor:

(a) Will it be a perpetual trophy, with the sponsor's name engraved on it, or will it only have the event name, so that it will be equally usuable for the event when it is supported by another sponsor? If it is a trophy using the sponsor's name, it will not be of any use to the event after termination of the sponsorship, so the agreement should state what will be done with it at that time. It would be reasonable to expect that replica trophies will also be provided by the sponsor to be retained permanently by the event trophy winner in each year.

(b) With the trophy will there also be prize money for the winner. If so, that could be allocated by the sponsored party out of the general sponsorship money. If it is to be a separate amount to be made available by the sponsor in addition to the sponsorship fee, that should be specified in the agreement.

7. Liabilities to sponsored party

4–30   As the major obligation of the sponsor is to provide funding and other support to the sponsored party, its major potential liability will be its failure to do so. The failure could be total or partial, *i.e.* payments being late where that causes the sponsored party a problem, or being on time but not being the full amount agreed. The sponsor should be absolved by the agreement from having to continue to pay any part of the sponsorship fee to the sponsored party if the latter is at that time in material default of any of its obligations under the agreement. The liability of the sponsor for a failure by it to fulfil its obligations will depend on the strength of the sponsored party's rights under the sponsorship agreement, such as by way of defining the extent of the sponsorship fee, and how it is to be paid.

The sponsor may have agreed to provide sponsorship money "up to a maximum of £....." with no specific minimum amount being stated. In the absence of any other indication of commitment by the sponsor to a specific amount, the sponsored party will not be entitled to claim for any more than what is eventually provided by the sponsor, even if that is well below the stated maximum figure. This manner of describing the possible amount to be paid by the sponsor may occur where the sponsorship is not considered by the sponsor to be of any major significance, and the sponsored party has not fixed at least a minimum amount. The happening or style of the event may at that time have been uncertain, and the sponsor wanted just to be of some help, such as for a charity fund-raising exercise.

4–31 If the wording is that the sponsor "will cover the cost of hiring the marquee", while that seems an indeterminate amount, it will be quantified when the bill for the marquee is submitted (see paragraph 4–14 for a similar set of circumstances). What may not be clear is exactly what is meant by the "hire" of the marquee. There may be a problem if the account submitted by the marquee proprietor states that the "hire costs" include £X for the marquee, £Y for transportation from the hirer's premises to the event and back, and £Z for five men's time to put it up and take it down. What exactly does the sponsor's obligation cover? The problem would only arise if the sponsor took a strict line, and said that its limit of obligation is £X. If the account simply stated "To hire of marquee" £X (*i.e.* including but not listing each of the other elements of £Y and £Z), the sponsor would appear to be responsible for the whole amount.

If the event is a local Round Table fund-raising project, and the sponsor knows from the relevant price list that the daily "hire" charge for the marquee is £50, but it received an overall bill of £250, it might query the detailed charges. This would be a good example of a sponsor being surprised at the cost of its liability by not being absolutely specific in describing what it thinks it has agreed to pay for. At that level of sponsorship neither the Round Table secretary nor the sponsored party will seriously consider the strict legal interpretation of a friendly letter confirming the commitment, assumptions are made on both sides. Nevertheless, the bill has to be paid.

4–32 The sponsor may have agreed to provide a specified sum of money, but on a purely voluntary basis without any detailed agreement or written confirmation by either party. This would only happen for a minor event and for a modest contribution by the sponsor. If the sponsor fails to pay all or any of it, there may be no legal agreement for the sponsored party to sue on. (See chapter nine for the minimum requirements for a legally binding agreement.) If the sponsored party is relying on the promise of the sponsor for that money, it should take the time to get it properly documented, if only by a letter to the sponsor thanking it for agreeing to pay £X as a sponsorship fee, and in consideration of some promotional rights granted by the sponsored party.

If there is no reference to payment dates in the sponsorship agreement, and the sponsor does pay but much later than a critical date by which the money is needed by the sponsored party, there may be no basis for a legal claim against the sponsor even if the delay has caused expense to the sponsored party, or has caused it to incur a liability it would not otherwise have had. After the agreement has been signed, the sponsored party cannot unilaterally impose on the sponsor an "of the essence" condition relating to the date by which the sponsored party then discovers it needs the money. The sponsor intends to help the sponsored party, and if the money is genuinely needed in a hurry or unexpectedly, the sponsor should be co-operative if approached in a reasonable manner.

The above examples show that it is essential for the sponsorship agreement to state specifically and in detail what the obligations of the sponsor are in respect of payment amounts and dates. The sponsored party will be entering into commit-ments of its own relying upon the sponsor to fulfil its obligations, and if the sponsor fails to do so, there can be an expensive knock-on effect for the sponsored party.

4–33　If a financial liability of the sponsored party depends on the payment by the sponsor of a sum of money by a given date, the clause dealing with that payment ought to state that fact, and should also state that if the sponsor fails to make the payment as agreed, it will be responsible also for any liability, loss or expense incurred by the sponsored party as a reasonably direct result of that failure. A sponsor of a major event should realise that sponsorship is not a game, a magnanimous gesture of generosity on its part; it is a serious business and should be treated as such when negotiating the sponsorship agreement. A safeguard for the sponsor should be built in to such a clause, such as the sponsored party should give the sponsor a seven working day reminder in writing, to avoid an unintentional administrative error creating a breach of contract.

4–34　There may be other ways in which the sponsor can cause the sponsored party to incur loss, liability or expense. If these are specifically identified and dealt with in the sponsorship agreement, it would be reasonable for there also to be a clause whereby if the sponsor fails to comply with its relevant obligations, it will indemnify the sponsored party accordingly. The sponsor, if not used to sponsorship responsibilities, may ask why it should potentially be responsible for the sponsored party's liabilities when the sponsor is trying only to help it by providing money, products or services for the event. The answer is that the sponsor is, in reality, buying promotional opportunities, and that the sponsored party is accepting that sponsorship payment as an obligation on which it will rely. The deal is a commercial transaction with legal implications, and the sponsorship agreement is negotiated and signed on that basis. Providing all the legal requirements for a binding contract are present, an informally worded letter agreement is no less "legal" than an imposing-looking document under seal.

CHAPTER 5

Obligations of Sponsored Party

1. Introduction

5–01   In order to attract sponsorship at a financial level and sponsor status appropriate to the event, the sponsored party has to make it commercially worthwhile for the sponsor, and justifiable as a marketing expense in its annual budget. This may not always be easy, depending on the kind of sporting, leisure or cultural purpose upon which the event is based.

The sponsored party is selling potential value to the sponsor, and should package the event accordingly so far as may be practical or allowed by any relevant rules applying to it. In doing so the sponsored party must ensure that it is not presenting the event in a misleading manner, in its anxiety to get sponsorship. It is not a *caveat emptor* position for the sponsor—the sponsored party should fully disclose all matters pertinent to the event, whether or not they have any direct impact on the sponsor, and whether or not they have been asked for. Any significant information may be relevant to the sponsor when it is assessing the viability of sponsoring the event, or when it is assessing the value of it for the calculation of the sponsorship fee. The sponsored party is not in a position to judge what the sponsor considers to be relevant for these purposes. The sponsor is providing financial assistance to the sponsored party, and must be dealt with on a good faith basis accordingly.

5–02   The obligations of the sponsored party may include the following:

(a) to run the event efficiently for the benefit of the participants and paying spectators;

(b) to ensure that the event is run in accordance with regulations of a sport-governing body;

(c) to fulfil all of its obligations to third parties which provide goods, services or facilities for the event;

(d) to fulfil all of its obligations to the sponsor in accordance with the sponsorship agreement;

(e) to deal with the sponsor in good faith in all things, and to disclose fully to the sponsor all relevant matters relating to the event;

(f) not to incur the sponsor in any expense or liability outside any authority given by the sponsor to do so.

5–03   When negotiating the sponsorship agreement, the sponsored party must ensure that any relevant matter under paragraph 5–02(a), (b) or (c) which affects, or which is affected by, the agreement is taken into account when drafting it. All of the relevant commercial and financial issues which the sponsored party considers to be important to the deal should be tabulated into separate categories of essential matters and of desirable matters, so that nothing important is missed in the course of negotiations with the sponsor. Essential matters must be dealt with and agreed between the parties. Desirable matters may be only useful, so the sponsored party has greater flexibility when negotiating them.

The obligations of the sponsored party will depend upon what the event is (such as an operatic concert or an athletics meeting) and who the sponsored party is (such as a racing driver or a football club first team). Set out in this chapter are, first, some general obligations which have a wider application to sponsored parties, and then some more distinctive obligations which may apply more to specific circumstances. Even within a specialised sponsorship area, different parties will want different things, whether unique to their deal, or based upon an item normally included in that specialised area. Personalised requirements can only be guessed at, so this chapter sets out those items which should come up for discussion in the normal course of negotiation.

2. To hold the event

5–04   If the sponsored party is the organiser of an event, the whole foundation of the sponsorship agreement is that the event will be held as specified in the sponsorship agreement, and that the sponsored party will perform its obligations under it. The sponsor will have studied the event before offering sponsorship, and its decision may have been based upon the happening of certain circumstances relating to it. For example, the event may be made more newsworthy if named participants turn up, such as world-class runners. It may be only commercially appealing if it will get TV coverage. If that is the case, then the sponsorship agreement must specify any aspect upon which the sponsor has relied as the basis of deciding to sponsor the event.

These might be peripheral activities which the sponsored party had said would be undertaken to enhance the appeal of the event, so as to attract top-level participants and to persuade a TV channel to cover the event. The sponsored party is never able to guarantee that all such items which depend on third-party performance will be in place on the day, and so it should not make any commitment, even an implied one, to that effect. Any obligations of the sponsored party to achieve these objectives must be clearly stated, either as being absolute or as being subject to best endeavours. They should only be absolute when they are wholly within the control of the sponsored party.

One-off event

5–05   The sponsored party may be trying to set up a one-off event, such as for charity, and is endeavouring to persuade sponsors to commit themselves, conditional upon the event being held. The obligations of the sponsored party should include the equivalent of producing a business plan, to demonstrate that the concept of the event is realistic, what major input is required from whom and at what cost and to include cost and income projections for the sponsor to consider.

At this preliminary stage it should be agreed by both parties that if there is no event, there will be no sponsorship. The sponsored party is itself taking all the financial risk prior to the event being confirmed. Depending on the proposed financial commitment of the sponsor, it would be well advised to add further conditions to its sponsorship commitment becoming firm, such as:

(a) there should be an agreed memorandum setting out the minimum requirements of the sponsor from the sponsored party for the event;

(b) there may be a time limit by which the event venue must be booked, and by which all major commitments from third parties to the event must be in place;

(c) if the sponsor is to be the sole sponsor of the event, the financial needs of the sponsored party must be within an agreed budget. If it exceeds that budget, the sponsored party will not be entitled to appoint a joint sponsor, so it will have to raise the excess cash requirements in some other way.

Regular event

5–06 The event may be a regular event, and therefore expected to happen each year. The sponsorship will also be on an annual basis for a specific number of years, so the consequences of failure to hold the event in any year will be dealt with in the agreement. If the event is well established, the sponsor is either taking over the sponsorship from a previous sponsor which has let its agreement expire or the event has only now considered sponsorship as an additional way of securing a minimum funding for a known period. This will enable the sponsored party to plan ahead, particularly if it owns or manages the event venue. Improvements to facilities can be undertaken, provided that the sponsor's funding is not to be applied only to specified items, such as prize money, or athletes' entry fees.

Postponement of event

5–07 There may be good reasons for the sponsored party postponing the event to a later date, or even bringing it forward in the year. This may be necessary (for example) due to the clash of international events for an athletics meeting, whereby none of the top-class athletes would be able to appear at the event; or the temporary incapacity of the star performer in a concert. This should not happen for a well-prepared athletics meeting, as the international events are fixed well in advance for the year, so the sponsored party has to choose a suitable date for the event. The incapacity of a star cannot be foreseen, and is likely to have occurred only a very short time prior to the event date. It may be impossible to postpone the event at short notice, so the sponsored party will have to make alternative arrangements to enable it to proceed as planned.

Because of all of the detailed arrangements and commitments which go into staging any event, postponement may not be possible because of the difficulty of immediately being able to find another date which would be suitable for all parties connected with, or participating in, the event. The sponsor may not be prepared to hold open indefinitely a commitment to sponsor the event, subject to reactivation by the sponsored party as and when it is able to reinstate the event. The sponsor should be entitled to treat an indefinite postponement as a total non-fulfilment and cancellation so that it can terminate the sponsorship agreement. The clauses in the sponsorship agreement dealing with the sponsored party's obligations should refer to postponement and cancellation. The sponsor may also want the first option to take up the sponsorship of the event when it is reinstated.

5–08 Regular events which are part of a larger event should not be subject to postponement in isolation, as it may not be practical, or because it may damage the main event. An example would be a horse race which is only one (although the crucial one) of an afternoon's racing. The 3.30 Widget Stakes cannot be postponed or cancelled, leaving a hole in the afternoon's race-card. If the whole day's racing is cancelled due to bad weather, or any other compelling reason, reinstating it within a packed racing calendar may not be possible, as all the suitable licensed courses may not have any free dates. Even if the race-day could be reinstated, the original horses and jockeys may have other commitments.

The adverse consequences of postponing an event may far exceed the benefits of doing so, even if the casual circumstances are beyond the sponsored party's control. It may be possible to retain the event as planned, but modified or reduced by whatever has happened to raise the subject of postponement. An assessment of the situation from all points of view should be made before taking what might be a drastic decision, particularly if the event date is close.

Substitution of venue

5–09 The event may still happen on its projected date, but it may have to be held at a different venue. Whether this will affect the value of the sponsorship to the sponsor will depend on whether the original venue had some special significance to it. The substituted venue may be adequate for the event activities, but may not have the prestige of the original venue or its convenience and accessibility. It may also lack facilities which the original venue had for spectators and participants, and also for the sponsor to use for promotional purposes. This might relate to entertaining facilities, or to arena facilities such as an electronic scoreboard, or to the crucial issue of no TV filming facilities being available at the substituted venue.

The cause of substitution of the venue may be valid, such as if the original venue burns down. In the case of some kinds of event, substitution of the venue may be difficult, due to the unusual requirements for the event. For example, the number of venues which would be suitable for holding horse show-jumping competitions in London is limited.

If the sponsor is the sole sponsor of the event, and if the identity of the venue is a crucial aspect of the deal, then the sponsor will need to be able to approve any substituted venue, assuming that it accepts the necessity to make a substitution. Changing the venue may have to be linked with a change in the date of the event, as all good venues are in constant use, and are fully booked well into the future.

A charity sponsored rock concert could be moved from Wembley to another major London venue, but a sponsored opera could not be moved from Covent Garden to the Odeon Hammersmith. A horse race traditionally held at Sandown is not likely to be moved to Haydock Park.

5–10 The reasons for substitution of a venue being considered may include the following:

(a) (i) There being a far greater demand for seats than the original venue has, and a suitable larger venue becomes available. All popular international artistes who are booked into the Albert Hall could have sold more tickets than there are available seats for their concert. But that is the booked venue, and there is no intention of moving the concert elsewhere, whatever the ticket demand is. The Albert Hall has character and image, and provides a special atmosphere. Also there is a certain prestige in tickets having a scarcity value. Sponsored events have to follow the same path unless exceptional circumstances prevail.

(ii) Where possible, the period for the staging of the event (such as an exhibition of ancient Egyptian relics) can be extended if the premises are free. The same can apply for a seated event, and sometimes the promoter of a concert will book the venue for two consecutive nights to accommodate the ticket demand. If the event is for one day only, and the venue is fully booked, an alternative venue would be the only way of extending the possibility of additional concerts.

5–11

(b) (i) If the event is an exhibition of, say, vintage classic and rare motor cars, and a much smaller collection than envisaged is entered, it would make sense to book a smaller hall if the original one would be only half full, and if there is time to do so. On the other hand, it would give visitors to the exhibition much more room to move about in, and to see all the cars without being crushed and uncomfortable.

(ii) The number of cars entered does not mean that the expected visitors will be less, so the gate receipts should not be affected. A smaller hall may be less expensive to hire for the exhibition, but better use can be made of the greater available space in the original hall. In these circumstances, a substituted venue may not be justified.

(c) The original venue is made unusable, such as being damaged by fire, or by having substantial crowd capacity or use limits being imposed by an authority which has the right to control such specifications. Damage to the venue may make it entirely unusable, and the ability of the sponsored party to find an alternative venue will depend on how close to the event date the fire or other damage was incurred. New limitations on the use of the venue are only likely after some disaster or other event has caused the question of safety or use to be raised to a higher than normal precautionary level.

5–12 The administration of a substitution of a venue may cause greater inconvenience and time spent than organising the event in the first place. Factors to be considered are as follows.

(a) Before agreeing to the new venue, the sponsored party should inquire whether the participants in the event, and other key people involved with it, will object to the change or will be unable to make the event if the substitution goes ahead. This may be likely if the venue substitution necessitates a change in the date upon which the event will take place.

(b) The views of the sponsor of the event should be considered. Even if there is no contractual obligation of the sponsored party to consult the sponsor, it may be well advanced in its planned promotions and advertising activities, where all printed or other media adverts refer to the original venue. If the substitution would only be a matter of convenience, the sponsor should not be forced to incur unnecessary cost if it objects. If a *force majeure* situation makes the substitution necessary, then both parties should co-operate to reduce cost and inconvenience to the minimum.

(c) If the event is being held under the auspices of a governing body, the sponsored party should check whether the proposed new venue complies with any minimum criteria applied by that body to the premises for eligibility of holding the event.

5–13

(d) When in doubt, check that the new venue is authorised by the local authority to hold the event, and that all licences and other regulations relating to it are fully observed. For events with a large crowd of spectators, safety is of paramount importance. Tragic incidents in recent years have put an even greater responsibility on the holders of events to ensure the safety of structures and the proper maintenance of crowd control. The local authority may lay down minimum requirements of security for the substituted venue for the event, which may not have been relevant for the original venue. This will affect the basic cost of holding the event, so sponsorship support and other means of raising funds may need to be extended to cover any such increase.

(e) Will the new venue enhance or be detrimental to the image of the event, and the image of the sponsor? The elements of (a) and (b), above, will be affected if the new proposed venue is considered to be a risk to the viability of holding the event.

Cancellation

5–14 The sponsorship agreement will not allow the sponsored party to cancel the event except in circumstances of *force majeure*, or where the sponsor agrees that it should be cancelled. If there was any doubt in the mind of the sponsored party as to the viability of the event when the sponsor was approached, then signing the sponsorship agreement should have been postponed until the event was secure. The points raised in paragraph 5–02 may be relevant.

Unauthorised cancellation would be a breach of contract by the sponsored party. The rights of the sponsor will depend on the terms of the sponsorship agreement, but its practical attitude may be different. It will depend on whether the event was to have been "one-off", or whether it is a regular event under a long-term sponsorship agreement.

5–15 The effects of cancelling the event will depend upon how long before the event is due to be held that decision is taken. If cancellation is not inevitable, but is a conscious decision of the sponsored party, an assessment should first be made of the potential consequences. For example, a list should be made of what commitments have been made which cannot be set aside without incurring any liability, or which must be paid for even though cancellation takes place. There should be another list of commitments in respect of which third parties will suffer no loss or expense as a result of the event being cancelled.

Any third-party loss or expense which is inevitable on cancellation of the event may be recovered from the sponsored party by the third party if it cannot reasonably reduce or eliminate the relevant loss or expense. Notwithstanding the contractual rights of the parties to an indemnity, there are circumstances in which any party which is adversely affected by the cancellation has a common law obligation to mitigate its loss where it can reasonably do so.

5–16 So far as the sponsor is concerned, the following points are relevant.

(a) It is not good publicity to be involved with a sponsored party or event which is cancelled in circumstances which are seen to be acrimonious, shady or which could be criticised as being unethical. If the cancellation causes a sport or the governing body of a leisure activity to declare that it will never again approve of the sponsored party as the organiser of an event coming within its jurisdiction, the sponsor should contact that governing body and ensure that the sponsor is not blacklisted in the future by having been associated with the cancelled event.

5–17

(b) (i) The sponsor should not be responsible for any payments to the sponsored party, and should not, even by implication, have any responsibility to third parties which may have claims against the sponsored party as a result of the cancellation. That will depend upon which obligations or responsibilities are undertaken by the sponsor in the sponsorship agreement.

(ii) An exception will be where the cancellation is directly caused by the default of the sponsor, such as where it has failed or refused to make a sponsorship fee payment properly in accordance with the sponsorship agreement. Any argument between the parties as to whether or not the refusal by the sponsor was justified should be resolved by arbitration before the claim escalates to legal proceedings.

(iii) For example, if part of the sponsorship cost was agreed as being the responsibility of the sponsor paying for the venue rent and other charges, that may have been done either by the sponsor signing the venue agreement and taking on the responsibility directly; or by the sponsor being committed in the sponsorship agreement to reimbursing the sponsored party for that specific cost.

(iv) In the first alternative, the sponsor would be liable directly to the venue management for any cancellation charges stated in the venue agreement, and the sponsor would then have to rely on its rights under the sponsorship agreement to obtain reimbursement from the sponsored party. That may prove to be difficult. In the second alternative, the venue cost liability is that of the sponsored party, and if the sponsorship agreement has been drafted properly, the sponsor will not be liable for it on cancellation of the event by the sponsored party.

5–18

(c) The sponsor should never be a guarantor of the performance of any obligation by the sponsored party, or of the payment by it of money to a third party. It is possible that, for an unknown sponsored party trying to get an event together, third parties may be persuaded to provide goods or services to the sponsored party because of the prestige and commercial standing of the sponsor. The sponsored party should be prohibited in the sponsorship agreement from using the sponsor's name as an influence, implying that it is, in a sense, guaranteeing the sponsored party's credit.

(d) The sponsor will have lost an opportunity to promote itself and its products. That is an inconvenience, but is not of itself a calculable loss, unless it is a regular event, and the sponsor can reasonably demonstrate that there is always an uplift of sales following the publicity connecting it with the event. Even so, that may not be a loss which can be sued for.

(e) If the sponsor is in the middle of a programme of advertising and promotion relating to the event, cancellation will be a commercial embarrassment. There will be a cost incurred in cancelling media bookings, wasted printing of promotional material, an unscrambling of any related business or social arrangements it has made, and the cancellation of any hospitality invitations it has already sent out.

Compliance with regulations

5–19   There may be conditions placed upon the staging of the event, either as to its management, or as to the conduct of the activities. Non-compliance with these may affect the event and the sponsored party should be obliged in the sponsorship agreement to establish which (if any) regulations might apply to the event, and to ensure that they are fully complied with in all respects.

5–20   Examples are:

(a) Local authority or similar requirements, mainly relating to the venue itself. These would include regulations for maximum numbers of seated and standing spectators; fire regulations; crowd control and other security and safety measures, the availability of alcohol on the venue premises and weekend or evening ending times for the event. A venue which holds events regularly as a business venture should already be complying with all of those regulations which affect it. The venue booking form may require the sponsored party to provide a listing of any activities or other matters which would be affected by, or which may bring into operation, any other regulations.

5–21

(b) Regulations imposed by a governing body of the activity upon which the event is based.

    (i) These regulations will refer to the holding of an event, how the activities are carried out, the results to be recorded, the eligibility of participants, whether the event is a championship or has some other qualifying status, and so forth. This would apply to competitive sports and other activities of a leisure nature. Failure to comply with any of these regulations may disqualify the event from the status it purported to have, and may make any results, including records, null and void.

   (ii) Any event which is subject to a governing body will relate to an established activity, and will have to be set up well in advance with the co-operation of the governing body. If the event is not recognised officially by the governing body, then it may not be worth holding, as the status of the event as an "outside" one may prevent the participation of those people who are needed for the event to be viable, and to be worth sponsoring. Particularly in sporting and athletic events, the calendar for the year is full enough for participants of national and international standing. They would not want to appear at an event which is not at the top level, or with the right competition, or without TV coverage or at least newsworthy.

5–22   The effect that any of the above matters may have upon the sponsor will relate either to the justification of the sponsorship fee, or to the value of the promotional use the sponsor can make from the event.

3. To promote the event

5-23 The sponsored party must be obliged to advertise and promote the event so as to make it as well known and successful as can be expected. This may depend on whether it has a broad or a specialised appeal, and on the level of public interest which can therefore be generated for it. The limitations on the efforts of the sponsored party will depend on where the event is going to be held, an assessment of the point at which the beneficial effect of additional advertising becomes marginal, and how to balance the maximising of profitability for the event against the cost of promoting it.

5-24 Apart from events put on to raise money for charity or other worthy causes, or where sponsorship money goes into governing body funds for the general benefit of that body's activity, the main purpose of sponsored events is not to be profitable for the promoters in the sense of a trading profit. It may be expected to be profitable for the purposes for which the event is held. "Profitable" refers to:

(a) maximising the income for the benefit of the participants (such as prize money), or to be able to provide first rate facilities at the event for spectators and participants, to cover all the costs of staging the event, and (where relevant) to put the balance to the general funds of the governing body, or association, under whose auspices the event is being held; and

(b) providing as much funding as can be achieved from the event, directly or indirectly, for sponsored parties such as those connected with the cultural arts, and which are always in need of more money.

5-25 The sponsor also wants the event to be a great success, and will encourage the sponsored party to undertake its own advertising and publicity programme. This is enhanced by whatever promotional activities the sponsor is prepared to carry out as part of its benefits of sponsorship, but the angle will emphasise the sponsor, not the event. As the sponsor is already providing funds to support the event's cost, the sponsor would not want to be subsidising the sponsored party's own advertising, unless that is part of an agreed budget. Promotion and advertising activities easily expand so that their costs match any budget made available for those purposes. Excessive enthusiasm, and blind belief in the power of media exposure, can damage any budget unless the costs are kept strictly under control.

Where the sponsorship is of an individual racing driver, tennis player or athlete, the obligations of that individual to undertake promotional activities will be limited. At this point sponsorship and endorsement become closely related, and the endorsement applications are dealt with in chapter seven.

4. Television coverage

5-26 The most valuable promotional facility, both for the sponsor and the sponsored party, is TV coverage of the event. This, where it is available, will be the responsibility of the sponsored party to provide. TV programme time is limited and therefore carefully scheduled, and the event would have to be slotted into the relevant category of the arts, sport or leisure. Within each of these categories the available time is even more limited, and to warrant TV coverage the event would have to be widely newsworthy and an important event within its category.

A major sponsorship deal may be conditional upon the likelihood, or even a guarantee, of TV coverage. Where it is relevant a portion of the sponsorship fee will depend upon TV coverage, and the extent to which it is given in prime viewing time. Part of the fee may be allocated on the assumption of a minimum period of TV coverage, with a pro rata reduction for (say) each 10 minutes by which the actual viewing time is short of the projected time.

It is the responsibility of the sponsored party to negotiate the TV rights and to conclude an agreement with a TV channel for filming and broadcasting. That will not of itself guarantee any broadcast time on the day if unforeseen circumstances arise, but an indication can be given of the likely viewing time. This may depend on whether the event is broadcast live, or whether highlights will be shown in an edited form at a later time that day. The sponsor should be entitled to see the TV contract, in confirmation of any express obligation set out in the sponsorship agreement.

5. Access to event venue

5–27   The sponsored party, whether it is the owner of the event venue or whether it is renting the venue, must enable the sponsor to get into the venue in good time before the event to instal its agreed banners, advertising material, product presentation kiosks, electronic timing equipment, sound and lighting equipment, or whatever else the sponsor has agreed to provide or is entitled to instal. The sponsored party must also have the agreement of the venue owner for all such installation, before committing itself to the sponsor. This will mean first establishing what is required. If some of the banners are not free-standing, but will need the support of any of the structure of the venue premises, consent will be needed. If the venue has flagpoles from which the sponsor would like to fly a flag containing its company name and logo, or that of the sponsor's product which is related to the event name, again consent is required. Normally these consents should not be controversial or difficult to obtain, but they must be organised in good time.

A venue premises plan may be needed so that the siting of the sponsor's banners, boards and other material can be agreed. The placing of arena boards for football matches is crucial for televised matches, but they would not need the proprietor's consent, as it should be a standard item in the agreement for the use of the venue. The provision of hospitality areas, either in the venue premises, or separately in a marquee, may be one of the sponsored party's obligations, and the size and siting of the marquee should be agreed. For a marquee the siting should be flexible, in that an ideal spot on a sunny dry day may be under water on a rainy day.

5–28   Whether the sponsor pays for its own food and drink, or whether that is provided by the sponsored party up to a limit of cost, should be agreed and set out in the sponsorship agreement. The cost of the marquee itself is to be agreed, and whether the sponsor contributes to any of its cost or pays for it all. That will depend upon whether the sponsor is covering the whole cost of staging a one-off event, or whether it is paying an established event a commercially negotiated fee based only on the value of the right to have the title of sponsor to the event. In the first case the sponsor will ultimately be paying the cost; in the second case (subject to the terms of the sponsorship agreement) the sponsor simply expects the hospitality facility obligations to be performed, whatever the cost.

If the hospitality facilities are set out in a large room in the permanent building of the venue premises, there should be no charge to the sponsor for such use; only the cost of food and drink should be allocated as agreed.

6. Special event areas

5–29 At most sporting events there are two special areas which separate the chosen few from the milling masses. These should be required by the sponsor in accordance with its reasonable needs, and should be provided free of charge by the sponsored party.

Special enclosure tickets for guests

5–30 What might be represented by the special enclosure depends on what kind of event it is, but it enables chosen guests to not be crowded, and to have the best view of the event's activities. The special enclosure may have a covered area for the guests to seek refuge from rain, and it is likely to have its own bar facilities and other comforts handy. Not to have to walk long distances and then to queue forever for a drink is a much-appreciated perk.

If there are secondary sponsors, and as the space in such a facility is limited, the primary sponsor will have the lion's share. If the secondary sponsors are relatively insignificant, the major sponsor may be able to obtain exclusivity of these facilities. Whether an official supplier will be entitled to use this facility will depend on its value to the event. For an athletics event the official timer, supplying all of the electronic timing equipment, might qualify for the perk.

Special parking area

5–31 If the event is an outdoor rock concert, the parking may be half a mile away, and much the same might apply to the parking for a major car racing track. The sole or primary sponsor of the event should be able to get a few of the special car park passes, to enable its top executives and guests to have the benefit of proximity car parking. This would not apply to all of those who get special enclosure tickets: the car park would be an extremely limited privilege. Special parking areas are normally subject to a different level of security, so each car pass would be issued only to a specific vehicle, marked with its registration number, so that the passes are not transferable.

If there is no sole or primary sponsor of the event itself, then the organisers of the event will allocate the passes in their normal way. Sponsors of individual teams of cars, or of individual racing drivers, may not qualify for passes: it depends on the event organiser.

7. General obligations of sponsored party

Appointment of subsidiary sponsors

5–32 Where the sponsor is the sole sponsor, the sponsored party will not be entitled to appoint any secondary sponsors, whatever title or rights they would be offered. The sponsorship agreement should set out which rights and limitations are placed upon the sponsored party appointing product manufacturers as official supplier of their goods. If the sponsor is a primary sponsor, that assumes there will be secondary sponsors and official suppliers. The primary sponsor and the sponsored party will agree how many of these may be appointed, what their minimum or maximum contribution will be, and their proportionate benefits. While the sponsored party would like to get in as much cash as possible, once the costs of staging the event have been covered, for some events an excess of secondary sponsors can detract from the marketing value of the event to the primary sponsor.

Warranty

5–33 The sponsored party will be required to warrant to the sponsor that its trade mark is original, that the sponsored party is the absolute owner of it, and that it does not infringe the rights of any third party. It will also have to indemnify the sponsor from any expense or liability which it might incur as a result of being associated with or using the trade mark should any of the sponsored party's warranties in that respect prove to be incorrect.

Indemnity

5–34 The sponsored party will be required to indemnify the sponsor from any liability (except one directly caused by the sponsor) relating to the event, or arising from anything connected with it. This serious obligation should be examined carefully by the sponsored party. There may be obvious risks, depending on the event, which may be specified in the indemnity, as well as it being otherwise all-embracing. The sponsored party should take out insurance against all the usual risks of running such an event, and all other business-related insurance which would be prudent.

The sponsor provides funding and any other assistance as a wholly independent concern. It wants to reap the benefits of being associated with the event and is not prepared to accept any liabilities flowing from it. Sponsorship is not a joint venture with the sponsored party or an investment by the sponsor. So far as the indemnity extends to breaches of contract by the sponsored party, the clauses in the agreement setting out the warranties and representations of the sponsored party must be absolute. Wording like "so far as the sponsored party is aware", or "to the best of the belief of the sponsored party" virtually nullify the effect of any warranty, and therefore of any indemnity relating to breach of that warranty.

The only qualification to this is where a sponsored party may seek to limit its liability in respect of loss of promotional opportunities to the sponsor as a result of a breach of contract by the sponsored party. In certain circumstances such a limitation may be considered to be perfectly reasonable.

Assignment prohibition

5–35 The sponsored party should not be entitled to assign the benefit of or any of the obligations under the sponsorship agreement. This prohibition should be absolute—there is no deemed reasonableness which can be applied by the sponsored party should it wish to assign the management of the event to another party. If the sponsor, on being consulted, agrees to transfer the sponsorship agreement to the new event proprietor, that is easily done. If, in the meantime, money has already been paid by the sponsor under the agreement, that will have to be sorted out between the parties to the sponsor's satisfaction. If the sponsor does not want to be involved with the proposed assignee, the sponsorship agreement should entitle it either to enforce the prohibition or to terminate the sponsorship agreement.

Chapter 6

Merchandising

1. Introduction

6-01 When a sponsored party owns and organises a successful high-profile event, there can be great potential in linking the promotion of the event name and logo with the sale of suitable merchandise. Each sponsor should be entitled to merchandising rights in respect of its product which is connected with the event. The terms should be set out in the sponsorship agreement, so that its limits can be clear.

Usually, merchandising will be done through sales promotion campaigns, as sponsors are not likely to be the manufacturers of T-shirts or other cheap consumer products widely available at the bottom end of the retail market. In any event, these will be rights which the sponsor can exercise, or not, as it sees fit, with no further obligation to the sponsored party arising from those promotional activities except possibly to pay royalties. Therefore this chapter concentrates on merchandising from the point of view of the sponsored party.

6-02 Any merchandising rights which are not taken up by the sponsor may be granted separately to a professional merchandiser, or may be exploited generally through a merchandising agency. Merchandising licensees are not sponsors of the event but the royalties from their product sales help to fund it. Efficient use of merchandising rights granted to licensees which have no connection with the event should be profitable.

If serious long-term merchandising is contemplated, it needs a carefully constructed agreement. This chapter deals with matters which should be considered, although they may not all be relevant or appropriate for every deal. The licensor will be the sponsored party, and the licensee will be the party granted the rights.

6-03 Merchandising is a competitive commercial business for those who take up licences from the sponsored party. A licensee must not take on commercial risks or responsibilities under a merchandising agreement beyond its reasonable ability to fulfil them. A licensee which is not familiar with the business of merchandising should take advice before extending its promotional activities by taking advantage of merchandising rights.

Considerable finance may be necessary for the licensee to set up the deal, depending on the type of merchandise to be manufactured and sold, and the media to be used for promotion and publicity to make the public aware of its existence. Sufficient stocks must also be readily available to fulfil the demand which is created once the licensee has established its market.

6-04 The concept of merchandising extends to the granting, by the sponsored party, of exclusive rights to produce and sell high-cost, high-quality products, such as commemorative medals or plates of the event. The value of these items is established by being produced by the most prestigious mint or pottery, and being produced in limited editions which are numbered and authenticated.

Detailed preliminary market research need not be necessary where the right to use the event logo is in connection with articles in everyday use. More careful planning may be necessary where the project is novel in its concept, or where the form of merchandise is unique, unusually expensive or with limited specialised appeal.

6–05　The sponsored party should put together a standard merchandise licence agreement, so that the same basic rights, obligations and restrictions will apply to all licensees. Individual cases may require modified or added terms to take account of matters peculiar to that product range, or to the licensee's agreed requirements.

If an event name or logo has a value for merchandise promotions, it may not be in the sponsored party's best interests to grant all the available rights exclusively to one party in case it is not fully able to take advantage of all the potential possibilities. Some areas of promotion will be more valuable than others. By negotiation with different interested parties, the value of those rights, and the ability of the parties to deal with them effectively, can be assessed more accurately.

6–06　From the sponsored party's point of view, merchandising is a means of making money for the event, and promoting it in a different way. The merchandise manufacturer depends on the public recognition of, and attraction to, the event and its logo to induce them to purchase the goods. That the event may thereby become more famous is incidental to the merchandiser, although the more popular the event becomes, the stronger will be the merchandiser's selling ability. In practice the licensee is able to sell the products as they are, and the addition of the event name or logo should simply generate a higher level of sales. It is not the logo which sells the product, unless the logo is currently "all the rage", when it can only be obtained by buying that product.

Many well-planned merchandise promotion schemes for event logos do not come up to expectation, both as to sales potential, and the royalty income. This can happen where the products are not right, or where bad business methods are used, or the licensee is selling over-priced, poor quality goods.

2. Management of licensed rights

6–07　The sponsored party should consider carefully whether it wants to spend the time and effort finding licensees, negotiating deals with them, and concluding the merchandise licenses. There may be continuing responsibilities to licensees during their agreement. As an alternative, there are some very experienced merchandising companies which provide a full service of licensing the name or logo, monitoring licences, inspecting sample products, receiving licence fees and generally running the business side of the merchandising activities. For this service the company will charge a commission of between 20 and 30 per cent of the net receipts from all the licences granted, depending on the level of their continuing obligations.

It may be in the sponsored party's best interests for all of the merchandise rights to be kept separate from the other event activities and income, such as by having the source rights vested in a company, which becomes the licensor. This would only be viable for major long-term events, where the value of the merchandising rights is substantial, and the name and logo are well established and will have a long commercial life. This separation will then distinguish between the different rights and liabilities of each commercial sector of the event. The decision may also depend on whether there is any tax or cashflow advantage in doing so. If the sponsored party is liable in damages for breach of contract or breach of copyright in respect of one activity, such as merchandising, it will be an advantage to the sponsored party if it is possible to prevent attachment of the income arising from the other activities connected with the event.

6–08　If the merchandise rights are granted through a limited company, the proposed licensee must satisfy itself that the company is entitled to act as it purports to, and that it can do so for the whole of the term of the proposed licence agreement. The sponsored party's professional advisers will guide it upon the corporate set-up for the merchandise rights, to minimise any tax liabilities, and to get the best advantage from the merchandising income. The sponsored party may appoint a merchandising agency to administer the merchandise company.

The value of the proposed merchandise promotions will be based upon the event name, logo and reputation, and the sponsored party should assign to its wholly owned merchandise company whatever rights will be legally required to enable the company to give and fulfil the usual warranties and undertakings contained in merchandising agreements. These will include some obligation on the sponsored party to promote the event to the best of its ability, which will help the merchandiser to ensure the success of all of the projects entered into by it to promote the merchandise. References in this chapter to "merchandising company" mean the sponsored party's wholly-owned company.

Because merchandising is a specialised method of representing and promoting the event whereby licensees spend the money and do the work to create the income from which a royalty is paid to the sponsored party, the responsibilities involved should be taken seriously by the sponsored party and the licensee for their mutual benefit.

3. Prior agreements

6–09　If the event has been involved in merchandising deals in the past, then before any firm offers are made to a licensee, or negotiations with a prospective licensee are concluded, the merchandise company must ensure that there are no existing conflicting agreements, or outstanding options, relating to any current merchandise deals. The merchandise company should maintain a register of current licence agreements, setting out which products they cover, the licensed territories and the periods of each agreement, including option periods. Any passive and non-profitable conflicting agreements should be terminated if possible. Previous options granted over merchandise rights which have yet to be exercised must be left to lapse. Prior licence agreements which have terminated must nevertheless be checked to ensure that there are no outstanding items to be dealt with.

Most merchandise agreements contain a non-exclusive right for stocks existing at the date of termination of the agreement to be disposed of within a specified time thereafter. Whether this clause has been complied with correctly will depend upon confirming the stocks existing at the date the licensee's right to manufacture ended, and comparing that figure with the shipments of stock and confirmed sales accounted for within the stock sell-off period, and the declared terminal stock held by the licensee. If a subsequent licensee will not be manufacturing and selling the same range of products, it would not affect it if the sponsored party authorises the previous licensee to sell and account for its terminal stock of merchandise for a short time after the expiry of the non-exclusive sell-off period. The decision to do so will depend on the length of the original sell-off period, the stocks held at termination, the efforts already made to sell stock, and whether an extension would be genuinely beneficial. In practice, the licensee will dispose of its terminal stock one way or another, so it might as well be on an authorised, royalty paying basis.

6–10   Any technical or legal requirements needed to complete the reversion of merchandise rights after the termination of each licence agreement must be complied with. Depending on the type of merchandise, and the form of the licence, included among those formalities, there may be:

(a) changing the registered licensee details in the local trade marks registry or completing or assigning any registered design or trade mark applications arising from the rights granted under the agreement;

(b) confirming the sponsored party's rights in the copyright and other proprietary rights of any original item of merchandise specifically designed by the licensee and permanently associated with the event. This will only occur when the merchandise is incapable of being put to any other use beyond its close association with the event. An example would be a mascot created solely for the English World Cup football team, or the replica of a famous trophy such as a horse statuette.

6–11   All sub-licences entered into by the licensee must be checked, to make sure they have also terminated, and that they were authorised in accordance with the original licence terms. Unless a licence agreement covers a wide territory, it will usually prohibit the original licensee from assigning any of its rights without the licensor's prior written consent. Each sub-licence can only grant to the sub-licensee rights which the original licensee itself is entitled to, and the sub-licence must also be subject to any conditions (including termination provisions) by which the original licensee is bound. If the original licensee has contracted to give the sub-licensee more rights than the licensee itself has, the sub-licensee may be able to sue the original licensee for misrepresentation. But the termination of the merchandising licence by the licensor effectively terminates any sub-licence as well.

If the original licensee itself does not manufacture the goods it merchandises, it must ensure that its agreement with the manufacturer is consistent with the rights granted by the licence. This will apply mainly to quantities and the quality of the finished article, and the satisfactory use of the event's name or logo. The sponsored party should have the right to inspect samples of the goods and to refuse to authorise the sale by the merchandiser of those not reaching the agreed specifications. If the goods are consumer goods which come within manufacturing or materials regulations for safety or otherwise, they must be complied with.

4. Rights granted to a licensee

6–12   As the merchandising rights in respect of a successful event are valuable, and as the quality and presentation of the products will reflect on the reputation of the event and of the sponsored party, the licence agreement must be sufficiently detailed and clear to protect them while giving the licensee a fair deal. Set out below are the major items which should be dealt with when negotiating what the licensee is entitled to.

5. Name and logo

6–13   The licensee will be given the exclusive right to use the name and logo of the event in connection with the manufacture and sale of specified categories of goods within a specified territory for a specified length of time.

If the event is represented by a famous caricature, image or invented person, with characteristics identified only with the event or the sponsored party, the licensee should be prevented from using or depicting that personification in any way uncharacteristically, or in such a manner as to alter materially the impression or qualities by which that representation has become known.

The name or logo, when it starts to be used in connection with the manufacture and sale of goods, becomes a trade mark. Trade marks are dealt with in paragraph 6–40, and it is important that the sponsored party does not lose any rights in the marketing of the event name or logo by not taking sufficient care in setting up merchandising deals.

6. The product category

6–14   Unless the sponsored party is licensing its merchandising rights without product category limitation to one licensee (such as to its wholly-owned merchandising company), the range of products to be included in the scope of the licence must be clearly defined as the sponsored party reserves all other product categories so that it can grant merchandise licences for them to other parties. Vague descriptions, such as "clothes and clothing accessories" will create confusion when there is a dispute as to what is meant by "accessories".

The sponsored party should decide the broad categories of merchandise which can usefully be promoted with the name or logo of the event. A prospective licensee may approach the sponsored party and propose its requirements by way of product and any other concepts. If it sounds sensible and will be profitable, there is no reason to reject the proposal.

7. Exclusivity and territory

6–15   To have any value, the licence must be exclusive to the licensee for its products within the licensed territory. Exclusivity eliminates authorised competition with the licensee by others in the rights it has acquired. Where different licensees are given different markets or territories on an exclusive basis, the sponsored party has to be very careful not to infringe the U.K. or E.U. legislation on restrictive or anti-competitive practices. Infringement of these legal requirements can have serious consequences, and can make the licence agreements defective so legal advice should be sought on the agreement. (See further chapter one, paragraph 1–65.

For the protection of the sponsored party there should be either a rewarding incentive, or a negative disincentive, to the licensee to ensure, so far as is commercially possible, that it does its best to promote the merchandise rights, otherwise there is a temptation for the licensee to remain inactive until it feels that the market will be most receptive. The positive incentive can relate to royalty rates and possible additional rights in a situation of great success. The disincentives can relate to termination provisions or minimum royalty payments to protect against inefficiency.

Where the name and reputation of the event are recognised worldwide, and there is no known conflict or similarity of name with any other event or party, they can be licensed over many countries. This is only likely to apply to an international event or sport of major status.

6–16   The description of the territory must be clear and precise. It must not be described, for example, as "Europe", or with any other general identification which may change geographically or politically during the period of the licence. Without a precise definition, "Europe" could mean Europe as constituted at the start of the licence, or whichever countries make up Europe from time to time.

If the warranty by the sponsored party in the licence as to its exclusive rights over the event name or logo is breached, the licensee will expect to be compensated for its loss of profit, reimbursed its expenses and indemnified against any consequences of acting in reliance on the warranty being correct. The sponsored party will be required to warrant that it has granted no other rights to third parties which would be breached by, or conflict with, the exclusive licence. Any warranty must be subject to the overriding provisions of the legal system governing commercial transactions in and between different licensed territories. For example, despite a licence being subject to English law, the country in which it is to be effective may have overriding local laws protecting a licensee upon termination, by having compensation payable to it. As warranties are representations in absolute terms, they should only be given if the sponsored party is confident that there is no risk of them being wrong or misleading.

An exclusive licensee may be entitled to take direct legal action against third parties which infringe its enforceable exclusive rights, such as by the production of unauthorised versions of the event name or logo upon similar merchandise. The sponsored party should assist the licensee in any reasonable manner at the licensee's expense, but should not commit itself to the risk of time and expense in being responsible for taking legal action against any infringer.

8. Infringement

6–17   Pirating of merchandising rights, or their unauthorised use, is a hazard facing every licensee which has an attractive and marketable product, a high investment in its stock of merchandise and a royalty liability to the licensor. If the pirated goods are shoddy, or even dangerous, they will also reflect adversely upon the event's reputation. The purchasers have no way of knowing that the sponsored party or the event is not involved in the unauthorised activity. Infringement of merchandising rights is only worthwhile to the pirate if it can sell a high volume of the product quickly with a good profit. Therefore pirating is only likely to apply to the merchandise rights of an event which has a wide appeal and is well known.

If a licence has not yet been granted by the sponsored party for that product category in the territory where the pirating is being carried out, the potential sales market can be either saturated to the extent of extinguishing its potential demand for the product, or it can be spoilt to prevent effective and economical authorised marketing. In either case there is not much incentive for any licensee to acquire the merchandising rights. The sponsored party loses potential income, and has no control over the quality of the unauthorised products being sold.

6–18   If an exclusive merchandising licence is already in existence in a territory where pirating occurs, the sponsored party can get into expensive legal difficulties if it has undertaken with the licensee in the merchandising agreement to prevent or to attack pirating by court action. Taking legal action against all infringers would be expensive, time-consuming and not always effective. The more popular the merchandised rights, the more likely will be the unauthorised use of them. The extent of the legal difficulty, and the commercial embarrassment, will depend upon the wording and intent of the warranties and undertakings by which the sponsored party is bound. Any assurance it gives to the licensee to police unfair competition through the sales of unauthorised products must be subject to its own opinion in good faith upon the chance of success, and the economics of trying to do so. In the context of a sponsored event such an obligation would be wholly impractical, and the sponsored party should never make such a commitment.

6–19 The following courses of action can be used to identify and stop infringements of the licenced rights. First it is necessary to define what constitutes an infringement. Copyright, such as of artistic logos or devices, is covered by the Copyright, Designs and Patents Act 1988. There is no copyright in an event name which may only be protected through trade mark registration or passing off (the nearest thing we have in the United Kingdom to the wider laws against unfair competition found elsewhere in Europe). Passing off is a common law concept, which is explained in paragraph 6–23.

Infringement of a copyright artistic logo or device, or of a registered trade mark (under the Trade Marks Act 1994), or of an unregistered trade mark which has an established valuable goodwill may occur when an unauthorised party publishes or makes use of such a logo or name for its own products or business and where certain fundamental conditions are satisfied. Infringement may be innocent, such as where the infringer can show that it genuinely did not know of the original item, and had not copied it for its own use. This may be possible in respect of a name or logo relating to an event which is not nationally publicised and newsworthy. Continuation of the infringement can be prevented, but the level of damages which may be awarded for the infringement would not be punitive.

6–20 Difficulty arises where the infringer is using a name or logo similar to that of the event, but deliberately designed to be superficially identifiable with the event, while (so the infringer hopes) not being so close a similarity as to be found by the court to be an infringement. Despite the dishonourable intentions of the "infringer", it may succeed if the similarities between its name or logo and that of the event are not close enough to be preventable. This is a matter of comparison which (as it is a matter largely of opinion) may not provide an absolute answer one way or the other. The comparison will be based upon how substantive the similarities are and, for copyright works, "substantive" can refer as much to the quality and feel of the logo as to the quantity of elements taken by the infringer, or its attempt to expand the substance of the design into something visually different over all. Many infringers do not bother to make any changes to, or adaptations of, the protected name or logo, on the basis that they may not be discovered, or no action may be taken against them, or that the penalty will be less than the profit they can make in the meantime.

9. Copyright, designs and trade marks

Copyright

6–21 Where the infringing item breaches the copyright in the original item, an action for breach of copyright will be available to whomever owns the copyright in the original item and their exclusive licensees. Examples are photographs used for posters and artwork used for T-shirts. It is immaterial for copyright protection purposes whether or not the authorised item has been licensed in the territory where the infringing article is made and sold.

Professional photographers and artists nearly always retain the copyright in their work, and receive fees for its reproduction in magazines and elsewhere. The licensee or the sponsored party would have to get a specific licence from the photographer or artist to use the photograph or artwork for merchandising purposes, even if the sponsored party has previously used the photograph or artwork, for example, on the cover of an event programme.

Registered designs and trade marks

6–22   Where the sponsored party grants a licensee rights over a graphic mark or name which is its property in connection with the event, and which is registered as a design or trade mark in the licensed territory, legal action is also available against infringers in that territory for breach of that registered right. An original design (*i.e.* shape, configuration, pattern or ornament), applied to an article of manufacture, is capable of protection through registration. The registration of trade marks is dealt with in paragraph 6–40. Subject to the terms of the licence and the Trade Marks Act 1994, the action can also be brought by a licensee of the registered device or logo, which may be more convenient to the sponsored party.

If the infringing goods use the registered event name or logo in a manner similar to that used for the products manufactured by the licensee, whether or not being visibly attributed to the licensor or the licensee, there may still be a claim against the infringer for trade mark infringement where a likelihood of confusion on the part of the public exists. In certain cases the use by an infringer of a similar mark but in relation to totally different goods will also constitute an infringement where the registered mark has a reputation in the United Kingdom and the unauthorised mark takes unfair advantage of, or is detrimental to, the reputation of the registered mark.

Passing Off

6–23   The infringer's intention is to cause confusion in the minds of purchasers who would assume that the infringing merchandise is the product of the licensee, or that the licensor or licensee has authorised its production. In fact the purchaser of such infringing goods probably has no such thoughts: he likes what he sees, and buys it. Nevertheless, the licensee has established its business and created the market for the goods. Each infringing item sold will wrongfully deprive the licensee of what would have been its profit on that item, and the sponsored party of what would have been its royalty on the sale of an authorised item.

However, there is a significant difference between the ease of taking infringement action where there is the statutory protection of trade mark registration, and having to produce the proof of confusion and damage necessary for a successful passing-off action. If the registration protection is infringed, then without having to prove intention or damages, a writ can be issued for an injunction and compensation. By contrast, in a passing-off action it is well established that there must be a misrepresentation which injures the business or goodwill of another trader (see chapter one paragraph 1–55). The *Teenage Mutant Ninja Turtles* (*Mirage Studios v. Counter-feat Clothing* [1991] F.S.R. 145) and *Spice Girls* (*Halliwell v. Panini SpA* (1997), unreported, Chancery Division, Lightman J.) cases demonstrate how difficult this can be to prove, particularly where there is no underlying copyright. (See further chapter seven, paragraph 7–11 *et seq.* in the context of personality rights.)

10. The merchandised product

6–24   The merchandise which is promoted through the use of the name and logo of the event must meet high standards of manufacture and presentation.

Shoddy goods, although not part of the sponsored party's business activities, may nevertheless be connected with its reputation in the minds of dissatisfied customers. Similarly, high-quality goods will reflect well on the sponsored party although its only connection with them is in a marketing capacity. Marketed merchandise does not hold out to the purchaser the same form of recommendation by the sponsored party as is implied where, for example, a sportsman endorses the goods, but the sponsored party does suffer to the same extent from the adverse effects of justified consumer dissatisfaction.

The following should be included in the sponsored party's rights under the merchandising licence:

(a) The right to inspect samples of the goods to ensure their manufacturing quality, if necessary in accordance with agreed specifications. The concern of the sponsored party is to ensure that its name and logo are being used only on reasonable quality goods and to check that any photograph or logo is being used in the correct style and colour, and with the right quality of presentation. This is normally achieved by the licensee having to submit a sample of each range of product which contains the event name or logo for approval prior to committing to manufacture. Approval should be required to be given in writing within (say) 14 days after submission. For the licensee's protection, the clause should state that if no response is received from the sponsored party within (say) 21 days after receiving the sample, approval will be deemed to have been given. Subsequent inspection by the sponsored party may be undertaken from time to time to ensure that the article as produced consistently conforms with the approved sample.

6–25

(b) The right to control the format of the combined presentation of the product and the event name or logo to the public by way of advertising and promotion. The licensee should not be able to advertise the product in such a way that it looks like an endorsement by the sponsored party of the products. For example, how and in what context will the identification of the event name or logo with the product be projected, and what representations and claims does the licensee make for the product which by implication are supported by the sponsored party, *e.g.* as to the quality or performance of the goods? The sponsored party and the event must not be involved in false or misleading representations, or those which otherwise bring the product and the event into disrepute.

6–26

(c) The right to be able to intervene, so far as it is legally able to, if the price structure of the merchandise is excessive, even allowing for adequate margins to cover the cost of royalties to the sponsored party. Similarly it may harm the image and reputation of the sponsored party and of the event if the goods containing the event name or logo are being mass-produced and sold at ridiculously low prices as loss leaders or as incentives for the purchase of other products. This is not a case of illegal resale price maintenance, but of establishing a fair price for the merchandised product consistent with its quality and the status of what it represents, *e.g.* the event. The ultimate sanction is termination of the licence agreement. Reasonable pricing depends on the product's comparative manufacturing and marketing costs, and the primary target sector of the public. An overpriced product may give rise to criticism of the sponsored party, although it is not connected directly with it. Damage to the event image can be difficult to repair in these circumstances.

(d) If the item licensed is a registered design, logo or trade mark, or if it is an unregistered artistic device, the merchandising licence must ensure that the correct copyright and registration credits are placed on each item of merchandise manufactured containing that mark. This is required for the protection of such rights, under international conventions and local laws. Wherever reasonably practicable, notification will be on the product itself, its packaging and in all publicity and promotional material and advertising.

(e) As the sponsored party has no connection with the design or manufacture of the merchandised products, it should have no liability to consumers if the product is defective or dangerous. All the sponsored party is doing is authorising the licensee to attach the event name or logo to those products. The licence agreement should contain a suitable warranty and indemnity from the licensee to the sponsored party covering this aspect.

11. Royalties

Fixed rate or percentage royalty

6–27   The financial return to the sponsored party is a royalty paid by the licensee upon sales of licensed merchandise. A fixed sum of money may be payable upon the sale of each article irrespective of the selling price, such as where the retail price is very low and is not likely to increase significantly during the licence period. Alternatively a royalty is paid on the sale of each article based upon a percentage of its retail selling price, or its net invoice value if not retailed by the licensee, excluding VAT in each case.

Fixed sum payments do not benefit the sponsored party where the article has more than a relatively nominal retail price, as the licensee can make a bigger profit by raising its price, and by doing so it is not obliged to pay a share of the increase to the sponsored party. Inflation is a good reason for the sponsored party not using the fixed sum system, except possibly where the fixed sum is paid to the sponsored party in advance and is so calculated that impressive sales have to be achieved to enable the licensee to reach the point of making a profit for itself.

6–28   The percentage royalty on the retail selling price or net invoice value ensures that the profit of the licensee arising from the sale of merchandise is proportional to the income of the sponsored party. This minimises the risk of the licensee finding some ingenious method of legitimately reducing the amounts to be paid to the sponsored party. This can happen where the royalty base price is a wholesale price, or any other figure which is within the control of the licensee. Trade discounts or incentives deducted from the base price can lead to the licensee being dishonest, such as by wholesaling to its own retail company at an unrealistic price, where the licensee is the wholesaling company. The merchandising licence should cover that position, so that if the licensee deals with any connected company, or other entity, which sells on the licensed product, the sales price on which the royalty is calculated is adjusted accordingly. The fact is that if a licensee wants to rip off the sponsored party it will be able to find some means of doing so.

6–29 Where the licensee is a manufacturer of goods but not a retailer, the royalty will be based upon its net invoice value, excluding any discount which is not acceptable to the sponsored party on a reasonable basis. If the licensee sells direct to consumers, whether or not it is the manufacturer of the licenced products, the royalty should be based on the retail price. If both scenarios apply, the two bases of calculation can be agreed to apply in each case as appropriate, and at the higher of the two possibilities. The rising prices of the items of merchandise, and the consequent increase in the amount of the royalty to the sponsored party, will keep it in pace with inflation.

If the royalty percentage is of recommended retail selling price, that is easily ascertainable, but there is a distinction between the recommended retail selling price and the price which may actually be charged. As the amount of discounts or other forms of price reduction are not permanent, and are not the same over the whole territory, it may not always be practical to base the royalty on actual retail selling prices. For example, if a discount is considered not to be a commercial bona fide arm's-length deal, it should be disregarded, and the royalty should be on the original invoice price prior to the discount.

Foreign currency royalties

6–30 Where an event has an international interest, foreign licensing may be carried out. If foreign licences are granted, the means of calculating the royalty become most important to the sponsored party. This will include the problem of rates of currency exchange, and which party is to take the risk or the benefit that may arise due to fluctuations in the exchange rates.

Agreement upon rates of currency exchange in relation to royalty payments is not so easy where, for example, the licensor is a U.K. company, the licensee is an American corporation, and the royalties are to be paid in Switzerland. A U.K. licensor will normally want to be paid in sterling for accountings relating to U.K. sales, or U.S. dollars for accountings relating to foreign sales. A great deal will depend upon what tax problems are involved. The rate of exchange can be determined as being the same rate at which the licensee exchanges its foreign royalty currency into sterling, or the rate applying on the due date of payment of its royalties to the sponsored party.

If the relevant currencies are not stable, and a licensee deliberately delays payment past its contractual date so as to take advantage of currency variations at that time, there can be a clause in the merchandising licence giving the sponsored party the option to treat the contractual date of payment as the date of the exchange rate calculation, to discourage such practices.

Sliding scale royalties

6–31 A sliding scale can be used to calculate royalty rates. One method is to impose a high royalty rate on marginal sales, and thereafter the greater the volume of sales the lower the royalty rate per item, in case the sales never become significant. Alternatively the reverse can be applied, where the royalty rate increases in accordance with increased sales levels. Once sales increase, the licensee's costs are lower per item, its profit margin is higher, and that is the time for the sponsored party to participate fully in the profits available.

If the licensee has a range of different goods under the agreement, will they all have the same royalty rate? If the rates are different, due to different profitability levels or projected sales levels, any applicable escalating royalty rate can be across the board, or more likely, related to individual lines of merchandise. The purpose is to have overall a fair royalty to the sponsored party, and a reasonable profitability to the licensee.

Royalty advances

6–32　Upon the execution of the licence agreement the licensee should pay a non-returnable advance on account of royalties to be paid to the sponsored party. The sponsored party receives an immediate income, and the licensee has to work to generate sales so that the royalties reach the level of the advance, because until then the licensee is out of pocket. Subject to any minimum royalty commitments, the licensee has no obligation to make further royalty payments to the sponsored party until sales of the merchandise have reached the volume at which royalties payable to it exceed the total of royalty advances already made.

The advance royalty payment must be specified to be "non-returnable", so that if the promotion of the merchandise fails, the sponsored party will not have to repay to the licensee the amount of the advance in excess of what would have been finally due on an accounting of royalties on actual sales. Any advance royalty payment must be recoupable only from the sponsored party's earnings in connection with the agreement. If the event is not staged, or if for any other reason there is nothing to promote, the merchandising rights are useless.

6–33　If there is a total failure by the sponsored party in this respect, the licensee should be able to terminate the merchandising agreement, and get back any advance payment it may have made to the sponsored party. Although the event may not have happened, the event name and logo will have been licenced to the licensee a considerable time before the event was due to take place. If the licensee has made and sold enough units of the licensed product to generate a royalty payment due to the sponsored party in excess of the advance, that will not be returnable.

If there are different licensed product ranges with different royalty rates, the sponsored party should consider whether the attribution and recoupment of advances should not also be separated accordingly. The difference is that if the advance is general, then it is possible for the licensee to recoup the advance from the sales of one or two of the licensed products, irrespective of whether the others have any sales at all. If the advances are allocated between the ranges of licensed products, then they each have to have sales to recoup their attributed advances. It also means that the licensee will be paying royalties in excess of advances on popular items of licenced product rather earlier, *i.e.* when their own advance allocation has been recouped. Popular ranges of products are therefore not subsidising unprofitable or unworked ranges of products.

Minimum royalty

6–34　To reduce the risk of a licensee doing nothing to promote its rights, and thereby earning nothing for the sponsored party in excess of any advance payments received on account of royalties, the merchandise agreement should contain a minimum royalty clause. The amount of the minimum royalty can be in addition to royalty advance payments, although it would normally be a top up at the end of a licence year if the total accounting due to the sponsored party falls short of the balance between the advance and the minimum royalty commitment. A minimum royalty provision would only be relevant if the licence period is for some years, and is therefore a significant commercial enterprise.

A minimum royalty clause is only necessary where it is important for the actual products to be sold to maximise the royalty potential of the merchandising rights, as opposed to the licensee simply acquiring the rights by agreeing to pay an advance. Otherwise the advance would be the only payment ever received under the merchandising agreement if the licensee did absolutely nothing to exploit the rights it has acquired. This is treated by the sponsored party as a positive inducement for the licensee to trade actively, rather than as a penalty for not doing so.

6–35   The licensee will have to pay to the sponsored party a minimum royalty in each annual accounting period, which can be based upon the estimated volume of sales the licensee should be able to maintain with a reasonable effort. This will ensure that the sponsored party has a minimum earning from the venture. The higher the minimum royalty required, the more serious the intentions of the licensee are likely to be, because it would need to be confident of being able to recoup its outlay and of making a profit. Subject to the recoupment of advances, the minimum royalty payments should be paid at the end of the relevant accounting period, if the total royalty accounting for that year would otherwise be less than the minimum royalty commitment.

The merchandise agreement should state whether a licensee, who has not achieved enough sales to cover the minimum royalty payments, can nevertheless maintain its rights by making up the difference in each accounting period out of its own pocket. The sponsored party is interested in the royalty income, not the products, so this should not be of any concern to it. Alternatively an exclusive licence could convert into a non-exclusive licence at that point, and/or the sponsored party may retain a right to terminate.

Accounting

6–36   Merchandise agreements should contain accounting dates and procedures to suit the capability of the licensee, its own accounting arrangements with third parties, and the requirements of the sponsored party. The accounting dates will be half yearly or quarterly, depending on the likely flow of income hoped to be generated. The licensee should undertake to produce its statement and payment within a reasonable specified time thereafter, e.g. 21 days after each June 30 and December 31. The accounting clause should have a provision for interest at a specified rate to be automatically payable on all royalties due to the sponsored party if they have not been paid by the due date.

If the licensee has a large territory and (with the prior consent of the sponsored party) sub-licenses some of the rights, or if it has regular major outlets for its products, the sponsored party should establish the dates by which the licensee expects to be accounted to by these third parties. It should make sure that the accounting dates to it from the licensee "catch" the most recent receipts by the licensee, otherwise that money will fall into the next accounting period. This is a question of cashflow efficiency. The statements rendered to the sponsored party by the licensee should set out in reasonable detail all sources of income and sales by category of product and when the sale was made.

6–37   The licensee must keep separate accounts for its activities under the merchandise agreement, and the sponsored party should have rights of inspection and audit upon giving reasonable prior notice of its intention to do so. If there is doubt as to the accuracy of the accounting, the sponsored party's auditor should verify the figures independently by contacting sales outlets and any manufacturers used by the licensee for the products. The audit clause should give such right of access, and the licensee should undertake to provide the necessary authority to such parties to disclose relevant information to the sponsored party's auditor.

If an audit shows that the licensee has underpaid the sponsored party, the clause should contain the provision whereby if that deficit exceeds (say) 5 per cent of the amount properly due over the audit period, the cost incurred by the sponsored party for the audit will be charged to the licensee.

12. Guarantor

6–38   A sponsored party with a valuable asset in the event and its name and logo should not grant any rights to a licensee which it considers does not have the ability, finance or organisation to promote and protect the merchandising rights properly. Where a small company is given exclusive merchandising rights, the sponsored party should consider requiring the licensee to provide a guarantor of the performance of its obligations. Small private companies can have an enormous and profitable business, in which case a guarantor should not be necessary. Large companies can be dangerously overtrading. The assessment of need of a guarantor should be addressed more to the substance and soundness of the company, rather than just to corporate structure.

A guarantor will normally be a director of the licensee company. The guarantor ought to be someone who is financially sound enough to be worth attaching as guarantor to indemnify the sponsored party against loss or expense should the licensee fail to honour its obligations. A guarantor stands in the place of the licensee if it cannot meet its commitments, so there is little point in having a guarantor who is financially worthless.

13. Law of licence

6–39   If the licence covers any territory outside the United Kingdom, it should specify which legal system will govern its interpretation and enforcement. If it is not specified, confusion can arise where, for example, the sponsored party and the licensee are resident in different countries, and the licensee's territory covers more than one country. In the absence of a specified legal jurisdiction, the possibilities are either the sponsored party's legal system, or the licensee's legal system. The decision will be influenced by where the agreement is signed, and where the operation of the rights granted will take place, but it is not a contractual term which should be left open to contention. For example, the clause can state that English law will apply to the interpretation and enforcement of the agreement, and that the English High Court will be the court of competent jurisdiction. This reference to the High Court should be stated otherwise a foreign licensee might try to take action in its country against the sponsored party, but in accordance with English law.

The sponsored party has the right to decide by which system of law it would like the contract to be governed. The laws relating to commercial contracts differ throughout the world; both as to the formalities necessary to constitute a binding contract, and what can and cannot be contained in a contract as enforceable obligations, limitations and incentives. Although two parties can agree to any matter to be contained in their contract (provided it is not illegal), whether any unusual term of the agreement is enforceable will depend upon the principles of the relevant law of the contract.

14. Trade marks

6–40 Any distinctive original name or logo which has been used by the event will have attached to it a goodwill value depending upon the extent to which it has become instantly recognisable in its own right as being connected with or representing the event. Therefore the name or logo has a proprietary right which is the property of the owner of the event, which for these purposes is assumed to be the sponsored party. If the party is proposing to grant merchandising rights in respect of the name or logo, then the best form of protection would be to apply for registration of it as a trade mark. Set out below is an explanation of trade marks with specific application to merchandising rights.

As explained in chapter one, paragraph 1–55, while any name or logo will be capable of having a considerable commercial value, not every one of them is capable of being registered as a trade mark. Registration of a trade mark in an individual country only protects the name or logo in that country, although there is now a Community Trade Mark system covering the whole of the European Union and a system of international registrations under the Madrid Protocol which is still growing in Member States. Registration in one country which is a member of the Paris Convention gives to that party the prior right within six months of making an application for registration of the mark within other Member States. Failing that, it is open to anybody to make a trade mark application in another country for the event name or logo where it is not so protected. Prior substantial unregistered use in that country is one ground for objection, *i.e.* the name or logo must have been used commercially in a substantive manner for a reasonable period in that country prior to the conflicting application being made.

6–41 Internationally there are established classes of goods, and classes of services, within which an application may be made for a trade mark. A trade mark has to be attached to specific ranges of goods or services, which have to be described in the application form, and so determine the class within which the application will be made. It is possible to apply in any number of classes which are appropriate to the goods or services, even if they are not at that time being distributed or provided, as the case may be. However, see paragraph 6–47, below.

If a trade mark which is not wholly original or unique is applied for in the class which covers, say, entertainment, and the same or a similar trade mark is applied for by another party altogether for, say pharmaceutical substances and medicines, it can do so. There should be no confusion between the relevant parties, their normal business activities and the products connected with the trade marks. However, if the trade mark is unique, such as the word "EXXON", the Exxon company may have good grounds to object to another party seeking to register the same word in relation to unrelated goods if the world would assume that the original Exxon is in some way connected with the independent trade mark application, or the use of the later mark would take unfair advantage of, or be detrimental to, the distinctive character or repute of the original mark.

Registrability of names

6–42 Not all names are registrable, however much they are in use to identify products or services, and however high the goodwill value there is attributed to them. Examples of words which are not generally registrable are personal names (see the *Elvis* case in chapter seven, paragraphs 7–29—7–30 (*Re Applications by Elvis Presley Enterprises Inc.* [1997] R.P.C. 543)), names of geographical places, and ordinary words which are not distinctive as being applicable to the goods or services in question. Also not registrable will be duplicated names in the same class without some fundamental distinction, and names confusingly similar to those already registered.

The application for registration of any name (although potentially registrable) may be successfully objected to by the proprietor of a well-used unregistered name which is the same or confusingly similar, within the same class of goods or services. To object successfully it would have to show substantial prior use over a significant period of time, and that a commercial value and a trade recognition is attached to the unregistered trademark. The Trade marks Registry has a helpful inquiries department which, free of charge, will give useful guidance. The advice is subject to the applicant making the proper searches, and if necessary, taking specific professional advice.

6–43　If there is a real doubt as to whether a name is registrable, *i.e.* where the rules are not definitive when applied to it, then it would be safer to make an application in any event. It may succeed and, if not, all the applicant has lost is the application fee and any other cost incurred in making it. The applicant would also know that anybody else who was minded to make a similar application would be unlikely to succeed.

6–44　If a name is considered by the registrar to be registrable, depending on how innovative it is and whether it contains ordinary words, the following rulings will be made affecting the registration. It would be possible for a reasonably similar trade mark to be registered within the same class if on a visual and aural comparison it will not be a cause of confusion between them. A relevant factor will be if the product range associated with each trade mark is quite separate. The proprietor of the first trade mark should not manufacture or distribute a product similar to that to which the second trade mark relates. Whether or not a trade mark for which registration is applied is considered to be confusingly similar to an existing registered trade mark, and therefore is rejected, is a matter of the opinion of the Trade marks Registrar.

Specially protected marks

6–45　Special rules apply to the registration and use of marks which consist or contain insignia resembling the Royal arms, crown and flags. These would not, generally, be registerable. The Olympic Symbol, etc. (Protection) Act 1995 also confers special protection on the Olympic symbol and certain words associated with the Olympic Games.

Registration timetable

6–46　A trade mark can take around 12 months to proceed from application through to registration, and even longer if there are objections and hearings at the Trade marks Registry to overcome the objections. Upon registration, the date of priority of right is retrospective to the date of application. Because of this time lag, forward planning is required if a specific name is going to be reserved for use in due course. During the application period the applicant would be well advised to make as much commercial and promotional use of the name as possible. This will help to protect it in the waiting period, and, if the application fails, a protectable and valuable goodwill will hopefully have been built up in it as an unregistered trade mark.

Abandonment of registration

6–47 If a trade mark is registered, but is never used commercially by the proprietor within a period of five years following the registration, or if it lapses from commercial use for five years for whatever reason, it is open for anyone to apply to the Registrar to revoke that registration, which would enable that party to make its own new application for the same or a similar trade mark in that class. As the registration of a trade mark creates a form of exclusivity of use of a limited nature, it is reasonable that if it is abandoned then that area of exclusivity should be opened up to other parties. It is considered that no commercial use for a continuous period of five years is reasonable evidence of abandonment. The application for revocation may not succeed if the current proprietor can show that the trade mark is to be used or reinstated imminently, with sufficient evidence being provided to satisfy the Registrar that such a statement is genuine.

15. Character merchandising

6–48 Character merchandising is very big business. A product manufacturer normally relates its trade mark to its own products, to give them a brand image on which promotions and advertising can be based. Character merchandising is the opposite. The proprietors of the rights in, say, Snoopy the dog, the Muppets or the Teletubbies, capitalise on the value of their creation by licensing other parties to merchandise their product using that creation. The pictorial image of the creations is protected, such as by copyright, and their names will be protected by trade mark registrations wherever possible.

Originally these creations would have been marketed in film animation, book or printed form and as toys, and they would have been protected by applications in the relevant classes of goods. In relation to merchandising, the proprietor will also want to make applications in all classes within which the creation could possibly have any further connection. Posters would come within the same class as books (paper and printed material), and items such as jigsaw puzzles would come within the toys and playthings class.

6–49 The Trade Marks Act 1994 did away with the original prohibition on "trafficking" in trade marks. Previously, unless the proprietor of Garfield was itself in the business of making and selling T-shirts, joke mugs, children's clothes or any other use to which the merchandising of Garfield has been put, the registrar might query the validity of a number of applications being made at the same time for trade marks in different classes on the basis that the proprietor was not retaining a sufficient degree of control over his registered users. The 1994 Act repeals all the previous restrictions. However, while the licensing of registered trade marks is no longer discouraged, the requirement to ensure that the use of the trade mark does not become misleading—for example, as to the identity of the manufacturer— remains. Accordingly, care must still be taken by a licensor to ensure that the use of its registered mark by a licensee is properly controlled.

To allow the licensee to make the application for the trade mark in its own name creates a security risk which can be overcome contractually, but is not recommended.

Trade mark registration is not a legal requirement to enable character merchand- ising to be undertaken, it is a legal precaution. However, it is possible to deal with the licence to use the name, logo or character purely as a contractual matter, relying on the accepted ownership of the underlying intellectual property rights being with the proprietor of them, which grants the licence on that basis. Any infringement would come under a claim for breach of contract, copyright or as a passing-off action (see paragraphs 6–21—6–23, above).

CHAPTER 7

Endorsement

1. Introduction

7–01 Sponsorship is seen as corporate support of an event for the mutual benefit of the sponsor and the sponsored party, and with the intention of promoting the image and reputation of the sponsor, and of any of the sponsor's brand products associated with the event.

Endorsement is the promotion of the company's product by means of the personal recommendation of an individual who is sufficiently well known and respected that he can influence the purchasing pattern of sections of the consumer public. In a sense, the personality sponsors the company's product, and is paid for doing so. It is a much simpler commercial arrangement than for sponsorship, and is a means whereby that personality can extend his own programme of self-promotion to increase his earning capacity, and to maintain a profile in the public eye. For that reason he has to choose carefully what he is going to endorse.

7–02 Endorsement is also a form of specialised advertising by the manufacturer of the endorsed product. The basic concept of the advertisement centres around the personality extolling the virtues of the product. Endorsement is mostly carried out through the printed media and television, but can be extended to branded goods with the name of the personality attached to them as a special line.

Merchandising is the generalised cashing-in of this asset to promote and sell almost anything with the name or features of the personality put on them in a decorative manner, subject to approval by the personality. Consumers do not believe that the personality is in any way connected with the products, or that they are endorsing or otherwise recommending the products, which tend to be subject to the impulse purchase trend, such as casual clothing, everyday articles and posters. Merchandising tends to be popular for cult personalities. If a personality licenses merchandising rights and is popular for endorsement work, he will have to ensure that the two areas are managed in a manner compatible with the image he wants to project on a long-term basis.

7–03 While the endorsed product is promoted and advertised in association with the personality's recommendation, specific items of the product sold do not contain any reference to him, except perhaps on the special packaging designed for the purpose, or if any leaflet containing a picture of the personality plus any quotations by way of recommendation is provided with the product. If the product manufacturer has a one-year endorsement agreement with the personality, it would not, as a business decision, saturate its advertising of the product using his name, as the impact wears off by becoming stale. There would be periods during the year, such as at Christmas and for special sales periods, when the style and presentation of the promotional material will be changed to emphasise the endorsement.

The products will already be well established in their own right within their market, and the endorsement by the personality is one of many methods of maintaining, and hopefully increasing, consumer awareness of that brand of product as against all other brands. Therefore the image or profile of the product is not wholly dependent on featuring the personality in the same way as merchandised products are for an event logo.

2. Marketable value of personality

7–04 A successful individual, such as an athlete, opera star, or media or sporting personality, has a valuable asset in his name and reputation, which is marketable in connection with products, and sometimes with services. The value depends on the public perception of the personality, and how established he has become in the "recognition factor" stakes. Different personalities appeal more to certain sections of the public than to others, so any endorsement deals are chosen carefully for that personality accordingly. Over a long period of being successfully associated with a specific product, a personality may become known as "Mr Widget". That is fine for so long as he continues to be used to promote widgets, but by being typecast the personality loses some versatility in being chosen by other manufacturers to promote their products. That is why many personalities refuse long-term endorsement offers.

Not every personality has the kind of appeal that is necessary for successful endorsement. Except for sports stars who endorse the product they use, endorsement by personalities who have no connection with the product is sometimes perceived as a down market commercial cashing-in of current status. Superstars do not seem to do it, except for top-status products or services, which are commensurate with the level of their own image, but not all personalities are superstars with incomes and assets to match. Nevertheless, properly done, endorsement is a growing legitimate marketing of a personality's stock in trade, *i.e.* his public recognition.

7–05 A personality may be used to endorse one product for so long that they become inseparable in the minds of the public. If the use of that personality eventually ceases to stimulate those to whom the advertisement is addressed, or if consumer interest in the product is turned off due to the familiarity of the personality becoming boring or stereotyped, it is time for the product manufacturer to change the personality upon which the endorsement campaign has been based. When a manufacturer finds that a personality has a high public acceptance factor and an expensive and extensive endorsement campaign is set up, the manufacturer is naturally reluctant to change a winning style. That may mean a long-term steady job for the personality endorsing that product, but it may make that personality of little value for promoting any other product.

Sometimes personality endorsement of a product does not work, despite quality advertisements and the efforts of both the manufacturer and the personality to promote public awareness. It is quite possible for the personality and the advertisement to be remembered, but for there to be a total failure to recollect the product that personality was endorsing in the advertisement. The advertisement has a very short-term impact, both at the time of any TV transmissions and during the media campaign as a whole.

3. Personality's personal recommendation

7–06 The endorsement of products is presented in the advertising material as the personal recommendation by the personality of those products, with the purpose of influencing people to purchase them. The psychological basis is that if a top athlete uses and endorses a manufacturer's special running shoes, budding and experienced athletes may be persuaded that part of the personality's secret of success is in the use of those shoes. Whether the product is a watch, or a new brand of aftershave lotion or scent, the urge to be trendy and to catch the mood of the moment makes it essential to match the product and the endorsing personality correctly.

The products endorsed by a sports personality will normally be related to the activity undertaken by the individual. For example, an athlete may endorse the running shoes he uses, a tennis player may endorse his racket, and a golfer his clubs. The purpose is to persuade other sportsmen to buy these products by association with the personality, and with the purchaser believing and possibly relying on the express or implied recommendation of the product by the individual. Well-known sports personalities may nevertheless not have universal appeal, and so will not necessarily be successful in the endorsement of a product or article with which he is not closely associated.

4. Voice-overs

7–07 Endorsed products are heavily advertised and promoted to give the association with, and recommendation of, the individual maximum exposure. It may be said that "voice-overs" used to back TV advertisements are a form of endorsement, although those speaking are not visible and are not named. However, they are chosen for the distinctive quality of their voice, the idea being that, subliminally, the familiar soothing voice recommends that product, and almost urges the listener or viewer to go out and buy it.

Because of the anonymity of the personality behind the voice it is not considered to be endorsement in the usual manner. Part of the interest in watching TV advertisements is in guessing the identity of the voice-over. But what about copy-cat voice-overs, where the listener believes the voice is that of a well-known personality, but in fact it is the voice of an imitator? Does a personality have proprietary rights in his voice? As he is anonymous and is given no credit for being the owner of the voice, does it matter whether or not it is his voice or that of an imitator? Why should an advertiser on television pay large sums to a personality, when a professional "voice" could be used? The answer is that voice-overs are very lucrative for famous voices, and an imitator is passing off his voice as that of the personality. This deprives the personality of the fee (as his voice was required by the advertiser but he was not used for the voice-over), falsely attributes to the personality an association with the advertised product, and is an unauthorised use of his public image. The distinctive voice is a business asset with valuable goodwill. But are the listening public confused?

7–08 What would be the position if the personality never does voice-overs on principle—is he being deprived by a professional "voice" and is there any infringement of a business asset which the personality has never developed or used? In those circumstances is there an actionable infringement by the professional voice, or is it just an encroachment on personal privacy, which is not actionable? As explained further in paragraphs 7–11 *et seq.* below, unless the personality can show that he is damaged in some way commercially or professionally, it may be difficult to prevent.

The voice-over is not an overt recommendation of the product by the personality whose voice it is, and so it is not a positive endorsement by him. Choosing the right voice for the product and the style of the TV advertisement is an art. Specific voices are chosen to fit the advertised product, the style of presentation of the advertisement and the background music. For example a "top person" product needs a cultured voice, and a young excited voice sells children's toys. Those with recognisable voices which associate themselves with categories of product are kept busy "voicing over" on TV advertisements for all sorts of products or services. They might not promote competitive products, but otherwise there is a free range.

It is of course possible to find someone whose natural voice is the same as the voice of a personality, so there is no actual imitation, although that is the clear intention. Because of the nature of the business, that transparent device will not work, the end result will still be a misrepresentation to the public, and a potential claim from the personality. Otherwise what would happen if an eminent teetotal personality's voice was imitated on an advertisement for a popular lager or spirits?

5. Monetary *Value of personality*

7–09 Where a personality is nationally known for whatever he does, and is not only associated with a limited activity, his endorsement value extends to almost anything else which itself has a status or reputation consistent with that of the personality. These products tend to be serious, more expensive consumer products, in contrast to the inexpensive merchandised everyday items.

The value of an individual for endorsement purposes if he is endorsing products related to his recognised activity or sport depends entirely upon his being a champion or top player, or a famous star, to give credibility to his recommendation of the relevant product. That value increases if he wins the next title, but eventually decreases if (for example) he ceases to be involved competitively with the activity for which he is famous. Unless the individual is a household name it is not likely that he will be asked to endorse an unrelated product. The value of a personality who has become a household name will be what is perceived as his "pulling power". The willingness of a product manufacturer to risk the high cost of a major advertising campaign based upon the personality depends on its assessment of that appeal. The endorsement fee will be negotiated accordingly.

7–10 The monetary value of endorsement to the manufacturer of endorsed product is limited to the extent that there is a market for the product, and by the sales competition it faces from other makes of a similar product. The additional cost of the personality is minuscule in relation to the total advertising budget, and to the anticipated success of the product sales promotion campaign based upon the endorsement. It also depends upon the product. If it is perfume at £100 per 100ml, the market is limited immediately to women, and then only to those who might choose it and who can afford it. If the product is a credit card, or any other universally used product, the endorsement campaign strategy is all about increasing the market share of the product.

What is the measure of success? There may be no dramatic surge of sales of the product during the endorsement campaign which can be identified as being the result of the campaign, but it may have helped to maintain a steady level of sales in a period of intense competition. Endorsement will usually be an additional promotional scheme for the product designed to be complementary to all other advertising. If the other advertising is kept to schedule, then any uplift in sales during the endorsement period can be largely attributed to its influence upon the market awareness of the product.

6. Personality Rights

Unauthorised endorsement

7–11 Although product endorsement has clear commercial advantages, companies seeking to enjoy them can run into at least two types of substantial problems. First, the personality may be too expensive for them. Secondly, and even more problematically, the personality may simply not want to endorse the product concerned.

Neither of these problems have necessarily stopped companies seeking to enjoy the advantages of a particular personality's endorsement. By way of example, there follows below a number of real-life American examples of how, despite their refusal to endorse certain products, personalities have been used to unwittingly endorse them.

7–12 (a) Tom Waits and Frito-lay. The well-known American singer Tom Waits had a very distinctive singing voice which, according to one fan, was "like how you'd sound if you drank a quart of bourbon, smoked a pack of cigarettes and swallowed a pack of razor blades . . . late at night after not sleeping for three days".

Mr Waits had, for the previous 10 years, maintained a strict policy of refusing to endorse products or do commercials. The advertising agency, Tracey-Locke Inc., created television commercials to advertise Frito-Lay's "Salsa Rio Doritos" snack chips. Knowing that Waits would refuse to participate in the TV commercial, the agency hired a professional singer, Steven Carter, who was an accomplished imitator of Waits's voice, to sing "Step Right Up". Mr Waits was not amused and brought a suit for voice misappropriation and false endorsement. A U.S. jury awarded him damages totalling U.S. $2.6 million (reference at paragraph 7–34).

7–13 (b) Vanna White and the Wheel of Fortune. The U.S. television gameshow programme "Wheel of Fortune" was hosted by Vanna White. Ms White endorsed various products. However, when approached by Samsung Electronics America Inc. to participate in a series of print advertisements for its product, each of which showed a Samsung product with a current popular item or celebrity set in the next century, she refused. The advertising agency therefore decided to run the advert using a robot dressed in a wig, gown and jewellery (specifically selected so as to resemble Ms White), posed next to the "Wheel of Fortune" game board, in a stance for which Ms White was famous. Above the board was the caption "Longest Running Game Show 2012AD". The U.S. Court upheld Ms White's claim on appeal (*White v. Samsung Electronics America Inc.*, No. 90–55840 (1993) WL 73915, 9th Cir. March 19, 1993).

7–14 (c) Motschenbacher. Mr Motschenbacher was a well-known racing driver in the United States. He was known for driving a very distinctive racing car. R.J. Reynolds Tobacco Company, without Mr Motschenbacher's consent, issued a TV commercial which featured a copy of Mr Motschenbacher's car, although Mr Motschenbacher himself was not featured in it. Mr Motschenbacher successfully sued R.J. Reynolds even though he was not personally featured in the advertisement (*Lothar Motschenbacher v. Reynolds Tobacco Co.*, No. 72–1419 (1974) US App. LEXIS 8275).

7–15 (d) Olivia Newton-John and Maybelline. The well-known Australian singer, Olivia Newton-John, would not endorse the soap "Maybelline". An advertisement was therefore issued showing an Olivia Newton-John look alike with the words "Olivia? No. Maybelline!" Ms Newton-John failed in her claim against the manufacturers of the soap (*Olivia Newton-John v. Scholl Plough Ltd* (1986) A.T.P.R. 40–697).

7-16 If a film star is photographed in a casual moment drinking from a can of Coca Cola, when printed as a news item of general interest that is not an infringement of any right the film star has in his personal marketability. The use is not in the course of trade, and is not by Coca Cola. If Coca Cola used the same photo in any context promoting their product, *i.e.* implying an endorsement, would that infringe the star's rights in his own marketability?

Another example would be where a personality, who is famous for always using a known tennis racket, is photographed unwittingly playing with a racket of another make. Could the manufacturer of the other racket use that photograph as an implied endorsement of its product? Using a racket and recommending it are two different things, especially if the personality is already contracted to endorse the racket with which he is professionally associated. There can also be an implied endorsement where, for example, an advertisement consists of a picture which contains the personality and (apparently only incidentally) the product. An advertisement for an exotic motor car, with nothing else in the picture but the personality casually leaning against the car exuding an aura of proud ownership, would be considered by most viewers to be an endorsement. In this example, there may also be registered trade mark issues.

Voluntary codes

7-17 In the United Kingdom, there are a number of voluntary advertising codes which address the issue of endorsement in advertising. These are not legally binding.

7-18 **The British Code of Advertising and Sales Promotion.** This states (Clauses 13 and 14):

> "Advertisers should obtain written permission in advance if they portray or refer to individuals or their identifiable possessions in any advertisements. Exceptions are made for crowd scenes, portraying anyone who is the subject of a book or film being advertised and depicting property and general outdoor locations. If an advertiser does not obtain prior permission from entertainers, politicians, sportsmen and others whose work gives them a high public profile, they should ensure that they are not portrayed in an offensive or adverse way. It is stressed that advertisements should not claim or imply any endorsement where none exists. However, prior permission may not be needed when the advertisement contains nothing that is inconsistent with the position or views of the person featured. Reference to anyone who is deceased should be handled with particular care to avoid causing distress or offence. Reference to the Royal Family, the Royal Arms and Emblems are normally not permitted."

7-19 The Code states clearly that advertisers should hold signed and dated proof, including a contact address, for any testimonial they use. Testimonials should be used only with the written permission of those giving them and must relate to the product being advertised.

There is specific guidance given regarding alcoholic drinks and cigarettes. Advertisements of alcoholic drinks should not be directed at people who are under 18 and not feature those under 25 years old drinking. In particular, advertisements should not feature real or fictitious characters who are likely to appeal particularly to people under 18. The same restriction applies to cigarettes.

7–20 The ITC Code of Advertising Standards and Practice. This controls TV advertising. It states clearly that no individual should be portrayed or featured in advertisements without permission (except in circumstances approved by the ITC). No reference should be either offensive or defamatory.

No advertisement for alcoholic drink should feature a personality whose example people under 18 are likely to follow.

7–21 Radio Authority Advertising and Sponsorship Code. The Code clearly states that individual living persons must not normally be portrayed or referred to in advertisements without their prior consent. If impersonations or sound-alikes of celebrities or well-known characters are to be used, the practice notes to the Code states that it is strongly advisable for advertisers to obtain advance permission.

As regards alcoholic drink endorsement, the rules state that advertisements for alcoholic drinks must not include any personality whose example people under 18 are likely to follow or who have a particular appeal to people under 18. It also states that advertisements for alcoholic drinks must only use voice-overs of those who are, and sound to be, at least 25 years of age.

Children's voices must not be heard in advertisements for alcoholic drink.

7–22 Press Complaints Commission. The PCC published a new Code of Practice in December 1997 which now includes tighter provisions on privacy, harassment, intrusion into grief, children and the public interest. In particular, the Code acknowledges that everyone is entitled to respect for his/her private and family life and disallows the use of long-lens photography to take photographs of people in private places. However, a breach of the Code does not result in any financial penalty.

Legal Rights

7–23 Unlike U.S. law, the law in the United Kingdom does not recognise any legal rights in a personality. It is therefore necessary to try and protect an individual's rights in his/her own personality by reference to other recognised legal concepts. As a result, in the United Kingdom there is a patchwork of legal protection against infringement of personality rights which is far from satisfactory from the personality's point of view.

7–24 Passing Off. The tort of passing off potentially offers equal opportunity for the manufacture and the endorser to protect certain rights. The burden of proof is not straightforward and falls primarily on the plaintiff to prove that a reputation or goodwill had been acquired by him in the trade, goods or mark in question. The key question is then whether, as a matter of first impression, a substantial portion of the public would see or assume a connection between the personality and the alleged passing-off article. For one trader to induce the belief, by deceptive suggestion, that his goods are made or licensed by another (trader) with an established reputation can amount to correctionable passing off.

It follows that if an advertisement were to confuse a significant number of people who saw the advert into believing that the personality had endorsed or sponsored the product, or had authorised the use of his likeness to promote the product, he need only prove damage in order to succeed in a case of passing off. It may also constitute misleading advertising by incorrectly purporting to be an authorised specific recommendation or endorsement of products. This is not, however, as simple as one might imagine.

7–25 In one high profile sporting case (*Cantona v. Cantona French Wines Ltd* (1996, unreported)), individuals registered the company names: "Cantona Pour Homme Limited" "Cantona French Wines Limited" and "Cantona French Brandy Limited". They sold cases of wine and brandy respectively. Advertisements were placed in the sports pages of a local newspaper containing the phrases "Ooh Aah!" and "Celebrate Manchester United's Incredible Double-Double in style". The wine also depicted the number 7 on the bottle. Clearly the whole sales campaign centred upon linking the goods to both Manchester United Football (soccer) Club and Eric Cantona, the French superstar footballer.

Cantona sued the companies, seeking an inquiry as to damages or an account of profits, delivery up of offending articles, the change of company names on the Register of Companies and generally that the associations between the goods and Eric Cantona cease. The case settled, and the directors agreed to the change of company names and to ending any association between Cantona and the merchandise. Clearly, although the connection between the sports star and the goods was apparent, whether or not this amounted to passing off would have depended upon whether a significant proportion of the public believed the product to have been endorsed by Eric Cantona. The claim would be that the use of Eric Cantona's name in association with the product would damage his business and reputation as an endorser and the goodwill associated with that business.

7–26 In the *Spice Girls* case (see paragraph 6–23) the judge refused to accept that the public care one way or another whether the product they are buying is "official" or not. In that case the Spice Girls applied for an injunction to prevent the supply and distribution of a sticker collection containing their image. The court held that it was unlikely that, in the absence of the word "official" on the defendant's product, the public would be led into buying the product in the belief that it was endorsed by the group.

The problem with passing off is that it relies on the personality having an established trade in the licensing of his or her name or image, and also on the need to prove confusion. This is not always an issue, as the purchaser of a T-shirt bearing a personality's likeness is buying that likeness—not a badge of origin—so where is the confusion? The court in the *Elvis* case (see under Trade Marks, below) also rebutted the suggestion that the *Teenage Mutant Ninja Turtles* case (see paragraph 6–23, above) gave authority for the proposition that the production of articles bearing the likeness of characters by unauthorised parties amounted to a misrepresentation that each of the characters was licensed by the characters or their "owners". The judge stated, "when people buy a toy of a well known character because it depicts that character, I have no reason to believe that they care one way or the other who made, sold or licensed it".

7–27 Defamation and Malicious Falsehood. Malicious falsehood may be used if the victim's trade has been harmed by a falsehood or misrepresentation. An endorsement which is not authorised could also be defamatory if it is contrary to the known attributes of the individual or derogatory to his image so that his personal standing and integrity, or professional reputation, would be substantially damaged in the eyes of those who assume the endorsement to be genuine. In the case of *Tolley v. Fry* ([1931] All E.R. 131) an amateur golfer took action in defamation as a result of a chocolate bar which bore his name. He argued that his reputation as an amateur had been sullied as a result of the implication that he had been paid in his capacity as a golfer, thereby affecting his reputation and integrity as an amateur.

Another example might be where there is created an implied endorsement of some hell's brew liquor by a teetotal personality, or an implied approval of the use of prohibited body-building or performance-enhancing drugs by an international superstar athlete. The circumstances would have to be untrue and professionally damaging to be considered defamatory.

If a tennis player always uses a certain manufacturer's racket but refuses to endorse it commercially, it may seem odd that the manufacturer cannot simply advertise that fact, which is already known to anyone involved in tennis. An advertisement stating a fact, if neutrally worded, should not give the impression that the payer is positively recommending the product.

7–28 Copyright. Under English law there is "nothing akin to a copyright in a name. This has been a part of our common law for a long time." In the case of *Du Boulay v. Du Boulay* ((1869) 2 L.R.P.C. 430) the Privy Council stated boldly that "we do not recognise the absolute right of a person to a particular name . . . whatever cause of annoyance it may be [this] is a grievance for which our law affords no redress". English law clearly states that if an injunction is granted restraining the use of a word or name, it is not granted to protect the word itself but the trade or goodwill which will be injured by its use.

Likewise an individual can have no rights in his own appearance. In the *Elvis* case (see paragraph 7–29, below) the judge mused that "during his life he [Elvis Presley] could not prevent a fan from having a tattoo put on his chest or a drawing on his car which looked like the musician simply on the basis that it was his appearance which was depicted". Clearly the owner of copyright in drawings, photographs or recordings of an individual can prevent them being reproduced or exploited by third parties, but this is quite different from any personality right.

There is one possible exception to this for an endorser or celebrity generally, and that is when an individual or celebrity creates themselves in a different form or media such as a cartoon character or other characterisation. The "El Tel" character reportedly created and owned by former English soccer coach, Terry Venables, is an example of this.

7–29 Trademarks. Trade marks in U.K. law provide little protection for personalities. The *Elvis* case clearly underlined the fact that, under English law, trade marks are badges of origin of goods and cannot be goods in themselves. Although this case was under the now-repealed 1938 Act, it is likely to be considered by the courts to reflect the situation under the current 1994 Act. The *Elvis* case follows in a long line of cases unfavourable to the idea of the protection of names by way of a trade mark.

The case of the *TARZAN* trade mark ([1970] R.P.C. 450) held that the name "Tarzan" was not registrable even though it was a made-up name. The ruling was given on the basis that "it seemed quite plain that the word "Tarzan" had by 1965 passed into the common language".

117

The judge in the *Elvis* case stated that "When a fan buys a poster or a cup bearing an image of his star, he is buying a likeness, not a product from a particular source." This is in many ways a near killer blow for protecting the rights of individuals who endorse products or services

One can only speculate as to where all this leaves personalities such as Paul Gascoigne and Alan Shearer, the well-known English soccer players, and Damon Hill, World Champion Formula One driver, not to mention the estate of celebrities such as James Dean. All of these have their names registered as trade marks at the U.K. Trade Marks Registry. Whilst these registrations were all accepted by the Registry in accordance with its internal guidelines or practice, this offers little comfort.

7–30   The Examiner in the *Elvis* case commented, when rejecting the opposition to the application to register "ELVIS" for Class 3 goods:

> ". . . I am aware that this was the Christian or first name of a very famous individual: . . . I cannot see that there is prima facie objection to it . . . the use of feminine proper names is generally regarded as non-distinctive . . . but no such objection is taken to masculine proper names used on that class of goods".

The court in the *Elvis* case took the contrary view and suggested that, while such a rule of thumb may have been useful in days gone by, eau de cologne, deodorants, antiperspirants, cosmetics and the like were now frequently sold to and targeted at men, and that if there was such a prima facie rule it should now cover both feminine and masculine proper names. However, in the end whether or not it is acceptable or not for registration must depend upon the particular mark in issue, the goods for which registration is sought and the nature of the trade into which they will be sold.

Thus the registration of names and signatures of James Dean, Alan Shearer, Damon Hill and Paul Gascoigne seem particularly vulnerable. Even would-be endorsers with unusual or made up names such as "Gazzer" or "The Artist Formerly known as Prince" cannot be certain of being able to take advantage of trade mark protection.

7–31   Breach of Confidence.   In the *Oasis* case the pop group applied for an injunction to prevent photographs of themselves taken at a photo shoot for their forthcoming album being further published in *The Sun* newspaper. The court held that there was a sufficient case for breach of confidence as it was arguable that the photographer had acted surreptitiously because he knew that photography was not permitted and that he was allowed to remain only on that basis. Although the photographer was lawfully at the scene that did not mean that he was free to take photographs.

Protection of personality rights outside the United Kingdom

7–32   The protection of personality rights is perhaps best most comprehensibly dealt with in the United States. There, so-called "publicity rights" take two basic forms: common law and statutory. Whilst taking very different approaches to the issues involved, both forms afford substantial protection to personalities—indeed, some personalities would say far too much protection and infringe upon the right for freedom of speech.

7–33 Common law rights. A series of cases in the United States during the late 1980s and early 1990s have clearly established a common law right of publicity. Neither deception nor confusion need be established to prove liability. The protection is broad and is not available merely for the name or appearance of a personality, but for any indication of one's identity.

In the *Bette Midler v. Ford Motor Co.* case (849 F.2d 460, 7 US PQ 2d 1398, 9th Cir. 1988) the court said that "a voice is as distinctive and personal as a face". The court stated clearly, however, that not every imitation of a voice was actionable—only those where there is a deliberate intention to sell a product by using the distinctive voice of a well-known professional singer.

7–34 In the *Tom Waits* case (*Waits v. Frito-Lay Inc.*, 978 F.2d 1093, 9th Cir. 1992), the court held that the right of publicity can be infringed by the imitation of a distinctive performing persona associated with the plaintiff. In the *White* case (see paragraph 7–13 above), the court held that it was not necessary for the robot to be Vanna White's likeness for the common law right of publicity to be violated. The issue was whether the defendants had "appropriated the plaintiff's identity"—not how it had done so.

Carson v. Here's Johnny Portable Toilets Inc. (810 F.2d 104; 1987 US App.) took a similar view over the use of the TV chat show host Johnny Carson's catchphrase "Here's Johnny" applied, without Carson's consent, to toiletries.

Thus U.S. common law provides substantial protection for personalities as regards the commercial exploitation of their personality during their lifetime.

7–35 Statutory rights. Statutory rights afford protection which is in some ways wider, yet in others narrower, than the common law. California has the most comprehensive legislation as regards publicity rights—probably due to it being the home of the film and television industries.

The California Civil Code provides publicity rights to both living and deceased personalities. The protection focuses upon the non-consensual use of name, voice, signature, photographs or likeness "in any manner, on or in products, merchandise, goods or services". Use of protected aspects of personal identity in a "play, book, magazine, newspaper, musical composition, film, radio or television programme, other than an advertisement or commercial announcement" are not protected by the Civil Code.

7–36 In order for the name, voice, signature, photograph or other likeness of a dead personality to be protected under the statute, it must be registered with the Secretary of State in Sacramento. It provides for a 50-year term of protection following the personality's death. Thus, Elvis, who died on August 16, 1977, is able to enjoy protection up to and including August 16, 2027, even though he did not live in California: the jurisdiction is determined on a transactional not domicility basis.

Other states with similar provisions include Oklahoma (100 years from death); Kentucky, Texas and Nevada (50 years); Florida (40 years); Virginia (20 years); and Nebraska (an indefinite period).

The California statute does not, however, afford protection against imitators as borne out by the *Midler* case, nor did it afford protection to the plaintiff in the *Vanna White* case as the robot did not amount to White's "likeness".

Many European Union countries also afford protection to image rights in one form or another.

Ineffective remedies in the United Kingdom

7–37 The court's traditional approach to trade marks in the *Elvis* case does not offer protection to a personality's publicity rights in the United Kingdom. The tort of passing off offers no protection to a personality against unauthorised merchandisers or others who, whilst commercially using the personality's "persona", do not confuse the public as to the origin of the goods/services involved. Copyright is of little or no use. Defamation and malicious falsehood and breach of confidence are antiquated and ineffective remedies. The Advertising Standards Authority is unable to award damages.

7–38 Given the commercial importance of endorsement and merchandising some might argue that there is a clear and obvious need for the creation of a new and distinct publicity right in the United Kingdom. The Human Rights Bill is not intended to, and is unlikely to, resolve the problem, and will fall far short of providing a right available to all individuals to prevent their "persona" from being commercially exploited by unauthorised third parties—without the need to prove confusion or damage. Confusion should be irrelevant. Damage should be relevant only in determining the remedy—injunctive relief, financial compensation and/or destruction or delivery up of the offending articles. Clearly, in view of present commercial practice the right must be accessible and assignable. It must also be divisible into different fields of exploitation. Non-commercial use must be allowed so as to allow a sufficient freedom of speech in the media. A post-death term of protection would seem to be appropriate, perhaps equivalent to that available to copyright.

The adoption of such a new form of intellectual property right in the United Kingdom would afford an appropriate level of protection to the legitimate commercial interests of individuals in a straightforward and easily utilised manner. It would allow the courts to escape from their present dilemma of either clumsily (and somewhat unsuccessfully) adapting existing legal doctrines to protect these relatively new rights, or affording them no protection at all.

7. Agreement period and exclusivity

7–39 The period of the agreement with the personality for the endorsement of the manufacturer's product should be for not less than one year if it is a consumer-related product, so as to catch regular trade, the Christmas market where there may be extensive media exposure for the endorsement, and then to mop up in the spring. The endorsement contract period limits the manufacturer's use of the endorsed advertisements accordingly. It should therefore ensure that its rights period is long enough for it to get the most out of the endorsement campaign.

The period of the agreement should be calculated to take into account the market season for the products, or the period during which the personality is most likely to be active. For example, if a golfer is endorsing the clubs he uses, the contract period should cover at least a season's worth of national and international tournaments. If the endorsement agreement is entered into half way through a golfing season, it should run for the period required to complete this season, and to cover the whole of next season. The same thinking applies to an athlete, where there is a defined athletics season. In the case of an athlete, if they are relatively close together, the agreement period should extend to cover the Commonwealth Games, or the European Championships, or the Olympic Games.

7–40 If the golfer or athlete has an "off" period during the agreement period, such as for illness, or to resolve some psychological block which has made him lose his form, there is no need to terminate the agreement. Any adjustment can be made in the calculation of endorsement fees, for the year in which the "off" period occurs, if a portion of the fees are dependent upon a level of performance and success, such as for bonuses. If the sponsor still has faith in the personality on the basis that everybody has an "off" period from time to time, the spoilt season can be compensated for by the sponsor being able to extend the period of its agreement until the end of the next season.

The endorsement agreement should be exclusive to the product manufacturer in connection with any directly or indirectly competitive products during which time certain reasonable restrictions may be placed upon the personality.

8. Restriction on personality

7-41 The personality should not be restricted unduly from endorsing general products which do not compete with any product related wholly to his activity, or any other category of product which he is endorsing under an exclusive agreement with a manufacturer. However, a product manufacturer is not likely to use a personality who has already featured in an extensive national campaign endorsing any other major brand product. The reason is that the public may become confused, having become used to the personality endorsing the other product. Personality uniqueness is crucial to the prestige of the endorsement of the product and a "used" personality may be thought of as second hand. Therefore an eligible personality has to be very careful in what he accepts from the choice of offers put to him for the endorsement of products.

During a short endorsement contract period for the national campaign to promote a major product, the individual should be restricted from endorsing any other product, whether or not it is competitive. It is a matter of marketing impact, to give the product a promotional hook for advertising which its competitors will not have. There will also be a restriction for a period after the contract expiry date on his endorsing any product which is competitive. This restriction period should not be punitive or excessive: it should only be for a period which is reasonably required to protect the product manufacturer's right to wind down its promotional operations, and (where relevant) to dispose of existing stocks of "personality product", such as personalised golf clubs, snooker cases or tennis rackets. The protection extends to the reputation and image of the endorsed products, the cost of the endorsement fee, and creating the advertising or promotional campaign for the products based upon the personality's endorsement. Taking the example of a successful professional golfer, playing in tournaments for prize money is his primary means of earning a living and he cannot be unduly restricted from doing so.

7-42 The restriction does not prevent a sporting personality from continuing to play with competitive products immediately following termination of the endorsement agreement—he is simply prevented during the restriction period from publicly and commercially endorsing them. The restriction would be limited to the United Kingdom, unless the product is marketed internationally, and the endorsed advertising will also be international. This will relate to the territory covered by the endorsement agreement.

If a top international golfer is dedicated to one manufacturer's clubs or ball, and becomes a well-known endorser of those products, the manufacturer has to assume that the association will be sufficiently long-term to warrant entrusting the endorsement element of the promotion of the product to the recommendation by that golfer. Because the choice of clubs is a very personal decision by a golfer, it is not something mechanical which can sensibly be controlled by a contract. The cause of a potential danger for such an endorsement agreement is as follows.

7–43   The golfer hits a bad patch and has a dismal showing in major tournaments. He loses all confidence and in frustration, having tried all else he uses a friend's clubs, and miraculously his form returns, and so does his confidence. In the absence of any other explanation he is convinced that the cure lies in the construction, balance and "magic" of these new clubs. Unfortunately they are made by a competitor of the product he is currently endorsing under a contract with six months to run. A fundamental clause in his endorsement contract states that he must use the endorsed products at all tournaments he enters during the endorsement period. What is he to do? The problems he faces are:

(a) Supreme confidence in the equipment used is psychologically essential to his tournament success in the future. He has lost all confidence in the endorsed product. Should he cease to compete for the balance of his contract period? That would probably be a breach of contract. Should he press on with the endorsed product and hope for the best, to see whether the bad patch is only temporary? Or should he approach the endorsed product manufacturer and explain the problem? The manufacturer might analyse the apparent properties of the other clubs, and design a new range of clubs to the golfer's own specification.

(b) If the endorsement agreement has just expired when the golfer has this revelation, he would be able openly to use the new clubs in tournaments. This will delight their manufacturer, who will want to sign the personality up to an endorsement agreement for those clubs. But the golfer may still be under a competitive endorsement restriction for a period of time after the expiry of his previous endorsement agreement.

Any contractual restriction will only be enforceable if it is genuinely necessary to the extent required to protect the legitimate interests of the manufacturer of the sponsored product. What can be considered reasonable will depend entirely on the terms of the deal. It could be said that a change of allegiance by the golfer is not unusual, and that it is not derogatory of the previously endorsed product, and that it does not damage its image. If that is the case, then it is likely that no post-contract restriction would be acceptable, except for the reasons set out in paragraph 7–41.

9. Defining endorsed products

7–44   Endorsement will normally be of one particular item, usually identified by the brand name of the product and its manufacturer, rather than of a general specification of goods. If the manufacturer has only one type of product, such as golf clubs, it still may have a vast range of the products from which to choose. The manufacturer may have a range of wholly different products, which are not related in any way. The personality must ensure that his endorsement agreement accurately sets out the limits of the rights granted to the manufacturer. The main difference will be whether the personality is endorsing a specific brand of product, or (but more unlikely) he is endorsing the manufacturer generally as to any product within a given range or specification.

For example, a consumer product manufacturer of all sorts of DIY equipment for a diverse range of needs may get a personality who is renowned for his DIY expertise as a hobby to endorse the manufacturer's product. It would be wasteful to restrict the endorsement to the range of electric drills, when all of the products are suitable for the endorsement. The deal would therefore extend the personality's endorsement across the whole of the manufacturer's DIY catalogue with emphasis now and again on different kinds of product.

7–45 For specialised products, such as golf clubs or a billiard cue, the manufacturer may design, develop and produce a product or range of products to the specifications laid down by the personality. These will then be sold as "personality widgets" and they will be heavily endorsed in promotional and media terms by the personality. Alternatively the manufacturer may allocate a specific range of the product to be those which will be known and promoted as the "personality widgets" although the personality has not had any say in their design or specification. There are two main differences between this style of endorsement of personalised product, as opposed to endorsing consumer branded goods in a generalised manner.

(a) As well as an endorsement fee, the personality will get a royalty on sales of the personalised products. This additional income is an incentive for the personality to promote the product whenever he can beyond his contractual obligations, because he benefits financially from their increased sales.

(b) The endorsement period will need to be long term, to make it worthwhile for the manufacturer to take the trouble and cost of creating and promoting the personalised product. The association between the personality and the personalised product is much stronger, and the promotional emphasis is more on the personality than it is upon straight endorsement of unrelated product.

10. Endorsement fees

7–46 The remuneration of the personality in consideration of endorsing a product will not usually be a royalty on sales of the product, but a fee to be negotiated. There is a distinction between endorsement and merchandising in this respect, as merchandising income is based upon a royalty on sales of the products merchandised in association with the name of the personality. The exception is referred to in paragraph 7–45(a) where, for example, the deal is a combination of an endorsement by a top snooker player of the cue, and a merchandising licence for the sale of those cues with the player's name inscribed upon it. The reasons for the difference are as follows:

(a) An endorsement fee will be a substantial sum of money irrespective of the success of the promotion of the endorsement campaign for the product. The endorsing personality has done his bit as contracted, and will be paid his fee. How effectively the product manufacturer markets the opportunity is beyond the control of the personality. The royalties payable on any U.K.-based merchandising agreement are not likely to be any where near the top level personality fee value, and may be paid half yearly over a considerable period of time. An endorsement fee will be payable wholly or substantially by the time the personality has finished filming, or still media photography, and whatever else he is obliged to do to set up the product promotional material. Additional fees may be payable to the personality on the happening of certain events, or the fee may be payable in tranches over a period of time, but their level is not dependent on the successful sales of the endorsed product.

(b) The amount of the fee will be stated in the endorsement agreement, and is not dependent on whether the manufacturer sells the product. The ultimate value of a merchandise fee is not known when the agreement is signed, and (subject to a minimum royalty) is wholly dependent on the sales of the merchandised product.

7–47

(c) (i) For a merchandising agreement an advance will be paid on account of eventual royalties. The advance should be set at an amount which would represent a significant level of sales, so that the merchandiser has an incentive to be active early and energetically. If it fails to do so, or if it goes bust in the near future, the personality is not out of pocket, and may even be in profit, as the advance will be stated to be non-returnable in the agreement.

(ii) An advance on account of the endorsement fee will normally be paid on signing the agreement. This is for cashflow purposes—as the fee has a known value—rather than as a form of security against an unknown ultimate entitlement.

7–48

(d) (i) The unit sales of the product connected with a personality which is sold by a merchandiser will be relatively small, and the merchandised product relies wholly for its extra appeal upon the reference to the personality contained on it. When a personality endorses a brand of product, his name or image will not usually appear on the product itself. That endorsement will be applied by way of advertising and promotion of the product nationally, or possibly internationally, but only at intervals. The "unit sales" will represent the manufacturer's entire sales of that product during the endorsement period, whether or not those sales have any connection with the intermittent endorsement-related advertising undertaken by the manufacturer.

(ii) A per unit royalty on endorsed products may be wholly unjustified, impractical and uneconomical for the manufacturer. The current sales of the product do not rely even marginally on the endorsement by the personality: his endorsement is intended to increase sales and to develop a greater public awareness of the product. The product had a growing volume of sales before the personality was involved, and will continue to sell after the expiry of the endorsement period. As with any other promotion cost, paying a personality a fee to recommend the product is just another method of advertising it and, to that extent, endorsement can be treated as an adjunct to ordinary media advertising.

7–49 The endorsement fee may be a flat fee, or it may have a potential increase structure calculated upon a greater than normally anticipated sales level of the endorsed product. This would be unusual, but might apply to a new range launch, or to some limited scale project. The fee will also take into account any restriction accepted by the personality as part of the deal, thus reducing the potential market within which he might be in demand as a means of promoting other manufacturers' products. That assessment is all part of the overall calculation of the personality's marketable value to the manufacturer.

The fee level may depend on whether the agreement extends beyond endorsement promotion of the brand product within the United Kingdom. A factor to be taken into account on territorial exposure is the advertising/promotion budget being allocated to the endorsed product. Media advertising on a regional or national basis will have different costs, and the greater the budget the less the impact upon it of a fixed endorsement fee paid to the personality.

11. Territorial limits

7–50   The endorsement agreement should state whether the rights granted to the manufacturer are in respect of the United Kingdom only, or whether they are, for example, European or even worldwide and for which medium. If the rights are to be exercisable outside the United Kingdom, the personality should ensure that his endorsement agreement deals with the following matters:

(a) How is the fee level to be calculated, and who is to be responsible for paying it? The contracting manufacturer may be the U.K. subsidiary or distributor of an international company. If international rights are granted (such as for Europe), how does that U.K. company ensure that the terms of the agreement will be fully observed and performed in those countries where the U.K. company has no control? For example, if the fee is topped up by factors relating to overseas budgets, what checks can be made by the personality to ensure that he is being paid correctly?

(b) What contract period will be needed to enable the other territories to fit in their own promotion plans? For an international sports personality the endorsement value is "now", and the period agreed for the United Kingdom will apply wherever the rights have been granted. For the tennis or golfing circuit, within any country of the territory there may be concentrated product promotion campaigns when there is a tournament being played within that country.

7–51

(c) Will agreed photos and quotations need to be modified to cater for different consumer tastes and markets? A range of photos and quotations will be approved by the personality, and the manufacturer should be able to make language translation to get the same message across, but not always literally.

(d) How can the individual approvals system be simplified for promotional material? The personality or his agent should give approval to a range of presentations, which can then be used by the manufacturer as it thinks best.

(e) Are there any regulations outside the United Kingdom relating to endorsement which need to be considered? What additional safeguards should the personality require in his endorsement agreement to cover the use of his name and image outside the United Kingdom? The manufacturer should be obliged to ensure that, for example, local codes of practice relating to advertising and promotions are complied with.

7–52   Any "United Kingdom only" rights must be considered within the broader E.U. market, particularly with the abolishment of trade barriers, and the effect of anti-competitive and trade restriction laws and regulations. Even if the product packaging contains the endorsement, limitations on distribution and sale within specific E.U. countries are illegal unless one of the exemptions apply. This complicated issue should not concern the personality, as he is not involved with the distribution and sale of the products he endorses. Any liability in this respect will not affect the personality, except for the reflection upon him of any adverse publicity which might arise.

12. Approval of material

7–53   The personality or his agent should approve all basic promotional and advertising material, to ensure that it is reasonable, accurate and truthful. If the material infringes any legal prohibition or requirement, or if it contravenes any relevant code of practice, the personality may be affected by such criticism. The precise wording of any quotation, direct or indirect, must be checked and agreed, to ensure that it reflects accurately what the personality is prepared to say by way of recommendation, as opposed to only urging the consumer to buy the product. Photos of the personality to be used by the manufacturer will also be agreed.

13. Product liability

7–54   Compared with ordinary media advertising, however enticing it may be, endorsement is a much more personal and direct appeal from the personality. He is assumed to have good grounds for recommending the purchase of the goods he endorses to all those who respond to the appeal by purchasing the product. Endorsement carries, in the mind of the person thereby influenced to purchase the goods, an assurance of quality and success in its use or application, implied by the assumption that the personality would not otherwise use or recommend such a product. Therefore the personality must be careful in his choice of endorsement, especially if he does not have personal experience of the product he is asked to promote.

Unlike a merchandise licence agreement, the role of the personality in endorsing a product is active in the sense of positively promoting it by recommendation. The manufacturer's hope is that the endorsement will influence consumers to purchase their product. While in this case the personality is not connected with the design, manufacture and sale of the endorsed product, the trend of consumer protection legislation suggests that it might soon be possible for a consumer who has been injured by defective or dangerous endorsed product to make a claim against the personality for recommending it.

7–55   If the wording of the quoted endorsement is careless, and can be interpreted as positive assurance by the personality as to the safety, structure, quality, and benefit of the product, and the injured consumer genuinely believed and relied on that representation, it would be worth the consumer joining the personality as a co-defendant to an action against the product manufacturer for damages. The endorsement would have to be a statement of fact, not opinion, and the claimant would have to show that it was reasonable for him to rely on the statement. As the statement could not be a contractual representation, the claimant would have to prove it to have been a tortious and negligent representation. The personality's defence would be that the representation was made in good faith based upon the facts as he believed them to be after making reasonable inquiries. He will have to show that he did take care in asking about the products, and that the information he was given should have been reliable. Where the personality uses the products in his career, at least he may be satisfied with them.

The endorsement agreement should contain a warranty and indemnity from the manufacturer to the personality in respect of the legality of all promotional projects and material which refer to the personality and his endorsement of the product. An indemnity should also be given by the manufacturer to the personality in respect of the product endorsed, should it be defective or should any other consumer-related claim be made against the personality in connection with it.

14. Termination

7–56 Two specific reasons for termination which should be included in the endorsement agreement for the benefit of the personality are the failure of the manufacturer to make any further agreed payments, and its material and persistent failure to comply with the agreed format of presenting the personality and the agreed wording by way of recommendation. Termination may not be practical if the personality is a user of the product, as it may be difficult to stop the manufacturer from making a carefully worded statement of fact as to the personality's use of it. Then the question of implied endorsement arises, for which see paragraph 7–11 *et seq.*, above.

15. Morality Clauses

7–57 An association with the wrong star can be more of a liability than a benefit and sponsors must take steps to protect the significant sums that such stars can now command. The success of the endorsement is almost wholly dependent on the endorser projecting a positive image of a product. Sponsors should therefore take the following steps before embarking on such an arrangement.

(a) Research the career history and prospects of the individual. An endorser who is at the peak of his career will not only command a high price, but could fall at the next hurdle. As much, if not more, benefit could be obtained by an association with an up-and-coming star who achieves success during the term of the endorsement deal with him or her. If surprises about the individual's personal life are to be avoided, he should be checked out as far as reasonably possible first. These considerations will have a bearing over how long it might be desirable to commit to the endorsement deal.

(b) In the agreement it should be specified what control the sponsor will have over his or her conduct, of any disciplinary hearings, and any press coverage relating to it. The sponsor always insert a "morality clause" to allow it to terminate the agreement if the individual commits any act that the sponsor considers to be damaging. Such clauses can be difficult to negotiate because of the subjective nature of what is damaging—would a car manufacturer care, for example, if its endorser declared himself to be having an affair with his next-door neighbour? The position might be rather more black and white if an endorser were to be convicted of murder, but in the "greyer" areas the sponsor should try to spell out in the agreement exactly what it (or more importantly) what it considers its customers would take offence to. After all, what might be thought damaging to one product will not necessarily be damaging to another. It will all depend on the product and its particular market.

7–58

(c) If a "morality" situation arises, the sponsor should ensure that the endorser is no longer able to associate himself with the sponsor's product. If the product is a professional golfer's favourite brand of club, it would not be reasonable for the sponsor to restrict the endorser from using that brand in the future, but at least the endorser should be required not to imply a direct association with the sponsor in the future

(d) Another way of controlling an endorser's behaviour is the "stick and carrot" approach—*i.e.* give them performance incentives to encourage continued success and good behaviour.

16. Restraint of Trade

7–59 The other specific issue that affects sponsorship of individuals is to ensure that any restrictions placed on the individual are enforceable and do not constitute an unreasonable restraint of trade. Therefore, any constraints imposed must be reasonable, taking into account the amount being paid, the duration of the restraint and its territorial scope. Particularly in relation to young up-and-coming players, it is important not to take unfair advantage of them, and to ensure that they are separately represented and properly advised.

17. Assignment

7–60 The manufacturer should be prohibited from assigning the benefit and obligation of the endorsement agreement. The agreement relates to a specific product, so the only circumstances in which it would be possible for the manufacturer to assign the endorsement agreement would be if it sold the whole of its rights in the manufacture, distribution and sale of the endorsed products to a third party. The identity of the manufacturer may not concern the personality, provided the assignee is as reputable and substantial as the previous manufacturer, and that it fully performs and observes all of the previous manufacturer's obligations under the endorsement agreement. This can be dealt with satisfactorily on a contractual basis.

CHAPTER 8

Sponsorship Taxation

1. Introduction

8–01 This chapter explains various tax aspects of sponsorship arrangements. The explanations are necessarily general in scope and detailed tax advice should be obtained on any particular sponsorship proposal.

Most sponsors will want to get a tax deduction for their sponsorship payments. This is considered in section 2, below. The sponsor and sponsored party should both be concerned that they understand the value added tax (VAT) implications of their arrangements, and that these do not cause difficulties. The VAT aspects of sponsorship for both the sponsor and the sponsored party are covered in section 3, below.

8–02 The overall tax position of the sponsored party is not considered in detail because so much is dependent on the sponsored party's tax status and the sponsored event involved. The sponsorship income will generally be a trading profit, on which corporation tax or, as appropriate, income tax is payable. Trading profits can include non-monetary receipts as well as cash sponsorship payments. The receipt of sponsorship income will generally only be part of the sponsored party's activities. Exceptionally, obtaining sponsorship can be a business activity in its own right. H.M. Customs and Excise accept that someone racing horses with a genuine view to income from sponsorship, appearance money and prize money can register for VAT purposes. The fact that an organisation or individual gets commercial sponsorship does not, however, necessarily mean that the sponsored party is carrying on a trade for income or corporation tax purposes.

8–03 There are likely to be many other tax matters for a sponsored party to consider in addition to those already mentioned, such as the taxation of merchandising arrangements (see section 4, below). The position of a charity involved in sponsorship arrangements is considered in outline (see section 5, below). The sponsored event itself may involve special considerations, such as the special rules on non-resident entertainers and sportsmen (see section 6, below).

Making the sponsorship payments is only part of the sponsor's business activities, there may be wider tax implications which should be considered. The position of joint ventures (see section 7) is an example of such wider considerations. The sponsor may also be involved in merchandising and endorsement activities. The tax table at the end of this chapter sets out tax data relevant to sponsorship and is correct as at April 6, 1998.

2. Tax deductions for sponsorship payments

8–04 A sponsor will want to get a tax deduction for its sponsorship payments as a trading expense and, generally, such a deduction will be available. This should be the case if cash is paid for what amounts to advertising or other publicity services. The technicalities of obtaining a tax deduction should not be overlooked:

129

if they are, it is quite possible to put at risk the obtaining of a tax deduction for all or some of the payments concerned. This is because sponsorship can be so closely involved with entertaining and patronage, and other objectives which can be prejudicial to obtaining a tax deduction.

A tax deduction in computing the profits of the sponsor is not available merely because the payment is made out of the sponsor's profits. Nor is a deduction automatically available because it has been made in computing the sponsor's profits for accounting purposes. There are various statutory provisions which must also be considered. In limited cases these may help in getting a deduction. For example, there is a statutory right to a tax deduction for an employer who incurs costs in temporarily seconding an employee to a charity. However, the statutory provisions mainly seek to disallow certain types of expenditure for tax purposes.

8–05   If a deduction is to be claimed, then the expenditure must be revenue and not capital expenditure; that is, it must be proper to deduct the expenditure in computing the income of the sponsor. If the sponsor is in effect receiving advertising services, then there should be no doubt that the sponsorship payments are revenue expenses. In the case of *Evans v. Wheatley* (38 T.C. 216) the court considered a clause in an agreement providing for certain sales promotion and advertising expenses. In the leading judgment it was stated: ". . . it is plain upon the face of that clause that the payments there contemplated to be made are payments essentially of a revenue nature. . .". If the sponsorship arrangements involve more than the provision of advertising then the question will probably need more detailed consideration.

8–06   As to what is to be defined as capital expenditure, an H.M. Treasury Memorandum (1982) concerning public and private funding of the arts (including sponsorship) gave as examples of capital payments: "any lump sum donation towards, for example, the building or modernisation of a theatre, or the purchase of a work of art". The examples are not explained in the Memorandum but give an indication of areas where concerns could arise. The Inland Revenue's internal manual indicates that sponsorship costs may be capital if they involve, for example, a contribution to a permanent exhibition providing an enduring benefit or expenditure on assets such as racehorses or racing cars. The main point is therefore to identify what benefit the sponsor is receiving for its payments. If the payments bring into existence an asset (or enhance an asset or advantage) for the enduring benefit of the sponsor, the expenditure is likely to be considered as capital expenditure. So if the sponsor is buying, say, advertising hoardings outright rather than merely hiring them, the sponsor is likely to be incurring capital expenditure. It is possible to get a deduction in computing trading profits for some proportion of capital expenses, but this would be under the capital allowance provisions rather than a trading expense.

8–07   The question may arise as to whether a well-established and successful sponsored event itself amounts to an enduring asset. It is suggested this would not be the case. The purpose of the sponsorship payments will be to advertise the sponsor's name and product, therefore the payments in question are of a revenue nature. It does not matter that the success of the sponsored event gives an enduring advantage to the sponsor. The case of *Cooper v. Rhymney Breweries, Ltd* (42 T.C. 509) considered the tax deductibility of expenditure on a campaign to remove prohibitions on opening licensed premises on Sundays. The case report refers to expenditure, such as on an advertising campaign to extend the business, producing an advantage of permanent benefit to the trade but still being tax deductible. The expenditure in question in the case was said to be near the line but was still held to be revenue expenditure. The Inland Revenue may nevertheless look closely at, in particular, heavy launch expenditure for a new product or brand to see if there is a case for classifying the costs as capital expenditure.

8–08 There must be a business purpose in incurring the sponsorship expenditure. In most cases there should be no difficulty in showing the commercial nature of the sponsorship arrangements. It is assumed that the sponsor is in business, otherwise it would not be interested in the tax deduction. There have been reported cases (especially in the context of VAT) where it has proved difficult to link the expenditure to business but it should be possible to establish a business purpose if there is a properly conceived and implemented sponsorship campaign. This involves taking into account the geographical scope of the sponsored event, whether the sponsor's products are linked to the sponsored event, and other relevant commercial matters for the benefit of the sponsor. Moreover, the business purpose established must be that of the payer. The Income and Corporation Taxes Act 1988 (the "Taxes Act 1988") makes it clear that a payment is not deductible unless it is laid out or expended for the purposes of the trade, profession or vocation in question. It is possible that the sponsorship payments are to be made by a parent company, whilst it is a subsidiary company's trade that will benefit. A tax deduction should not be claimed in such cases by the parent company sponsor unless it can show that in making the sponsorship payments there is a purpose relating to its trade, and that the benefit to the subsidiary is incidental.

8–09 One problem may be that the sponsor is entering into the sponsorship agreement solely for personal reasons. A sponsorship agreement could be made solely to further a hobby of the sponsor or of a shareholder or director of the sponsor. If that is the case then the sponsorship payments will not have a business purpose and so will fail the above statutory test. Expenditure is also expressly disallowed by statute if it is, in respect of any domestic or private purposes, distinct from the purposes of the trade, profession or vocation of the sponsor. This issue is more of a concern, in practice, to the Inland Revenue in the case of sponsorship by smaller businesses.

It is a further requirement for deductibility that the sponsorship payments are wholly and exclusively laid out for business purposes. In strict terms, a deduction is only available if there is *solely* a business purpose. This matter came up for consideration in respect of solicitors' entertainment expenses in *Bentleys, Stokes and Lowless v. Beeson* (33 T.C. 491). It was stated:

> "Entertaining involves inevitably the characteristic of hospitality. Giving to charity . . . involves inevitably the object of benefaction. An undertaking to guarantee to a limited amount a national exhibition involves inevitably supporting that exhibition and the purposes for which it has been organised. But the question in all such cases is: was the entertaining, the charitable subscription, the guarantee, undertaken solely for the purposes of business, that is, solely with the object of promoting the business or its profit earning capacity?"

This is different from the position for VAT purposes where apportionment is allowed if there is a duality of purpose.

8–10 The above case makes it clear that if some other purpose exists then this prejudices the claim, even if the business motive may predominate. However, the case recognises that:

". . . if in truth the sole object is business promotion the expenditure is not disqualified because the nature of the activity necessarily involves some other result, or the attainment or furtherance of some other objective, since the latter result or objective is necessarily inherent in the act".

If the sponsored event is, say, a charitable fund-raising event it is a question of fact as to whether a deduction can be claimed for a sponsorship payment. If the sponsor makes payments only because it sees the event as a valuable advertising opportunity, then a deduction should be available. If the sponsor makes the payments partly for advertising purposes and partly to support the charitable object, then the statutory requirement has not been met. In the latter case, the sponsor should recognise the duality of purpose of the sponsorship, and make separate payments in connection with each of the separate objects. If a single payment is made it should be made clear that this represents various categories of expenditure, including which amounts are attributed to which of the objects.

8–11 Expenditure on business entertainment is expressly disallowed under section 577 of the Taxes Act 1988. Entertainment includes hospitality of any kind and gifts (for example, free tickets). There is generally no longer any exception from this rule for expenditure on entertaining overseas customers. The case of *Fleming v. Associated Newspapers Ltd* (48 T.C. 382) went to the House of Lords in establishing the scope of what is disallowed. The case concerned hotel and restaurant expenses incurred by journalists in their dealings with informants and contributors. The report explains that:

"experience has shown . . . that the desired relation with such 'contacts' can best be built up and maintained over an occasional meal or drink, or, depending on the circumstances, by regular or bi-weekly meals or drinks, at a suitable hotel or restaurant. . .".

The taxpayer tried to establish a distinction between entertaining suppliers and entertaining customers. The taxpayer failed in its assertions that it should get a tax deduction for entertaining its suppliers (of information) so, neither type of expense is deductible.

8–12 To the extent the sponsorship agreement provides the sponsor with the means of business entertainment, the expenses connected with that entertainment are disallowable. If the sponsorship agreement involves such expenditure it is advisable that it is separately itemised from any allowable expenditure. This makes it easier to prepare the sponsor's tax computations. The *Associated Newspapers Ltd* case provides further support for the deductibility of any expenses attributable to advertising. There is a statement in one of the judgments that: "advertisements of goods for sale are normally deductible as trading expenses in computing profits . . . chargeable to tax". Implicit recognition of this is given in section 577(10), which makes it clear that the prohibition on deducting entertaining expenses does not apply to expenditure with the object of advertising to the public generally, gratuitously (*e.g.* free samples given to the public). Entertainment provided by a sponsor to members of its staff (including directors) is not caught by the business entertainment prohibition, although consideration then needs to be given to the tax position of the employees or directors concerned. The entertainment may be taxable on them as a benefit in kind. If the provision of entertainment to staff is merely incidental to the provision of entertainment to others, then the business entertainment rules will still apply.

8–13 Sponsorship payments will generally be paid under the terms of the contract, which will help in establishing that there is a business purpose in connection with the payments, and what it is. There are circumstances in which voluntary payments, including donations, can still be tax deductible. For example, the sponsored event could get into particular difficulties and, to resolve them, a sponsor may make voluntary payments beyond those provided for in the sponsorship agreement. The business purpose could be to prevent the sponsor suffering any adverse publicity from the event failing, and to ensure that the sponsor's products are advertised as planned. In such a case, a tax deduction should be available.

If the sponsor is merely making a donation to a charity then it is unlikely that it can claim a deduction for that donation as a trading expense. A case could perhaps be made out on the basis that the sponsor will be identified and that the payment would promote its trade. It would also be preferable that a series of relatively small donations are made, rather than a larger single donation. A one-off payment could be disallowed as a capital expense. If voluntary payments are to be made it is particularly advisable that the reasons are well documented. If the sponsor's inspector of taxes raises questions he can be shown copies of, say, the relevant board minutes in support of the tax-deduction claim. Payments to charities are considered further below. If a small donation is made to a local body which is not a charity, but is otherwise dedicated to social ends, then a deduction may be given by concession (ESC B7).

8–14 It should be remembered that tax deductions are generally only given for actual expenditure. If the sponsor wants a tax deduction in a particular accounting period, it should actually incur the expenditure in the relevant period, although an accrued liability recognised in the accounts can still be deductible. For example, under the terms of the sponsorship agreement the payment may be due, but for some reason there is an administrative delay in making the payment in the relevant accounting period. In this case a deduction can still be claimed. Difficulties will arise in respect of claiming deductions for what is still only a future or contingent liability, although in some circumstances a provision made in the sponsor's accounts in respect of such liabilities may be allowable. Deductions should not be claimed if the sponsor has merely set aside the money to be paid, but has not yet committed itself to making the payments.

Payments by way of loans do not give rise to tax-deductible expenditure. If a sponsor lends money to the sponsored party, perhaps in addition to sponsorship payments, no tax deductions are available for the loan. Payments may not be described as loans, but could be made on terms giving the sponsor the right to demand immediate repayment, which means that they are, in effect, loans. Similarly, a tax deduction should not be claimed for such payments. In a reported case, a company making contributions to a trust found its payments were non-deductible because, under the terms of the trust, it could obtain its money back at will. Careful consideration must be given to the tax deductibility implications of any repayment provisions in a sponsorship agreement.

8–15 The preceding paragraphs have identified some aspects which may prejudice the tax deductibility of certain sponsorship payments. In practice and with self assessment of tax liabilities, the sponsor's local inspector of taxes may not investigate the sponsorship arrangements in detail. But this should not mislead the sponsor into thinking there are no difficulties in getting a tax deduction.

3. VAT and sponsorship

8–16 As for other taxes, there are no special provisions relating to VAT and sponsorship as such. The VAT aspects of sponsorship are therefore determined by the general principles of the VAT system.

H.M. Customs and Excise publish some guidance as to how the VAT system applies to sponsorship arrangements. Notice 701/41, "Sponsorship", outlines how VAT must be accounted for on sponsorship income. The latest edition of this notice is reproduced in full in Appendix VIII. H.M. Customs and Excise notices and leaflets which refer to sponsorship and the related matters mentioned below should be available from any local VAT office.

Particular VAT-related questions which may arise on the sponsorship arrangements include the following:

(a) Is VAT applicable to sponsorship payments?

8–17 The starting point, assuming the sponsored party is registered for VAT purposes, is that VAT is applicable to sponsorship income. Sponsorship as described in this book means commercial sponsorship in which the sponsor receives something in return for its financial support. The something received could be advertising of the sponsor's name or product or any other type of benefit. The VAT treatment is the same whether or not there is a written sponsorship agreement. It makes no difference that the something is described as free (for example, free tickets to a sponsored event). This is misleading. Where the sponsorship is conditional upon the supply of clearly identifiable benefits in return, this is a taxable supply for VAT purposes, so the normal VAT consequences apply to the making and receiving of such a supply. The sponsored party charges VAT. The sponsor is charged VAT, but if it is VAT-registered it can generally claim a credit for the VAT it pays to the sponsored party (its input tax) against the VAT it charges its own customers (its output tax). In the same way, the sponsored party can offset its input tax on third-party invoices against the VAT it charges the sponsor. In this way, the sponsored party only has to account to H.M. Customs and Excise for tax on the difference (the value added). Apart from the administrative inconvenience and cashflow implications, the fact that VAT is charged should not cause problems if the sponsor is VAT registered and can get full credit for its input tax against output tax. As explained below, some supplies involved in or relating to sponsorship arrangements may fall outside the scope of VAT or otherwise may not be subject to VAT at the standard rate.

(b) Can the sponsored party avoid charging VAT by not being VAT registered?

8–18 If the sponsored party does not have to register for VAT, the answer is yes. VAT is not chargeable if the sponsored party is not registered, or is not required to be registered. As well as not charging VAT, the sponsored party would avoid the administrative inconvenience of making VAT returns and maintaining VAT records. It could be that the sponsorship is received for something which is not a business (or, in European law terms, an economic activity), such as a hobby or worthy cause, in which case it may be possible to avoid registration for VAT purposes. However a local authority, for example, that granted advertising facilities to sponsors of child safety and anti-smoking campaigns failed in its argument that it was not making supplies in the course or furtherance of a business. The scale and regularity of activities are important factors. If the sponsored party supplies goods and services, the charges for which would normally be subject to VAT, then the key to avoiding registration is to keep the value of such supplies below the registration limit. In this way it may be possible to avoid registration, or to delay the date of registration. The sponsorship income itself could cause the sponsored party to become liable to register. The sponsored party, if not already VAT registered, will usually become liable to be registered if at the end of any month the value of the supplies made by the sponsored party in the last 12 months exceed the prescribed threshold. If it is unlikely that the value of supplies will be sustained at or above the threshold in the next 12 months, then H.M. Customs and Excise may agree that there is no need to register. Alternatively, the sponsored party can become liable to be registered if at any time (for example, after signing a sponsorship agreement) there are reasonable grounds for believing that the value of supplies in the next 30 days will exceed that threshold. Notice 700/1, "Should I be registered for VAT?", explains the registration provisions in more detail.

(c) What is disaggregation?

8–19   One method of avoiding registration is to separate individual activities into different entities, each of which do not make taxable services exceeding the registration limits. The Howell Report on Sports Sponsorship (1983) came to the conclusion that:

> ". . . sporting organisations which derive their income from various sources should consider arrangements whereby certain of the income is paid to a separate legal entity (entities) such as a private limited company if the effect of the move is to separate income into two or more funds, none of which qualify to register for VAT".

Such a separation is known as disaggregation. Disaggregation must be approached with some caution, as H.M. Customs and Excise have and do exercise the power to treat separate entities as if they are one for VAT purposes. This would apply particularly if the separation has no reasonable commercial basis and the main reason, or one of the main reasons, for disaggregation is to avoid a liability to VAT registration.

(d) What if money is donated?

8–20   Donations—that is unconditional gifts of money—are outside the scope of VAT. When a payment is made by one party and nothing is due from the other party in return, the payment is not subject to VAT. This is to be contrasted with the position of a sponsor who does not, for whatever reason, receive what it is contractually entitled to under the sponsorship agreement. In this case, there may still have been a supply for VAT purposes. Because charitable or other donations are not subject to VAT, there is no obligation to account to H.M. Customs and Excise for what would otherwise be the VAT element of the amount received. The downside is that any input tax attributable to obtaining those donations is not available as a VAT credit, even if the sponsored party is VAT registered.

(e) What if the donor gets some benefit?

8–21   There are various ways in which a donor may get some benefit from the donation. Care must be taken that this does not bring the donation within the scope of VAT.

(i) It may be that a mixture of sponsorship payments and donations are made by a sponsor. Where in addition to a sponsorship fee paid under a sponsorship agreement, a donation is made by the sponsor independently and on a voluntary basis, there should be no problem. It is generally accepted by H.M. Customs and Excise that donations can be made as well as sponsored payments. However, to avoid difficulties there should be a written acknowledgment that donations may be made as well as sponsorship payments. This is to make it clear that not all payments by the sponsor are to be subject to VAT. A document can contain a commitment to make a donation, provided that this is not a condition of the sponsor getting its sponsor's benefits. The amount of the sponsorship payments must be realistic in relation to the benefits received by the sponsor so that it is not possible to say the donation is a disguised payment for the benefits. This aspect has been commented on in detail by H.M. Customs and Excise in relation to charges for admission to charity balls, dances, first-night performances, concerts and other fund raising functions. The comments in Leaflet 700/22/89 ("Admissions") are worth repeating because they illustrate the points of detail the VAT authorities consider in such matters. It is assumed that a basic minimum charge is made for admission with an invitation to make an additional donation. Only the minimum charge will be subject to VAT provided:

"(1) you state clearly on all tickets and in all relevant advertising material and programmes that any person paying only the basic minimum charge, will be admitted to the function without making any further payment;

(2) the additional payment does not secure admission to a particular part of the auditorium or any other benefit [if, for example, the publicity material suggests that those paying the additional amount are more likely to be admitted than those paying merely the basic ticket price, then the additional amount becomes subject to VAT];

(3) any reference to donations on tickets or in advertising material or programmes makes it clear that it is entirely up to the ticket holder to decide whether to make a voluntary donation over and above the basic admission charge, (as long as this is made clear you may indicate the desired level of donations which you hope to receive);

(4) in the case of film or theatre performances, concerts, etc., the stipulated minimum charge is not less than the usual price for the particular seating accommodation at a normal commercial performance of the entertainment in question;

(5) in the case of balls, dances, dinners and similar functions, the minimum total sum upon which [the organisers] will be liable in principle to account for VAT will not be less than the total costs incurred . . . in putting on the event."

8–22

(ii) The donor may know it will get some publicity through its name being included in a published list of donors or perhaps by having something named after it. H.M. Customs and Excise accept that the donor can have a general understanding as to how the money will be used by the sponsored party. In an official release, "VAT and donations to Universities" (84/88), the point is again made that: "pure donations, *i.e.* financial contributions with no strings attached, are not liable to VAT". The *mere acknowledgment* of support by the recipient will not render the donation subject to VAT. For example, naming a building or a university chair after the donor is acceptable. This is as long as the payment is not made on condition that the acknowlegment is given. Other examples of simple acknowledgments are set out in Appendix VIII.

(iii) The sponsored party may use the payment to buy, say, goods from the donor. This need not prejudice the treatment of donations as being outside the scope of VAT, provided that the underlying principle—that it must not be agreed the donor will get something in return for making the donation—is maintained.

(iv) Certain benefits received by the sponsors of research and development projects may be ignored—for example, technical reports and loan of samples. This would apply to benefits that can be justified as necessary safeguards to ensure money is spent correctly. It helps if the benefits are minimal in relation to the amount of the funding and can be seen as incidental to the primary purpose of the project.

(f) What if services are donated?

8–23   True donations of services are, like donations of money, outside the scope of VAT. This covers, for example, telecommunications companies donating the use of telephones for good causes. VAT would apply if the sponsor bought in the donated services and recovered VAT on those bought in services.

(g) What if goods are donated?

8–24   Not all gifts are outside the scope of VAT. If the recipient has to do something in return for a purported gift, this is a form of barter which H.M. Customs and Excise will treat as a supply for VAT purposes. True gifts out of the assets of a business are generally deemed to be supplies for VAT purposes whether or not there is any consideration paid by the sponsored party. Computer equipment may be given to schools. Goods may be donated as prizes in newspapers and magazine competitions. If these are true gifts, by a VAT-registered sponsor, then the sponsor must account for VAT. There is an exception for donations of gifts which cost the donor £15 or less or on which the sponsor had not originally recovered VAT. There are other special rules for certain donations to charity.

(h) How is the VAT calculated?

8–25
(i) There is a prescribed standard rate of VAT. This is either charged in addition to the sponsorship payments or is included in those payments, depending on what has been agreed. In the absence of agreement, a sponsorship fee is generally taken as being VAT *inclusive*.

(ii) The general principle is that VAT is charged on the value of the supply. The calculation of VAT is relatively straightforward when only cash payments are involved. Normally, all payments made under a sponsorship agreement will be subject to VAT unless they can be shown to be genuine donations. H.M. Customs and Excise expect, for example, payments of prize money and payments direct to the sponsored party's contractors and other third parties all to be taken into account in calculating VAT. There is, however, authority that VAT should not, in all cases, be charged on payments by sponsors to finance cash prizes. A VAT tribunal decided that particular sponsorship payments did not form part of the award organiser's turnover and, based on European law (the *Glawe Spiel* case C–38/93; see also [1994] S.T.C. 543), VAT should not be charged. This decision was confirmed on appeal (*CEC v. Emap MacLaren Ltd* [1997] S.T.C. 490). The sponsorship payments were not consideration for any supply of benefits by the awards organiser to the sponsor. This case must be considered carefully when reviewing the VAT aspects of sponsorship arrangements, particularly those involving payments to third parties.

8–26

(iii) If part of the sponsorship cost is provided in goods or services, then normally their open-market value will be taken into account for VAT. If goods or services are provided by the sponsor in exchange for the sponsorship rights then this is a form of barter and each party needs to account for VAT on the relevant values of the supplies. In particular, the sponsored party will be charged VAT as well as charging it to the sponsor.

(iv) If goods are donated then their value is taken, broadly, as the market value of the goods. Another method may be for the sponsor to donate cash to the sponsored party, out of which it buys, from the sponsor, the goods required. If the sponsored party buys the goods at below cost, VAT would only be charged by the sponsor on the price paid, rather than on the higher market value. If goods are loaned by the sponsor in a barter situation then the value for the calculation of VAT is based on what the hire charge for those goods would have been in the open market. Even though the end result is the same, in that goods are received by the sponsored party, the VAT implications will depend on which method is used to provide them.

(v) If the fees payable under the sponsorship agreement can vary, then VAT is charged on what is actually payable.

(i) When is the VAT due?

8–27 The rules which determine when VAT is due should be taken into account when considering the payment and invoicing arrangements for sponsorship fees, whether in cash, goods or services. VAT is charged at the rate of tax at the time the supply is made, which is normally the earliest of the following:

(a) the date when the services are performed, or the goods are delivered or made available to the customer (unless a tax invoice is issued within 14 days);

(b) the date when payment of sponsorship fees is received for the supply; and

(c) the date when the invoice is issued.

A credit can only be claimed for VAT if the claimant holds a tax invoice as proof that it has been charged VAT.

(j) What if the sponsor pays the sponsored party's supplier?

8-28

(i) The assumption is that the sponsored party has contracted with the supplier, but the sponsor is paying the supplier's invoice. The supplier will be charging VAT, and there may be confusion as to whether the sponsor or the sponsored party can claim back that VAT. In the circumstances outlined the sponsor must not claim back that VAT. The goods or services were actually supplied to the sponsored party, so only it can reclaim the VAT on those supplies. The sponsor should receive a VAT invoice from the sponsored party (assuming it is VAT registered). It is the VAT on that invoice that the sponsor will reclaim. The position will be different if the sponsor contracted with the supplier, or if the sponsor had agreed to be the sponsored party's agent (see below).

(ii) For cashflow or other reasons the sponsor may be prepared to contract with the supplier. The sponsor could then pass on the goods or services to the sponsored party in consideration of the grant of the sponsorship rights. In this case, there should be no problems in the sponsor recovering the VAT in question. This is because the input tax of the supplier will still be attributable to an onward business supply. It is irrelevant whether or not the sponsored party is VAT registered.

(k) What if an agent is involved?

8-29

(i) The existence of an agent which is appointed by a sponsored party to manage its sponsorship affairs will not remove the need to charge VAT on the granting of sponsorship rights. A supply of sponsorship rights from the sponsored party to the sponsor will continue to be subject to VAT. The agent would normally create its own separate supply of organisational services, for which it is paid a fee or commission. This is also a taxable supply and a VAT invoice must be issued by the agent in respect of it.

(ii) The involvement of the agent needs careful attention if it acts as a buying agent on behalf of the sponsored party for third-party goods or services. Agents can be an exception to the normal rule prohibiting the reclaiming of another party's VAT, so that VAT charged on goods supplied to a sponsored party through its agent can be recovered by the agent. But this does not mean that the sponsored party avoids its liability to pay VAT. Although the supplier invoices the agent, the agent must in turn invoice its principal, the sponsored party. An agent cannot alter an invoice it receives to show the name of the sponsored party, but must actually issue a new invoice.

(iii) The amount of VAT charged by an agent can be unnecessarily high if certain amounts are not invoiced in the best way. It is helpful to separate out expenses which are disbursements for VAT purposes, so as to avoid an unnecessary VAT charge on them. This is generally advantageous where no VAT is chargeable on the supply. To be treated as disbursements, goods or services must be received and used by the sponsored party and be clearly additional to the agent's services; this means the agent's travelling, telephone bills and postage are not normally disbursements.

(l) What if there is an overseas sponsor?

8–30

(i) A sponsor may belong outside the United Kingdom (the Isle of Man is deemed part of the United Kingdom, and the Channel Islands are not in the United Kingdom). This is likely to affect whether VAT is charged on the supplies made in return for the sponsorship payments. Various categories of services supplied internationally are outside the scope of VAT. The principle behind this is to enable U.K. providers of services to compete equally internationally, so a U.K. supplier does not have to add VAT to its charges when competing with an overseas supplier.

(ii) If a sponsored party grants sponsorship rights to a sponsor outside the United Kingdom then the supply of those rights should be outside the scope of VAT. A sponsor belonging in another E.U. Member State will, however, have to account for that Member State's VAT under what is known as the reverse charge procedure. Notice 741, "Place of supply of services", gives examples of services which have this treatment:

> "(1) Supplies of advertising services in the media, for example, of radio or television advertising time; of the right to place an advertisement on an existing hoarding; or of advertising space in any publication.

> (2) Supplies of publicising another person's products with a view to encouraging their sale (or the supply by a personality of an advertising performance directly to the person whose products are advertised).

> (3) Supplies in return for sponsorship which involve display of the sponsor's name, or product, by the sponsored person or team.

> (4) Supplies of services which are the means of advertising, *i.e.* services which are of use only in connection with specific advertising promotion or sponsorship. For example, the supply of a master advertising film, tape, record, poster, picture or photograph, or an advertisement printing block."

8–31

(iii) Therefore if what the sponsor receives is wholly advertising services, all the sponsorship payments will be outside the scope of VAT. But it may be that not everything can be covered by the definition of advertising services. It may be preferable to separate out items outside the above categories and pay specific fees for them, to preserve them outside the scope treatment in respect of advertising services.

(iv) In the early stages of preparing for the event, the sponsored party may provide the sponsor with consultancy services, which would be outside the scope. Consultancy services for this purpose include market research, and research and development (but exclude any services relating to land).

(v) If VAT is charged then an overseas business sponsor may be able to obtain a refund under one of the various refund schemes (Notice 723, "Refunds of VAT in the E.C. and other countries").

(vi) For a sponsored party there are advantages in seeking overseas sponsors, as it might not be required to account for VAT on the sponsored payments received and yet it may still be able to recover input tax in full.

This is because supplies that are outside the scope of VAT, by reason of the sponsor belonging outside the United Kingdom, would have been taxable supplies, had the sponsor belonged in the United Kingdom. A sponsored party receiving mainly overseas funding may find itself in a VAT refund situation, where it has paid excess input tax, which is then repaid by H.M. Customs and Excise. If this applies, the sponsored party should submit monthly VAT returns, rather than quarterly returns, so as to receive regular repayments. This is efficient cashflow management.

(vii) If it is the sponsored party or sponsored event that is overseas then the sponsor may have to account for VAT on the supply it *receives*, under the reverse charge procedure. Advertising services received from overseas are relevant services for the purposes of the reverse charge procedure. Notice 741, "Place of supply of services", explains this procedure in more detail.

(m) What if the sponsor is a bank or insurance company?

8–32

(i) A sponsor may be what is known as an exempt trader or a partially exempt trader. These are businesses which are not able to recover any or all of the VAT they are charged, because supplies they make are exempt from VAT. Many supplies connected with finance are exempt, hence the particular problems faced by banks and insurance companies in sponsoring events. This does not stop such sponsorship, but the sponsored party should be prepared to be flexible in meeting the wishes of such sponsors as to how payments are made. Care must obviously be taken to avoid misunderstandings as to whether or not a sponsorship payment is VAT inclusive. Sponsors who cannot get full input tax recovery may choose to make donations, rather than incur irrecoverable VAT. They may prefer the sponsored party not to be registered for VAT or for it to make zero-rated, or exempt, supplies to the sponsor.

(ii) As a very general rule, supplies relating to land are exempt. It may be possible to arrange, for example, for a sponsor to pay for the hire of an advertising site, for its use, which would be an exempt supply of land However, the grant of certain sponsorship rights connected with land, such as any right to occupy a box, seat or other accommodation at a sports ground, theatre, concert hall or other place of entertainment, is subject to VAT at the standard rate.

8–33

(iii) An exempt or partially exempt business may have an associated company with a better ability to recover VAT. The sponsored party should consider approaching that company for sponsorship. Alternatively, the sponsorship could be provided by an overseas affiliate (preferably with no U.K. branch or establishment).

(iv) Books and other printed material may be zero rated and sponsorship payments could be made in respect of the supply of such items to a sponsor. It is possible to zero rate certain advertisements in charity brochures.

(v) The impact on the sponsored party of making exempt supplies (for example, of land) should not be forgotten. Any input tax attributable to making such supplies will not be recoverable by the sponsored party. If exempt supplies by the sponsored party are small in relation to its taxable supplies, then there is a rule which may enable the exempt supplies to be disregarded.

(n) What if the sponsor or its employees receive hospitality?

8–34

(i) As a general rule, VAT incurred on goods or services used for business entertainment purposes is not available for credit, in the same way that a trading deduction cannot be claimed for such expenses. So it is also important to check from a VAT point of view whether the sponsorship rights enable the sponsor to provide business entertainment, which includes hospitality of any kind. If the directors and employees of the sponsor are not acting as hosts and only they benefit by receiving meals, free tickets and so on, then input tax recovery will not be refused because this is not business entertainment. But if the entertainment goes beyond this, so that the sponsor's customers or suppliers benefit, then difficulties will arise. H.M. Customs and Excise consider such arrangements in detail, which is evident from the reported cases in this area. Credit has even been disallowed where the entertainment has been provided for people who work for a company on a self-employed basis.

(ii) There are concessions which may assist in limited circumstances, such as where recognised representatives of sporting bodies necessarily provide accommodation and meals to amateur sport persons, the input tax incurred may be deductible (Notice 48, "Extra-statutory concessions"). At one time, VAT on hospitality for overseas customers could be reclaimed, but this is no longer the case.

(iii) If input tax is to be disallowed, the hospitality has to be provided free to the recipient. If it can be shown that there are contractual obligations to provide hospitality then the business entertainment provisions are not applicable. An association (the City of Chicago Board of Trade) sponsored receptions at conferences. It was invoiced for the reception costs, and paid them, not the conference organiser. The delegates paid to attend the conferences (which expressly included the receptions) and so did not receive, in VAT terms, hospitality. The input tax charged to the association could not therefore be disallowed as incurred for business entertainment purposes. The output tax consequences of such arrangements must not be overlooked. The provision of entertainment under a contractual obligation will normally be the subject of an onward supply and VAT will be due on it.

(o) Must the sponsorship serve a business purpose?

8–35 A very important consideration is whether or not the VAT has been incurred for the purposes of the sponsor's business. If VAT is attributable to non-business supplies it is not recoverable. There are many reported cases on this topic and the outcome in each depended very much on the facts. A crucial factor is that the sponsorship must make sense commercially. It is important to have documentary evidence of the commercial rationale of the sponsorship arrangement. It is obviously easier to justify expenditure on the sponsorship of, for example, racehorses or motor racing if the sponsor's business is in some way connected with such activities. H.M. Customs and Excise will look at all the circumstances surrounding each claim for input tax recovery, including:

(a) the nature of the goods or services, how they are related to the sponsor's business activity, whether (or not) they are of a kind suitable for private use and whether the cost is out of proportion to the claimed business aims;
(b) the sponsor's intention at the time the supply was made; and
(c) the actual use to which the goods or services were put.

8–36 If there is any duality of purpose then it is possible to agree an apportionment of the VAT in question. In the case of certain goods acquired by a sponsor, even though there is both a business and a private use, it may be possible to claim input tax recovery in full. This is through relying on European law (the *Lennartz* case 97/90 [1995] S.T.C. 514). However, the sponsor must then also account in full for output tax in each accounting period on the private use.

There may also be VAT aspects to consider regarding the sponsored event itself, including the VAT aspects of holding competitions, the letting of facilities for sport and physical recreation, and admission fees.

4. Merchandising and endorsement

8–37 The merchandising agreement will generally involve the sponsored party or related company receiving a recurring fee (or royalty) from the licensee who has the merchandising rights. If the recipient of this fee is carrying on a trade, then the fee would usually be part of the income of that trade. The licensee would normally get a trading deduction for its expenditure. It would also pay the fees gross. Whether this is the right tax treatment in a particular case depends mainly on whether the recipient is in fact trading in respect of the fees it receives. The tax status of character merchandising was considered in the case of *Noddy Subsidiary Rights Co. Ltd v. CIR* (43 T.C. 458). It was decided that the company receiving the Noddy royalties was trading. In this case the company went out and found licensees (or they came to it), and supervised acts done under the licences granted. The company also looked out for infringements of copyrights. So, if the sponsored party or other recipient is carrying out these functions it should be treated as receiving trading income.

8–38 The other main possibility is that the person granting the licence is, in effect, an investor obtaining a return on its investment. This means the fees it receives are classified in tax terms as pure income profits. The fees are still taxable but there are other consequences. The licensee, instead of claiming a trading expense deduction, will need to claim a deduction as a charge on income. This in itself is unlikely to cause difficulties. What could be a problem is the fact that the licensee would usually have to deduct tax from the payments (section 349 of the Taxes Act 1988) at the basic rate of income tax then in force. The tax deducted is accounted for to the Inland Revenue. The licensee could end up paying more than it expected, if there is a clause in the merchandising agreement that provides for the grossing-up of payments if tax deductions are made. If the licensee did not deduct tax then it could still find itself being assessed for that tax by the Inland Revenue. If the licensor receives less than it expected then this will affect its cash flow. If a royalty is paid in respect of a patent then this tax-deduction treatment must be applied (section 349(1)(b) of the Taxes Act 1988). If the merchandising agreement involves, as is more usual, the licensing of copyrights or trade marks then, as explained above, it depends on the relevant circumstances. If the sponsored party will not in the normal course of its activities receive the fees as trading income (as may be the case for a charity) then it may be advisable for a separate company to be established, as a trading company, to act as the licensor.

8–39 If a lump-sum payment is made by the licensee it should check that it can still claim a trading deduction. As mentioned previously, a one-off payment suggests that a capital payment may have been made, in which case it will fail one of the tests of being deductible as a trading expense. If the licence is only of a limited duration and limited territorial scope then it should still be deductible, in the same way as a recurring licence fee.

The merchandising fees will usually be subject to VAT at the standard rate, assuming that the licensor is VAT registered. The VAT situation may need to be looked at in more detail, particularly if the licensee is based outside the United Kingdom or if the licensor is treated as receiving pure income profits (as described above).

8–40 Stamp duty is payable on certain types of documents. A document cannot be produced as evidence in court (except in criminal proceedings) if it is not properly stamped. Copyrights, trade marks and certain other intellectual property rights are property for stamp duty purposes, so agreements transferring an interest in them could be subject to *ad valorem* stamp duty, in the same way as stamp duty is paid on land transfers. If an exclusive irrevocable licence is granted then stamp duty is payable. It does not matter that the licence is for a limited period or extends only over a limited territory. The dutiable consideration will include any lump sum or other initial payment and, possibly other sums payable under the agreement. If the agreement provides for a minimum or basic amount of consideration, then duty will be paid on that amount. If a maximum amount is stipulated then duty is paid on that maximum amount, even though in the event a lesser amount may be paid. No duty (or duty at a reduced rate) is paid on transfers certified as being not more than a specified sum. This means that a certificate in the following terms is included in the agreement:

> "It is hereby certified that the transaction effected by this instrument does not form part of a larger transaction or series of transactions in respect of which the amount or value or aggregate amount or value of the consideration exceeds [*specified sum*]."

Perhaps more significantly, no duty is, in practice, payable if the licence is revocable. A licence is accepted as revocable if either party can terminate it by notice.

8–41 Endorsement fees will usually be received as trading income of the personality, if he is providing his services directly. The personality may be employed by a company which arranges the supply of the personality's services, in which case the company would receive the endorsement fee and the personality could in turn receive a salary from the company. The payments should be tax deductible as trading expenses of the sponsor or other payer. The fees will be subject to VAT, assuming the personality or the company is VAT registered. Stamp duty would not usually be payable (just as no duty would usually be payable on a sponsorship agreement). More detailed consideration is needed of the tax position, particularly if there is an international element.

5. Charities

8–42 Sponsorship arrangements could include a charity, particularly in relation to sponsorship of the arts and, to a certain extent, of sport. In structuring sponsorship arrangements it may be advantageous from tax and other viewpoints to ensure that a charity is involved. Whether or not this is possible depends on what is being sponsored or what use will be made of the profits of a sponsored event. The sponsored party could itself register as a charity if it is eligible to do so. Another possibility is that the sponsored party is a company owned by a charity.

In broad terms, charitable purposes cover the relief of poverty, the advancement of education, the advancement of religion and other purposes beneficial to the community. It is the latter category which includes promotion of the arts, and this enables art galleries, and opera houses to establish associated trusts or companies which have charitable status. To register as a charity an entity's objects must be exclusively charitable—the promotion of sport alone is not enough to be charitable. As an example, a gift to provide a prize for the encouragement of yacht racing was held not to be charitable. If the promotion of sport is part of a wider charitable purpose then it may be accepted as charitable. The objects of the F.A. Youth Trust were eventually accepted as charitable by both the Charity Commission and the Inland Revenue, being:

> "to organise or provide or assist in the organisation or provision of facilities which will enable and encourage pupils of schools and universities in any part of the U.K. to play association football or other games or sports and thereby to assist in ensuring that due attention is given to the physical education and development and occupation of their minds".

Therefore, by linking sports promotion to schools and universities generally, or a particular school, sport can be charitable under the heading of the advancement of education. The provision of recreational facilities could also be charitable if linked to the relief of poverty. The Recreational Charities Act 1958 also enables the provision of facilities, including sporting facilities, in the interests of social welfare to be charitable.

8–43 Charitable status makes it easier for financial support to be obtained through donations. As has been seen in relation to VAT, donations are not the same as sponsorship payments, although in practical terms the end result may be similar. Even with donations the donor can achieve a limited level of publicity for its name without, for instance, making the donation subject to VAT. If there is uncertainty as to the tax deductibility of sponsorship payments then perhaps certainty could be achieved by making gifts to a charity. There are various tax efficient methods of supporting a charity. The Inland Revenue publications IR64 ("Giving to charity") and IR113 ("Gift Aid—a guide for donors and charities") provide useful information. These publications should be available from any Tax Inquiry Centre. A corporate sponsor should consider the following.

(a) Deed of covenant

8–44 Annual payments under a deed of covenant to a charity are allowable as charges on income. A sum equal to the basic rate of income tax needs to be deducted and accounted for to the Inland Revenue but the charity can reclaim the tax deducted. The period of the covenant must be capable of exceeding three years.

The terms of the covenant could provide for termination on the happening of certain events (but only those which are outside the control of covenantor). Unlike a sponsorship payment, the covenantor must not be entitled to receive any benefit in return.

(b) Gift aid

8–45 Gift aid is a tax relief for single outright cash gifts. Tax at the basic rate of income tax is deducted from each gift. There is no restriction on the amount that can be paid by a company unless it is, in tax terms, a close company. In very broad terms, a close company is one that is under the control of five or fewer people. Each gift by a close company must exceed a specified amount (after deducting tax). Even so, this is a very flexible form of obtaining tax relief in comparison to deeds of covenant. Also, it avoids the uncertainties that can arise when claiming payments as trading deductions.

(c) Trading deduction

8–46 This method of getting a deduction has been considered above. Gifts to charities can be justified as tax-deductible expenditure if they are made wholly and exclusively for the purpose of the donor's trade and are not of a capital nature. The Inland Revenue do accept payments made to sponsor a charitable activity as tax deductible, if the payer's sole purpose is to get publicity for the payer's name or product and that publicity is in line with the amount paid.

(d) Seconding staff

8–47 The costs of temporarily seconding staff to work for a charity are tax deductible.

8–48 Charitable status brings various tax advantages to the charity itself. If it has funds to invest pending their use for charitable purposes, then the investment income and gains will generally be tax exempt. Charities do not, however, have a wholesale exemption from tax. For example, they only have an exemption for a limited type of trading profits. The trade must either be the primary purpose of the charity, or the work of the trade must be mainly carried on by the beneficiaries. By concession, profits from gymkhanas, fireworks displays, and similar activities meeting certain conditions are not charged to tax (ESC C4). Other exemptions from rates and stamp duties may be relevant, but a charity is not so privileged in relation to VAT. If a charity makes taxable supplies and its taxable turnover exceeds the registration threshold, it must register for VAT. There are a few special VAT reliefs. Care must be taken if these are used in "avoidance" schemes (see, for example, the arrangement to acquire equipment without incurring VAT that failed in *University of Wales College, Newport and another* (LON/97/145). Many charities have no business activities because it is difficult for them to be compatible with charitable status and so they cannot recover VAT.

There is a helpful VAT exemption relating to one-off fund-raising events by charities (and certain non-profit-making bodies). The exemption covers an event such as a fête, ball, bazaar, gala show, performance or similar event which does not form part of a series or regular run of like or similar events. The one-off limit is aimed at preventing charities and other eligible bodies from gaining an unfair tax advantage over the activities of commercial organisations that have to charge VAT. The exemption applies to goods and services supplied by a charity in connection with a fund-raising event organised for charitable purposes by a charity or jointly by charities. It covers goods and services supplied in return for sponsorship of such events. Notice 701/1, "Charities", explains the exemption in detail.

8–49 Because of the conflicts between commercial fund-raising and charitable status, it is usual for a charity to establish a subsidiary company which can carry out the business activity. The trading subsidiary then covenants with its shareholder, the charity, to pay out an annual sum equivalent to the company's profits. The arrangements need to be worked out carefully but this should avoid tax being paid on the profits. The charity will receive tax-free covenanted income rather than having to argue that it comes within the limited exemption for trading profits. The VAT exemption for one-off fund-raising events now also covers such events when undertaken by a trading subsidiary.

6. Non-resident entertainers and sportsmen

8–50 The sponsored event may involve entertainers and sportsmen who are not resident in the United Kingdom for tax purposes, in which case the rules requiring the deduction of tax from certain payments must not be overlooked. These rules were introduced to counter non-payment of tax by such non-residents. When a payment is made in respect of an appearance in the United Kingdom by a non-resident entertainer or sportsman, the person making the payment has to deduct tax at the basic rate of income tax. The definition of entertainer or sportsman for this purpose is wide. The payer must make a return to the Inland Revenue and account for the tax deducted. The non-resident receives a net amount and a certificate showing the tax deducted.

It is therefore important to identify who is the payer for the purpose of the rules because of the duties involved. If the sponsor is making payments under the terms of the sponsorship agreement to the non-resident in question, then the sponsor will clearly need to consider its position. If a payer fails to deduct tax, the payer may be assessed by the Inland Revenue. Even if the payments are made indirectly to the entertainer or sportsman, perhaps through a tax-haven company or trust, then the tax-deduction rules still apply. The tax-deduction rules apply to payments in kind and transfers, such as the loan of property, as well as to cash payments. There are special rules to calculate what tax is due on non-cash payments.

8–51 Payments connected with sponsorship are caught, as much as payments for actual appearances. The point was emphasised by the Inland Revenue in a press release issued when the rules were introduced: "In addition to fees, etc., for actual appearances, other income associated with appearances (from for instance advertising, sponsorship or endorsement) will be included." This is brought out in the detailed rules of the scheme which contain an express reference to sponsorship. If the rules are to apply there must be an individual entertainer or sportsman who is non-resident when he performs what are called relevant activities. This covers, among other things, activities in connection with a commercial occasion or event. An event includes one which is: "designed to promote commercial sales or activity by advertising, the endorsement of goods or services, sponsorship, or other promotional means of any kind". This is a rare express reference to sponsorship in tax legislation.

8–52 It is possible that tax does not need to be deducted from every payment, or deducted in full. No deduction is required if another tax-deduction scheme applies, or for payments in respect of proceeds of sale of records. No deduction is required from payments totalling £1,000 or less in the tax year. Payments to certain third parties at a normal level for services ancillary to the performance (such as hire of stage hands, premises, equipment, etc.) can be paid gross. There is scope to agree a reduced rate of tax deduction with the Inland Revenue. There is a special Inland Revenue section to which such applications are sent, which is the Foreign Entertainers Unit, Royal House, Prince's Gate, 2–6 Homer Road, Solihull, West Midlands, B91 3WG. This unit can also be contacted to check the entertainer's residence position.

This book is not the place to explain the tax-deduction rules and other provisions relevant to entertainers in detail. The entertainer must, in particular, take into account any relevant double tax treaty provision with the United Kingdom.

7. Joint ventures

8–53 Genuine sponsorship arrangements do not amount to joint ventures or investment arrangements. The distinction is as important for tax purposes as it is commercially. If the sponsor is only making payments for sponsorship services, then there will be no question of the arrangement being, say, a partnership for tax purposes. But if the arrangements include, for example, the sharing of the profits of the sponsored event, then the tax aspects must be considered carefully. It is important that the right label is put on events. If the status of proposed arrangements for a sponsored event is unclear, it is preferable that the proposal is moved into a recognisable category. This is so it is clear to all involved (including the tax authorities) what the status of the venture is for tax and other purposes.

The sponsorship arrangements as a whole may involve some joint venture aspects. There is the possibility of the sponsor joining with a television company to support the making of a documentary film, in which case the basis for the tax treatment of the arrangement needs to be established. In many cases what is described as a joint venture between two separate entities actually amounts to a partnership. Relevant factors are whether or not expenses, profits and any losses will be shared, and whether a joint bank account and joint administrative arrangements exist; if they do then the relationship between the parties is likely to be a partnership. The tax consequences of being in partnership then follow, for example, the parties probably have to make a separate VAT registration of the partnership business. Because of various factors, it may be preferable to establish a joint venture company in which each of the joint venturers owns shares.

Tax Table

Value Added Tax

Standard rate	17.5%	From April 1, 1991
VAT fraction	7/47	From April 1, 1991

Example:

A sponsorship agreement provides for a payment of £23,500 (including VAT). The amount of VAT included in this payment is £3,500 (that is 7/47 × £23,500 = £3,500). The VAT exclusive amount is £20,000.

Small business gifts limit	£15	From November 29, 1995
Registration threshold	£50,000	From April 1, 1998
Deregistration threshold	£48,000	From April 1, 1998

Stamp duty

Conveyance or transfer on sale with appropriate certificate of value (not stock transfers)

Consideration:

Not more than £60,000	Nil	From March 23, 1993
More than £60,000 but not more than £250,000	1%	From July 8, 1997
More than £250,000 but not more than £500,000	2%	From March 24, 1998
More than £500,000	3%	From March 24, 1998

Income tax

Basic rate of income tax	23%	From April 6, 1997

Non-resident entertainers and sportsmen

Payments threshold	£1,000 each tax year	From May 1, 1987

Gift Aid

Single gift by close company (or individual)

Minimum amount (after deduction of tax)	£250	From March 16, 1993

CHAPTER 9

Basic Contract Points

1. Introduction

9–01 Sponsorship and all of the activities arising from it are marketing, promoting and selling concepts, each of which is ultimately set out in a legal agreement between the relevant parties. These agreements contain the rights and obligations of each of the parties to the other, and set out all of the legal, financial and commercial terms which will govern the transaction they have entered into. In most cases the preliminary discussions and more detailed negotiations will have been undertaken directly between the parties, after which they give the deal over to their lawyers to tidy up the paperwork. In some cases the parties set out their agreement in a letter or a more formal document to which they have both contributed the drafting without taking legal or accounting advice, and they both sign it.

9–02 Many agreements created in this less formal context are inadequate in legal and commercial terms because:

    (a) the basic rudiments of what can constitute a legally binding agreement have not been understood or followed;

    (b) due to the lack of drafting skill or experience the wording may be contradictory, incomplete or capable of being construed in different ways;

    (c) there may be illegal or unenforceable provisions, such as excessive restrictive covenants or territorial restrictions;

    (d) the agreement may not cover all of the commercial and financial terms which are necessary for the proper operation of the deal and for the reasonable protection of both parties.

This chapter is designed to give those persons a simple explanation of the basic needs and safeguards, and things to do or not to do, so that they can be more aware of the potential pitfalls of "do-it-yourself" contracts. For anything more than a simple deal the cost of competent legal advice will be worth the peace of mind.

2. Oral and written agreements

9–03 There should be no mystery about a contract, which is a document containing the terms governing the agreement between the parties, *i.e.* it is a set of commercial rules. To be binding in law a contract need not necessarily be in writing. A written contract may confirm the terms of a previous oral agreement, which itself can be legally binding, but is usually the result of completed negotiations.

150

Assuming that the discussions end in an understanding that all the terms the parties can think of have been agreed, the position will be either that they will now consider the total deal before being committed; or they now agree to be committed on those terms. The next step is to formalise the agreement in writing. There is a difference between an oral agreement, which is intended to be legally binding on both parties without a written document signed by them; and an agreement which has been negotiated, but which will not become legally effective until there is a document signed by both parties. In the second case, if no agreement is signed, neither party is committed. If there was no such distinction, the ordinary commercial process of negotiation would become technical and complicated.

9–04 If, in anticipation of the formal document being drawn up, the parties start to become actively involved in the organisation of the event, and the sponsor pays to the sponsored party a portion of the sponsorship fee for preliminary matters, or if a merchandiser is authorised to start to manufacture merchandise, there would be sufficient part performance of the negotiated agreement to create some legal obligations between the parties notwithstanding the absence of a formal document signed by them. A written agreement avoids having to rely on memory in the event of subsequent disagreement upon what was originally negotiated. An oral agreement still needs to contain the essential formalities necessary for a binding contract, which are:

(a) a specific unconditional offer;

(b) a specific unconditional acceptance of that offer; and

(c) the passing of consideration, such as money, or an undertaking to do some act or perform some service, or to forego some right.

9–05 If the terms of an oral agreement are not put in writing, a plaintiff in a court action may have difficulty in proving its case where a disputed term of an oral agreement is to be identified, interpreted or enforced. Correspondence between the parties may be useful evidence of what was agreed, and so will be any actions undertaken by the parties after the conclusion of negotiations. An oral agreement gives the parties greater flexibility than a written agreement in the interpretation of what they thought they had agreed.

The contract as set out should represent accurately and completely what is agreed between the parties. To agree something in conversation, and to put that agreement into writing effectively to represent precisely and unambiguously what is meant, are two different matters. The parties should consider all the likely consequences of the terms of their deal. These can then be dealt with specifically in the agreement to avoid future problems. A hurriedly and inadequately prepared written contract may be more dangerous than not having one at all, if it does not reflect the true agreement between the parties.

It is commonly found that when the parties get down to agreeing the written document, which means analysing what they have agreed in negotiations, further issues emerge as being relevant but which have not yet been addressed. These may be side issues or they may be of major significance. In normal circumstances this should be looked upon as extending the negotiations, not the necessity for complete renegotiation.

3. Private arrangements

9–06 The reason for having a clear definition of what should constitute a legally binding contract is because the parties may only want to come to a private arrangement. An informal or private arrangement, whether oral or written, sometimes called a "gentleman's agreement", is one which both of the parties never intended to be legally enforceable, but to be binding upon them in honour only. To avoid any misunderstanding, if this is really intended, it should be made absolutely clear by both parties before they consider doing a deal on these terms. No business arrangement should be on this basis, the concept of entering into specific obligations, but their not being enforceable, is incompatible.

If a private arrangement is entered into, it is assumed that none of the parties intend to create a legal business-like relationship. It is no more than a statement of intent between them. However, there will always be people who habitually do their business on the basis of a handshake, considering the deal to be legally binding. They do not realise that such an arrangement may be inadequate in law if the essential elements for a binding contract do not exist. To avoid any misunderstanding, the parties should make the basis of the deal clear, even by confirming it in a letter without delay. Another benefit of doing so is that if there has been any misunderstanding during the course of discussions, that may be discovered when the letter is received.

9–07   Mutual intention to create a legal relationship between the parties is the crux of an enforceable agreement. This has to be a positive frame of mind. If no such intention is present, such as in a private arrangement, there is a presumption that no legal contract arises; the matter rests as one of trust and honour. If the trust in the honour is broken, the disappointed party must put it down to experience. Where a contract comes into existence through negotiation with professional advice, and is incorporated in a formal document, it is presumed to be intended to be legally binding in law.

A private arrangement, notwithstanding its informality, may have been intended by one or both of the parties to be legally binding. Consternation will follow if, when clinically put to the test of whether or not it was a contract in law, it fails. Where the contract appears to be legal and binding on the face of it and if one party intended to be legally bound, but the other did not, that other party would have difficulty in pleading mistake, or that it was intended by him to be only a private arrangement. Ignorance of the law is no defence, even where unforeseen hardship arises through it. If it were a defence, the legal system would break down, and the security of properly drawn up commercial agreements would be at risk.

4. Recitals to an agreement

9–08   Recitals are the preamble of an agreement: the "whereas" part at the beginning. These describe briefly the context in which the agreement is entered into. They should not contain any grant of rights or obligations unless they are also fully set out in the main part of the agreement, as the legally enforceable part of the agreement starts after the heading "Now it is agreed as follows", or a similar heading followed by the contract clauses. Recitals can be useful if there is a dispute at a later date, as the legal advisers (who may not be those who negotiated the agreement), will have some explanatory background to the deal.

Recitals become necessary to avoid confusion where the same parties enter into an agreement which is supplemental to the principal agreement, or if they enter into different agreements dependent upon or related to each other. This can happen where the parties enter into a sponsorship agreement, and then sign related agreements for merchandising or other matters. The risk of errors arising when drafting associated agreements will be reduced, and each agreement will have an easily recognisable identity of its own.

5. Contents of an agreement

9–09 An agreement should contain in sufficient detail all of the fundamental points agreed upon by the parties, together with all the necessary ancillary matters needed to make it operate effectively and the usual clauses which are relevant to commercial agreements. It is dangerous to rely upon unwritten understandings which form part of the deal, but which are not thought worthy of inclusion in the formal document. To the contrary, there should be a clause stating that only the terms contained in the written agreement will apply.

Drafting the agreement provides the opportunity to ensure that it sets out everything upon which each party wants to rely. There is no point, and it is dangerous, to have relevant contractual terms which are not set out in the written agreement. If they are not referred to in the agreement they should be disregarded. It may not always be possible to keep the agreement simple, but it is a false economy to leave relevant details out only for the sake of brevity.

9–10 Litigation is frequently caused either by ambiguity in the drafting of clauses, or by a dispute as to whether or not a specific point which was not included in or referred to in the written agreement should be deemed to be included in it as (so it is alleged) having formed a fundamental part of the negotiations upon which the plaintiff claims to have placed reliance. If the parties were legally represented, and if the drafting of the agreement went through various stages and was carefully examined prior to being signed, how is it that only afterwards the plaintiff raises this claim? If the omission is obviously a typist's error that is one thing, but in the absence of an acceptable explanation showing mutual intention to include the missing clause in the agreement, the claim may well fail.

Terms can sometimes be implied into an agreement from a relevant unwritten universal commercial understanding, or an established trade custom and usage, providing both parties understand and accept that position. Any representation, warranty or undertaking offered as a substantial inducement to a party to enter into the agreement should be recorded fully in it, if it is to be relied upon. See paragraph 9–32, below.

9–11 Even if there is a clause in the agreement to the effect that the written terms are the only ones binding the parties, and that the agreement can only be amended by a document in writing signed by both parties, it may be possible for a written term to be varied effectively by the unrecorded but accepted actions of expedience or custom of either party. These would have to be known by the other party and positively approved, ratified or acted upon by it. An example may be where a sponsor unofficially releases some restriction placed upon the sponsored party in the agreement. With the full knowledge of the sponsor, the sponsored party then does whatever he was previously restricted from doing. The sponsor could not later claim that the sponsored party is in breach of that restriction just because there is no written confirmation of that variation.

An exchange of correspondence would be adequate to confirm the variation in writing, it does not have to be another formal agreement. If the parties get along well, and both believe they fully understand the variation, it may not occur to them that its details should be confirmed in writing. The point will only be raised if there is a subsequent dispute on the variation.

6. Options

9–12 An option granted to a party to enable it to extend the period of an agreement, or for any other purpose, must be supported by consideration in order for it to be specifically enforceable, unless it is contained in a deed. If an option is not specifically enforceable, then it is treated as being voluntary, and may be revoked at any time. A revocable option can only be revoked prior to its exercise; but if it has been properly exercised by the party to which it was granted, it will remain binding upon all the parties. If the option to extend the period of a principal agreement is contained in a supplementary agreement, it should have a consideration independent of any expressed in the principal agreement. Past consideration is not legally effective.

The clause containing an option should set out all the conditions affecting its exercise. For example, it is useful to make the exercise of an agreement period extension option limited in time to not after, say, 30 days prior to the date of expiry of the agreement. This gives the grantor of the option adequate time to decide what to do if the option is not exercised. Exercise of an option should be in writing, and should be actually received by the grantor, rather than being effective if posted to it by a given date. An option should be stated to be irrevocable during the period within which it is exercisable. If an irrevocable option has no specified period, it may be revoked at any time by written notice given by the grantor of the option: it cannot be perpetual.

Upon assignment of the benefit of an agreement containing an option which has been granted to a third party to it, written notice of the assignment should be given to the third party to make it aware that any exercise by it of the option will be against the assignee of the benefit of the agreement.

7. Signature

9–13 The proper completion of the legal formalities relating to the signing and dating of agreements is important. These are the first things to check when considering their validity. All the parties should have signed the agreement, and should have initialled all alterations made to its text. This prevents a signed agreement subsequently being amended or added to in a prejudicial or fraudulent manner without the knowledge and consent of the party affected by the amendment. If alterations are not initialled, that does not invalidate the contract, but the alterations can be challenged by the party affected by them.

All signatures should be witnessed, and the witness should also state his address and occupation. Lack of a witness does not invalidate the agreement, but where it was signed with nobody present it is possible for a party to claim that it is not his signature at all. A witness to a signature can give evidence that it is genuine. To maintain impartiality, none of the witnesses should be a party to the agreement.

A signatory to an agreement on behalf of a company or a partnership should be prepared to provide reasonable evidence that he is entitled and authorised to commit the party, and to sign the agreement for it. For a company, a verified copy of a resolution of the board of directors authorising the signatory to execute the agreement would be best. If the signatory is a director of the company, or is well established as having signatory powers, his signature will bind the company, whether or not there is a previous board resolution.

8. Date

9–14 Strictly, the date of the agreement should be the date of signing the agreement. Where necessary there can be a clause stating that the agreement is to take effect from a specified date before or after the actual date of signature. The same result is obtained by merely pre-dating the agreement to its genuine starting date, unless the intended effect of pre-dating is to deceive, or to obtain a fraudulent benefit, or to deprive others of rights which they would otherwise have, or to preserve rights which would otherwise have been lost. Pre-dating an agreement is not recommended.

9. Original and counterpart documents

9–15 Although it is not legally necessary, it is preferable for an agreement to have all its original copies signed by all parties. Each party then has a completely executed original copy of the agreement. If there are only two parties, it is as easy to have each party sign one of the copies, and exchange it for that signed by the other party. The one signed by the grantor of the rights will be known as the original copy, and the other will be known as the counterpart.

10. Termination of agreements

9–16 An agreement can be terminated in the following ways.

(a) By effluxion of time

9–17 Where an agreement is stated to run for a specified time only, when that time has expired the agreement ends. If the parties to that agreement disregard that date, and continue in business as if that date had not been reached, the agreement becomes an agreement at will, terminable by reasonable notice in writing at any time by either party.

(b) Upon completion of its purpose

9–18 Whatever may be the intended period of the agreement, it may contain a provision for termination by either party giving to the other notice of intention to terminate the agreement on a certain date, or upon the happening of a certain event. The notice should be in writing, and where possible should be given not less than a specified minimum period of time before the termination is to take effect. Notice provisions should always be contained in agreements which do not have a fixed terminal date.

(c) Bad faith

9–19 In the absence of specific notice provisions, notice of termination can be given by one party where the other party has so acted in bad faith, or is in such default of his obligations that the injured party is entitled to deem the agreement at an end on the basis that the other party has totally repudiated his rights under it. That might precipitate a legal argument over whether the termination is lawful, questioning whether the grounds are genuinely fundamental. The purported grounds of termination, and the surrounding actions of the parties, will be significant in deciding the issue. If the court decides that the termination was not proper, the consequences of the purported act of termination may cause the terminating party itself to be in breach of contract.

(d) By notice upon breach

9-20

(i) Any agreement should specify a procedure to be followed should a breach of contract occur. For example, written notice of the breach should be given by the complaining party to the breaching party, with a requirement that it must be remedied within a specific time. Failure to comply with the notice creates the right to terminate. Non-compliance may be either a total disregard of the notice, or it may be because, despite all reasonable efforts of the breaching party, the remedy will happen, but not in the specified time. It is possible that the breach will not be remediable, whatever efforts the breaching party makes. The time stated in the clause should be sufficient to enable the party to remedy the breach if it gets down to it promptly. There is no point in having an unrealistically short time period.

(ii) Substantial or irreparable breach of a fundamental term or condition in an agreement may entitle the injured party to terminate the agreement for that reason, whether or not that right is contained in the agreement.

(e) Breach of fundamental term

9-21 Depending on the nature and purpose of the contract, it may also be agreed that a breach of certain fundamental terms, specified to be "of the essence" of the agreement, will give rise to a right of termination. This avoids a dispute as to whether the breach is sufficiently substantial, or whether the term breached is sufficiently fundamental, to create a right of termination under the general law. This will normally be where an event or the performance of some obligation is crucial to the deal, without which it is not intended that the deal will proceed. This procedure will be necessary for a matter which in the context of the deal is vital, but which ordinarily would not be considered to be fundamental. An example would be where something has to be done by a specified time. The clause must state clearly that the event is "of the essence of the agreement".

(f) Automatic termination

9-22 The agreement may state that it will terminate automatically upon the happening of specified events, such as:

(a) the liquidation of a party being a company;

(b) the party being a company or business ceasing permanently to trade;

(c) the bankruptcy of an individual party;

(d) the attempted assignment by a party of the benefit of the contract, or of a right connected with it, which is specifically prohibited.

(g) By mutual agreement

9-23 Any agreement can be terminated or amended in any way at any time with the consent of all of the parties to it. The unanimous consent relates to rights and obligations between the parties themselves, but will not affect any continuing rights of, or obligations to, independent third parties contained in or arising from the agreement.

(h) By substitution of agreements

9–24 Where a subsequent agreement is made between the same parties, which effectively takes over all of the rights and obligations contained in a prior agreement between them, the prior one should be specifically terminated. If it is not terminated, but thereafter is totally ignored in favour of the new agreement, the previous agreement will be deemed to have been terminated. It is more likely that a subsequent agreement will only amend certain aspects of the original agreement, which then remains in force subject only to the alterations.

(i) By the actions of the parties

9–25

(a) It is possible for an agreement to be terminated by the party which is bound to perform the obligations under it if the other party (which is entitled to the benefit of the agreement) so behaves with reference to the agreement as to indicate clearly and unequivocally that it no longer requires the terminating party to be bound to fulfil any of its obligations under it. It may be difficult to decide whether the rights have been abandoned or whether the agreement has only become temporarily dormant.

(b) The interpretation of what a course of behaviour means, and what the consequences are, is usually a matter of opinion. The party believing itself to be released should obtain written confirmation from the other party that the agreement has ended. It will then find out whether its view is correct. Because the abandonment has simply evolved, there is unlikely to be any clear date upon which it occurred. If confirmation of termination is forthcoming, a specific date of termination should be agreed, so that dealings with the rights in the agreement prior to and after that date can be separated, if necessary.

(c) The termination of most contracts will still leave outstanding matters between the parties which need to be cleared up. The termination document should deal with the details of who does what and who gets what.

11. *Force majeure*

9–26 The *force majeure* clause deals with all those possible but unexpected events which are outside the control of the parties, and which by their nature or effect prevent the fulfilment of a contract. The law recognises that if certain intervening events, which could not have been reasonably foreseen, either nullify the entire objective of the contract, or make it impossible to achieve, the contract can be ended without any liability by either party arising from that event, except possibly, in the context of sponsorship, a refund of part of the sponsorship fee. The termination does not "wipe out" other obligations, rights or liabilities already existing under the contract, and which are not affected by the *force majeure* event.

The *force majeure* event may only cause a delay in fulfilling the contract, and it may not be a total frustration of it. Where the time lost due to a *force majeure* event only deprives the injured party temporarily of what it has contracted for and, provided that performance of the prevented event on the due date was not of the essence of the contract, one alternative is to agree to extend the term of the agreement for the period of lost time.

12. Mistake

9–27 It is possible for a party to terminate an agreement on the basis that it signed it by mistake. This may be difficult to explain satisfactorily. The mistake must be of fact, not of law, and must be either as to the fundamental basis of the agreement, or as to a fundamental term of it. In this context "mistake" is not just an error of judgment or the result of carelessness. It means that the document which was signed bears no legal relationship to what was agreed or intended by the party wishing to terminate it.

9–28 The mistake must be that of both parties, except where the mistake by one party is such as to indicate clearly that the agreement as a whole is completely different in content and purpose from that intended to be entered into. Two guidelines are that:

(a) An agreement will not be enforceable if the party claiming mistake signed it under the genuine misapprehension that it was another document of a totally different legal nature and intent;

(b) mistake cannot be pleaded as a ground for termination of the agreement if the general purpose of the agreement as set out was intended, but the party pleading mistake merely had not read the document carefully, or at all, or had not inquired sufficiently into what he did not understand, though given adequate opportunity to do so. These are not legal mistakes, they are decisions of an arbitrary nature taken with the benefit of hindsight.

The burden of proving that a genuine legal mistake, as defined above, has occurred is high. Negotiation, however inadequate, must have preceded the drafting of the agreement, when the nature of the agreement should have been clear and understood, or when a fundamental issue should have been raised. Had the complaining party read the document before signing it, it should have realised something was wrong. If it did read it, but at that time did not spot what is now being complained about, it could not have been an important issue in the negotiations.

13. Misrepresentation

9–29 To affect the validity of a contract, a representation must be a statement of fact, and not just of an opinion. The representation may be inferred by conduct, which leads the other party reasonably to assume the fact tacitly being represented. A representation which is clearly not intended to form part of the contract, or which is not used to procure or induce the signing of the contract, does not of itself affect its validity or enforceability.

For a claim of misrepresentation to be successful, the claimant must act promptly on discovering it. The claimant should also make it clear that further negotiation to deal with the misrepresentation after it has been discovered will be without prejudice to its rights in respect of the misrepresentation if the negotiations fail. If the misrepresentation was not a fundamental one leading to a claim of repudiation of the agreement, the claimant will need to show that it has suffered some loss or disadvantage which can be quantified for compensation.

9–30   There are three categories of misrepresentation:

(a) Innocent misrepresentation: these are misleading statements, but where they are free from fraudulent intent. The representee can repudiate the contract if the misrepresentation is substantial, fundamental and strikes at the essence of the contract. It cannot obtain damages unless the misrepresentation was in connection with an essential term of the contract.

(b) Negligent and fraudulent misrepresentation: the representee can repudiate the contract and claim damages as well, whether or not the representation was in connection with an essential term of the contract.

9–31   There are two further points to consider:

(a) where third parties have innocently acquired rights under the contract, which will be prejudiced by its repudiation, the court will not necessarily grant repudiation, so as to protect the third party's interests;

(b) where misrepresentation induces in one of the parties to the contract a fundamental mistake as to the nature of the contract, *i.e.* where the entire basis of the contract is mistaken, the contract can be rescinded, *i.e.* treated as void *ab initio*. This means it is treated as never having been entered into in the first place, and therefore as never having had any legal effect. Where that happens, whatever has been produced or done in the meantime has to be unscrambled, so that the parties can be put back to square one.

A third party may not be able to protect rights purported to have been granted by the "non-existent" contract, because all rights ceased to exist when it was repudiated. If the third party is damaged it would have a claim against the party from which it got its rights, *e.g.* for breach of warranty.

14. Rectification

9–32   An agreement is construed and enforced by the court in accordance with its clear and unambiguous language setting out the intentions of the parties to it. If the principal terms of the document are incomprehensible or contradictory, the court will not attempt to create an agreement between the parties by deciding what they might have intended. The court may use common sense and the evidence of the context in which the agreement was entered into to interpret its meaning, where the lack of clarity is caused only by inadequate use of the English language. If the document is so vague as to be meaningless, there may well be no agreement enforceable in law. The same rules apply to oral agreements as well as to written ones. The main difficulty in oral agreements is to prove the existence of the terms which have to be relied upon to support a claim.

Evidence of prior representations claimed to be relevant to the meaning or operation of the agreement, which ought to have been, and which are not, contained in the formal document, will only be allowed if it is to prove fraud or mutual mistake. When one party later alleges that previously agreed oral terms have been omitted entirely from, or are only partially set out in, the written agreement, if both parties agree the omission, there is no problem. Further documentation can be signed to bring those oral terms into the written agreement. Otherwise the aggrieved party must issue legal proceedings to attempt to get a court order to rectify the error. That is why it is useful to have a clause which makes it clear that any item which is not set out in the document will not be part of the agreement.

9–33   If the court accepts the plaintiff's claim, and can be satisfied that a typist's error, or some other genuine reason, resulted in the omission; or that the error was on both sides; or that there was unilateral fraud, it can order the agreement to be amended accordingly. The remedy of rectification will not be available where one party subsequently thinks of something which it would have liked to include in the agreement if only it had thought of it at the time. That is not an omission, it is hindsight.

Where alterations to an agreement are negotiated after its execution, the parties should either enter into a supplemental agreement if the subsequent variations are minor, or they should sign an entirely new agreement in substitution for the previous one if the variations are extensive. Applying to the court for rectification is not a procedure to be used where the entire agreement is to be attacked; it is only to amend or complete the text of an agreement in special circumstances.

15. Undertakings

9–34   Where there are services to be performed, even the best of efforts in good faith may fail to achieve the objective required. For this reason the wording of the obligation in the contract determining its legal effect upon the party who has to fulfil it must be considered carefully. To agree to do something is itself enforceable if the obligation is not conditional on some uncertain factor yet to occur.

It is more positive and absolute to require an undertaking from a party to a contract to perform or to procure the performance of an obligation, rather than for it just to agree to do it. To undertake to do something where it is not certain that such an objective can be fulfilled is a hazard which beats a well-worn path to the courts. The belated explanation that fulfilment had become impossible or inconvenient for whatever reason will not necessarily remove the obligation for that party to compensate the other for loss arising from the breach of the undertaking.

9–35   It would become unnecessarily complicated for the party to give conditional undertakings, because the conditions would have to be specified and interpreted strictly. If ordinary commercial prerequisites are the conditions, then the force of an undertaking is lost. For these reasons obligations in sponsorship and related activities are normally made subject to the exercise of "the best endeavours" of the party being bound to perform. If best endeavours are used, but even then the obligation is not fulfilled, the party bound has discharged its duty, providing it used good faith. What is the difference between "best endeavours" and "reasonable endeavours"? There is no absolute bench mark below which an effort is only reasonable, and above which it becomes best. "Reasonable" implies a lesser effort on an objective basis than for "best" which implies that no financial or other limit may apply.

16. Warranties and Indemnities

9–36   Warranties in contracts are statements or representations concerning the truth of facts, or the existence of circumstances, which have particular relevance to the contract, and upon which fundamental issues to the contract are based. They confirm to other parties to the contract facts they can rely on, as the same warranties may be passed on by them to third parties in subsequent contracts. The financial aspects, guarantees, or the passing of title to property dealt with in a contract may be subject to warranties being proved correct, which is why they should not be treated casually or drafted carelessly. Many warranties are intended to replace the necessity for the other party to ascertain facts independently, and they are used also where the facts or circumstances are only within the knowledge or responsibility of the warrantor.

Most warranties are the subject of indemnities by the warrantor, where breach of the warranty might involve loss, damage or expense to the party relying upon the warranty. If the validity of a warranty is specified to be "of the essence" of the agreement, breach of the warranty will entitle the other party to terminate the agreement. To avoid confusion this right should be clearly stated.

9–37   As an indemnity is a form of insurance policy, the warrantor is only liable for losses which have actually been incurred. In many cases the loss cannot be quantified, but appropriate factors will be taken into account if damages are awarded by the court.

In an extreme case of misrepresentation, the aggrieved party may be entitled to rescind the contract altogether. To "rescind" means to nullify the contract, *i.e.* to treat it as never having been entered into. Rescission for breach of warranty will not be an available remedy if the parties have so acted or progressed during the period of the contract that they cannot be put back to square one.

17. Conditions

9–38   Conditions are terms in a contract which have to be fulfilled either before the contract becomes binding, or before certain aspects of it come into effect. The intention is that if a condition is not fulfilled, the event dependent upon that condition will not occur. For example, the sponsored party may hold the agreement open for the sponsor provided the sponsorship fee is paid by the June 1. If the fee is not so paid, the sponsored party is released from the obligation to hold the agreement open to the sponsor. Conditions normally relate either to statements to be relied upon but not yet proved, or to future events the outcome of which will determine the action of the parties.

Conditions can either be precedent to, or subsequent to, the event in question. If a condition precedent upon which the whole contract depends fails, the contract does not come into effect. Where an existing contract contains a condition subsequent which fails, the agreed effect of the failure should be set out in the agreement.

18. Licence and assignment

9–39   A licence grants a restricted legal right of use for a specified period of time. The restrictions are reservations by the licensor of all matters to be excluded from the licence, the terms governing the exercise of the rights, and the specific right of termination of the licence on the happening of certain events. Meanwhile, the underlying beneficial ownership of the rights remains with the licensor. As a guide, the outright sale of a right will be by an assignment, while the granting of a temporary use of a right will be by a licence.

In an unconditional assignment, the legal and beneficial ownership of the subject passes absolutely out of the hands of the assignor to the assignee with no right of recall. If the assignment is conditional upon, for example, the completion of instalment payments, it will not be effective until all the payments have been made. In that example, care must be taken in drafting the assignment to ensure that it is not complete on payment of the first instalment, leaving the assignor only the right to sue for the balance of unpaid instalments.

9–40   There cannot be licensed or assigned any rights which are not either owned by the licensor or the assignor, or which are not theirs to call for from a third party. If there is any difficulty on the part of the licensor or assignor in giving warranties of title to the rights, and if time is of the essence in concluding the deal, an unsatisfactory compromise is to give a conditional contract. That means if the condition is fulfilled the contract comes into operation, but if it is not fulfilled, it does not. The condition would be the ascertaining of the title to the rights in question, and there should be a time limit on doing so. Meanwhile nothing should be done under the agreement which would be considered to be sufficient part performance to nullify the effect of the condition not being fulfilled.

Appendices Contents

Sponsorship Questions and Answers

Q1: What should I sponsor, and how do I go about it?

A1: To be able to make a sensible choice, you should consider the following points:

(a) First, basic commercial decisions should be made, such as:

    (i) fix a monetary limit to the sponsorship budget, as that will set the scope of what can be sponsored;

    (ii) decide whether you want to sponsor one event this year to get experience, or whether you want to have a medium-term deal for, say, three to five years;

    (iii) how you want to project your company's image. Would you prefer to sponsor an individual (such as a car racing driver), a sporting event (such as a horse race) a competitive event (such as an athletics meeting) or an arts or cultural event (such as an opera or exhibition)? Outside these areas the choice is wide.

(b) There are three basic ways of progressing the search for a suitable party which either does not currently have sponsorship, or whose sponsorship has or is about to expire:

    (i) if you have identified an area of activity which will be suitable, you can approach the governing body, if there is one, or any other association or organisation which administers the activity. They may have a list of events which are looking for sponsorship;

    (ii) approach the organisations set out in Appendix IV for guidance;

    (iii) use the services of a sponsorship consultancy to find you an acceptable party to sponsor. An added benefit will be that the consultancy will also have the experience to advise you, and to negotiate the sponsorship deal for you.

Q2: Is sponsorship a worthwhile marketing strategy?

A2: If your products are related to a specific sporting or leisure activity, you may prefer endorsement to sponsorship. If your products are major consumer products (such as a drinks manufacturer), or if you provide consumer services (such as a bank), sponsorship can be a very effective means of heightening consumer awareness. Sporting events are supported on a national basis, and generate considerable personal emotions among the relevant supporters. Sponsors are identified with whatever they sponsor, and as sponsorship is a visible and positive support of the event, the public who follow that sport become aware of the sponsor in a different and more personal way. Sponsorship may not produce dramatic improvements in business for the sponsor, but nor does any other form of media advertising.

Q3: What will sponsorship cost?

A3: Worthwhile sponsorship with a high public profile will not be cheap, but there is no general rule which states that for so much funding you get so much exposure or value from a given sponsored party. Sponsorship can eventually cost whatever you are prepared to spend. The sponsored party will agree a fee with you, but the added cost of marketing depends upon your budget. Always assume for safety that the real cost will be greater than projected cost, and have a suitable contingency built into your budget. However, compared with TV advertising, the overall cost of sponsorship in the right circumstances could be significantly greater value for money. If the sponsored event (such as a top snooker tournament) is also given significant TV coverage, the cost effectiveness of the sponsorship is even greater.

Q4: What will I get out of sponsorship?

A4: The purpose is to achieve media exposure, and to create a platform for product advertising and sales promotion activities. This may extend to merchandising, if your product is suitable. If media exposure is your prime aim, then choose an event which will have TV coverage agreed for it. At that level, the event will be important and prestigious to warrant that attention, and so the cost of sponsorship will be pitched accordingly. Single events or annual events have a limited period of public interest, whereas a seasonal sponsored party (such as a football team) has a much longer period. Again, the question of cost is a key factor in the choice.

Q5: What are a sponsor's responsibilities?

A5: Apart from the sponsorship fees to be paid, or services or products to be provided by the sponsor, the sponsorship agreement will set out any further obligations relating to the event itself. These will depend mainly on what kind of event it is, and may include advertising the event, providing trophies, and administrative support on an event committee. (See chapter four.).

Q6: What are the sponsored party's obligations?

A6: Primarily, the sponsored party's obligations are to hold the event as contracted, and to grant the promotional rights to the sponsor as set out in the sponsorship agreement. It should use its reasonable endeavours to ensure that the event is staged as intended, and that if the sponsor needs any assistance within the exercise of the sponsorship rights, it is provided with it. (See chapter five.)

Q7: Is sponsorship tax effective?

A7: The tax ramifications of sponsorship are dealt with in chapter eight. As sponsorship is a marketing and promotional activity, provided that there is a reasonable connection between the business of the sponsor and the sponsored activity, it should be as tax deductible as any other form of promotion.

Q8: Which is better: sponsorship or endorsement?

A8: They are different means of appealing to consumers, and depend upon which product the company is promoting. Endorsement is the personal recommendation by a personality of a product, usually one with which he is associated in his sport or other activity. Leisure and sports goods are therefore more likely to benefit from endorsement, as the promotion is aimed at the sector of people who participate in that activity. Sponsorship can relate to any activity, so the choice is wider. Endorsement rights are granted for a year or for a greater period; sponsorship can be of one event where the marketable interest in it may only extend over a few weeks, or even less. Sponsorship or endorsement may seem to be trendy, but it is a serious commercial decision to be taken, and in a manner most suitable to the promotion of the particular product.

Q9: How can ambush marketing be controlled?

A9: Where a company which is not an official sponsor of an event associates itself with an event in an unofficial capacity, this is known as ambush marketing. It may occur where a party buys up advertising or sponsorship time during or around the broadcast of the event; buys billboard advertising around the event venue; carries out promotions which falsely imply a link with the event; gives away free samples or products to spectators if they are approaching the event venue.

The ramifications of ambush marketing are loss and damage to both the sponsor and the sponsored party. The risk of ambush marketing is enhanced in relation to new events, or those which take place in public arenas. As there are no proprietary right in an event as such, the ability to prevent ambush marketing rests on:

(a) the extent to which the identifying features of an event have been registered as trade marks or are protected by copyright (see, for example, *F.A. v. Trebor Bassett* and *Panini v. Merlin* cases—the first case denied trade mark protection to the Three Lions logo which appeared on collector cards which featured England players in their England kit. The latter case, on the other hand, held that Merlin was breaching Panini's copyright by reproducing the team strip and emblems on its football stickers);

(b) the use of an effective contract with the sponsored party to ensure that they do not grant conflicting rights to competitors, and take all adequate steps to control access to the environment in which the event takes place.

Q10: How can I ensure that my merchandise is not sold at the wrong price?

A10: Price fixing is unlawful. The Resale Prices Act 1976 prohibits the supply of goods on the condition that the retailer sells the goods at a minimum price, or to discriminate against retailers on the basis of price charged. The Office of Fair Trading has powers to take action against such resale price maintenance. However, there is nothing to prevent you stating a recommended retail price.

Q11: What sort of insurances are available to protect against risks associated with sponsorship?

A11: There are four main types of insurance which should be considered in relation to any sponsorship.

(a) Liability insurance—public liability insurance should always be considered in relation to potential claims by members of the public for damage to person or property which might arise whilst attending an event. Errors and omissions insurance can cover negligence on the part of persons in a position of responsibility such as umpires. Product liability insurance should be sought in relation to products supplied to events and merchandising. Employers liability insurance is compulsory for all private company employers.

(b) Buildings and contents insurance may be applicable depending on the type of event.

(c) Personal insurances, such as travel, life, medical expenses and personal accident insurances, may be appropriate for the benefit of individual sports persons.

(d) Cancellation and curtailment insurance should be considered to guard against contingent events such as bad weather, strikes, etc., which could lead to cancellation or curtailment of an event and loss to both parties. Insurance against legal expenses and consequential loss caused by business interruption may also be appropriate.

Example Agreements

This Appendix contains example agreements in connection with sponsorship, endorsement and merchandising. Their contents and layout are not an exhaustive or comprehensive list of relevant clauses. Brevity and clarity are advantages, provided the agreement contains all that is needed. However, if the deal is complicated then a detailed and lengthy agreement may be necessary. As with any legal contract, these combine the financial and commercial terms which are negotiated between the relevant parties, and so each individual contract will have different matters to be incorporated into it. Therefore, these examples have been drafted on a wide basis, to try to refer to the most important aspects which are likely to be the subject of negotiation within that kind of deal. They have been devised to provoke thought and indicate a viable structure, rather than to be used as the last word in draftsmanship.

In every agreement there are "boiler plate" clauses, *i.e.* those of a nature common to most agreements and which do not depend on who the parties are, or what the agreement is about. These are set out in the Sponsorship Agency Appointment Agreement from clause 10 onwards. They are not repeated in the subsequent examples, but are brought in by the note "[Insert standard clauses]". The standard clauses on termination and *force majeure* may need to be adapted to the particular deal.

At the end of each example agreement is a commentary on specific clauses in the example which may be adjustable, or which may be affected by the negotiations for that agreement. The substantive clauses are not to be taken as being "standard" and therefore strongly recommended; the whole agreement is an example to be considered. The same clause which is set out in different example agreements may be differently worded. This is to show slightly different approaches to the point and to demonstrate that the person who drafts the agreement does not have to be hide bound in the wording of it. Through experience much the same wording is used for common clauses, but it is not necessary, providing that any freestyle drafting is clear, unambiguous, and sets out exactly what both parties mean.

SPONSORSHIP AGENCY APPOINTMENT AGREEMENT

THIS AGREEMENT is made the [   ] day of [   ] 19[   ] BETWEEN [   ] of [   ] (hereinafter called the Client) of the one part and [   ] of [   ] (hereinafter called the Agent) of the other part.

WHEREAS

    (a) The Client is the organiser and proprietor of the events described in the First Schedule to this Agreement in respect of which the Client wishes to obtain the financial and other support of sponsors.

(b) The Agent is in the business of representing its clients in the procuring of sponsorship and as a consultant upon marketing and the Client has agreed to appoint the Agent as its sole and exclusive representative in the sponsorship activities of the Client.

NOW IT IS AGREED as follows:

1. Definitions

In this Agreement the following words will have the following meanings:

"Events" means the arts, sports and leisure events set out in the First Schedule hereto and such other Events which may be undertaken by the Client during the period of this Agreement.

"Sponsor" shall mean any person firm or corporation which shall enter into an agreement in writing with the Client for the provision to the Client of money and/or services or products in respect of a stated Event in consideration of being granted rights by the Client in connection with that Event.

"Sole Sponsor" means a Sponsor which shall have the sole and exclusive right to sponsor any specific Event.

"Primary Sponsor" shall mean any Sponsor which has acquired the primary right but not the sole right to sponsor an Event including the right to have the name of the Event contain its name or the name of such of its products or services which will be connected with the Event.

"Secondary Sponsor" shall mean a Sponsor which is granted limited rights in an Event which has a Primary Sponsor.

"Official Supplier" shall mean a manufacturer of goods or supplier of services which is granted the exclusive right to associate its product or service with the Event and to supply the Client with those products or services for the Event.

"Promotion Rights" shall mean those rights set out in the Second Schedule hereto.

"Sponsorship Fees" shall mean the gross income in money or money's worth (net of value added tax) received by the Client or by any other party on its behalf from a Sponsor in any sponsorship period and in accordance with a Sponsorship Agreement.

"Money's worth" shall mean the most economical cost or expense which would have been incurred by the Client in acquiring a product or using a service which is provided by a Sponsor whether or not such product or service was a contractual commitment under the Sponsor's Sponsorship Agreement.

"Sponsorship Agreement" shall mean any agreement in writing between the Client and a Sponsor under which the Sponsor agrees to pay the Client Sponsorship Fees.

"Merchandise Rights" shall mean the right of a party to a Merchandise Agreement to use such at the Promotion Rights as are granted by the Client to that party in connection with the manufacture and sale of the products of that party.

"Merchandise Agreements" shall mean an agreement in writing between the Client and a third party to which the Client grants Merchandising Rights in respect of stated categories of Promotion Rights and for convenience herein all references to "Sponsor" and "Sponsorship Agreement" and any rights or obligations relating thereto procured negotiated or managed by the Agent hereunder shall be deemed to refer also to Merchandising Rights and Merchandising Agreements and the rights and obligations set out herein.

2. Appointment

The Client hereby appoints the Agent as its sole and exclusive agent and representative for the purpose of procuring suitable Sponsors for the Client in respect of each of the Events and the Agent accepts such appointment subject to and upon the terms and conditions herein set out.

3. It is of the essence of this Agreement that the Agent shall provide the personal services of Mr [   ] who will be primarily responsible for supervising the business of the Client and the obligations of the Agent as set out herein provided that during his absence for any reason but of a temporary nature the Agent shall provide the personal services of such other person as the Client may accept in his place [in its absolute discretion] [which acceptance shall not be unreasonably withheld or delayed].

4. Period of Agreement

This Agreement will commence with effect from the [date hereof] [   ] day of [   ] and will remain in force for the period of [   ] years subject to termination as set out herein.

5. Agent's obligations

During the period of this Agreement the Agent will exercise its best endeavours using its skill, experience and contacts to perform the following obligations to the reasonable satisfaction of the Client and the Agent will:

(a) make known, publicise and promote the Events in its normal manner in the seeking of Sponsors;

(b) advise the Client upon all material aspects of constructing or devising the Events to enable the Agent to commercially exploit and promote the Events to attract Sponsors;

(c) procure and negotiate on behalf of the Client Sponsorship Agreements with Sole Sponsors, Primary Sponsors and Secondary Sponsors in that order of preference for the sponsorship of the Events;

(d) procure and negotiate agreements with other parties for the marketing, exploitation and commercial use of the Promotion Rights subject only to any limitation thereon due to prior rights having been granted to Sponsors under Sponsorship Agreements;

(e) procure and negotiate on behalf of the Client agreements with Official Suppliers for the supply of goods or the provision of services to the Client for the benefit of an Event each such Official Supplier to be limited to one exclusive category of goods or services unless the Client shall otherwise agree.

(f) on behalf of the Client supervise the due performance of all Sponsorship Agreements Official Supplier Agreements and Promotion Rights Agreements by the respective other parties thereto.

[NOTE: The following clause is on the basis that the Agent runs the commercial side of the Client's business, relating to sponsorship and rights exploitation, and that it receives all the fees and income, and accounts to the Client accordingly].

6. Accounting procedures

During the period of this Agreement the Agent will receive on behalf of the Client all monies which are due from any Sponsor or any other party under any agreement entered into by the Client hereunder and in respect thereof the Agent will:

(a) Receive all such money into a separate bank account nominated "[Client] Trust Account" which shall be a deposit account with the interest thereon accruing to the benefit of the Client, and the Agent undertakes not to pay into that account any money which is not the property of the Client and not to make any payments out of that account except as authorised under this Agreement.

(b) Within 21 days after the end of each [month] [quarter] give the Client a detailed statement of all money received by the Agent within that previous [month] [quarter] and all payments made during that period to or on behalf of the Client and after deducting all commissions and expenses due to the Agent during that period the Agent shall pay to the Client the balance remaining on that statement.

(c) On each accounting date also inform the Client of any failure of any contracting party to make full and timely payments under its contract so that in consultation with the Agent the Client can decide what is the best method of resolving the difficulty.

(d) (i) Maintain separate and full books of account in respect of all monies received or paid on behalf of the Client and upon giving not less than 14 day's prior notice in writing the Client or its properly authorised representative shall be entitled to inspect such accounts and take copies thereof but not more frequently than once in each calendar year.

 (ii) In the event of there being a discrepancy in the accountings from the Agent which are found upon any such inspection to be more than 5 per cent less than the correct amount due to the Client under the accounts which are the subject of the audit the reasonable cost of the inspection to the Client will be paid by the Agent together with the amount of the under payment.

(e) Upon the termination of this Agreement the Agent will make up the accounts as at the end of the then current [month] [quarter] and at the same time as submitting them to the Client it will return to the Client all of the invoices, payment slips and other third-party payment and accounting documentation relating to all such contracts, together with any further relevant or necessary information or documentation reasonably required by the Client to complete the accounting records handed over to the Client by the Agent.

(f) Thereafter, for so long as the Agent is entitled to receive commission on any contract procured by it during the period of this Agreement the Client will provide the Agent with a [monthly] [quarterly] accounting statement of such commissions due and shall pay such amounts to the Agent.

(g) Maintain all VAT records which may apply to all receipts and payments related to all sponsorship income and disbursements dealt with by the Agent.

7. Contract negotiations

(a) The authority of the Agent to represent the Client in accordance with this Agreement is limited to seeking potential Sponsors and other contracting parties and it is not empowered (and it undertakes not) to make any representation offer or commitment on behalf of or to pledge the credit of the Client without the Client first having approved thereof in writing.

(b) If the Client receives any inquiry from a potential Sponsor it will direct that inquirer to the Agent and the Agent will undertake all negotiations with third parties relevant to this Agreement in accordance with the following terms:

   (i) The Agent will first consult with the Client upon all offers received by the Agent or procured by it and the Client will decide whether such party is suitable and whether the initial proposals made by them (if any) are acceptable in principle.

   (ii) For any inquirer, the Agent and the Client will agree what are the minimum commercial and financial terms which will be acceptable to the Client, and the Agent will undertake negotiations with the inquirer accordingly and (where appropriate) the Agent will ask for and take up such business and other references as the Agent considers desirable or the Client may request.

   (iii) When those negotiations have been concluded in the sense that the inquirer, has indicated that the terms offered are agreed by the inquirer, then the Agent will consult with the Client thereon to see if the deal as a whole is acceptable to the Client.

   (iv) The Client's decision will be given by the Agent to the inquirer and if it is to proceed then the Agent will be requested to prepare the contract and to finalise the negotiations accordingly.

   (v) When the final version of the contract is approved by the Client it will be executed by the Client and the inquirer and exchanged, together with any payment which may be due from the inquirer on signing the contract.

(c) During the period of contractual negotiations the Client will have the right to be in direct communication at any time with the inquirer to discuss the operative needs and wishes of both parties in respect of the marketing possibilities of the relevant Event and any other appropriate matter provided that the Client will keep the Agent informed of any matter which may be pertinent to the negotiations being conducted by the Agent with the inquirer.

173

8. Agent's commission

(a) In consideration of the Agent procuring sponsorship and other offers for the Client and negotiating and managing the Sponsorship and other agreements entered into by the Client pursuant to the activities of and procured or negotiated by the Agent during the term hereof the Agent in accordance with this Agreement, the Client agrees to pay to the Agent the following commissions upon the income derived from all such agreements:

    (i) [   ] per cent of all Sponsorship Fees received by the Agent or the Client or by any party on the Clients' behalf and paid by a Sponsor;

    (ii) [   ] per cent of the gross fees (net of VAT) paid by any party appointed as an Official Supplier;

    (iii) [   ] per cent of all royalties or other income (net of VAT) received from the granting of Merchandising Agreements or any other agreement entered into for any other use or exploitation of the Promotion Rights.

(b) The commission payable to the Agent under this Agreement includes the remuneration due to the Agent in respect of all management and supervisory activities undertaken by it in respect of all such agreements.

(c)   (i) The Client will not be responsible for any of the expenses incurred by the Agent at any time or for any purpose hereunder unless it is an unusual expense which the Agent would not have incurred ordinarily and which the Client has first approved in writing.

    (ii) If the Agent incurs any minor expenses (being less than £[   ] per item) for and on behalf of the Client as a convenience and which would otherwise have been properly an expense payable by the Client, then the Agent shall be reimbursed those expenses upon providing the Client with the receipt and satisfying the Client that the expense was reasonably incurred and that it is liable for that expense.

(d) After the expiry of this agreement [the Agent will be entitled to receive commission upon the income received by the Client from all such agreements for the remainder of the original or initial period of the relevant agreement but not for any extension of the period of such agreement but the commission rate shall be reduced by [50] per cent to take account of the fact that the Agent is no longer managing the relevant agreement or the Event].

[Alternative 8(d): The Agent will be entitled to continue to receive its commission on the income derived from all such agreements at the full rate of commission but only for the next following [year] of the relevant agreement.]

(e) Accountings will be made by the Client to the Agent in accordance with Clause 6(f).

(f) The commission rights of the Agent under this Clause will be subject to the terms of Clause 10(c)(iii).

9. Intellectual property rights

(a) The Agent acknowledges that any and all copyright trade mark rights, goodwill and other rights in the nature of intellectual property rights in the Promotion Rights and any other matter referred to in Sponsorship and other agreements is the sole property of the Client (the Property Rights).

(b) The Agent will ensure that in all Sponsorship and other agreements the Property Rights shall be protected so far as they can reasonably be in connection with the activities of the other party.

(c) If the Agent becomes aware that any of the Property Rights are being infringed by any party it shall notify the Client promptly in writing and if required to do so will advise the Client on the most effective way of preventing such infringements.

10. Termination

(a) Either party may terminate this Agreement by [3] months prior written notice or forthwith by giving written notice to the other party if that other party:

(i) remains in breach of a material obligation under this Agreement for more than [21] days after the injured party has given the breaching party a written notice specifying the breach and requiring its remedy; or

(ii) enters into liquidation or any composition with its creditors, or has a resolution passed to wind up (except for amalgamation or construction) or has a receiver or administrator appointed over all or any part of its assets; or ceases permanently to trade or threatens to do so;

(b) The Client will be entitled to terminate this Agreement by giving the Agent written notice in writing if the services of Mr [   ] as referred to in Clause 3 cease to be provided by the Agent to the Client and the Agent is unable within [3] weeks of such cessation to provide an alternative person acceptable to the Client [at its absolute discretion] [such acceptance not to be unreasonably withheld or delayed.]

(c) Upon expiry or termination of this Agreement the following shall be done:

(i) the terms of clause 6(e) shall apply;

(ii) the Agent will arrange an organised hand over to the Client of all then current matters relating to any Event and any contract which is currently being discussed or negotiated with another party;

(iii) the accounting for commission by the Client to the Agent will be in accordance with Clause 8(d) except that if the Client has properly terminated this Agreement in any of the circumstances referred to in Clause 10(a) then the Agent will only be entitled to its commission on Sponsorship Fees of the Client received within the next [month] [quarter] following that in which the termination is effective.

(d) Termination of this Agreement howsoever will not affect any rights or obligations of either party which have accrued as at that date.

11. Waiver

If a party waives any breach by the other party that will not be deemed to be a waiver of any other breach whether or not of a similar nature. For the purposes of this sub-clause a party will be deemed to have waived a breach if in the full knowledge thereof no action is taken against the breaching party in respect thereof within [12] weeks after becoming aware of the breach.

12. Confidentiality

Each party agrees with the other that it will maintain as confidential and will not make any unauthorised use of any private or confidential information about the other party and its business or its private and financial affairs, as the case may be.

13. Assignment

Neither party shall be entitled to assign the benefit of this Agreement or any of its obligations hereunder to any other party without the prior written consent of the other party which may be withheld in its absolute discretion.

14. Notices

Any notice to be given under this Agreement shall be in writing and to be effective shall be delivered or sent by recorded delivery to the addressee at its registered office. Such notice shall be deemed to have been received within 48 hours after the date of posting.

15. Entire Agreement

(a) This document contains the entire agreement between the parties and any prior representation statement or assurance which is not set out herein will not be effective.

(b) Each party agrees and confirms that there is no representation or statement upon which they have relied in entering into this Agreement and which is not set out herein.

(c) This Agreement may only be modified by a written instrument signed by both parties.

16. Force majeure

Neither party will be deemed to be in breach of any of its obligations if prevented from carrying them out due to circumstances beyond their control provided that:

(a) if it is possible to achieve the purpose of the obligation in any other reasonably expedient manner the breaching party will do so;

(b) as soon as the preventing circumstances cease to apply the breaching party will promptly fulfil any outstanding part of the obligation;

(c) the parties will co-operate to minimise any adverse consequences during the period of the intervening *force majeure* circumstances;

(d) if the *force majeure* event continues for more than [3] months either party may terminate this agreement by written notice to the other.

17. Schedules

Any Schedule or attachment hereto shall be deemed to be incorporated herein provided that if there shall be any conflict between the terms of this Agreement and any schedule or attachment then this Agreement shall prevail.

18. Applicable law

This Agreement shall be construed and enforced in accordance with the Laws of England and the English High Court will be the court of competent jurisdiction.

19. Invalidity

If any part of this Agreement is found to be invalid due to the application of any U.K. or EEC law or legal principle then that invalid part will be deemed removed from this Agreement and the parties agree to use their best endeavours in good faith to achieve the same objective by a lawful means.

[20. Legal advice

Both parties confirm they have taken legal advice on the construction obligations and consequences of the terms of this Agreement which affect them and that they are fully understood and agreed.]

21. Clause headings

The headings to the clauses are for convenience only and are not to be taken into account in the interpretation of any part of this Agreement.

IN WITNESS whereof the hands of the parties have been hereunto affixed the day and year first above written.

The First Schedule

Description of the Events

The Second Schedule

The Promotion Rights

Note: These will differ depending on the Event, but the following are included for possible reference. Those applicable should be described in reasonable detail:

1. The right to be the Sole Sponsor, the Primary Sponsor, a Secondary Sponsor, or an Official Supplier in respect of the Event, as the case may be.

2. The marketing and merchandising of the Event name and logo.

3. The granting of rights to have stalls or display facilities in the Event premises to promote products.

4. The negotiation of TV and radio rights.

5. The provision of hospitality facilities.

6. The publication of official books or the making of authorised TV or video documentaries.

7. The provision (by Sole or Primary Sponsors) of trophies.

8. The creation, recording and exploitation of an official event song.

SIGNED FOR AND ON BEHALF OF
[the Client] Limited
in the presence of:

SIGNED FOR AND ON BEHALF OF
[The Agent] Limited
in the presence of:

Comments using clause numbers

1. "Sponsorship Fees" in this example include "money's worth", where goods or services are provided, as well as or instead of cash, for the purposes of calculating the agent's commission. If their value is significant, the client will have to find the commission from other resources, which might of itself affect the amount of sponsorship cash required. An alternative is to have commission payable only on cash payments.

2. "Promotion rights" will consist of whatever the event can provide by way of facilities and marketing opportunities. These will differ according to the kind of event.

3. If the client has only appointed the agent because of a key man there, this clause will enable the client to ensure that it is not left with an agent it does not know or like if the key man moves job. Unless the key man is the owner of the agency, such a key man clause is not popular because it puts a substantial power in the hands of an executive. If the key man leaves the agency the client will be entitled to terminate its agreement with the agent. Subject to any restrictive covenant contained in the executive's service contract he can open his own agency and take on the client as his first client.

4. The agency period should be looked at from two points of view, such as how long a sponsorship period will the client get with a major sponsor; and what sponsorship management activities is the agent to be asked to do? This also has an effect on clause 8 (commission).

5. Is the agent's job just to find sponsors, or will it additionally negotiate all deals, and manage the operation of all agreements?

6. For a single sponsor of one event the money should go direct to the client. If the client is a sports association supported by an industry of sponsorship and merchandising, a professional manager may collect and account for income, especially if it is to be paid in different directions.

7. This depends on whether the agent will manage the negotiations, or whether the client would prefer to. In practice they would consult and co-operate closely.

8. There are two aspects of commission rates: those applying during the agency agreement, and those payable afterwards, while those sponsorship and other agreements continue. There are no absolute rules as to what the commission rates will be.

9. These will normally apply to copyright material, protectable logos, trade marks and the goodwill generated by the event.

10. Being an agent, and having the client rely on the agent for a measure of success, makes agency a personal business. A clash of personalities is not a normal ground for termination. This may be taken care of by the key man provision. The major bone of contention arises from the concept that if the agent goes bust, or the agreement is terminated for good reason by the client, why should the agent (or its liquidator) continue to benefit indefinitely?

MERCHANDISE AGREEMENT

THIS AGREEMENT is made the [   ] day of [   ] 19[   ] BETWEEN [   ] of [   ] (hereinafter called the Licensor) of the one part and [   ] (hereinafter called the Licensee) of the other part.

WHEREAS the Licensor is the organiser of the [sporting] event known as [   ] (hereinafter called the Event) and is the proprietor of the marketing and merchandising rights in the name and image of the Event.

NOW IT IS AGREED as follows:

1. Definitions

In this Agreement the following words will have the following meanings:

"The Territory" shall mean [   ].

"The Products" shall mean [   ].

"The Rights" shall mean the right to manufacture, distribute, promote and sell within the Territory the Products which contain or upon which are exhibited the Logo.

"The Logo" shall mean the name of the Event and the official Logo connected therewith as set out in the schedule hereto.

"The Term" shall mean the period commencing on the date hereof and terminating on the [   ] unless previously terminated as set out herein.

2. Grant of rights

(a) In consideration of the Licensee paying the royalties to the Licensor and observing and performing all of its other obligations hereunder the Licensor hereby grants to the Licensee exclusively the Rights within the Territory during the Term.

(b) The Licensor undertakes not to grant to any other party any exercise of the Rights within the Territory during the Term.

3. Intellectual Property

(a) The Licensor warrants that the Logo is the sole property of the Licensor in the Territory and that so far as it is aware the Logo does not infringe the rights of any third party.

(b) The Licensor confirms that the Logo is [not] the subject of a trade mark registration or application within [the Territory] in Class ( ) under number ( ).

4. Use of Logo

(a) All uses of the Logo upon the Products will be in accordance with the terms of this Agreement and no modification may be made to any part of the Logo which shall always be used in the format set out in the schedule hereto.

(b) If the Licensee becomes aware of any unauthorised use of the Logo within the Territory it will promptly notify the Licensor in writing with appropriate details.

(c) No other logo device or wording will be used on any of the Products together with the Logo except with the prior written approval of the Licensor.

5. Approval of Products

(a) The Licensee will submit to the Licensor for approval samples of each version of the Products which contain the Logo and (where applicable) their packaging and any intended advertising and promotion material which will contain or refer to the Logo, such samples to be of the same quality of the Products which is intended to be sold.

(b) The Licensor shall notify the Licensee within [21] days whether approval is given and any modifications which may reasonably be required to ensure the proper depiction of the Logo and the quality of the Products.

(c) If any new Products are to be made or produced by the Licensee during the Term or if the design of the Products will be changed significantly whereby the use of the Logo or the quality of the Products is modified then new samples must be submitted to the Licensor as in (a).

(d) Failure by the Licensor to notify the Licensee of approval in time will [not] be deemed to be approval.

6. Quality Control

The Licensee undertakes that all items of the Products:

(a) will conform in all respects to the quality of the samples submitted to the Licensor for approval and which are approved by the Licensor and (where applicable) will conform to any statutory or other regulations on safety of materials or design or otherwise within the Territory and the Licensee will supply the Licensor with [two] samples of each of the finished Products as manufactured for sale to check their standards of quality;

(b) will not breach third-party copyright, trade mark, design rights or any other rights in any respect;

(c) will not be defective in workmanship or materials and will not be constructed of dangerous materials or those materials which are not suitable for the Product in relation to its intended or reasonably anticipated use.

7. The Licensee shall take out adequate product liability insurance naming the Licensor as an additional insured on the policy and shall indemnify the Licensor from any claim, loss, damage, expense or liability arising therefrom or from any breach of any obligation of the Licensee set out in this Agreement.

8. Sales

(a) The Licensee will use its reasonable endeavours to promote and sell the Products within the Territory throughout the whole of the Term.

(b) If the Licensee has not commenced sale of commercial quantities of the Products within [   ] months after the date hereof, then the Licensor shall be entitled to terminate this Agreement forthwith by written notice.

(c) The Licensee will not distribute or sell the Products outside the Territory nor will it sell them to a third party within the Territory who the Licensee is aware (or ought reasonably to be aware) intends to distribute or sell those Products outside the Territory.

(d) The Licensee shall ensure that all Products shall retain at all times the same quality as the samples approved by the Licensor and shall promptly take all steps necessary to remedy any failure to achieve such level of quality, and shall not distribute or sell any articles of the Products which are not in accordance with the approved quality standards.

9. (a) The Licensee at the time of submitting the Products to the Licensor for approval will notify it of the proposed wholesale price thereof from the Licensee to third parties or the retail price direct to consumers (as the case may be), and the Licensee undertakes to notify the Licensor of any significant changes therein when commercial quantity sales commence.

(b) Subject as set out herein the Licensee shall be entitled to sell the Products howsoever it decides provided that the Licensor is accurately accounted to for royalties on sales and Provided that if any of the Products are sold by mail order or under any other promotional schemes the Licensee undertakes to comply with all legal regulations applicable thereto and with any applicable Codes of Practice issued by the Advertising Standards Authority or any other appropriate body.

10. If the Licensor requires reasonable quantities of the Products for its own purposes and not for onward sales or distribution the Licensee agrees to supply such Products on a cost basis royalty free.

11. Royalties

The Licensee will pay to the Licensor royalties at the rate of [   ] per cent calculated on the net invoice value from the Licensee of sales of the Products subject to Clause 9(a) and excluding VAT or other sales tax. If any cash discount is given by the Licensee otherwise than in the normal and proper course of business on an arm's-length basis to a party unconnected with the Licensee or the Licensee's shareholders or directors the royalty will still be calculated upon the proper full invoice price which should have applied before the discount.

12. Advances

On the execution of this Agreement the Licensee will pay to the Licensor the sum of U.S. $[   ] as a [non-] refundable advance against the royalties to be paid by the Licensee hereunder.

13. Accounts

(a) The Licensee will render accounts of sales of the Products to the Licensor within 30 days after each [Quarter Day] [June 30 and December 31] in each year and within 30 days after the termination of the period referred to in clause 17(b) together with payment by [banker's draft] for the amount due to the Licensor after recoupment of outstanding advances.

(b) All accounting statements will show the number of items sold the invoice price and any other material details to enable the Licensor to check the validity of the accounts.

(c) All payments to the Licensor hereunder will be made in [£ Sterling] [U.S. $] [at the exchange rate calculated at the due date of payment or the actual date of payment, whichever is more favourable to the Licensor].

14. The Licensee undertakes to:

(a) Maintain accurate books of account in respect of all quantities of the Products which have been manufactured and all sales of the Products and to make the accounts available for a period expiring 12 months after the termination of this Agreement to take account of the sell-off period referred to in clause 17(b) and of the rights of the Licensor under clause 14(b) below.

(b) Permit an authorised representative of the Licensor to examine the accounts of the Licensee not more than once each year and within 12 months after the termination of this Agreement upon the Licensor giving the Licensee not less than 14 days' prior written notice of its intention to make such an inspection.

(c) If such an inspection indicates that the Licensee has under accounted by [5] per cent or more overall up to the inspection date then it will pay the Licensor the balance due and any interest thereon and the reasonable costs incurred by the Licensor in connection with the inspection.

15. (a) If there are currency transfer restrictions in the Territory the Licensee shall notify the Licensor promptly in writing and will open a separate bank account in the name of the Licensor and will pay into it all sums due to it arising within that Territory.

[(b) If the Licensee is obliged by law to deduct a withholding tax on royalty remittances abroad it will provide the Licensor with a valid tax deduction certificate to enable the Licensor to obtain the benefit of any relevant double tax convention.]

16. Interest at the rate of [   ] per cent per annum over [   ] Bank base rate from time to time calculated on a daily basis will be charged on all overdue royalty accounts from the date due to the date of payment.

17. Effects of termination

(a) Upon termination of or the expiry of this Agreement the Licensee shall forthwith cease manufacturing the Products and within [21] days thereafter the Licensee shall notify the Licensor in writing of the level of all existing stocks of Products in its possession and under its control.

(b) The Licensee shall be entitled for [90] days after termination on a non-exclusive basis to sell off existing stocks which sales shall be accounted for to the Licensor hereunder and any stocks then remaining will be destroyed unless the sell-off period is extended by the Licensor in writing.

18. The Licensee is an independent contractor and this Agreement does not constitute a partnership or joint venture between the parties.

[INSERT STANDARD CLAUSES]

The Schedule

The Logo

IN WITNESS, etc.

Comments using clause numbers

The licensor may be the event owner, or a company set up to separate commercial ventures from the event being sponsored so the agreement would have to be modified accordingly.

1. The territory is likely to be the United Kingdom for domestic events, but may be wider for international events.

2. The logo may only be the name of the event. If that is in a specific artistic style, a copy should be scheduled as the format to be followed precisely.

3. If there are trade mark registrations within the territory they should be described and this sub-clause modified. This is only likely to be the United Kingdom, except where the event has international connections.

4(a). The logo is known and protected as it is set out in the schedule, therefore it should not be modified by the licensee.

5. Approval may not always be practical or necessary, but the right should be there. Clause 5(d) could be for the benefit of the licensee, as if there is a long delay approval may be deemed. If the licensor wants to have changes made to what is submitted, it will have to notify the licensee in good time.

8(a). The Licensor could impose minimum sales targets and for advertising spend on the Licensee which, if not achieved, could provide a right to terminate.

8(b). As there is no time within which the licensee must provide samples to the licensor, there has to be a means of ensuring that the licensee gets going reasonably promptly. If not, the rights can be granted elsewhere.

8(c). This sub-clause could not be included for any U.K. or E.U. licensee due to the Treaty of Rome and U.K. anti-restrictive legislation. For a domestic event, granting the U.K. rights should not produce a problem so far as other markets are concerned.

11. If there are different products with different rates of royalty then set them out in a schedule.

12. The Licensor should take as high an advance as possible, if it is unsure of the trading liability of the Licensee as future accountings may leave a lot to be desired.

12 and 13(c). Outside the United Kingdom the usual currency for accounting is U.S. $ but it can be whatever is agreed.

ENDORSEMENT AGREEMENT

THIS AGREEMENT is made the [   ] day of [   ] 19[   ]
BETWEEN WIDGET GOLF CLUBS LIMITED of [   ]
(hereinafter called Widget) of the one part and PERSONALITY LIMITED of
[   ] (hereinafter called the Company) of the other part.

WHEREAS

(a) Mr X (hereinafter called the Personality) uses exclusively Widget Golf Clubs and has agreed to endorse them as herein set out.

(b) Widget is the designer and manufacturer of the Products as defined below.

(c) The Company [is wholly owned by the Personality and] has an exclusive agreement with the Personality in connection with his worldwide sporting personal services and is the beneficial owner of the commercial promotion and exploitation rights and activities relating thereto.

NOW IT IS AGREED as follows.

1. Definitions

"The Products" shall mean all of the range of golf clubs currently manufactured by Widget or which may be manufactured by Widget during the period of this Agreement.

"Widget" shall mean and include in respect of the grant of rights under Clause 2 and Clause 4(g) hereof all Widget subsidiary and associated companies, licencees and distributors throughout the Territory (as defined below) to enable Widget to exercise its rights hereunder effectively throughout the Territory.

"The Territory" shall mean [the World].

"The Rights" shall mean the grant of rights to Widget by the Company as set out in Clause 2 hereof and the obligations of the Company under Clauses 10 and 11 hereof.

"The Tournaments" shall mean those Golf Tournaments set out in the First Schedule together with any other tournaments which are added to the Schedule by mutual agreement.

"The Fee" shall mean the payments to be made to the Company under Clause 4 and the free provision of Products to the Personality by Widget under Clause 13.

"The Period" shall mean the period commencing on the date of this Agreement and terminating in accordance with clause [   ] subject to the right of Widget to extend the Period upon mutually agreed terms if the Personality is still using the Products at the expiry date of the initial Period.

2. Grant of Rights

In consideration of the payments to be made by Widget and the other obligations of Widget set out herein the Company hereby grants to Widget the following rights:

(a) Widget shall be entitled during the Period and throughout the Territory to:

    (i) use the name, image and reputation of the Personality in the promotion and advertising of the Products by any lawful and reputable means and within any media;

    (ii) use a selection of agreed photographs of the Personality in approved promotional material produced by Widget relating to the Products;

    (iii) use a selection of agreed quotations to be attributed to the Personality in any promotional material.

(b) To call for the Personality to make himself available at reasonable times to be agreed during the Tournaments (but no more than once on each occasion) and at such other times and places as may be agreed for personal interviews and promotional activities for the Products in a manner fitting to the status of the Personality.

(c) To personalise a range of the Products as the "Personality Clubs" provided that:

    (i) they are similar to the clubs ordinarily used by the Personality;

    (ii) the manufacture and sale of the clubs will only be during the Period and for 12 months thereafter.

(d) Subject to any overriding rules and regulations at all Tournaments the Personality will:

    (i) use a golf bag provided by Widget upon which is conspicuously contained the name and logo of Widget;

    (ii) use clothing accessories (such as an umbrella and wind-cheater or jersey) upon which is set out the Widget name and logo.

(e) In all other respects when it is appropriate for him to do so the Personality will use his reasonable endeavours to promote the Products and to this end Widget may submit any proposals for doing so and will give the Personality any assistance reasonably required from it in the planning and undertaking of such additional promotional activities.

3. The Company undertakes during the Period:

(a) to ensure that the Personality fulfils all of the obligations herein set out which affect him personally;

(b) that neither the Company nor the Personality will grant any rights to any other manufacturer of golf clubs conflicting with the rights granted to Widget under this Agreement;

(c) that neither the Company nor the Personality will permit actively or passively, directly or indirectly, any other such manufacturer to use the name, image or reputation of the Personality in connection with the marketing or promotion of its products.

4. Fees

In consideration of the Company providing the services of the Personality as set out herein and subject to Clause 5 Widget agrees to pay the Company the following fees and bonuses:

(a) A basic fee in each year of $ [   ] payable in advance in two half-yearly instalments on [   ] and [   ].

(b) The following sums in each year of the Period for entering all of the Tournaments payable in quarterly instalments in arrears:

First year	$[ ]
Second year	$[ ]
Third year	$[ ].

(c) The fee for each year is calculated on the basis that the Personality plays in each of the Tournaments in that year and in the event that for any reason the Personality fails to play in any Tournament then the fee for that year will be reduced by $[   ] for each such Tournament.

(d) If the Period is extended then the fees payable to the Company will be negotiated in good faith at that time.

(e) If the Personality wins any of the Tournaments in any of the years of the Period then the Company will be paid a bonus for each such win of:

First year	$[ ]
Second year	$[ ]
Third year	$[ ].

(f) If during any Tournament during the Period the Personality gets a "hole in one" [which is televised] then the Company will be paid a bonus of $[   ] [and if the hole in one is televised then the bonus will be $[   ].

(g) In the event that Widget manufactures and markets "Personality brand" Products in accordance with Clause 2(c) Widget will pay the Company a royalty on sales being [   ] per cent of net invoice value (excluding VAT and other sales tax), the accounting for which will be in accordance with Clause 12(e) below.

5. Payment of any of the fees and bonuses are conditional upon:

(a) the Company and the Personality not being in breach of any material obligation under this Agreement;

(b) the Personality using his personal items of the Products exclusively for all Tournaments and other competitions he plays during each year of the Period.

6. If Widget requests the Personality to undertake personal promotion activities for Widget under Clause 2(e) then Widget agrees to pay the reasonable expenses incurred by the Personality in doing so in accordance with a budget agreed between Widget and the Company.

7. If the law in the United Kingdom or in any other country requires Widget to deduct withholding tax from any payment due to the Company then Widget will be entitled to do so and Widget shall:

(a) Pay over the withheld amount to the relevant revenue authority.

(b) Give the Company a tax deduction certificate to enable the Company to take advantage of an appropriate double tax convention.

8. If appropriate, all payments to the Company will be subject to the additional payment by Widget of VAT on the fees and bonuses.

[**9.** All payments to the Company will be subject to any Exchange Control Regulations which may be in force when the payments become due and which arise in countries to which such regulations apply.]

10. Obligations of the Company

The Company will ensure that during the Period the Personality will not use professionally any golf clubs other than those manufactured by Widget, but this shall not oblige the Personality to use the "Personality brand" Products in preference to any other of the Products.

11. The Company undertakes that it will ensure that the Personality will perform those obligations herein set out which refer to his personal services to be provided to Widget.

12. Obligations of Widget

The obligations of Widget are as follows:

(a) (i) to agree with the Personality the basic different layouts or usages of pictorial and text advertising material containing those matters referred to in Clause 2(a) and for that purpose to submit all basic concepts to the Company for written approval which shall not be unreasonably withheld or delayed by the Company;

    (ii) if the Company has not made any written comment to Widget within [10] days after receiving any such material for approval then approval shall be deemed to have been given.

(b) To ensure that all printed material containing any of the approved concepts will comply with the approved version and that it will also comply with all relevant laws and regulations relating to the publication of advertising and promotional material and in particular that it will not be misleading or in breach of third-party rights and that it will project the Personality in a proper manner.

(c) If Widget manufactures and markets any "Personality brand" Products in accordance with clause 2(c) that all such Products will be:

(i) of the top range of the Products produced by Widget;
(ii) of the latest Widget design and personalised in a tasteful manner;
(iii) manufactured to the highest standard of materials and workmanship of any Widget Product;
(vi) packaged, distributed and sold in accordance with any description or assertion in those respects set out in the relevant advertising and promotional material relating thereto.

(d) Make payments to the Company as set out in Clause 4 hereof.

(e) In respect of any Personality brand Product marketed by Widget under Clause 2(c) and in connection with the royalties due to the Company under Clause 4(g) Widget undertakes that [subject to Clause 9] it will:

(i) Make all such payments to the Company and provide it with a supporting account detailing where the sales were made and whether the income arose under Clause 4(g) within [14] days after June 30 and December 31 in each year of the Period;
(ii) maintain accurate books of account in respect of all such sales and licences and the Company's authorised representative will be entitled by giving Widget not less than [14] days prior written notice to inspect such books of account provided that such inspection will be not more than once in each year and within [12] months after the termination of this Agreement;
(iii) pay the reasonable audit costs of the Company if the audit shows that the Company has been underpaid by not less than [5] per cent of the accountings being audited;
(iv) Pay interest at the rate of [   ] per cent on any over due payments and on any underpayments established by an audit from their due date of payment to their actual date of payment.

(f) If a licenced manufacturer of Personality brand Products is within a country subject to Exchange Control Regulations, Widget will deposit all royalties due to the Company from sales within that country into a deposit bank account in that country in the Company's name.

13. (a) Widget agrees to provide the Personality free of charge with [one] complete set of golf clubs from the Product range to the choice of the Personality in each year of the Period and will modify free of charge any Widget club to the individual specifications required by the Personality from time to time.

(b) Widget agrees that it will not disclose to any other party the details of any personalised modification it makes to any club at the request of the Personality without the prior approval in writing of the Company nor will it without such approval produce any "Personality brand" or other club utilising any such personalised modifications made for the Personality.

[INSERT STANDARD CLAUSES except as follows]

14. Assignment

Widget will not be entitled to assign this Agreement to any other party provided that:

(a) If Widget sells its worldwide right title and interest in the manufacturing and selling of the Products to an unrelated party on a full value arm's-length basis, Widget shall be entitled to assign the benefit and obligations of this Agreement provided that the purchaser/assignee enters into an agreement with the Company upon the same terms as herein set out and for the remainder of the Period.

(b) Widget will be entitled to licence the Rights to any bona fide and reputable manufacturer of the Products under a licence from Widget and to any territorial authorised licensee or distributor of the Products upon the distributor agreeing in writing with Widget to observe and perform all of the obligations of Widget set out herein in connection with the exercise of the Rights provided that Widget shall nevertheless be fully liable to the Company for any default of such licensee or distributor.

15. Effects of termination

Upon termination of this Agreement for whatever reason:

(a) Widget will stop producing any new promotional and advertising material referring to the Personality but will have a period of [four] months within which to wind down and cease publishing all such material already in the course of creation or distribution throughout the Territory;

(b) Widget will stop the manufacture of "Personality brand" Product but will have the period of [twelve] months within which Widget and its licensees and distributors may dispose of stocks of the Products existing at the date of termination;

(c) the rights referred to in Clause 15 (a) and (b) above will be on a non-exclusive basis;

(d) the Company will not be entitled to grant endorsement rights in respect of the Personality to any other manufacturer of golf clubs during the period of [six] months from the date of termination of this Agreement.

16. General

During the Period Widget will be [will not be] entitled to enter into any endorsement agreement for the Products with any other golfer.

189

The Schedules

The Tournaments referred to in Clause 4b

Personality's side letter

To Widget Golf Clubs Ltd
from the Personality.

Dear Sirs,

With reference to the Agreement: you have entered into today with Personality Limited (the Company) for my exclusive services for the endorsement of the Products (as therein defined), and as an inducement to you to do so (upon which I understand you have relied as a fundamental condition of the Agreement) I confirm and undertake as follows:

1. I have an exclusive service contract with the Company which covers the obligations of the Company to you under the Agreement.

2. The Company is fully entitled and authorised by me to enter into the Agreement. I also confirm that I have taken independent legal advice on the Agreement which I have read, fully understand and agree with.

3. I undertake that if for any reason the Company fails to fulfil its obligations to you under the Agreement, and if you give me written notice, I will promptly fulfil any such obligations personally.

4. During the Period of the Agreement I agree to use only Widget Products.

    Yours sincerely,

Comments using clause numbers

Major personalities normally use a company which contracts with third parties for the Personalities' services, for tax reasons and for convenience. If there is no company involved the contract will be personal to the Personality.

Whatever the "Products" may be, from the manufacturer's point of view they should be reasonably widely defined. From the personality's point of view, the definition will depend upon whether it is a sportsman endorsing product he actually uses, or whether it is an unrelated product, when its definition is a matter of agreement. This decision will affect several significant clauses in an endorsement agreement.

"The Period", whenever it starts, should have an end date to fit in with the conclusion of the last of the tournaments to be played in the last year of the agreement. This is not likely to be the anniversary date of the signing of the agreement.

2. The rights reflect the ability of the manufacturer to use the name and image of the personality to promote the products. This clause should be worded appropriately for the personality and the products.

4. The fee structure depends on the circumstances of the deal. For non-U.K. based personalities the usual currency is U.S. $.

9. This currently does not apply, but is inserted as a reminder that these controls have existed in hard times. They do exist in certain countries, and the obligations of

the manufacturer under clause 4(g)(ii) would be onerous to it in respect of those countries, if the safeguard of clause 9 is not available.

15. There should be a sensible winding down provision because, *e.g.* printed media advertising may be in progress for publication quite a while later.

16. Depending on the definition of products, the personality may not be prepared to have a competitor also endorsing the same product. Properly used endorsement rights can be valuable promotion for the personality. Check that this is consistent with clauses 10 and 15(d) so that there is no unreasonable restriction on the personality.

Side letter. This is the personality's personal guarantee that the company has the rights which are granted to the manufacturer.

SOLE SPONSORSHIP OF ANNUAL SNOOKER TOURNAMENT

THIS AGREEMENT is made [   ] day of [   ] 19[   ] BETWEEN
THE SNOOKER CENTRE LIMITED of [   ](hereinafter called The Company)
of the one part and WHIZZO WIDGETS LIMITED of [   ] (hereafter called
the Sponsor) of the other part.

WHEREAS

(a) The Company is the proprietor and organiser of the annual snooker
    championship held at its premises (as hereinafter defined).

(b) The Sponsor has agreed to sponsor the championship as hereinafter set
    out.

NOW IT IS AGREED as follows:

1. Definitions

"The Event" shall mean the snooker championship referred to in Recital (a).

"The Premises" shall mean the Company's premises at [   ] or such other
suitable premises at which the Event will be held.

"The Event Period" shall mean the [14] days during which the Event will be held in
each year during the month of [   ].

"The Event Title" shall mean the title "Widget Snooker Championship" or such
other title as the Sponsor shall request which shall not be unreasonably refused by
the Company.

"The Event Logo" shall mean the original device by which the Event is identified.

"The Sponsorship Fee" shall mean the sums of money referred to in Clause 3
hereof.

"The Products" shall mean such products of the Sponsor as may be agreed to be
provided by it to the Company from time to time hereunder.

"The Term" shall mean the whole of the period during which the Sponsor shall be
the Sponsor of the Event under Clause 5 of this Agreement.

"The Rights" shall mean the rights set out in the first Schedule hereto.

2. Grant of Rights

(a) Subject to and upon the terms and conditions herein set out the Company
    hereby appoints the Sponsor to be the sole sponsor of the Event and
    hereby exclusively grants to the Sponsor all of the Rights during the Term.

(b) The Company undertakes not to grant any Rights to any other party which
    will enable them to adopt the description of "Sponsor" of the Event and if
    the Company shall accept any financial or other payment or support from
    any party in respect of the Event it shall specifically prohibit that party
    from referring to itself officially or unofficially as a Sponsor of the Event

and from promoting itself or any of its products or services in association with the Event.

(c) (i) With the prior approval of the Sponsor (which shall not be unreasonably withheld) the Company will be entitled to grant "Official Supplier" status to any party for the provision to the Event of specified goods or services.

   (ii) No Official Supplier will be appointed whose products or services are competitive with the business or products of the Sponsor or which are in any related or similar field of activity even if not directly competitive.

   (iii) No more than [two] Official Suppliers shall be appointed so as not to dilute the value of the marketing opportunities of the Event for the Sponsor.

   (iv) Subject to (ii) and (iii) above, the grant of Rights by the Company to any Official Supplier shall be submitted to the Sponsor for approval which shall not be unreasonably refused or restricted by the Sponsor.

3. Sponsor's obligations

In consideration of the Grant of Rights by the Company to the Sponsor and the Company performing its obligations herein set out the Sponsor agrees to do the following things in each year of the Term:

(a) To pay the following sums of money:

   (i) The initial sum of £[   ] towards the cost of the Company staging the Event at the Premises to be paid as to [75] per cent upon the Sponsor being satisfied that the entry list of participants for the first elimination round of matches has been filled from those who are eligible to enter the Event but no more than [   ] weeks prior to the start of the Event and [25] per cent within [seven] days after the completion of the Event.

   (ii) The total sum of £[   ] in prize money and bonus money as set out in the Second Schedule hereto, the payment of which shall be made directly by the Sponsor to the winner and the runner up at the presentation of the Trophy and the payments due to any qualifiers up to the final match will be made to the Company no later than seven days prior to the start of the Event for payment by the Company to the appropriate qualifiers as they are knocked out of the Event.

   (iii) The further sum of £[   ] within seven days after the conclusion of the Event, conditional upon the Company obtaining not less than [   ] hours' national television coverage of the Event, while it is being held in any year, and if that coverage is reduced for any reason then the further sum will be reduced by £[   ] for each hour or part thereof by which the actual coverage falls short of [   ] hours in total.

(b) To publicise and promote the Event in such manner as the Sponsor thinks fit in the course of exercising the Rights.

(c) To provide a prestigious perpetual Trophy for the Event to be known as "The Widget Challenge Cup" to be held by the winner of the Event for one year and an annual replica for permanent retention by the winner.

(d) To co-operate with the Company in the media and other promotion possibilities for the marketing exposure of the Event subject to approving any cost for which the Sponsor will be wholly or partly responsible to be incurred in excess of the payments to be made by the Sponsor under Clause 3(a) above.

4. Company's obligations

In consideration of the payments to be made by the Sponsor hereunder the Company undertakes to do the following things in connection with the Event:

(a) Provide the Premises

(i) The Company will provide the Premises for the staging of the Event for the Event Period free of charge for each year of the Term.

(ii) In the event that for any reason the Premises shall not be available for the Event in any year (which may only be due to major circumstances beyond the control of the Company) the Company will obtain other suitable premises in consultation with the Sponsor as to its suitability and as to any additional cost which may [require] [justify] an increase in the sponsorship fee provided that the Sponsor shall be entitled to reduce the Sponsorship Fee by [   ] per cent if the Company does not otherwise make the Premises available for the Event.

(iii) The Premises will be booked for the period extending to [   ] days prior to and after the Event Period to ensure that the tables seating commentary box and rest and practice areas are provided installed and tested to be in full operating order not less than [24] hours prior to the first day of play.

(iv) The Premises will not be used for any televised major snooker or billiards competition with world Ranking points within [three] months before and after the Event.

(b) Rules of the Event

Subject to (c) below, the Event shall be an open competition and the Event rules and the status of eligibility of entrants to the Event are set out in the Third Schedule hereto.

(c) Event registration

(i) If the Event becomes eligible for world-ranking point status or otherwise becomes eligible for or is required to be registered with the World Professional Billiards and Snooker Association to enable and encourage world class players to enter the Event then the Company shall so register the Event and shall ensure that it complies with all of the regulations applicable to a registered Event.

(ii) If as a result of registration of the Event or as a result of any other fundamental competition requirements affecting the Event changes need to be made in the structure of the Event and so require modification of this Agreement to comply therewith the Company and the Sponsor will in good faith negotiate upon the changes required to be made but they will be subject to the final decision of the Company.

(d) Event publicity

(i) The Company will ensure that the Event will be publicised at the earliest opportunity and that all eligible players and their representatives are provided with the Event details and entry procedures and rules to ensure that the Event is fully subscribed.

(ii) Out of the maximum entry of [   ] players not less than [   ] places will be reserved as a priority for top world-ranking players such priority of entry to be held open until [   ] days prior to the start of the Event, the validity and operation of such priority reservations being subject to the applicable regulations governing the management of the Event.

(e) Television coverage

(i) The Company confirms that it has concluded an agreement with [   ] Television for live and recorded televised coverage of the Event and a copy of the agreement is attached hereto for identification.

(ii) In the event that for any reason the Television agreement is terminated by [   ] Television the Company will use its best endeavours to obtain other television coverage of the Event to the same national extent.

(iii) Upon the expiry of the above agreement the Company will use its best endeavours to obtain an extension of it.

(iv) The failure of the Company to obtain national television coverage of not less than [ ] hours during the Tournament period in any year will entitle the Sponsor to exercise its rights under Clause 3(a)(iii) above.

5. Period of Agreement

(a) This Agreement shall be for the initial period of [   ] years and thereafter the Sponsor shall have the right to extend the period of this Agreement by further periods of [ ] years each subject only to agreeing with the Company the sponsorship funding levels as set out in Clause 3 to apply in each of those additional periods.

(b) In the event of the termination of this Agreement or the expiry without renewal of the initial period or any subsequent period the Sponsor shall be entitled to enter into an agreement with any other party for the staging of "the Widget Snooker Championship" to be sponsored by the Sponsor.

[ADD STANDARD CLAUSES]

The First Schedule

The Sponsor's Rights

1. (a) To have the Event staged and publicised as "The Widget Snooker Championship".

   (b) To provide a permanent Trophy as approved by the Company to be known as "The Widget Challenge Cup" which will be suitably inscribed by Widget and which will be awarded annually to the Winner of the Event.

   (c) To provide a replica of the Widget Trophy to be presented to and owned by the Winner of the Event in each year.

   (d) To present the Trophy and cash prizes to the winner and the runner up of the Event in each year.

2. To an allocation of [   ] free tickets for each of the days of the Event with [   ] free tickets for the finals. The tickets will be in the top price seat area.

3. The Sponsor will be entitled to use its sponsorship connection with the Event and the Event name and logo to promote and advertise its Products in any form or media.

4. The ownership of the Event title and the Event logo and all of the goodwill attached thereto shall be the absolute property of the Sponsor.

Second Schedule

Prize Money List

Third Schedule

Event Rules

Comments using clause numbers

Recital (a). The event could equally be wholly organised by an experienced party for the sponsor which does not own the premises, in which case the premises contract will be an important element, and there should be a clause in the agreement relating to it.

1. "The Event Period" This depends on what qualifying rounds will be undertaken before the competing players fill the available 32 (or however many) places. The draw for players in the initial round of the event will be contained in the event rules set out in the third schedule.

"The Rights" will to some extent depend on what the sponsor wants out of the sponsorship, and can be added to or modified accordingly.

2(c). An official supplier is only likely to be in respect of the supply of the tables to be played on, or hospitality and practice facilities. The sponsor will probably choose not to have any dilution of the marketing and promotion value available from the event.

3. Payment of the money will depend on how the expenses are incurred. An important issue will be whether the company provides the premises rent free as its contribution to the event, or whether the company's actual running cost has been calculated and is included in the sponsorship fee.

4(c). If there is any "break-away" governing body or another association set up to rival the current association then this sub-clause will need to be modified accordingly.

4(e). Television coverage is most important—the current successful snooker events are televised. Without television, snooker is not a significant spectator sport, and an untelevised match will not attract major sponsorship money.

5. For an established televised event it is almost unthinkable for the sponsor to terminate the deal, short of there being some substantial circumstances which make it impossible or uneconomical for the sponsor to continue. If the ITC prohibit any indirect advertising or promotion of cigarettes, Embassy may be prevented from continuing to sponsor their successful event. But the company cannot be committed to the sponsor for ever, and at some time it will want to check out the market rate for the event, as a basis for negotiating future fees from sponsors.

SOLE SPONSORSHIP OF FOOTBALL CLUB

THIS AGREEMENT is made the [   ] day of [   ] 19[   ] BETWEEN UTOPIA FOOTBALL CLUB LIMITED of [   ] (hereinafter called the Club) of the one part and WIDGET ELECTRONICS LIMITED of (hereinafter called the Sponsor) of the other part.

WHEREAS

(a) The Club's first team (hereinafter called the Team) is in the Second Division of the Bootlace League (hereinafter called the League) for the football season commencing in 19[   ] and the Club is desirous of obtaining sponsorship as herein set out to enable the Club to maintain and develop its Club facilities and to strengthen the Team by the acquisition of new players.

(b) The Sponsor is the manufacturer and distributor of electronic equipment which is marketed under the brand name of Widget (hereinafter called the Products) and the sponsor is desirous of sponsoring the Club as is hereinafter set out.

NOW IT IS AGREED as follows:

1. (a) Subject to and upon the terms and conditions herein set out the Club hereby appoints the Sponsor to be the sole and exclusive sponsor of the Club and the Sponsor agrees to sponsor the Club as herein set out.

   (b) The exclusive sponsorship rights granted by the Club under this Agreement extend to the United Kingdom and Europe.

2. Grant of Rights

In consideration of the Sponsor paying the sponsorship fees set out in Clause 4 hereof the Club hereby grants the Sponsor the exclusive right to all of the following rights (hereinafter called the Rights):

(a) To publicise its appointment as sponsor of the Club in any suitable manner.

(b) To use the name and logo of the Club and photographs of the Team in the promotion of the Sponsor's Products including the use of incentive promotions and competitions, the prizes for which may be free tickets to specified home games of the Team and for the winners to be invited to the Club on specified occasions at home matches to meet the Team and to receive VIP hospitality, provided that all such arrangements will have been agreed and arranged in advance with the Club.

(c) To have the name of the Sponsor prominently displayed on all programmes and other promotional material which may be published by the Club and to be acknowledged as the sponsor of the Club in all advertising relating to it and its fixtures which is undertaken by the Club.

(d) To have the Team "strip" contain the name and logo of the Sponsor as prominently as may be allowed by the ITC rules and any other applicable regulations, and to have the Team use the distinctive kit bags which will be provided by the Sponsor.

(e) At all home matches the Sponsor will be entitled to have [two] arena boards placed on the pitch perimeter in positions chosen by the Sponsor as being most effective.

(f) If the Club has an electronic scoreboard then the Sponsor will be entitled to have its sponsorship of the Club advertised on the board at the beginning of each game and at half time and at the end of each game such advertising to be in a manner agreed with the Club.

(g) At each match played by the Team at home the Sponsor will be entitled to receive [ ] free seated tickets in the top-price covered grandstand and at all away games and any league or other major competition semi-finals and finals in which the Team participates the Sponsor will be entitled to receive [ ] of the best tickets from the ticket allocation allowed to the Club for those matches.

(h) At each home match the Club will provide the Sponsor with VIP hospitality at the cost of the Sponsor for food and drink consumed [free of charge] for not more than [ ] people on any occasion such hospitality being provided within the [Director's Bar] or at such other suitable facilities agreed with the Sponsor and available upon the Club premises.

(i) To call upon the Club to provide at the reasonable request of the Sponsor a Team member chosen or agreed by the Sponsor to be available as a star personality to attend prestige functions given by the Sponsor to promote the Sponsor and its Products provided that:

   (i) any such request made by the Sponsor will only relate to a date and time suitable and convenient to the Team and to the personal commitments of the Team member;
   (ii) the Sponsor will either make arrangements with the Team member for transportation to the promotion venue and back home or it will reimburse the Team member the reasonable costs he incurs in travelling;
   (iii) the Team member will be prepared to be photographed for newsworthy or promotional purposes of the Sponsor which photographs will only be used in promotional material of a general nature referring to the Sponsorship of the Club or to the promotional event at which the photographs are taken;
   (iv) the Sponsor will not be obliged to make any payment to the Club for its authorising the Team member to make the personal appearances and the Sponsor will pay the Team member a fixed fee of £[   ] for making each personal appearance.

[(j) with the prior approval of the Club (which shall not be unreasonably withheld or delayed) the Sponsor will be entitled to enter into a personal endorsement agreement with any Team member for the promotion of any of the Sponsor's products in which case the Sponsor will pay to the Club [ ] per cent of the endorsement fee which the Sponsor pays to the Team member.]

[(k) (If the Sponsor is a drinks company) the beer-related products which the Club will provide in its private and public bars will be only the products brewed by the Sponsor.]

(l) On home match days to place at agreed sites on the Club premises banners and placards of an agreed size referring to the Sponsor and to its Products.

3. Term of Agreement

(a) The initial period of this Agreement will commence on the date hereof and will cover the football seasons for the years 19[   ] to 19[   ] inclusive and will expire on the [   ] subject as set out below.

(b) In the event that in any year of this Agreement the Club is relegated to the Third Division [due to lack of success in the season] the Sponsor will be entitled to terminate this Agreement within [30] days after the last match of the season played by the Club by giving the Club written notice to that effect.

(c) In the event that the Club has a successful season in any year and is promoted to the First Division and is still there at the end of the initial period or if the Club wins any United Kingdom or European Championship within the last year of this Agreement the Sponsor will have the right to extend the period of this Agreement for a further [two] years upon giving the Club written notice within [60] days after the last match of that Season played by the Club or within [30] days after the Club has received formal notification that it has been promoted to the First Division, whichever period will expire the later.

(d) If the Sponsor is not entitled to extend the period of this Agreement under (c) above but nevertheless it wants to do so, it will give the Club written notice to that effect within [30] days after the expiry of the initial period and (subject to receiving such notice) in the absence of the parties reaching an agreement by negotiation the Club hereby grants to the Sponsor the exclusive right to match any other offer made by a potential sponsor of the Club which will operate as follows:

(i) the Club will submit to the Sponsor in confidence the details of the highest bona fide offer received unconditionally from a potential sponsor (the Offer Notice);

(ii) the Sponsor will have [14] days within which to match that offer by giving the Club written notice of the acceptance of a new agreement for sponsorship of the Club upon the terms set out in the Offer Notice submitted by the Club under (i) above;

(iii) if the Sponsor accepts the terms of the Offer Notice and notifies the Club accordingly then this Agreement will be extended as modified by the new or substituted terms constituted in the Offer Notice, and the confirmation agreement will be signed by the parties within [14] days after the Sponsor has accepted the new terms;

(iv) if the Sponsor fails to accept the terms of the Offer Notice then the Club will be entitled to grant the Sponsorship rights to any other party provided that, if the party which submitted the terms contained in the Offer Notice does not proceed with the Club and the next bona fide offer is significantly lower than those terms, then before committing itself to the next lower offer party the Club will submit to the Sponsor a fresh Offer Notice containing those lower terms, and (ii), (iii) and (iv) of this sub-clause will operate for that fresh Offer Notice.

4. Sponsor's Obligations

(a) During each year of this Agreement the Sponsor agrees to pay to the Club the following fees (hereinafter called the Annual Fees):

First year	£[	]
Second year	£[	]
Third year	£[	].

(b) Subject to (f) below, the Annual Fees will be paid by the Sponsor in [four] equal instalments in each year commencing on the date hereof.

(c) In addition to the Annual Fee the Sponsor will pay to the Club the following bonus amounts upon the happening of any of the following events at any time during the initial period of this Agreement:

(i) £[   ] for attaining promotion to the First Division.
(ii) £[   ] for being the top team in the Second Division.
(iii) £[   ] for reaching the finals of the League Championships.
(iv) £[   ] for winning the League Championship.

It being agreed that each of the above amounts is cumulative where one or more of the events occur in any one year of this Agreement and any amount due to the Club will be paid within [14] days after the occurrence of the event which gave rise to the relevant bonus entitlement.

(d) In the event that the Sponsor becomes entitled to and extends the period of this Agreement in accordance with Clause 3(c) above then in the absence of any agreement to the contrary the payments to be made by the Sponsor to the Club will be as follows:

(i) The annual fee will be increased to:

First renewal year	£[	]
Second renewal year	£[	]

(ii) The bonus payments referred to in Clause 4(c) will be increased by [   ] per cent.

(e) In the event that the Sponsor renews the period of this Agreement in accordance with Clause 3(d) above then the payments to the Club will be in accordance with the provisions of the accepted Offer Notice.

(f) If this Agreement is properly terminated by the Sponsor at any time due to the default or breach of a material term of this Agreement by the Club, then any instalments of the Annual Fee payable after the termination date will not be payable and the only bonuses payable will be those in respect of which the event giving rise to the bonus payment has occurred prior to the date when notice of termination was given.

(g) Where applicable VAT payments will be paid by the Sponsor on all the fees and bonuses to be paid by the Sponsor provided a proper VAT invoice is supplied.

5. Sponsor's products

During the period of this Agreement the Sponsor agrees that it will provide:

(a) Free of charge to the Club such products manufactured by the Sponsor as the Club may need for its own use provided that the [trade] price value of such Products taken by the Club does not exceed £[   ] in total over the initial period of this Agreement.

(b) (Subject to Clause 8 below) to each member of the Team at [   ] per cent of the retail price thereof such products of the Sponsor as that member shall choose provided that the overall attributed value of such Products taken by each Team member shall not exceed £[   ]

6. It is a condition of the Sponsor providing items of its Product under Clause 5 that the Products are only for the use of the Club or the personal use of the Team members (as the case may be), and that such Products are not sold or otherwise disposed of within [twelve] months after delivery by the Sponsor.

7. All of the Products supplied by the Sponsor under Clause 5 will have the benefit of the standard consumer warranty relating to them in respect of maintenance and repair and the Sponsor will provide the necessary documentation accordingly.

8. The definition of Team member for the purposes of clause 5(b) shall be:

(a) the permanent First Team members as at the signing of this agreement and the full First Team and [two] substitutes as at the commencement of each season all of whom shall be confirmed by the Club in writing as holding that position;

(b) any new permanent First Team member appointed during the initial period of this Agreement.

[Note: This definition should be agreed between the Club and the Sponsor, as the Club may have a permanent squad from which the Team members for any match are picked. There needs to be a balance between how Team members are chosen, and the maximum exposure of the Sponsor over the period of the Agreement on this cut-price perk.]

9. Obligations of the Club

The Club's obligations hereunder will be to grant the Rights to the Sponsor and to do all that may be reasonably required of it by the Sponsor to enable the Sponsor to exercise those Rights fully and including:

(a) ensuring that all agreed banners, placards, arena boards and other advertising material to be placed upon or in the Club premises are not removed, defaced or damaged, and to repair any such damage where practical;

(b) ensuring that all local advertising and promotional material issued by the Club refers to the Sponsor in the agreed manner;

(c) publicising the Sponsor and its association with the Club whenever reasonably possible.

[STANDARD CLAUSES]

Comments using clause numbers

Recital (a). The fee payment clause (Clause 4) contains no reference to the Club having to spend the fees in any specific manner. Such a requirement would be very unusual unless a special sponsorship deal is for the specific purpose of raising money only for a new stand or some other nominated cause.

1(b). World rights would do no harm, but the United Kingdom and Europe are the only likely territories in which to be active.

2. The Rights will depend to some extent on what size the Club is, and whether it is known nationally or only locally.

3(c). The same comments as in 2 will apply.

4. The fee levels will depend on the level of public interest in the club. The bonus fees may need lower targets to suit the status of the club and whether it is in a national or local league.

5(b) and 8. There may be other means of enabling team members to acquire the perk of cheap product, such as for goal-scoring individuals or "man of the match" players. The difficulty is to define those who, over a period of, say, three years, are to be deemed team members for individual purchase eligibility. The squad idea may be best, it depends on the price of the products and the total amount the sponsor wants to be limited to on such a commitment.

6. If the club has good reason to dispose of any such product provided to it by the sponsor, and the sponsor agrees, then the club should be able to do so. It should not expect replacement equipment, and the sponsor may want the right to have the excess equipment returned to it, although by then it will be second hand.

PRIMARY SPONSORSHIP OF RACING DRIVER

(Where the whole financial budget is sponsored)

THIS AGREEMENT is made the [   ] day of [   ] 19[   ] BETWEEN WIDGET ENGINE TUNING LIMITED of [   ] (hereinafter called the Sponsor) of the one part and of [   ] (hereinafter called the Driver) of the other part.

WHEREAS

   (a) The Sponsor's business is [ ] and the Sponsor wishes to extend the marketing and promotion possibilities for its name image and products.
   (b) The Driver has raced for the last season in Formula Ford and has sought sponsorship which the Sponsor is prepared to provide as herein set out.

NOW IT IS AGREED as follows:

[Condition Precedent

The Sponsorship fee payable to the Driver is [75] per cent of the total amount of financial support required by the Driver in accordance with the Budget referred to in Clause 4 below, and this Agreement is conditional upon the Driver obtaining a firm written agreement with a third party (subject to Clause 6) for payment to the Driver of the balance of the Budget (such agreement to be first approved by the Sponsor as to all of its material terms which will not grant that sponsor any greater rights than those granted to the Sponsor under this Agreement) and this Agreement will become effective on the signing of that approved agreement provided that such event shall occur no later than the [   ] day of [   ], failing which this Agreement shall be deemed to be null and void.]

[*Note*: Any such condition precedent must accurately state what is agreed, and must have a specific mechanism for making this sponsorship agreement come into effect, such as delivery to the Sponsor of a copy of the signed agreement with the sponsor for the 25 per cent.]

1.   (a) Subject to and upon the terms set out herein the Driver hereby grants to the Sponsor the exclusive right to be the Primary Sponsor of the Driver.

   (b) The Driver warrants that he has not granted to any other party any rights which may be in conflict with this exclusive appointment and the Rights granted to the Sponsor hereunder and the Driver undertakes that he will not appoint any other party [except such sponsors as are contracted under the operation of the above condition precedent] to be his sponsor during the period of this Agreement nor will he grant to any other party officially or unofficially sponsorship promotional and other rights as granted herein to the Sponsor.

   (c) (i) For the avoidance of doubt, nothing in this Agreement is intended to prevent the Driver from accepting any offer of financial or other support from any source provided that any provider of goods or services is only entitled to use the title of "Official Supplier of . . .

[   ]" in its capacity as a sponsor of the Driver and in any advertising or promotion undertaken by it of such goods or services in connection with the Driver.

(ii) The identity of all "Official Suppliers" will be agreed with the Sponsor before the Driver authorises the use of such title by any party and no such authorisation will be made in respect of any party providing goods or services similar to or competitive with the business of the Sponsor.

2. Grant of Rights

In consideration of the sponsorship fees paid hereunder to the Driver and all other obligations of the Sponsor (and subject to the 25 per cent sponsor obtained under the condition precedent above) the Driver hereby grants exclusively to the Sponsor the following Rights (hereinafter called the Rights):

(a) To call itself the Sponsor of the Driver and to use that title in all advertising and promotional material of the Sponsor relating to its corporate image and any of its brand products.

(b) To use the name and image of the Driver for all of the matters referred to in (a) above and whenever being interviewed and at other appropriate times to refer to the Sponsor as being his Sponsor.

(c) To have the Sponsor's name and the name of a nominated Sponsor's product prominently displayed:

(i) on the sides and front of the Driver's racing car;

(ii) on the sides of the Driver's racing car transporter and any other support vehicles or substantial equipment used by the Driver in his racing capacity;

(iii) on the front of the Driver's helmet and on the front and back of the Driver's racing overalls and the overalls or jackets of the Driver's racing manager, mechanics and all other team personnel who attend any race practice and race meetings;

(iv) wherever else it can reasonably be displayed in consultation with the Driver for the benefit of the Driver and of the Sponsor;

(v) wherever reasonably possible when the Driver gives official interviews or authorises the publication of any biographical or promotional material relating to his motor racing activities.

(d) All such displays and uses referred to in (c) above shall be subject to any applicable regulation made by the relevant Broadcasting Authority for television coverage of motor-racing events and any national or international motor-racing governing body, but otherwise shall be in a position and of a size agreed with the Sponsor.

3. Sponsor's obligations

In consideration of the Rights granted by the Driver, the Sponsor agrees to pay to the Driver the following fees:

(a) (i) The total sum of £[   ] in accordance with the Budget referred to in Clause 4 within the first year of this Agreement payable in [monthly] equal amounts in advance [in accordance with the cash-flow requirements as set out in the Budget] (receipt of the first payment being acknowledged) subject as set out in (c) below.

(ii) The Driver acknowledges that the purpose of this Agreement is for the Sponsor to pay for or contribute to [the whole of] [75 per cent of] the projected racing costs of the Driver for the championship races set out in Schedule One hereto (hereinafter called the Races) provided that those costs are actually incurred.

(b) A bonus in respect of each of the Races:

For winning a race	£[	]
For coming second in a race	£[	]
For coming third in a race	£[	].

(c) In the event that the Driver for any reason (not being caused by the Sponsor) does not start in any Race then the amounts to be paid to the Driver subsequently shall be reduced by the sum of £[   ] per non-start provided that the sponsorship fee shall not be reduced below the amount of £[   ] in any event.

4. (a) The sponsorship fee is calculated as the amount being reasonably required to enable the Driver to be competitively equipped with a racing car and support equipment and personnel in accordance with the cashflow budget prepared by the Driver and set out as Schedule Two hereto (the Budget).

(b) The Driver confirms that the Budget has been prepared with due and careful consideration for all the reasonable anticipated expenditure together with a contingency considered to be adequate in the experience of Formula Ford racing.

(c) In the event that the expenditure of the Driver exceeds the Budget in the aggregate and therefore that the sponsorship fee in total is not adequate for the cash needs of the Driver and if the Sponsor is not prepared to increase the sponsorship fee, then the Driver may seek additional financial support but he will not be entitled to grant such supporter any sponsorship title or rights other than as an "Official Supplier" if, on a bona fide basis, the supporter justifies that status title.

(d) In the event that the sponsorship fee exceeds the ultimate expenditure of the Driver in the racing season within the period of this Agreement in accordance with the Budget then the Driver shall reimburse [50 per cent] of the excess to the Sponsor or (as the case may be) the Sponsor may rebate the final payment of the Sponsorship fee accordingly.

5. In the event that the number of Races is reduced by the [RAC] for whatever reason then the Sponsorship fee shall be reduced in accordance with Clause 3(c) and if the number of Races is increased then if the Sponsor is not prepared to increase the Sponsorship fee then Clause 4(e) will apply.

6. Driver's Obligations

The Driver agrees not to appoint to any sponsorship status any party which is or whose products are competitive with the Sponsor or its products or which are in an industry or business which is similar to that of the Sponsor.

7. If the Driver undertakes any other Formula or Series or Championship racing for sports cars or any other vehicle not being Formula Ford then he undertakes that:

(a) It will not interfere with his Formula Ford racing in respect of which the Sponsor has been granted rights under this Agreement.

(b) It will only be on a casual race basis and he will not enter any full race programme during this Agreement otherwise than Formula Ford without the prior approval of the Sponsor which shall not be unreasonably withheld or delayed.

8. (a) The Driver will maintain his racing car at all times in as competitive a mechanical and structural condition as is reasonably practical within the Budget.

(b) The Driver will maintain an adequate support of mechanics and other essential pit personnel to assist him in transporting preparing and racing his racing car.

(c) The Driver will ensure that he books in for all of the Races and uses his best endeavours to start each race and to perform well in it.

(d) The Driver agrees that without the prior approval of the Sponsor he will not drive in the United Kingdom during the period of this Agreement in any of the Races any vehicle other than his racing car upon which the Sponsor's identity logos and name are set out as agreed herein and if he does so then the Sponsor will be entitled to exercise its rights under Clause 3(c) as if such Race had been a non-start for the Driver.

(e) The Driver agrees that he will do all reasonable things proposed by the Sponsor to benefit the Sponsor and its products and he will at the Sponsor's request appear personally from time to time at substantial promotional events relating to the Sponsor and its business provided that they do not clash with any existing commitments of the Driver and that the Sponsor will pay the Driver's reasonable expenses incurred in doing so and that there will not be more than [4] such requests during the period of this Agreement or in each year of this Agreement as the case may be.

(f) The Driver will ensure that he and his mechanics and other support team wear their overalls and jackets with the Sponsor's name and logo whenever reasonably practical at race practice and on race days.

9. Period of Agreement

(a) This Agreement will commence on the date hereof and will terminate on the [   ] subject to any earlier termination as set out herein.

(b) The Sponsor will have the exclusive right to be the Primary Sponsor of the Driver for the next racing season by extending the period of this Agreement to [   ] day of [   ] 19[   ], provided that:

(i) the Driver and the Sponsor agree upon the sponsorship fee for the next racing season in accordance with a realistic budget to be prepared by the Driver and submitted to the Sponsor no more than [45] days prior to the end of the period of this Agreement;

(ii) the Sponsor will be entitled to exercise the option by written notice given to the Driver within [30] days after the submission to the Sponsor of the Budget whatever the date of its submission to the Sponsor;

(iii) The renewed agreement (except for the sponsorship fee and also except for this sub clause (b)) will have the same terms as herein contained.

[Additional termination provision:

The Sponsor will be entitled to terminate this Agreement and to make no further payments to the Driver if the Driver is prevented from driving for the rest of the season due to incapacity or any other cause beyond his reasonable control or if he should lose his RAC Competition Licence, provided that the Sponsor will pay from the Sponsorship fee all cost commitments which are non-cancellable at that date and which are included in the Budget].

[STANDARD CLAUSES]

Schedule one

[List of Formula Ford Races]

Schedule Two

[Cashflow budget]

Comments using clause numbers

If the driver is being provided with the car and back-up team, spares and equipment by a car manufacturer, this sponsorship agreement will be with that car manufacturer, but related to the driver. The sponsorship will then be joint billing, but that is no disadvantage to the sponsor. The clauses would need modification accordingly. This would apply to the higher (and therefore more expensive) levels of motor racing, where the driver ceases to be an independent owner/entrant.

Condition precedent. This may be included in the agreement or in a side-letter, and applies where the sponsor will carry the bulk of the cost of the total sponsorship fee required by the driver, but requires the driver to obtain the rest of the money from other sources. This may be a matter of cost, or a matter of principle.

2(c). This is a matter of choice. How the car, clothing and equipment depicts the name depends on good artistic design, any applicable rules, and name visibility for TV cameras.

3 and 4. The sponsorship fee features which need to be dealt with are:

(a) preparation of realistic budget;

(b) will the sponsor cover the whole of or only part of the budget?

(c) how is the sponsorship fee to be paid?

(d) will the sponsor get back/retain any part of the sponsorship fee not spent at the end of the racing season?

7. The driver should only cover one level of racing in the season, but what is to happen if he combines Formula Ford and sports-car racing? The practicalities of economics and time may prevent this, but it should be looked at.

8. This clause assumes that the sponsor is not a Formula Ford car manufacturer.

OFFICIAL SUPPLIER AGREEMENT

THIS AGREEMENT is made the [   ] day of [   ] 19[   ]
BETWEEN SUPERSTAR MARKETING LIMITED of [   ] (hereinafter called SML) of the one part and WHIZZO GADGETS LIMITED of [   ] (hereinafter called Whizzo) of the other part.

WHEREAS

(a) Event Promotions Limited of [   ] (hereinafter called EPL) is the organiser of [   ] (hereinafter called the Event) and EPL has assigned to SML the exclusive worldwide right to enter into all sponsorship merchandising and marketing agreements on behalf of EPL in connection with the Event.

(b) Whizzo wishes to avail itself of such promotional, advertising and marketing rights and opportunities on a worldwide basis.

NOW IT IS AGREED as follows:

1. Definitions

The following words will have the meanings set against them:

"The Products" shall mean [   ].

"The Marks" shall mean the logo and device which is identified in the First Schedule hereto.

"Premium" shall mean a product bearing Whizzo's trade mark and/or trade name together with any of the Marks given away free of charge or sold at a subsidised price for advertising or promotional purposes by any party (including the parties to this Agreement).

"Event Rights" shall mean the rights granted to Whizzo under Clause 2b.

"Site" shall mean the location of the Event [and shall include the stadium and press centre].

"Territory" shall mean the world.

2. Grant of Rights

SML warrants that Recital (a) is correct and that it will remain correct during the period of this Agreement and SML hereby grants to Whizzo for the term of this Agreement the Event Rights in respect of the Products as follows:

(a) Status Rights

(i) The exclusive right in connection with the Event to be designated within the Territory "Official Supplier" of the Products, and SML undertakes not to grant to any other party any Official Supplier status or any Event Rights where that party is in a business or manufactures distributes or sells products or services which are similar to or competitive with the Products.

209

(ii) The exclusive right to use within the Territory the Marks in connection with the manufacture, marketing advertising and promotion of the Products.

(b) Event Rights

(i) The exclusive right to advertise on two arena boards within the angle of the main television cameras in the Site as specified in the stadium plan set out in the Second Schedule together with any additional placard or promotional material which SML authorises Whizzo to put up around the Site.

(ii) The exclusive right to have one colour page advertisement free of charge in the official programme of the Event and Whizzo will provide the completed artwork for such advertising to SML by the [   ].

(iii) The exclusive right to have free of charge Whizzo's logo and identification as "Official Supplier" printed on official printed advertising materials of the Event such as press releases and the reverse side of tickets.

(iv) The exclusive right to have franchise and display rights for the Products at the Site and at positions set out on the plan in the Second Schedule.

(v) The right to receive [   ] free tickets within the best seating sector of the Site and Whizzo shall have the priority right to purchase up to [   ] additional tickets at face value for the Event provided that its purchase requirements are notified to SML in writing by the [   ] and all such tickets shall be used by Whizzo for hospitality and promotional purposes and may not be resold.

3. Obligations of SML

SML agrees that during the period of this Agreement it will grant or provide the following support rights to Whizzo to no less a degree than it gives to any other sponsor of the Event which has "Official Supplier" status.

(a) SML will refer to Whizzo as the Official Supplier of the Products in press campaigns in major markets organised by SML and in any TV documentary or other programme produced by or with the authority of SML relating to the Event.

(b) Where appropriate, the right to obtain from SML research reports with respect to the Event showing:

(i) the countries which have taken the television broadcast;
(ii) viewing figures and ratings on the television audiences;
(iii) an analysis of the time exposure on television of the Site advertising boards.

(c) Any additional services and research are subject to agreement with SML as to level of services and fee structure.

4. Site Boards

(a) The size of each board shall be [   ], unless there are applicable regulations which require a reduction in such size, in which case all Site boards will be proportionately reduced in size.

(b) (i) Whizzo shall submit to SML for its approval the proposed text design and layout of the Site boards within [ ] days prior to the date of the Event and SML shall advise Whizzo of its approval or disapproval within [ ] days after receipt. SML shall base its approval or disapproval of such proposed text design and layout on the regulations which govern such forms of advertising including the television regulations applicable to the Event, the colour combinations proposed and their relationship with neighbouring boards.

    (ii) Whizzo agrees to indemnify and hold SML harmless against all claims and damages arising out of any unlawful content of Whizzo's Site boards.

(c) SML shall be responsible for, and shall pay the cost of, the original production of each Site board with the approved text, design and layout and undertakes to have the Site boards produced accurately. [SML shall also be responsible for, and pay the cost of, the installation, maintenance and removal of such boards.]

5. Use of the Marks

(a) Whizzo shall not obtain any title to or any interest or licence in or to the Marks except as specifically set out herein.

(b) Any use of the Marks by Whizzo shall include the appropriate copyright notices and/or trade mark legend as instructed by SML.

(c) Whizzo shall not use the Marks in any manner which compromises or reflects unfavourably upon the good name reputation and image of SML and the Event.

(d) (i) Whizzo agrees to submit to SML for its prior written approval samples of each of the Products in respect of which Whizzo will be using the Marks including packaging materials within a reasonable time before such use is to be made and samples of the basic concepts of the major advertising promotional or other display material to be used by Whizzo in connection with the Marks a minimum of [ ] working days prior to their release to the public provided that if, commercially, the submission of such proposed Products and samples is unduly burdensome or impracticable for Whizzo then Whizzo agrees to provide to SML full photographic representations adequately depicting such Products for SML's prior written approval.

    (ii) SML agrees that it shall not unreasonably withhold or delay its approval and approval shall be deemed to have been given in the absence of SML giving Whizzo written notice of disapproval thereof within [ ] working days of receipt of such samples or photographic representations and any disapproval shall give detailed reasons to enable Whizzo to remedy the matter.

(e) SML's approval of a particular product or advertising material using the Marks in one format will extend to substantially similar uses and in any other media provided that context is not materially changed, and Whizzo may compile a manual governing various conditions of usage of the Marks by Whizzo and after such manual is approved by SML all materials which conform to its provisions will be deemed approved by SML.

6. Premiums

In order to protect SML's and EPL's contracted sponsor's exclusive association with the Event within their product or service category Whizzo Products are not to be used as premiums by third parties in connection with the distribution and sale of goods.

7. Product Supply to Event

(a) Whizzo shall provide to EPL, free of charge, agreed quantities of the Products to be used in connection with the Event [including at ceremonies, press conferences and other official events relating to the Event as well as at VIP and press areas during the Event in reasonable quantities].

(b) SML shall endeavour to make available to Whizzo other opportunities to promote the Products through the Event including (where the Products are suitable) opportunities for the presentation of gift packs to VIPs and Event officials, and/or to have display and sampling facilities in VIP and press areas.

8. Assistance by SML

To assist Whizzo in the utilisation of the rights and opportunities granted by SML hereunder. SML agrees to make staff available without additional charge to co-ordinate and supervise the communications between Whizzo and SML in the implementation of Whizzo's advertising and promotional programme relating to the Event.

9. Fees payable by Whizzo

(a) In consideration of the rights and benefits granted to Whizzo herein Whizzo shall pay to SML the following amounts (excluding VAT):

Date   Amount

(b) All amounts outstanding after their due date of payment shall bear interest at the rate of [   ] per cent per year calculated on a daily basis until the date of payment.

10. Term

(a) This Agreement shall commence on the date of the execution hereof and shall expire on [   ] unless previously terminated pursuant to the terms hereof.

(b) Upon the expiration or earlier termination of this Agreement, the Event Rights shall revert to SML and thereafter Whizzo shall not use or refer directly or indirectly to the Marks, the Event or SML with respect to the manufacture, marketing, advertising or promotion of the Products, provided that Whizzo shall have the non-exclusive right to continue the distribution and sale of the Products currently in stock for an additional [   ] months after the expiration or earlier termination of this Agreement.

[STANDARD CLAUSES]

The First Schedule

Logo and device

The Second Schedule

Stadium plan for arena boards

Comments using clause numbers

[*Note*: Because each product category which has official supplier status will have a different effect on the deal, and it may be a product or a service, it is not possible to have a general draft which can be used as a template for all needs.]

Recital EPL could equally well have been the contracting party, but having SML is to show how an appointed agent would work.

1. "Site" could be a sports stadium or a large conference complex or a theatre. References in this example relate mainly to a stadium.

2. There is no reference in this example to whether TV coverage will be a fundamental requirement. If it is, then references in prior examples can be used as a basis of drafting.

4(c). Whether SML or Whizzo pays for the site boards is a matter of agreement, and will probably depend on which of them makes the boards.

5(d). It is important to arrange for the approval system to be practical and rapid, especially where modifications to artwork have been made.

6. The use of merchandise as loss leaders or premiums debases the image of the event. Whether the possibility is real will depend on the type of product that Whizzo manufactures.

7. To justify the official supplier status Whizzo has to supply an amount of its products to the event. The limits of what is to be given will depend on what kind of products they are, and their intrinsic unit value.

9. The fee structure and level will depend on the event and the status of the official supplier.

CHARITY CONCERT SPONSORSHIP AGREEMENT

THIS AGREEMENT is made the [   ] day of [   ] 19[   ] BETWEEN GIZMO PROMOTIONS LIMITED of [   ] (hereinafter called Gizmo) of the one part and UPMARKET INSURANCE LIMITED of [   ] (hereinafter called the Sponsor) of the other part.

WHEREAS

(a) Gizmo is a promoter of concerts and other entertainment which has submitted the concept of the concert (as herein defined) to the sponsor.

(b) The Sponsor supports cultural and Arts events and has agreed to sponsor the concert.

NOW IT IS AGREED as follows:

1. Definitions

The following expressions shall have the meanings set out against them for the purposes of this agreement.

"The Concert" means the production of [opera] at Olympia for the five days commencing on the [   ] and ending on the [   ], both days being inclusive.

"The Venue" means Olympia.

"The Fee" means all sums paid by the Sponsor to Gizmo hereunder but specifically the sums set out in Clause 13 hereof.

"The Rights" shall mean the rights granted by Gizmo to the Sponsor under this Agreement.

"The Charity" means the Great Ormond Street Hospital for Sick Children.

"Net Proceeds" shall mean the balance of income received from whatever source by Gizmo arising from the Concert and/or audio visual recording of the Concert after deducting all reasonable and proper expenses incurred by Gizmo in connection with the Concert.

"ABSA" means the Association for Business Sponsorship of the Arts.

2. Purpose of Sponsorship

The purpose of holding the Concert is to raise money for the Charity and the Sponsor has entered into this Agreement on that fundamental basis and Gizmo undertakes that the Net Proceeds shall be paid to the Charity within [14] days after the last performance of the Concert.

3. Grant of Rights

(a) In consideration of the payment by the Sponsor of the Fee and of the Sponsor fulfilling its other obligations hereunder, Gizmo appoints the Sponsor to be the sole Sponsor of the Concert upon the terms and conditions herein set out.

214

(b) Gizmo warrants to the Sponsor that it is the proprietor and responsible organiser of the Concert and that it has the absolute and unconditional right to appoint the Sponsor and to grant it the Rights and Gizmo confirms that all parties connected with Gizmo in the staging of the Concert approve such appointment.

(c) Gizmo undertakes with the Sponsor that Gizmo will not appoint any other party with the title of Sponsor of the Concert without the prior approval of the Sponsor, which shall not be withheld if the proposed additional sponsor;

  (i) is of similar reputation and status as the Sponsor;
  (ii) the Concert and therefore the Charity will receive a substantial benefit from it; and
  (iii) it is not in a business competitive with or similar to the business of the Sponsor.

4. Specific Rights granted to the Sponsor by Gizmo are the right to:

(a) Promote its name as being the Sponsor of the Concert, such promotion being in any media or through any normal promotional and advertising means providing that all references to the concert will be in the correct context and that all promotional and advertising material will be in good taste and of a quality of presentation which is consistent with the standing of the Concert and the reputation and status of the Charity.

(b) Have its name prominently displayed with the title of Sponsor of the Concert on all advertising material and on the front cover of the Programme of the Concert, and wherever else publicly the Concert is referred to by Gizmo, such as in local radio advertising "spots".

(c) Have one free page of advertising in the Concert programme, provided the sponsor provides or pays for the production of the advertisement.

(d) Have [   ] free seats in the best seating area for each performance of the Concert, provided that they are used for the private benefit of the Sponsor and that they are not otherwise disposed of to the public. If the Sponsor does not take up its whole allocation of free tickets within [7] days prior to the first performance of the Concert, the tickets which are not taken by the Sponsor will be sold by Gizmo in the normal manner.

(e) Have placed at the Venue such advertisement boards and banners as the Venue proprietors will agree to and which will be provided by the Sponsor and set up by Gizmo provided that Gizmo will not be liable for damage to or loss of such boards and banners otherwise than caused by its employees.

5. ABSA Applications

(a) The Sponsor confirms that its sponsorship of the Concert represents new sponsorship of the Arts in compliance with the rules of the ABSA Scheme, and Gizmo agrees to make an application to the ABSA Scheme for an award, and the Sponsor agrees to provide Gizmo or the administrators of the ABSA Scheme with any information they require in order to satisfy the relevant criteria of the ABSA Scheme.

(b) Subject to the Rules of the ABSA Scheme, the Sponsor authorises Gizmo to make use of any ABSA award in respect of the Concert as it sees fit for the promotion of the Concert and the benefit of the Charity.

6. Gizmo's responsibilities

(a) Gizmo undertakes to hold and promote the Concert as set out herein and if for any reason (including *force majeure*) it is not possible to hold the Concert on the date referred to herein then, in the absence of the approval of the Sponsor of an alternative date (which shall not be unreasonably withheld or delayed), the obligation of the Sponsor to pay the Fee shall terminate upon the Sponsor giving Gizmo written notice to that effect, and any part of the fee which shall already have been paid to Gizmo will be fully refundable without any deduction.

(b) This Agreement is conditional upon Gizmo having signed agreements with the Venue to hold the Concert and the Concert stars, performers, musicians and other essential people all of such contracts to be in place within [40] days from the date hereof, and the Sponsor authorises Gizmo to publicise the fact that the Sponsor will be the Sponsor of the Concert.

(c) The Sponsor will be entitled to have copies of any such contracts it requires to see which will be provided promptly to the Sponsor upon such a request being made.

(d) If some but not all of such contracts have been signed within the [40] days, the Sponsor will not be entitled to terminate this Agreement provided that there is reasonable evidence (in the sole opinion of the Sponsor) that any outstanding contract will be completed in good time to enable the Concert to proceed on a timely and professional basis.

7. The Venue will be booked with enough time before and after the Concert to enable the staging and other equipment to be installed, tried and tested to Gizmo's satisfaction and to have all such equipment removed from the Venue safely.

8.   (a) Gizmo will prepare [has prepared] the budget attached hereto as Schedule One, thereinafter called the Budget, within [14] days after the date hereof to estimate as accurately as possible what the cost of the Concert in total will be and wherever possible Gizmo will get all parties connected with the Concert to provide their services free or for a nominal amount.

(b) Gizmo will maintain detailed and accurate books of account in respect of all income and expenditure (including contingent liabilities) relating to the Concert and will permit a representative of the Sponsor and of the Charity to examine all such accounts of Gizmo relating to the Concert within [six] months after the conclusion of the Concert.

9. Gizmo will be responsible for the design, creation and installation of the staging, all theatrical effects and any special effects, and the sound system for the Concert, and all other requirements necessary to enable the Concert to take place.

10. Gizmo will ensure that all risks pertinent to the holding of the Concert will be covered adequately by insurance.

11. (a) Gizmo will promote and advertise the Concert to whatever extent it reasonably considers desirable to ensure that all performances are fully subscribed.

(b) Gizmo will give the Charity a number of free seats in the best seating area which will be agreed in consultation with the Charity, and it will also consult with the Charity upon any VIP Guests the Charity would like to invite to any performance of the Concert and any hospitality which should be made available for such VIP Guests.

(c) Gizmo will agree in a letter to the Charity all of the other matters which affect the Charity such as references to the Charity as the beneficiary of the Net Proceeds of the Concert in the Concert Programme and advertising material for the Concert.

[12. Gizmo undertakes that it will not directly or indirectly promote or be connected with an Arts-related concert within [three months prior to the Concert or [one month] afterwards for the purpose only of ensuring maximum exposure for and interest in the Concert for its benefit and that of the Charity.]

13. The Sponsorship Fees

(a) In consideration of the Rights granted by Gizmo the Sponsor agrees to pay Gizmo the sum of £[   ] to support the financing of the Concert provided that for the purposes of ascertaining the Net Proceeds of the Concert the Fees will be treated as income.

[(b) (i) The Sponsor has agreed to make a contribution of £[   ] to the Charity by means of assisting Gizmo to stage the Concert which will create a much greater income for the Charity.

(ii) To enable Gizmo to finance the staging of the Concert, the Sponsor agrees to make a loan of £[   ] to Gizmo which agrees to repay the loan interest free but as a first charge out of the Net Proceeds of the Concert.]

14. (a) The fees will be paid to Gizmo as to £[   ] on the signing of this Agreement and £[   ] no later than [   ] weeks prior to the Concert and £[   ] within seven days after the last performance of the Concert in each case upon the submission of an invoice plus VAT if applicable.

(b) If the Sponsor agrees to pay any other sums in excess of the aggregate of £[   ] in Clause 13(b), such further payments shall be treated as an addition to the amount loaned by the Sponsor to Gizmo under Clause 13(b)(ii).

15. Recording of the Concert

(a) Gizmo has entered into an agreement with [   ] whereby [   ] will film the Concert for the purpose of making a television documentary film of the Concert.

(b) Gizmo has entered into an agreement with [   ] whereby [   ] will record the Concert and will release a long-playing album of the Concert.

(c) Gizmo agrees to ensure that within each of the agreements referred to above:

(i) there is a royalty or fee payable directly to the Charity from each of the relevant parties and that they have entered into agreements directly with the Charity to that effect;

(ii) in the TV, film, screen and advertising credits and on the sound album sleeve the Sponsor will be credited as the Sponsor of the Concert.

(d) Within each of the filming and the recording agreements it will be the responsibility of the film or recording company (as the case may be) to obtain all third party and performers' consents and to ensure that the regulations of any applicable trade union will be observed and complied with.

16. Sponsor's Option

If Gizmo decides to promote a series of concerts or annual concerts whether of an operatic or popular music nature in support of the Charity the Sponsor is hereby granted by Gizmo the first option to accept the Sponsorship terms applicable to them and to continue to sponsor such concerts connected with the Charity.

[STANDARD CLAUSES]

Schedule One

[The Budget]

Comments using clause numbers

If the concert is going to be profitable, why does it seek sponsorship? Two reasons may be that it is a means of increasing the net proceeds for the benefit of the charity, and there may be significant expense to cover before there is any income. A compromise solution may be as referred to in clause 13, where a sponsorship fee is paid and temporary financial support is provided by way of a loan.

5. The ABSA scheme only applies to new or additional sponsorship of the Arts. It enables a discretionary grant to be applied for by the sponsored party, to be used for the benefit of the sponsor.

6(a). This is to cover the position where the concert is postponed and never reinstated. The sponsor's judgment must be used sensibly, as it does want the concert to take place.

6(b). That is probably the most time-consuming part of getting the concert fixed, particularly with the effects of clause 15.

13(c)(ii). This is temporary financing to enable Gizmo to get the concert commitments on their way.

15(c)(ii). These agreements should be put together carefully, as they can be quite complicated.

Appendix III

Contract Contents Checklist

While sponsorship contracts relating to the same kind of event will tend to have similar contents, each of them will be different in detail because of the specific needs of the different parties. Appendix II contains a variety of example sponsorship agreements to show how they are constructed, and the possible different approaches to negotiable matters, such as sponsorship fees and sponsorship rights. To assist a potential sponsor or sponsored party, set out in this Appendix is a checklist of items which ought to be considered by the parties before starting to negotiate the deal. The object is to address the important issues in the first place, which will save time, patience and expense in the course of concluding the sponsorship deal. This list is not exhaustive; different deals will have different primary and secondary priorities.

1. The Parties

(a) Is the sponsor contracting with the rights owner or an agency. If the latter, who is the agency acting for? Consider the need for a direct covenant from the rights owner.

(b) The capacity of both parties to enter into the particular deal needs to be checked and an authorised signatory must execute the document.

(c) The sponsor should undertake its own due diligence on the right of the sponsored party to grant the sponsorship rights, which may be vested in a hierarchy of participants such as the governing body, clubs, teams and players. If the sponsor is sponsoring the broadcast, ensure the broadcaster has acquired the necessary rights.

(d) The sponsored party should consider the advisability of obtaining a parent company guarantee where the sponsor is a new or financially unstable company.

(e) What is the nature of the parties' relationship? It should be stated if it is not one of partnership or agency.

2. The Event

(a) Is it a new joint event? Who owns it and can continue to promote it at the end of the sponsorship period?

(b) Agree the title. Will it include the name of the sponsor? If not, what title-related credit will the sponsor receive, *e.g.* "X Event sponsored by Y" or "Y presents the X Event", or whatever is suitable for the event.

(c) State where the event is to be held, even if it is always at the same race track or athletics stadium. Allow for the possibility of a venue substitution if the original venue becomes unusable or unsuitable.

219

(d) State when the event is to be held. If there is a traditional date, such "the first two weeks in June", ensure that the contract with the venue covers that period, plus enough access days each side to allow for "getting in and getting out", and for an extension of time due to weather or other prevailing circumstances.

(e) State the duration of the event, such as it being a two-day athletics meeting, a three-day horse trial or a two-week tennis tournament. Any significant change in the event duration may affect the level of sponsorship fee for that year.

(f) State whether it is a one-off event or whether it has been an established regular event, or whether the event is to be the first of what is hoped will become a regular established event.

3. The Sponsorship Fee

(a) What is the basis of calculating the fee, *i.e.* is it:

   (i) the shortfall between income and expense where the event is not intended to be profit making. A maximum exposure should be stated; or

   (ii) a contribution to the cost of the event by paying for a specific item, such as the venue hire charge or the advertised prize money; or

   (iii) a global negotiated figure irrespective of the event finances, *i.e.* the commercial value of the rights granted to the sponsor.

(b) If the sponsorship agreement is for longer than one year, is the fee increased in the second and third year? If so, the increases should be agreed at the onset for anything up to three years. After that, depending on the type of event, it may be difficult to assess a fair fee when the contract is signed. To avoid a deadlock dispute, the contract can include a formula for assessing the increases, whether it is the RPI, a fixed percentage or some other reliable and applicable benchmark.

(c) Will there be additional bonus incentive payments or penalties related to performance, such as for an athlete, a football club or a racing driver?

(d) Will the fees be payable in advance or in arrears, in one lump sum or in instalments upon given dates? To whom will the fees be payable?

(e) Will there be additional income payable by the sponsor, for example under a merchandising agreement or upon the sale of "personality brand" products, such as endorsed golf clubs or snooker cues? If so, then:

   (i) On what basis will the royalties be calculated?
   (ii) State the accounting dates for payment.
   (iii) Insert accounts and audit provisions.

(f) State the effects of termination of the sponsorship agreement on outstanding or future payments.

(g) Has the sponsor agreed to provide any of its products to the sponsored party. If so, upon what terms, *e.g.*:

(i) is the product loaned during the sponsorship period or is it given outright, or is it available at a nominal price?

(ii) what are the sponsor's obligations in respect of maintenance, repair and insurance?

(iii) if the sponsorship agreement terminates prematurely, loaned equipment will be returned to the sponsor. Will product purchased at a nominal value have a "penalty" uplift if, say, the sponsorship is properly cancelled during the first year?

4. The Sponsor's Rights

These will depend on the type of event, but may include the following:

(a) Is the sponsor to be the sole sponsor, the primary sponsor, a secondary sponsor or an official supplier of a product?

(b) What level of exclusivity will the sponsor have? To be exclusive sponsor within the same product category? Are competitor's advertisements in the programme and on ticket backs also prohibited? What about competitor sponsored broadcasts?

(c) Will it have its name in the event title?

(d) Will there be a "sponsor trophy"?

(e) The right to use the event name and logo in advertising and sales promotion activities to benefit the sponsor and its products, or the specific brand product the name of which is connected with the event.

(f) The event providing:

  (i) hospitality and display facilities;
  (ii) free seats and preferential purchase seats;
  (iii) preferential car parking;
  (iv) facilities for the sponsor's banners and placards at the event venue;
  (v) arena perimeter boards for stadium-based events, with specific placing to their best advantage for televised events;
  (vi) free advertising in the programme;
  (vii) agreed style of credit for the sponsor on all poster and other advertising done by the event.

(g) The sponsored party prominently placing the name and logo of the sponsor on clothing, *e.g.* a footballer's or athlete's shirt, a racing driver's overalls, the saddle blanket for a showjumping horse, and on advertisements for the event.

(h) If TV coverage is essential to the sponsorship, state clearly what the contractual rights are, and what is to happen if there is less TV coverage than contracted for. The most obvious consequence is an adjustment of the fee.

  (i) Will the event sponsor have first option rights to sponsor the event broadcast, or vice versa? Ascertain who they are. Will the broadcast be on domestic and/or satellite/cable television; live, delayed or highlights? Does the sponsorship comply with the BBC/ITC/Radio Authority rules on broadcast of a sponsored event regarding advertising, signage and credits? For trans-border broadcasts, check local laws and regulations.

(j) If the sponsored party is an athlete, a football club, a showjumping horse or any party as opposed to a static event, the sponsorship rights should be exclusive throughout the territory within which that party may compete or play.

(k) To be kept informed of progress of the event and additional promotional opportunities if they arise.

(l) Merchandising rights—for which product in which territory? Is subcontracting permitted? Is a royalty payable? What quality control procedures are there?

5. Sponsored Party's Obligations

These will normally relate to the rights granted to the sponsor, but there may be other obligations agreed upon, depending on the kind of event, such as:

(a) Undertaking to maintain the quality of the event.

(b) For an athletics event, is it recognised by the national and international governing bodies and does it comply with any applicable rules?

(c) For a rock or operatic concert being held at a recognised venue, does the venue need local authority or other consent to hold the event, and does it comply with all fire regulations, crowd safety regulations, and any other regulation covering the holding of such an event.

(d) What obligations does the sponsored party have to monitor and control ambush marketing?

6. Sponsorship Period

(a) For an annual event a reasonable initial period would be three to five years.

(b) The sponsor should have the right to extend that initial period, subject to agreed uplift of fees (see 3(b) above).

(c) If the sponsor wants to extend the agreement beyond the second period, the fee may have to be freely negotiable to establish its then market value. To protect the sponsor it should have built into the sponsorship agreement a matching offer clause.

7. Termination of Agreement

(a) Apart from the normal commercial termination causes, the right of the sponsor to terminate the agreement will usually be based upon failure of the sponsored party to perform. Examples are a venue which fails to provide TV coverage, a football team which fails to win a match all season, an athlete who is permanently injured or who breaches his or her "morality clause", or a racing driver who always crashes on the first bend.

(b) The agreement must also state the consequences of termination, *i.e.* what rights are extinguished or continue, is any of the sponsor's product returned to it and what about outstanding fees?

8. Warranties and Liabilities

(a) Include warranties concerning the fundamental issues to the contract such as sponsored parties' title to the rights, and concerning the performance of third parties.

(b) It may be appropriate or reasonable for the parties to limit their respective liabilities under the contract, *e.g.* the sponsored party may limit its liability for failing to provide the sponsor with promotional opportunities to refunding the sponsorship fee. Consider whether consequential loss should be excluded.

9. Intellectual Property

(a) Have the event name and logos been protected in the sponsor's product category? If not, consider trade mark registration for the territories of the event.

(b) Who owns the rights and goodwill to jointly created logos?

(c) What warranties of ownership are there? Have full assignments from the designers been obtained?

10. General

(a) If either the sponsor or the sponsored party are not based in the United Kingdom, or if the event is to take place outside the United Kingdom, the contract should state which legal system will apply to its interpretation and enforcement.

(b) What method of resolving disputes is appropriate? Court, arbitration or ADR?

(c) The usual "boiler plate" clauses should be included, particularly regarding termination, cancellation and postponement.

11. Financial Considerations

(a) Are there any tax or VAT considerations whereby either party, or the ultimate beneficiary of funds raised by the event, might get a substantial advantage if an appropriate scheme is set up before any commitments are made? If so, take appropriate advice at an early stage in the planning of the event.

(b) Will the sponsorship deal qualify for the application to the Association for Business Sponsorship of the Arts or Sportsmatch for a grant under their Business Sponsorship Incentive Schemes?

(c) The whole question of what insurances should be taken out by the sponsored party should be examined. Public liability cover should be taken out by the sponsored party and the sponsor should be named as an additional insured. Cancellation and curtailment insurance should also be considered.

Relevant Names and Addresses

As sponsorship is involved in all areas of funding and fund-raising, and as it is used as a commercial means of promoting the name and products of companies which manufacture goods or provide services, there are many organisations which have some connection with sponsorship. They may provide active services or advisory services. Any party wishing to be a sponsor, or looking for sponsorship, and which is not familiar with the sponsorship industry, has difficulty in finding at first the right guidance of an impartial nature backed by experience and expertise. Set out below are the names and addresses of some of the organisations which may be able to help and give information and advice, depending on what the party seeking the advice is looking for. This list is not comprehensive, but between them most aspects of sports- and leisure-related sponsorship will be covered.

Association for Business Sponsorship
of the Arts (ABSA)
Nutmeg House
60 Gainsford Street
London
SE1 2NY
Telephone: 0171 378 8143

ABSA Scotland
100 Wellington Street
Glasgow
G2 6PB
Telephone: 0141 204 3864

ABSA Wales & SW England
16 Museum Place
Cardiff
CF1 3BH
Telephone: 01222 303023

Arts Council of Great Britain
14 Great Peter Street
London
SW1P 3NQ
Telephone: 0171 333 0100

British Institute of Sports
Administration (BISA)
24 Southfields
East Molesey
Surrey
KT8 0BP
Telephone: 0181 971 2296

British Olympic Association
1 Wandsworth Plain
London
SW18 1EH
Telephone: 0181 871 2677

Central Council of Physical Recreation
Francis House
Francis Street
London
SW1P 1DE
Telephone: 0171 828 3163

Commonwealth Games Federation
197 Knightsbridge
London
SW1 1RZ
Telephone: 0171 225 5555

European Sponsorship Consultants
Association (ESCA)
16 Partridge Close
Chesham
Bucks.
HP5 3LH
Telephone: 01494 791760

Incorporated Society of British
   Advertisers (ISBA)
44 Hertford Street,
London
W1Y 8AE
Telephone: 0171 499 7502

Independent Television Commission
(ITC)
33 Foley Street
London
W1P 7LB
Telephone: 0171 255 3000

Institute of Public Relations
15 Northburgh Street
London
EC1V 0PR
Telephone: 0171 233 5151

Institute of Sports Sponsorship (ISS)
4th Floor
Warwick House
25–27 Buckingham Palace Road
London
SW1W 0PP
Telephone: 0171 233 7747

National Coaching Foundation
114 Cardigan Road
Headingley
Leeds
LS6 3BJ
Telephone: 0113 274 4802

Radio Authority
Holbrook House
14 Great Queen Street
London
WC2B 5DG
Telephone: 0171 798 5418

Sports Council
16 Upper Woburn Place,
London
WC1H 0QP
Telephone: 0171 388 1277

Scottish Sports Council
Caledonia House
South Gyle
Edinburgh
EH12 9DQ
Telephone: 0131 317 7200

Sports Council for Northern Ireland
The House of Sports
Upper Malone Road
Belfast
BT9 5LA
Telephone: 01232 381222

Sports Council for Wales
The Welsh Institute for Sport
Sophia Gardens,
Cardiff
CF1 9SW
Telephone: 01222 397571

The Rules of the Business Sponsorship Incentive Schemes for Arts and Sports

The purpose of these business sponsorship incentive schemes are to raise the overall level of business sponsorship of the arts and grass roots sports in Great Britain. See chapter one, paragraphs 1–58—1–64 for information.

These extracts are for information only. They are intended to provide an indication of the kind of criteria any successful applicant will be expected to meet, rather than exhaustively describe the schemes. Any potential applicant is advised that they should contact ABSA or Sportsmatch (as appropriate) before applying, and obtain from them the official forms on which applications must be submitted.

RULES OF THE ARTS PAIRING SCHEME

Reproduced with the kind permission of ABSA and the Department of Culture, Media and Sport. These Rules apply to applications for sponsored events starting between April 1, 1998 and March 31, 1999.

1. We can never guarantee to give an award. The Scheme is competitive and Awards are made at the discretion of the Pairing Scheme panel. The Pairing Scheme has an annual cash limit. We will guarantee, however, to review all applications submitted to us on time fairly, equally and on their full merit, within these criteria.

2. BSA must be satisfied with the eligibility, legal status and financial accountability of arts organisations and business sponsors who apply under the Scheme. ABSA's decision regarding eligibility for the Scheme is final.

Submission of applications

3. The deadline for submission of applications is determined by the month in which the sponsored project begins and applications must be submitted in time for the relevant panel meeting. Dates of panel meetings and application deadlines are available from ABSA and form a part of these Rules. The start date of the project is the public opening or when the business first receives a major sponsorship benefit, whichever is earlier. We do not normally take pre-publicity (such as press announcements or sponsorship credits in leaflets, posters, etc.) as being the major sponsorship benefit in this instance. If you have a query or are co-ordinating an application involving a festival or a competition, you are advised to clarify the start date with ABSA well in advance of submitting an application. Applications received after the relevant closing date cannot be guaranteed consideration by the panel. Retrospective awards can never be made.

Please note that dates of panel meetings may change. In such circumstances, submission deadlines will remain the same.

4. All applications will be acknowledged by ABSA. If you have not received an acknowledgment card, you are advised to confirm receipt of your application with your local office. ABSA cannot accept responsibility for late submission of an application as a result of postal or courier delays.

5. pplications received which do not include all information requested on the application form from the arts organisation, the business sponsor(s) or the third party co-ordinator (where applicable) will not be guaranteed consideration by the panel.

Eligibility of arts organisations

6. To apply, you must be an arts organisation which is either a recognised charity (Scottish arts organisations must be accepted as a charity by the Inland Revenue Claims branch) or legally constituted as a non-profit distributing company. Non-profit distributing organisations must submit their Memorandum and Articles of Association with their application.

7. If Rule 6 does not apply, you may be eligible to apply for an award when undertaking an arts project, if you are:

- a public body such as Arts Councils, Regional Arts Boards, educational establishments, local authorities or local authority arts facilities who have received business sponsorship. For local authorities or local authority arts facilities, we will ask for an external reference on the project.

- conducting projects or annual programmes which are funded via arts related budgets of a public funding body. We will ask for independent confirmation of this funding.

- a local or amateur organisation. We require certain information (guidelines should be requested from ABSA) to establish your non-profit distributing status.

- a charity or legally constituted non-profit distributing company which is undertaking an arts project as part of its core activities. Please check eligibility with ABSA before applying.

Please contact your local ABSA office for more details.

8. Individual arts organisations operating within an umbrella body (such as a local authority museum) may be considered as separate applicants. To do this, we will need to see that you are operating independently by looking at how your management structures, accounting systems, publicity material and offices are set up. If we are happy that you can prove independence in three or more of these criteria, then you may be eligible to make separate applications, with our prior consent.

How we apply the Scheme to different types of arts organisations

9. In the case of festivals, or other events which may have non-arts elements, we can only consider the arts elements for an award. In these cases, we will calculate awards in direct proportion to the arts content featured in the programme.

10. Cash sponsorship and sponsorship in kind as outlined in Rule 11 is eligible for matching under the Scheme. We regret the following cannot be matched under the Scheme, even if your organisation is eligible:

- appeal funding;
- commissions of works of art to which the public will not have permanent, open access;
- corporate membership;
- donations, including those to capital projects, covenants and money paid under the Government's Gift Aid Scheme;
- film, television or video projects which are not guaranteed a public showing;
- food and drink;
- non-arts activities;
- payments for advertising outside a sponsorship agreement;
- payments made by sponsors to third parties to cover expenditure incurred by an arts organisation;
- payments of fees to agents, such as sponsorship consultants;
- payments of less than £1,000;
- payments to individuals;
- private events which are not open to the general public.

11. Sponsorship in kind is eligible for matching only where it is for tangible goods which can be given a monetary value that can be verified and must be at cost price. The maximum sponsorship which can be matched under this Rule is £5,000. Because this is a pilot category, applications will not be accepted under the Rules for three-year contracts or established sponsors.

12. Sponsors eligible under Rule 11 must be able to demonstrate that their overall commitment to the arts (including both cash and in-kind sponsorship) has not decreased. However, previous in-kind sponsorship will not be considered when determining a sponsor's eligibility for an application to match cash sponsorship.

Eligibility of business sponsors

13. Arts, entertainment and leisure promoters, or other businesses who have a commercial interest in either an event or the promoter, whether directly or indirectly, are not eligible as sponsors under the Scheme unless such sponsorship is over and above existing commercial relations. Full disclosure of these relationships must be made to ABSA, who will determine eligibility.

14. Sponsorship money must derive from a business sponsor's own funds. Money that has come to a business from a third party for the specific purpose of paying for the sponsorship will not be eligible for matching under the Scheme.

15. A business may choose to pay its sponsorship through a promotional agency (*e.g.* a sponsorship or public relations consultancy) working on its behalf. We can only match the sponsorship money finally paid to the arts organisation.

In such cases, we suggest the application should be submitted by the arts organisation and the business, and co-ordinated by the agency.

16. When sponsorship payments for a single project are spread over more than one of the sponsor's financial years, we consider the sum eligible for matching the total of payments made in advance of or during the financial year in which the sponsorship starts (*i.e.* when the sponsor first receives a major sponsorship benefit—see Rule 3).

17. Recognised charities and their commercial arms are not eligible as sponsors, nor are organisations or agencies that receive 25 per cent or more of their income in the form of core funding from U.K. public sources (*e.g.* from central or local government). For these purposes, "core funding" is not intended to include income earned on a competitive basis, and at arm's length from the public bodies in question. Where businesses are in receipt of public funds but are nevertheless eligible for the Scheme, we require relevant details and written confirmation from the business and from its sponsoring body (*i.e.* its parent Department or other provider of public funding) to establish that the organisation in question is an eligible body under these provisions.

18. Different business units within a company may be considered eligible as sponsors in their own right. They will need to demonstrate three or more of the following:

- separate, identifiable budgets;
- a separate decision-making management process, *i.e.* separate personnel;
- a separate business structure, such as a subsidiary, division or branch which is shown separately in the company's annual report or other literature;
- active promotion of a separate identity or function.

19. Trade associations or business clubs may apply if they are legally constituted as a business and the sponsorship actively promotes that business.

How we apply the Scheme to different types of business sponsors

20. New sponsors are those within the first three years of arts sponsorship. These sponsorship years do not need to be consecutive. In addition, if you have sponsored the arts in the past, but not within your previous five financial years, we will consider you a new sponsor. We may be able to match 25 per cent of your sponsorship for each project, provided that:

- your business's overall commitment to arts sponsorship has not decreased;
- your financial commitment to your partner arts organisation has not decreased;
- your investment is at least £1,000 for each sponsored project for which an application is made.

The minimum award is £500. Sponsorships between £1,000 and £2,000 will be eligible for an Award of £500.

21. Established sponsors are those in their fourth year or more of arts sponsorship. We may be able to recognise your sponsorship for each project with a certificate and a reception hosted by a Minister from the Department for Culture, Media and Sport, on the same provisos:

- your business' overall commitment to arts sponsorship has not decreased;
- your financial commitment to your partner arts organisation has not decreased;
- your investment is at least £1,000 for each sponsored project for which an application is made.

Details of how to apply under this category will be available from ABSA.

Exceptional access

22. s a first-time sponsor (*i.e.* you have never sponsored an arts project which would have been eligible under the Scheme—see Rules 8, 11 and 12), you may apply for an exceptional access award. We may match 50 per cent of your sponsorship. The sponsored project must be seen by the Pairing Scheme panel to provide exceptional value to the arts in one or more of the following categories:

- bringing new audiences to artforms or new artforms to audiences;
- offering specific access to disabled people;
- developing a new education programme;
- interaction between arts groups and/or schools with the local community.

The sponsored project must be wholly concerned with providing exceptional access to the arts. It must also be beyond the arts organisation's usual range of activities.

Three-year contracts

23. As a first-time sponsor, you may wish to commit in advance to sponsorship of the same arts organisation for three consecutive years. We may match your sponsorship on a 100 per cent basis in the first year only. In order to be eligible for the three-year Pairing Scheme Award, a sponsor must not have sponsored an arts organisation before.

24. The sponsorship paid under a three year contract may be the same in each year or may increase in years two and/or three. It must not decrease in years two and/or three. Other sponsorships undertaken by a business in this period will not affect this contract.

25. The three-year sponsorship must continue for three consecutive years. This means that the sponsored events must start in three consecutive calendar years, three consecutive Pairing Scheme years, or three consecutive financial years of the arts organisation.

26. If a sponsor decides to increase their sponsorship under a three year contract after the panel has approved the award in the first year, the panel will treat this as new sponsorship (as defined in Rule 20) and may match this extra sponsorship on a 25 per cent basis. A separate application will need to be made.

27. If any applications with other arts organisations are made by a sponsor during the three year sponsorship period, the business will be treated as a new sponsorship within the first three years of arts sponsorship (as defined in Rule 20) and any award granted will be on the basis of 25 per cent of the sponsorship.

28. If approved, an award at 100 per cent recognises the full three years of the sponsorship. Recognition of the sponsor's commitment in years two and three will be by certificates signed by the Secretary of State for Culture, Mediate and Sport in both of these years. No application for a cash award can be made in years two and three, but the sponsor and the arts organisation will be required to credit the Scheme and to provide confirmation of sponsorship payment (see Rule 36). Guidelines will be available from ABSA.

Procedure in the event of budgetary pressures

29. A percentage of each monthly budget will be "ring fenced" to fund projects which meet required quality standards and which provide exceptional access to the arts (see Rule 22) or involve new three-year contracts (see Rules 23–28). Ring fenced budgets will be allocated before other applications are considered.

30. The following represent key priorities for the Department for Culture, Media and Sport and ABSA. Subject to Rule 29 and in the event that demand for awards exceeds the funds available in the panel's budget, the priorities listed below will apply. Relevant evidence must be attached to the application.

Sponsors who have demonstrated commitment to the arts by:

- entering into a long-term agreement (*i.e.* three years or more) with an arts organisation;
- encouraging staff involvement in the sponsored arts organisation;
- involving the sponsored arts organisation in the business process or including it in a strategic marketing strategy;
- increasing their *overall* commitment to arts sponsorship by a minimum of 25 per cent over their previous year's total spend. This increase need not be to the arts organisation which is the subject of this application;

and projects which demonstrate a commitment to widening access to the arts by:

- placing an emphasis on education or training, including developing skills in new technologies;
- developing links with schools, educational establishments or youth groups;
- building or developing links within a community;
- encouraging the participation of people with disabilities.

In determining priorities, the Pairing Scheme panel will take into account the number of criteria fulfilled in its opinion by the sponsorship (and not the proposed use of any Award money). The panel's decision will be final.

Use of an award

31. Awards are made on the basis that the money is used by an arts organisation to supply an additional range of benefits which would not otherwise be available to them or their sponsor. The sponsored project, however, must be able to take place irrespective of the outcome of the application. The award money should be used to offer the stated benefits within six months of the sponsored event.

32. We ask all applicants to give careful attention to these extra benefits and to list them clearly on the Application Form. We will expect applicants to show that at least 50 per cent of money awarded is used for this purpose. The food and drink element of corporate hospitality cannot be included, nor can the money be used to fund prizes, but the benefits may be items such as:

- additional marketing for the sponsorship;
- maximum publicity and exposure for the sponsored event to the target audience;
- the cost of corporate membership or the sponsorship of an additional, related event;
- other activities of specific benefit to the sponsor as a direct result of participating in the Scheme.

We ask this as we wish all businesses to be attracted by, and committed to, sponsorship of the arts.

Crediting the Scheme

33. The Scheme must be credited correctly in all relevant material. We will send you detailed guidelines on how to do this if an award is given. Please do not credit the Scheme before your application is approved. You must send us at least one item of printed material where the Scheme is credited.
We ask this as not only are the Pairing Scheme awards public money, but also because we wish others to be aware of the benefits of the Scheme.

34. Previous applicants only: failure to credit the Scheme satisfactorily for any previous awards may prejudice the decision about your current application.

35. Where an award of £15,000 or more is given we will require as a condition of the award, a report on the sponsorship and use of the award money. A separate form will be sent to you for completion.

Transfer of award money

36. Once an award is approved, we will pay the money directly to the arts organisation by bank transfer when we have received written confirmation from their bankers that the sponsors have paid their total sponsorship contribution, giving the date(s), amount(s) and source(s) of payment. We may also need separate, independent confirmation of the payment in writing from the sponsor. Guidance notes are available from ABSA. New applicants are strongly advised to check with ABSA what information needs to be provided.

37. Before paying an award, we may require satisfactory accounting information and/or examples of Pairing Scheme credits for previous awards. Please contact your local ABSA office for details.

38. Sponsorship is normally liable for VAT. The Pairing Scheme award matches sponsorship exclusive of VAT. Award money from the Pairing Scheme, however, is not normally liable for VAT.

39. If we give an award, the arts organisation is required to keep full and complete accounting records of the use of the award and may be required to provide an audited statement of the use of the award. ABSA shall be entitled to inspect all such records relating to the award and the sponsorship.

Termination

40. ABSA must be notified immediately in writing of any change to any contract or agreement.

Any contract or agreement may be terminated immediately by ABSA if:

- either the sponsor or the arts organisation enters into any arrangement for the benefit of its creditors or has a receiver or liquidator appointed over any of its assets, or becomes subject to an administration order;

- either the sponsor or the arts organisation goes into liquidation;

- either the sponsor or the arts organisation ceases, or threatens to cease to carry on business or, in the case of a sponsor, changes in status during the terms of any sponsorship which may affect that sponsor's eligibility to participate in the Pairing Scheme;

- we find that any information contained in the original application or any other information or representations made to either ABSA or the Department for Culture, Media and Sport is misleading or inaccurate or that the award, or any part of it, was not used for the purposes for which it was provided;

- we do not receive satisfactory confirmation that the sponsorship money has been paid to the arts organisation.

In addition to the above in the case of a three-year award, any contract or agreement may be terminated immediately by ABSA if the sponsor ceases to pay the sponsorship or the arts organisation ceases to provide the sponsor with the agreed benefit at any time during the three year period.

41. On termination of any contract or agreement either for any of the above reasons or due to any breach of the Rules we shall be entitled to our absolute discretion to require the repayment of some or all of the award money. The arts organisation and business sponsor will be jointly and severally liable for the return of all funds.

42. Any arts organisation or business sponsor who is knowingly involved in arrangements designed to secure an award under the Pairing Scheme contrary to the Rules or the objectives of the Scheme will be disqualified from participating in the Scheme at ABSA's absolute discretion.

Appeals

43. Applicants may appeal against the panel's decision in certain circumstances. Full details of the appeals procedure are available from ABSA.

The Department for Culture, Media and Sport and ABSA reserve the right to change these Rules at any time.

Contact ABSA for the official application form.

SPORTSMATCH RULES

Reproduced with the kind permission of the Institute of Sports Sponsorship and the Department of Culture, Media and Sport.

What is Sportsmatch?

- It is designed to improve the quality and increase the quantity of business sponsorship of grass-roots sport in particular by:

  — introducing new businesses to grass-roots sponsorship;

  — encouraging sponsors of major evens to extend their involvement into the grass-roots; and

  — existing sponsors of grass-roots sport to increase their support.

- The scheme is funded in England by the Department for Culture, Media and Sport (DCMS) and managed by the Institute of Sports Sponsorship (ISS), a national non-profit-making organisation representing business sponsors of sport.

  In Scotland and Wales the scheme is funded by the Scottish and Welsh offices respectively and managed by the Scottish and Welsh Sports Councils.

- Whilst many applications will be for an event or activity taking place in one country, it is possible to apply for an award for the same event or activity in more than one country (see *How to apply*).

- Decisions on awards are made by an independent panel appointed by the Secretary of State for the DCMS and representing both business and sport.

How Sportsmatch Works

Provided:

  — an application is jointly prepared and submitted by the organising body and the sponsor;

  — it conforms to the rules of the scheme;

  — an award is approved by the award panel;

  — the business is either a first-time sponsor of grass-roots sport or is increasing its amount of sponsorship;

  — the sponsor is contributing a minimum of £1,000;

then, for the first year of an award, every £1 from the sponsor will be matched with £1 from Sportsmatch up to a maximum for any one event or activity of £50,000.

(For a second or third year sponsorship see *How does the award panel decide?*).

What are the benefits?

Sportsmatch encourages a business to sponsor a grass-roots sport which it may not otherwise have considered. Consequently, the business sponsor enjoys all the commercial benefits resulting from the sponsorship fee and the Sportsmatch award and the organising body benefits by securing double the income for its project!

- As Sportsmatch award recipients, the extra benefits will include:
  - the prestige of receiving an award;
  - commemorative certificates;
  - the increased publicity to be gained from Sportsmatch ceremonies and related press releases;
  - government endorsement received through receptions held for award recipients.

Who can apply?

Sponsored organisations

- Any properly constituted organising body involved in sport and operating mainly in England which has attracted potential sponsorship from a commercial organisation. This includes governing bodies, sports clubs, charities, local authorities, schools and voluntary youth organisations.

- The organising body must be either non-profiting-distributing or if profit-distributing (such as a professional football club) be prepared to set up a separate cost centre and bank account for the purpose of administering and reporting on the sponsored activity and the income and expenditure involved including the Sportsmatch funds.

- The ISS must be satisfied with the eligibility, legal status and financial accountability of the organising body prior to the application being submitted to the award panel.

- Non-profit-distributing bodies must submit evidence of their legal status such as a copy of their Memorandum and Articles of Association or school prospectus. Other organising bodies must submit a copy of their Constitution unless their status is evident (such as local authorities). All documents must be submitted on official letterheading and signed and dated by two authorised representatives of the organising body with names and titles clearly printed.

Sponsors

- Any eligible business which is either a first-time sponsor of grass-roots sport or an existing sponsor investing additional money.

- The key question to be answered positively is "will the business sponsor's expenditure on grass-roots sport in its current financial year compared to the previous year be increased by at least the amount applied for under the Sportsmatch scheme?"

- To qualify as a "business" for the purposes of the Sportsmatch scheme it will be necessary for the applicant to demonstrate that it is trading with the intention of distributing any profits made to shareholders, owner-directors, etc. It will not be sufficient to show that profits have been made if those profits are simply retained within the organisation as in the case, for example, of a members' club.

- A business must have a trading or operations presence in England and be able to nominate a British-based representative to speak on its behalf.

- Where a company replaces an affiliated company as a sponsor of a grass-roots event or activity, it will be for the applicant to satisfy the award panel that it is a different and separate entity from the previous sponsor. An award will not be made unless the overall amount of money going into sport from the affiliated companies is increasing.

- Separate divisions and subsidiaries of businesses may be treated as separate sponsors provided their sponsorship budgets are independent of the parent or sister companies, *e.g.* local branches, franchises.

- Where a business sponsor's budget is not independent of a parent, division or subsidiary, details of sponsorship history and budgets must be given for the whole company or group.

- Each business sponsor must be either a first-time grass-roots sponsor contributing £1,000 or more in England or an existing grass-roots sponsor who is contributing equivalent additional money.

- More than one business sponsor can apply for a combined award together with the organising body provided each is obtaining a satisfactory commercial return and each is contributing at least £1,000. However, the panel will look more critically at applications with more than two sponsors and will normally only consider an award where each sponsor is sponsoring a specific activity, *e.g.* athletics, football, swimming within an overall programme of grass-roots sports.

Who cannot apply?

Sponsored organisations

- Profit-distributing bodies are ineligible unless they conform to the accounting procedures outlined in the previous section.

Sponsors

- Charities

- Professional and Trade Associations, Enterprise Agencies, Livery companies and business clubs.

- Organisers or agencies receiving more than one quarter of their income from public funds (*e.g.* national or local government).

- Sports promoters for events they are promoting.

- The alcohol and tobacco industries if the events or activities sponsored involve a majority of participants or spectators aged under 18. Sponsorships by the alcohol industry of motor sport events or activities will also not be eligible for awards.

What is eligible?

- Eligible events or activities are those which fall within the definition of "sport" as agreed by the DCMS for the purposes of Sportsmatch.

  They should be competitive or otherwise challenging and should involve physical effort and skill. Decisions on whether an activity falls within this definition will be made by the award panel and will be final.

  An illustrative list of eligible sports, recognised by the English Sports Council, can be found at Appendix A. Where there is any doubt the scheme managers will be able to give advice prior to the submission of the formal application.

- The award panel will require evidence that the sponsored event or activity encourages increased participation and/or improved performance at grass-roots level and does not apply unduly restrictive conditions of entry/participation.

- In the event of demand for awards exceeding likely funds available, applications which can be seen to benefit young people, disabled people, schools and schools-related projects, ethnic minorities and/or events or activities in urban or rural recreationally-deprived areas with community involvement will be given particularly favourable consideration.

- Revenue activities or essential capital equipment directly related to sporting activities such as nets, balls, bats, canoes are eligible.

- Capital projects with a total budget of less than £5,000. However, where the business sponsor is also the contractor or one of the contractors involved in the project, the tender submitted by the business sponsor/contractor must be subjected to verification by an independent surveyor under the control of the ISS but at the expense of the organising body. The tender must also be at cost price.

- Only the sporting elements of a project such as a festival are eligible. Awards may be given in relation to the proportion of sport within the festival as a whole.

What is ineligible?

The following are ineligible whether or not submitted by an eligible organising body:

- — Capital projects such as buildings, new stands, changing rooms, playing surfaces and fixtures costing £5,000 and over.

- — Sponsorship in kind *EXCEPT* sporting equipment and other non-personal items directly related to sporting activities, including kit, which remain in other organising body's possession. The item(s) must be capable of being given a monetary value which can be verified and must be at cost price.

- General administration and other running costs of the organising body that are not related to a specific event or activity.

- Non-sports events/projects.
- Appeal funding and donations.
- Commercial entertainment, commercial tours, and investment in commercial activities.
- Payments to agents and consultants in public relations, advertising or sponsorship for obtaining the sponsorship and for promoting the event or activity for the benefit of the organising body and/or the sponsor. However, appropriate payments can be included in the project costs for organising/ managing the event or activity.
- Corporate memberships.
- Sponsors' private events, not open to the general public.
- Individual sportsmen and sportswomen.
- Conferences.
- Hospitality.
- Where any material relationship other than the proposed sponsorship agreement exists between the organising body and the business sponsor, this may render the sponsorship ineligible (see the application form for examples).
- Professional sport. However, this does not necessarily exclude a professional body from applying provided the event or activity being sponsored is for the benefit of non-professionals, *e.g.* coaching schemes using professional coaches to teach sporting skills, where the coaching services do not form part of that person's normal job, then it would be reasonable to build into the sponsorship suitable remuneration charges. Events or activities which provide for both non-professional and professional sport may also be eligible in respect of the non-professional element.
- International and national major events. However, nationally organised grass-roots schemes for local implementation would be acceptable.
- Events or activities taking place outside Great Britain would not normally be eligible.

How to apply

- Please check the rules of the Sportsmatch scheme to ensure that you are an eligible applicant and that you are in a position to comply with the rules.
- If you have any queries about the rules or the Sportsmatch scheme in general or require an application form please contact the appropriate Sportsmatch office.
- Applications for awards or the same event or activity in more than one country should be sent to each office identifying the amount of award requested in each country and providing details of the event or activity taking place in that country.
- The Sportsmatch scheme manager or his/her deputy will discuss each application with the nominated co-ordinator before presenting the application to the award panel.

- Applications should be received at least 12 weeks before the start of the sponsored event or activity in order to give adequate time for processing, award panel consideration and for the Sportsmatch funds to be made available prior to the event or activity taking place.

- An award cannot be made in respect of an event or activity which commences before the application is considered by the award panel. Applications received less than five weeks before the next scheduled award panel meeting will be submitted to the following meeting, unless the event or activity starts before this date. In these circumstances, unless the start date can be postponed until after the panel meeting, every effort will be made to process the application within the remaining weeks, but this cannot be guaranteed.

- If a sponsorship agreement is signed between a sponsor and the organising body, and/or the sponsor has handed over any sponsorship monies before the award panel has met then, in these circumstances, the application will not be considered by the award panel. If the event or activity will take place without a Sportsmatch award, then evidence must be given that the award will significantly enhance the event or activity and therefore the benefits to the sponsor (see section 4.5 of the application form).

- The start date of a sponsored event or activity will be the date it commences or takes place; if an activity such as capital building works, it will be when the award panel considers that the sponsor first receives a major sponsorship benefit. The start date will be agreed with the scheme manager or his/her deputy when the application is submitted. Any changes to the start or end date after the award has been approved must be discussed, agreed with the scheme manager and put in writing to the ISS.

- All applications must be on the standard form. Whenever possible applications must be handwritten in block capitals. Faxes must be followed by originals and incomplete applications will not be accepted.

- An application must be signed on behalf of the business sponsor(s) and organising body by authorised signatories who are entitled to represent their organisations and agree to answer questions on the application. Agents cannot sign the form as an organising body or on behalf of a sponsor. However, they can act as co-ordinator.

- Where priority has to be given in order to remain within the funds available, the judgement of the award panel, taking into account the priority groups identified under "What is eligible", will be final.

- If there is more than one sponsor, the sponsor section on the application form may be photocopied for the other sponsor(s).

- The organising body, sponsor or an authorised third party may co-ordinate the application. The co-ordinator is responsible for submitting the completed application form and supporting material on time to the ISS and in accordance with the rules of the scheme, ensuring that the information is correct and comprehensive.

THE CO-ORDINATOR MUST ENSURE THAT ALL PARTIES TO THE APPLICATION HAVE READ THE RULES AND AGREE TO ANSWER QUESTIONS ON THE APPLICATION.

How does the award panel decide?

- Listed below are the key questions the panel will be asking about each application:

  — Will the sponsored event or activity lead to increased participation and will it improve standards?

  — Is it genuine sponsorship as opposed to donation or patronage, *i.e.* are there sufficient commercial benefits being obtained?

  — Is it "new" money, *i.e.* is the business a first time sponsor of grass-roots sport or increasing its funding of grass-roots sport?

  — Is it a new or additional event or activity, *i.e.* not part of the normal ongoing costs of running the sporting organisation or a replacement/ refurbishment expense for which provision should be made?

  — Does it fall within a priority group (see *What is eligible?*)?

  — Is Sportsmatch critical to the sponsor's support, *i.e.* has the business already committed its support through payment and/or signing a sponsorship agreement?

  — Will Sportsmatch funding either enable the event or activity to take place or significantly enhance it?

  — Is the organising body non-profit-distributing or able to set up a separate non-profit-making account for the Sportsmatch event or activity and is the sponsor a business trading for profit?

  — Is proper credit and publicity being planned for the Sportsmatch award. This will also be taken into account when considering future applications (see *Following payment*)?

- Sportsmatch is selective and discretionary. There is no guarantee that an award will be made, especially since funds are limited. Decisions of the award panel are final.

- There is no set limit to the number of applications for new events/activities that can be put forward by a business sponsor or organising body. Each application which conforms to the Sportsmatch rules will be capable of qualifying for a Sportsmatch award, subject to the decision of the award panel and to the rule about second and third year sponsorships (see third point, below). However, in the event of demand for awards exceeding supply the panel has the right to take the number and quality of awards previously received into account.

- To qualify for an award payment, the sponsorship of the event or activity that is the subject of the application must not have commenced before the award has been approved. The total amount of the sponsorship being matched by the award must have been paid by the business sponsor to the organising body, but not until after the award panel has met.

- The initial application must state the length of the sponsorship agreement and an application must be submitted for each subsequent year's sponsorship for consideration by the award panel. If not stated initially, any subsequent application will not qualify unless additional sponsorship money is made available in which case only the extra money may qualify for a matching award.

- If a Sportsmatch award has been approved for the first year of a grass-roots sporting project where the sponsor has committed up-front to sponsor the project for a further two or three years the panel may agree to an award in the second and third years. If so, the maximum award in the second year will be 50 per cent of the amount the sponsor originally committed for that year and in the third year will be 25 per cent. This also applies to all applications applying for second- and third-year funding from December 1996 onwards.

- Please note, that the minimum award remains £1,000. Therefore, if, as a result of the above rule, the award would be lower than £1,000, Sportsmatch will agree to pay the minimum amount of £1,000. Awards for the same project can only be given for a three-year period and the maximum amount provided by Sportsmatch for the same project is £50,000.

- Both parties to the application must provide evidence to the Sportsmatch award panel either (a) that the event or activity would not take place without the financial support available from Sportsmatch, *i.e.* that the business sponsor would not have been able to provide the sponsorship required, or (b) that the event or activity will be significantly developed and enhanced by the Sportsmatch award.

What are the business benefits?

- Business sponsorship is defined as the payment of money or the provision of goods in kind by business to an organising body for the purposes of promoting the business name and/or product. Sponsorship is part of a business's general promotional expenditure. Whilst it can encompass a sense of corporate or social responsibility, it does require some commercial benefit from the sponsorship unlike a donation from which no commercial return is required.

- The sponsorship must therefore in the opinion of the award panel given the business sponsor a level of publicity and commercial return appropriate for the money involved and this must be reflected in the sponsorship agreement.

What further conditions must be observed?

Before panel approval

- An application for a Sportsmatch award will not be considered by the panel if the sponsor has already paid the organising body before the panel has met to review the application.

— Prior to the award panel meeting a draft agreement must be submitted to the ISS unsigned, unless any signed agreement contains a clause stating that the sponsorship is conditional upon a Sportsmatch award being approved.

— Sponsorship, either cash or in kind, is liable for VAT if the organising body is VAT rated. The sponsor must agree to pay the VAT in those circumstances, otherwise the award panel will consider the sponsor's payment to be a donation and not a genuine business sponsorship and therefore not eligible for an award.

— If the organising body is not registered for VAT it may need to be—the registration turnover is revised annually.

— It is likely that a sponsor will be able to reclaim the VAT as most will be VAT-registered businesses.

— Sportsmatch can only match the sponsor's contribution net of VAT.

— Any Sportsmatch award payment is not liable for VAT.

— The award money received by the organising body is intended to be beneficial to all parties including Sportsmatch. Applicants are required to give full details of the benefits to the business sponsor, the organising body and Sportsmatch that will result from any award. The use of any award money received must fall within the rules of the scheme.

After panel approval but before payment of the award

— The award will be paid to the organising body only on receipt of the following:

- a declaration form signed by two authorised representatives, normally the co-ordinator and treasurer, stating that the award conditions will be observed;

- a signed and dated sponsorship agreement;

- evidence that the sponsorship money has been paid.

— Evidence of sponsorship payment should consist of a letter from the organising body's bank certifying that the sponsorship money has been paid and giving the date(s), amount(s) and source(s) of payment.

— This should be obtained at the time the sponsorship money is paid and should be sent to the Office Manager at the ISS, after notification that the award has been made. An exception to this requirement may be made where an authorised finance officer of a local authority acknowledges in writing receipt of sponsorship money.

— Where sponsorship in kind is to be provided the award will be paid on receipt of a certified statement from the organising body confirming that such sponsorship is in place. It should be noted that in the case of sponsorship in kind, the equivalent monetary value applied for should be calculated at cost price to the sponsor and similarly for a capital project the cost should be calculated for materials, labour and other relevant charges at cost, *i.e.* without any profit element. A certified costing must be supplied by the sponsor.

— The award will be paid only when the total amount of the sponsorship for that year, being matched by the award, has been paid. All Sportsmatch payments will be made directly to the organising body not to a third party. Sportsmatch payments will not be made by instalments.

Following payment

— Within 12 weeks of the completion of the sponsored event or activity or at the end of the first year whichever is sooner, the ISS will require an audited or certified statement clearly showing that the sponsorship and Sportsmatch award have been used in the way specified in the application. Any likely delay in submission of the statement should be communicated in writing to the ISS.

— All Sportsmatch awards over £10,000 require an audited income and expenditure statement contained within the appropriate yearly accounts or if not part of the audited accounts verified by the organising body's auditors.

— For accounts of £10,000 or less the statement can be certified by the Treasurer and signed by the Chair or equivalent. (These requirements are explained in Appendix C [not reproduced here].)

— All publicity material, such as certificates, press cuttings, posters, programmes, leaflets, etc., featuring the sponsorship and matching Sportsmatch award must also be submitted at this time unless previously supplied. Photographic evidence will be accepted. If all the required information is not provided then Sportsmatch reserves the right to have access at anytime in the site/equipment and to view the accounting records (invoices, etc.) to ascertain whether the event or activity took place as set out in the application. Failure to supply these elements of information could lead to the Sportsmatch award being reclaimed.

— If extra administration costs are incurred as a result of failure without good reason to comply with the above rules then the ISS reserves the right to charge an administration fee (normally up to £1,000).

— In general, if the conditions of an award are not met, the ISS reserves the right to request the repayment of all monies on behalf of the award panel and the DCMS.

— It is a requirement of the scheme that both parties in receipt of an award must as a minimum acknowledge the award in all relevant publicity materials as follows:

— "The sponsorship of .... (organising body) by .... (business sponsor) has been recognised by an award under the Government's Business Sponsorship Incentive Scheme for Sport (Sportsmatch) which is administered in England by the Institute of Sports Sponsorship (ISS)."

Wherever possible the Sportsmatch logo (a bromide of which will be supplied) should be used in conjunction with the copy.

Appendix A (to Sportsmatch Rules)

Eligible Sports

Aikido
American Football
Angling
Archery
Arm Wrestling
Association Football
Athletics
Badminton
Ballooning
Baseball
Basketball
Billiards and Snooker
Bobsleigh
Boccia
Bowls
Boxing
Canoeing
Caving
Chinese Martial Arts
Cricket
Croquet
Crossbow
Curling
Cycling
Disability Sport
Dragon Boat Racing
Equestrian
Fencing
Fives
Flying
Gliding
Golf
Gymnastics

Handball
Hang Gliding
Hockey (field)
Hockey (ice)
Hockey (roller)
Hockey (skater)
Horse Racing
Hovering
Hurling
Judo
Ju Jitsu
Kabaddi
Karate
Kendo
Korfball
Lacrosse
Lawn Tennis
Life Saving
Luge
Modern Pentathlon
Motor Cycling
Motor Sports
Mountaineering
Movement and Dance,
    Exercise and Fitness
Netball
Orienteering
Parachuting
Paragliding
Petanque
Polo
Pool
Quoits
Racketball

Rambling
Real Tennis and Rackets
Rounders
Rowing
Rugby League
Rugby Union
Sailing and Yachting
Sand and Land Yachting
Shinty
Shooting
Skating (ice)
Skating (roller)
Skiing
Softball
Sombo Wrestling
Squash
Sub-Aqua
Surfing
Surf Life Saving
Swimming
Table Tennis
Taekwondo
Tang Soo Doo
Tenpin Bowling
Trampolining
Triathalon
Tug-of-War
Unihoc
Volleyball
Water Skiing
Weight Lifting
Wrestling
Yoga

APPENDIX VI

Sponsorship and Broadcasting

Under the Broadcasting Act 1990 (the Act) the Independent Television Commission (ITC) is responsible for devising and enforcing a code of governing standards and practice in advertising and in the sponsoring of programmes on television.

THE ITC CODE OF PROGRAMME SPONSORSHIP

Reproduced with the kind permission of the ITC.

Last revised in Spring 1997, the Code applies to all television programme services licensed by the ITC under the Act. At present these are Channel 3 (ITV and GMTV), Channel 4, S4C, Channel 5, non-domestic satellite services (*e.g.* BSkyB) which operate from the United Kingdom but do not use broadcasting frequencies allocated to the United Kingdom, and licensable programme services. Compliance with the Code is a condition of a ITC licence.

The Code distinguishes between programme sponsorship and television coverage of sponsored events. Sponsored events which have a bona fide non-television status may contain a range of sponsored references provided that these can clearly be justified by the editorial needs of the programme itself. Events which do not have a non-television status are subject to more limited restrictions on sponsored branding.

The Code is concerned with those aspects of television programme services which entail advertiser involvement in programming or promotional (rather than advertising) time. It applies in some respects to programmes which are not themselves sponsored in the conventional sense of the term and licensees should therefore read this Code in conjunction with the ITC Programme Code, the ITC Code of Advertising Standards and Practice and the ITC Rules on Advertising Breaks. The detailed rules set out below are intended to be applied in the spirit as well as the letter.

1. Definition of Programme Sponsorship

1.1 General

A programme is deemed to be sponsored if any part of its costs of production or transmission is met by an advertiser with a view to promoting its own or another's name, trade mark, image, activities, products or other direct or indirect commercial interest.

Advertiser is defined as any organisation or person other than the broadcaster or television producer.

1.2 Advertiser-supplied programmes

Programmes sometimes referred to as "advertiser-supplied" are deemed to be sponsored if the programme funder(s) have contributed towards or funded the programme for a promotional (see rule 1.1), rather than solely for an investment, purpose.

The Commission may deem programmes made by a production company closely associated with an advertiser to be sponsored.

1.3 Barter

The provision of a programme in exchange for advertising airtime (barter) does not in itself bring the arrangement within the definition of programme sponsorship (and hence make it unacceptable).

1.4 Merchandising and licensing arrangements

For the avoidance of doubt, merchandising or licensing arrangements based on one or more programme characters or elements are not deemed to be sponsorship. However, if the programme or its transmission were to be funded in any way whatsoever by the product manufacturer or licensee (or their agent) this would be considered to be sponsorship and the programme would be regarded as having an unacceptable promotional purpose.

2. Sponsorship and Advertising

2.1 General

One of the main principles governing the regulation of programme sponsorship is maintaining the distinction between advertising and sponsor credits, in order to ensure that credits are not used as a means of extending allowable advertising minutage.

2.2 Advertising which refers to sponsorship

Advertising which refers to sponsorship of a specific programme may not be transmitted in advertising breaks within or immediately adjacent to that programme (see note (ii)) to rule 5(c) of the ITC Code of Advertising Standards and Practice).

2.3 Application of Code of Advertising Standards and Practice

No sponsorship may breach the principles or spirit of the ITC Code of Advertising Standards and Practice. The detailed rules contained in the advertising code should be applied to sponsorship credits as appropriate.

Note: For other advertising related matters, see rules 1.3 (Barter), 3 (Scheduling), 4 (Prohibited and restricted sponsors) 8.8 (Advertising campaigns), and 10.1(ii) (Similarity between programmes and advertisings).

3. Scheduling

Without the previous approval of the Commission, no sponsored programme may be broadcast at a time or in circumstances where the sponsor would be restricted from advertising under the ITC Rules on Advertising Breaks.

4. Prohibited and Restricted Sponsors

4.1 Prohibited Sponsors

The following are prohibited from programme sponsorship.

   (i) **Political interests.** Any body whose objects are wholly or mainly of a political nature (see rule 10 of the ITC Code of the Advertising Standards and Practice).

   (ii) **Tobacco products.** A manufacturer or supplier of tobacco whose name is chiefly known to the public through its tobacco business, even though it may market other non-tobacco products or services.

   (iii) **Pharmaceutical products.** Any person whose business consists wholly or mainly in the manufacture or supply of pharmaceutical products available only on prescription. (This rule is under consideration as part of the review of the E.U. Directive on Television Broadcasting from which it derives.)

   (iv) **Prohibited advertisers.** (Without the previous approval of the Commission) any other product or service which may not be advertised under the ITC Code of Advertising Standards and Practice.

4.2 Restricted sponsors

Sponsorship by companies whose business consists wholly or mainly in the provision of betting and gaming services or whose name is chiefly known to the general public as a supplier of betting or gaming services is permissible subject to the following restrictions:

   (i) **Bookmaking.** Where the relevant service is bookmaking, the company concerned may not sponsor programmes devoted wholly or in part to the coverage of horse or greyhound racing or the results of such racing.

   (ii) **Gaming.** Where the relevant service is gaming, the company concerned may not sponsor television game shows which closely resemble the gaming that takes place in bingo clubs or casinos.

   (iii) **Children's programmes.** No company with betting or gaming interests may sponsor programmes specifically designed for or aimed at children.

Note: In certain cases sponsorships not precluded by rule 4.2 may not be permissible because of the prohibition of promotional material content (see rule 10.2) e.g. sponsorship of a pools check service by a football pools company.

5. Sponsorable Categories

Sponsorship is allowed for:

   (i) whole programmes or substantive programme strands;
   (ii) "showcases" or themed programme blocks provided all the constituent programmes are eligible for sponsorship by the sponsor;

(iii) "seamless" channels (*i.e.* channels which do not have distinct programmes) may, subject to compliance with the other requirements of this Code, be sponsored;

(iv) some specialist news reports (see rule 6.1 below).

No other element of the television service may be sponsored, including items of station presentation or continuity.

6. Unsponsorable Programmes

6.1 News

Programmes and news flashes comprising local, national or international news items must not be sponsored. However, some specialist news reports (for example, cultural, sports, traffic, travel or weather) presented outside the context of a general news programme *may* be sponsored. Such sponsored reports must be separated from the news programme in some clearly apparent way, *e.g.* by programme end credits or a commercial break.

6.2 Business and financial reports

Business and financial reports where they contain interpretation or comment must not be sponsored.

6.3 Current affairs

Current affairs or other programmes which mainly deal with explanation or analysis or current events must not be sponsored. This definition includes programmes dealing with matters of political or industrial controversy, or with current public policy.

6.4 Use of news presenters in sponsored programmes

Presenters of unsponsorable programmes must not be used (in vision or voice-over) in sponsored programmes scheduled adjacent to the unsponsorable programme in which they have appeared. This restriction does not apply to presenters of incidental reports or minor items.

News presenters may, however, be used in voice-over only in sponsored specialist reports following the news (*e.g.* weather, travel news). They must be separated from the news programme as required in rule 6.1. News presenters may not be used in sponsorship credits (see rule 8.10).

7. Restricted Programmes

7.1 Consumer advice programmes

Programmes or series offering or including reviews or advice on the purchase or rental of products or services, including where to go or what to see, may not be sponsored by advertisers whose businesses involve the marketing or provision of products or services of the type featured. Instructional ("how to do") programmes which do not include purchasing advice or reviews ("what to buy") do not fall within this category and may be sponsored by advertisers who supply products or services relevant to the area of interest concerned, provided there is no conflict with the other provisions of the Code (see, in particular, rules 9.1 and 9.2, and 10.2).

7.2 *Controversial connections*

Programmes may not be sponsored if the programme refers to issues about which there is significant public controversy and in relation to which the sponsor has a direct interest.

8. Credits

8.1 *Transparency requirements*

Surreptitious sponsorship is not allowed. Any sponsorship must be clearly identified at the beginning and/or end of the programme. There may also be bumper credits (*i.e.* entering and/or leaving any commercial break). Credits may be aural and/or visual.

8.2 *Placing of credits*

There must be no programme sponsor credits within programmes.

    (i) Front sponsor credits must precede and not be integrated within any part of the programme apart from its title sequence (including title music), provided that sequence does not include, nor is preceded by, extracts from the programme itself.

    (ii) End and bumper credits may overlap the programme for not more than five seconds.

8.3 *Credit lengths (Channels 3, 4 and 5 only)*

    (i) Front credits. A front credit must not exceed 15 seconds in length where one sponsor is involved and 20 seconds where there is more than one. Where the credit is integrated within a programme title sequence which is longer than the permitted length for sponsor credits, the sponsor credit will be deemed to start with the commencement of the title sequence and all sponsor references must be contained within the first 15 (or as the case may be, 20) seconds. However, there may be one additional reference to the sponsor within the title sequence provided this is included within the overall limit for the credit.

Example: In a title sequence lasting 30 seconds it would be permissible for the last 5 seconds to contain a reference to the sponsor provided all other sponsor references were contained within the first 10 seconds.

This applies only to integration within ordinary programme title sequences and not to any additional sequences, *e.g.* "showcase" sequences referring to a programme series. If these sequences carry sponsorship references, the sequence as a whole will be regarded as the sponsorship credit and must not exceed 15 seconds.

    (ii) Bumper and end credits. Each bumper or end credit must not be more than 10 seconds in length (even where multiple sponsorship is concerned).

    (iii) Short programmes and programme segments. The credit entitlements referred to above do not apply unless the running time of the sponsored material net of the credits themselves is at least 50 seconds. If not, the combined total of front and end credits may not exceed 10 seconds or one half of the running time, whichever is greatest.

8.4 Sponsorship message

The front credit, or where there is none, the end credit, must identify the sponsor and explain the sponsor's actual connection with the programme, for example, "sponsored by", "in association with" or "produced by". It must not suggest that the ITC licensee's broadcasting responsibilities have been ceded to the sponsor or compromised in any way. Expressions like "brought to you by" are, therefore, not acceptable. Where programmes have a substantial child audience, it is particularly important that the sponsorship relationship is explained in a simple, straightforward manner.

8.5 Explanation of business

Credits may indicate the connection between a sponsor and a brand or the nature of the sponsor's business, for example, "sponsored by company x makers of brandy", or ". . . makers of widgets".

8.6 Straplines

Credits may include audio and/or visual straplines which clearly refer to the programme itself, or to the sponsor's relationship to the programme. Straplines or slogans of a general nature which are used in the sponsor's advertising, which do not refer to the programme or sponsorship, may appear in static, visual display only. However, in no circumstances may straplines directly encourage the purchase or rental of the sponsor's goods or services, for example by making specific references to the attributes or prices of those products or services, or by including injunctions to purchase.

8.7 Product representations

Credits must not feature the sponsor's specific or branded product (whether or not packaged) or any visual representation of their product or service. In no circumstances may specific product or service benefits be shown or referred to.

8.8 Advertising campaigns

There must be no visual or aural extracts from, nor elements which closely resemble, the sponsor's television advertising in any sponsor credit, or any trailer or sponsored programme.

8.9 Trade marks

Subject to the restrictions in rules 8.6 and 8.7 above, any credit (with the exception of end credits under rule 12.3 below) may include the sponsor's name, trade mark or logo without restriction as to size. Animation and musical effects may be employed.

8.10 Presenters

Care must be taken to ensure that sponsor credits are not confused with items of station continuity or actual programmes. Station continuity presenters and leading programme performers (including animated characters) should not present sponsor credits either in vision or voice-over, even if they are not otherwise associated with the sponsored programme. In any case, no performers or characters who appear in a sponsored programme may be used at all, either in vision or voice-over, in the sponsor credits for that programme. The only exception to this is appearances in title sequences where the credits are fully integrated with these sequences but in such cases there must be no interaction, explicit or implied, between the performer and the sponsorship material.

8.11 Sponsors' names in programme titles

(i) **Channels 3, 4 and 5.** A sponsor's name must not be used in a programme title except when the title is that of a sponsored event covered by the programme (*e.g.* the Coca Cola Cup Final).

(ii) **Other channels.** Where a sponsored event is covered in a programme which is itself sponsored and titled with the programme sponsor's name, this must not be done in such a way as to imply that the programme sponsor is the event sponsor if this is not in fact the case.

Licensees must also pay due regard to the need for appropriate recognition for the event sponsor (see rule 13.3).

For the purpose of this rule a sponsored event is as defined in rule 13.2.

8.12 Trailers

The main purpose of a trailer is to alert viewers to a forthcoming programme or to provide general information about the licensee's programme service. The sponsor's presence should therefore remain secondary. There may only be one simple reference to the sponsor, which can be aural and/or visual, lasting not more than five seconds.

9. Programme Integrity

9.1 Sponsor influence

A core principle of this Code is the preservation of programme integrity by not allowing programme agendas to be distorted for commercial purposes. No sponsor is permitted any influence on either the content or the scheduling of a programme in such a way as to affect the editorial independence and responsibility of the broadcaster.

9.2 Programmes directly funded by the sponsor

In the case of programmes made or funded by the sponsor, licensees must take special care to ensure that their responsibility is in no way compromised. Where such programmes have been commissioned (rather than acquired after viewing), the licensee must maintain sufficient contractual rights to secure their position to assert editorial control throughout the production process.

9.3 Commission guidance

Licensees are invited to request specific guidance from the Commission in cases where they are unsure whether a proposed sponsorship relationship would be acceptable. The Commission reserves the right to impose restrictions on sponsorship associations between particular categories of advertiser and particular programmes going beyond those in this Code.

10. Promotional References

10.1 General requirements for all programmes

(i) **Undue prominence.** Section 10.6 of the ITC Programme Code forbids undue prominence for commercial goods and services in programmes of any kind (whether sponsored or not).

(ii) **Similarity between programmes and advertising.** Except where programme footage is allowed in television advertising under rule 5 of the ITC Code of Advertising Standards and Practice, close similarity between a programme's content and an advertiser's advertising might constitute grounds for regarding the programme as having an unacceptable promotional purpose. This is likely to be the case if a character created for advertising or marketing purposes is developed for use in a programme, regardless of whether the advertiser is involved in making the programme or not.

10.2 Sponsor references in sponsored programmes

In the case of sponsored programmes, it is unlikely that any reference at all, whether visual or aural, to the sponsor will be editorially justified. The financial relationship between a sponsor and a broadcaster or programme maker may create a higher presumption that the inclusion of a sponsor reference (whether within the programme or in a credit under rule 12.3) is deliberate and/or promotional. Generic references to the sponsor's (unbranded) product, service or business may amount to promotional references for the purposes of this rule.

10.3 Single interest channels

The ITC is prepared to apply a less stringent test in this area to advertiser-supplied programmes broadcast on single interest channels provided the identity of the advertiser supplier is made transparent to viewers at the beginning of the programme. For example, travel programmes funded by a tourist authority would be acceptable on a themed travel channel. Such programmes must not, however, contain material which directly encourages the purchase or rental of the sponsor's product or service, *e.g.* by providing information on prices, exhortations to purchase or contact details.

10.4 Infomercials

For the avoidance of doubt, the ITC has no objection to the broadcast of "infomercials" (advertising features of programme length) within the allocations in the ITC's Rules on Advertising Breaks for advertising minutage and, if relevant, home shopping, provided their advertising purpose is clearly signalled to viewers. (On Channels 3, 4 and 5 extended advertising features are permissible only between midnight – 6.00 a.m.)

10.5 Music videos

Music videos featuring advertisements, or extracts from advertisements (whether previously televised or not), where the advertiser has contributed towards the funding of the video are themselves considered advertisements.

10.6 *Masthead programming*

(i) **Channels 3, 4 and 5 only.** Masthead programming (programming made or funded by periodical, newspaper, book or informational software publishers which incorporates the name of the publisher's product in its title and which has editorial content similar to that of the publisher's product) is not allowed.

(ii) **Other channels.** On other channels masthead programming is permitted but there may be no in-programme cross-promotion with the parent publication.

Masthead programming is not permitted by magazines that are supplementary marketing initiatives to other types of business.

Magazines which are used for masthead programming may not be regarded as programme support material for the purposes of rule 15 of this Code nor Section 10.3 of the ITC Programme Code.

The following rules apply to advertiser references in game shows and viewers' competitions included within programmes whether sponsored or not.

11. Game Shows and Viewers' Competitions

11.1 *Game shows*

(i) Advertisers may donate prizes and they may be their own products and services.

(ii) There may be two mentions of the brand of the main prize or prize donor (if this is different) which may include brief factual and/or visual references (normally no longer than five seconds). Descriptions should avoid promotional statements.

(iii) Trailers, teasers or reminders for game shows may not contain brand references.

(iv) End credits under rule 12.3 are only allowed for the brands or donors of prizes which have not been identified during the programme.

11.2 *Viewers' competitions*

(i) The licensee must retain full responsibility for the competition. Competitions in programme time must either occur within the body of a programme or as part of a programme promotion in presentation time. Competitions cannot stand alone as programmes in their own right.

(ii) Advertisers may donate prizes and they may be their own products and services. Where editorially justified, there may be a single mention of the brand of the main prize or prize donor (if this is different) which may include brief factual and/or visual references (normally no longer than five seconds). Descriptions should avoid promotional statements.

(iii) Prizes may not be branded products or services which are referred to elsewhere in the programme. Prizes connected with programme items concerned with sports, music, film, video, theatre and book titles are exempt from this provision.

(iv) The questions should have a clear thematic connection with the programme in which they appear. They may not refer to the products or services of the prize manufacturer or donor. Questions connected with sports, music, film, video, theatre and book titles are exempt from this provision.

(v) Trailers containing competitions, teasers or reminders for competitions may not contain brand references.

(vi) If the competition relates directly to a sponsored event of the kind described in rule 13 and the event sponsor's name is part of the title of the event, that title may be included in the name of the competition.

(vii) Where the programme title incorporates the broadcast sponsor's name that name may also be included in the name of the competition.

(viii) Sponsors may not donate their own products or services as prizes in viewers' competitions contained within programmes they are sponsoring.

(ix) Where the licensee is jointly running a competition with an advertiser there can be no mention of this on-screen.

(x) End credits under rule 12.3 are allowed for brands or donors of prizes which have not been identified during the programme.

12. Product Placement

12.1 Definition

Product placement is defined as the inclusion of, or reference to, a product or service within a programme in return for payment or other valuable consideration to the programme maker or ITC licensee (or any representative or associate of either). This is prohibited.

12.2 Restrictions on donated goods and services

Where their use is clearly justified editorially, products or services may be acquired at no or less than full cost. Provision of the article must not be conditional on any specific agreement as to the manner of its appearance in the programme.

12.3 End credits

Except in programmes prohibited from sponsorship under rule 6, a basic text acknowledgment lasting no more than five seconds may be included within the end credits of the programme for the product or service acquired under the terms of rule 12.2, but only where the identity of the product or service is not otherwise apparent from the programme itself.

Note: Please note that Section 10.6 of the ITC Programme Code, which prohibits undue prominence, applies irrespective of the means by which the product or service is acquired.

13. Coverage of Events

13.1 Sponsored events

Programme coverage of events and locations (*e.g.* the Fosters' Oval) which have been sponsored, or at which advertising or branding is present, may itself be sponsored. An event or location sponsor may also be the programme sponsor.

13.2 Advertising at events

Visual or aural references to any advertising, signage or branding at an event must be limited to what can clearly be justified by the editorial needs of the programme itself.

Such advertising or branding is acceptable providing the event has a bona fide non-television status. Three conditions of that status must be satisfied:

(i) the development and running of the event must be done by a body whose existence is independent of television, advertising and promotional interests;

(ii) television coverage must not be the principal purpose of the event;

(iii) the event must be open to members of the public irrespective of whether or not it is televised.

On-site advertising and branding arrangements are otherwise a matter for agreement between the relevant official body and the licensee.

13.3 Acknowledgment of event sponsors

Aural and visual references in the programme coverage to event sponsors should be sufficient to identify the events or elements (*e.g.* individually sponsored races or a sponsored prize ceremony) within it, and should provide appropriate recognition to the event sponsor. They must, however, clearly be justified by the editorial needs of the programme itself. In order to give fair recognition to an event sponsor whose identity is not otherwise apparent, a basic end credit lasting not more than five seconds identifying the event sponsor(s) may be included within the end credits of the programme with the exception of event sponsors prohibited from programme sponsorship under rule 4. A credit may be particularly appropriate for programmes such as those covering arts events where the event is not titled with the sponsor's name and signage or branding is not shown.

13.4 Tobacco sponsorship and branding

Coverage of tobacco-sponsored events, or events at which there is branding, signage or advertising for any tobacco company, must be consistent with the requirements of the Voluntary Agreement reached between the Minister for Sport and the Tobacco Manufacturer's Association dated January 31, 1995 or any replacement thereof.

13.5 Electronic imaging systems

The use of electronic imaging systems during event coverage must comply with the ITC Sponsorship Guidance Note on "Virtual Advertising".

14. Information Services

A programme may include technical informational services (*e.g.* timing or other specialised data) electronically generated directly on screen at reduced or no charge in return for an on-screen acknowledgment to the technical provider, which may appear when the information is displayed. The technical provider must not additionally sponsor the programme. Informational services may not themselves be sponsored. The provision of information on-site at any event is not covered or restricted by this rule.

15. Sponsored Support Material

Programme support material as defined in Section 10.3 of the ITC Programme Code, and promoted in accordance with it, may be sponsored subject to the following rules.

15.1 Unsponsorable programmes and support material

Programmes which are not eligible for sponsorship under rule 6 of this Code cannot have programme support material sponsored.

15.2 Prohibited and restricted sponsors and support material

Sponsors prohibited or restricted from programme sponsorship under rule 4 of this Code are subject to the same prohibitions and restrictions regarding sponsorship of support material.

15.3 Transparency requirements for support material

The sponsor must be identified when details of how to get the support material are given. The sponsor credit must be limited to a simple, factual audio and/or visual reference to the identity of the sponsor, lasting no longer than 15 seconds (or 20 seconds where there is more than one sponsor). It must be separate from, and not integrated with, the programme sponsor credits. A brief visual display of the sponsor's trade mark or registered logo may be included with the sponsor's name.

15.4 *Web sites*

For the purposes of rule 15.3, in order to determine whether an Internet web site is sponsored, support material on Internet web sites will be considered to be sponsored if the homepage is sponsored or if more than one-third of the editorial material on the site over which the licensee has control is sponsored.

Note: See Section 10.3 of the ITC Programme Code for the rules that apply to published programme support material.

16. Acquired Programmes

The Code applies also to acquired programmes, including those programmes acquired from outside the United Kingdom. Films made for the cinema and coverage of sporting and other events taking place outside the United Kingdom, however, may deviate from the Code where this is unavoidable.

17. Children's Programmes

Licensees should consider carefully the appropriateness of any sponsorship of children's programmes. In particular, for programmes addressed to younger children, it is important to remember that the status of a sponsorship relationship may be difficult for younger children to understand. Some parents may also have reservations about how far those producing goods and services for use by children should be able to use for commercial purposes children's enthusiasm for a particular programme or programme character through the particularly close association that sponsorship involves.

Appendices 1 and 2 to the Code contain further specific rules on programme sponsorship by religious and charitable bodies.

THE RADIO AUTHORITY ADVERTISING AND SPONSORSHIP CODE

Reproduced with the kind permission of the Radio Authority.

The Act also makes it the statutory duty of the Radio Authority to devise and enforce a Code which sets standards and practice in advertising and programme sponsorship on independent radio. Radio Authority licensees are responsible for ensuring that their broadcast material complies with the Code. The Code was last revised in March 1997. The rules are divided into three sections. Only the section which deals with programme sponsorship is reproduced here.

Sponsorship principles

1. "Sponsorship" in this Code refers to any item of publicity, other than an advertisement, broadcast in return for payment or any other valuable consideration to a licensee.

2. Editorial control of sponsored programmes must remain with the licensee.

3. All sponsor involvement must be declared so that the listener knows who is paying/contributing and why.

4. The sponsorship rules are intended to be applied in the spirit as well as the letter.

Advance Clearance of Sponsorship

The Authority does not require sponsored programming to be cleared in advance. Licensees must ensure that their sponsored programmes comply both with this Code and with the Authority's Programme Code.

The Radio Authority's advertising staff will give general guidance to licensees on sponsorship proposals if requested.

Programme Sponsorship

1. Definition

A programme is sponsored if it is broadcast in return for payment or other valuable consideration (which includes the provision of the programme itself) to a licensee.

Practice Note. The rules which follow apply to sponsored competitions and promotions but not to contra deals (where the licensee exchanges advertising time for facilities or services, related or unrelated to programming).

2. Sponsorable Programmes

All programmes may be sponsored with the exception of news bulletins.

Practice Note: Bulletins comprising local, national or international news items must be presented with impartiality and accuracy which sponsorship might appear to compromise. A simple single acknowledgment of the source of the news, whether a news agency or local newspaper, is not regarded as sponsorship. Such an acknowledgment should not be presented in a way which appears to be a sponsor credit.

3. Direct Links

A direct link between the sponsor's commercial activities and the programme's subject-matter is acceptable in all sponsored programmes.

4. Editorial Control

Ultimate editorial control of sponsored programmes must remain with the licensee.

5. Programme Contribution from Sponsors

Sponsors may contribute to the editorial content of all sponsored programmes, except:

> news features;
> news magazines;
> current affairs;
> business/financial news or comment;
> programmes/documentary items addressing matters of political or industrial controversy or relating to current public policy.

Practice Notes. A contribution to editorial from a sponsor may be information, advice or ideas for a programme's content or presentation. For example, a supermarket chain which sponsors a programme on healthy eating may produce the programme, contribute to production costs and include specialist advice from its nutritionalists. Material broadcast must be balanced and impartial and an appropriate range of views should be represented where necessary.

The types of programme listed at above may be sponsored but sponsors may not contribute in any way to editorial content. The sponsorship must represent financial assistance only which must be made clear in the sponsor credit. For example, "The Business Programme brought to you with financial help from Barclays Bank".

6. Product Endorsement

Endorsement of a sponsor's product or service within editorial is not permitted.

Practice Notes. A sponsor must not seek to sell its own products within editorial. Sponsored competition prizes should not be described in such a way as to constitute advertising, nor should competition questions include the gratuitous mention of the sponsor's brand.

7. Sponsor Credits

Sponsor funding and contribution to programmes must be clearly acknowledged. Sponsor credits must be brief, precise and capable of substantiation. Any link between the programme's subject-matter and the sponsor's commercial activities must be made clear.

Frequency

(a) Programmes/items of up to 15 minutes long must contain at least one sponsor credit, at the beginning or end of the programme/item.

(b) Longer programmes must contain at least one sponsor credit at the beginning or end of the programme and, where there is a link between the sponsor's commercial activities and the programme's subject matter, at least one sponsor credit approximately every 15 minutes.

Content

Sponsor credits, whether in the course of the sponsored item or in the trails for the item, must contain all of the following information:

(a) the programme/feature title;

(b) the name of the sponsor;

(c) an expression of the sponsor's contribution, where it is other than or additional to financial support, if the contribution is not self-evident;

(d) a brief identification of the sponsor's commercial activities, where they are not self-evident.

Credits must be, and sound like, acknowledgments, not advertisements. Such short branding statements should not generally include telephone numbers, full addresses, prices or details of special offers.

[NB: *Identification of the licensee or, if relevant, the programme provider is optional*].

Practice Notes. Listeners must be able to recognise unmistakably sponsored programmes and any contribution to editorial content from sponsors.

Sponsor credits may include sponsors' advertising slogans or copylines and brand or corporate names. Sponsors' names may appear in programme titles.

Any link between the programme's subject-matter and the sponsor's commercial activities must be made clear.

Style and presentation may necessitate that an "end" credit appears in the closing segment of the programme, rather than at the very end. The same applies to any "top of the hour" credits.

There are no requirements regarding the frequency of programme trails, but those which credit the sponsor must also include the elements listed under "Content" above.

Examples of suitable credits and taglines include:

(a) Haig Whisky, fine blended malt from the Highlands, sponsored coverage of the Edinburgh Festival firework concert (on Radio Forth);

(b) The Texas Homecare DIY Show (was produced by Zebra Productions) (for Red Dragon Radio);

(c) The Coca Cola Album Chart is made and produced by Coca Cola Productions (for Independent Radio);

(d) Weather Update with Peugeot, the lion goes from strength to strength;

(e) The Birthday Bonanza Competition with prizes donated by Thomson Holidays Cardiff;

(f) Traffic and Travel from the AA, courtesy of Fiat Motors;

(g) (Beacon's) Cricket Coverage, brought to you by Summer Sports of Wolverhampton;

(h) Canada Day (on GWR) is supplied by Labatts, Canadian Lager for the first time in the U.K.;

(j) The Fashion Report, courtesy of Unilever, makers of Persil;

(k) Homebuyer's Spot in association with First Place Ltd, Estate Agents of the Midlands.

[NB: Information in brackets is optional].

8. Sponsor Advertisements

Sponsors may buy advertising spots in and around the programme they sponsor.

Practice Note. If the format and style of an advertisement sounds similar to the format and style of the programme, it must be separated by other material such as a jingle/station ident or by scheduling it in the middle of an advertising break.

9. Prohibited Sponsors

(a) Those who are prohibited from advertising under any Advertising Code Rule may only sponsor programmes with the prior written approval of the Authority.

(b) Religious programmes and programmes/features directed particularly at children (*i.e.* those aged 15 and below) must not be sponsored by companies whose commercial interests involve sanitary protection, family planning, contraceptives, pregnancy testing and anti-AIDS and anti-drugs.

(c) Religious programmes and programmes/features directed particularly at people under 18 must not be sponsored by companies whose commercial interests involve alcohol, cigars or pipe tobacco.

10. Sponsorship by Betting and Gaming Companies

Companies with betting and gaming interests may sponsor programmes, subject to the following restrictions:

(a) football pools companies may not sponsor programmes devoted wholly or in part to results bulletins of football matches on which football pools competitions are based;

(b) bookmakers may not sponsor programmes devoted wholly or in part to horse or greyhound racing coverage or the results bulletins of such racing;

(c) gaming companies may not sponsor competitions or features which closely resemble the gaming that takes place in casinos;

(d) companies with gambling interests may not sponsor programmes specifically designed for or aimed at children (*i.e.* those aged 15 or below);

(e) sponsor credits for betting and gaming companies (excluding football pools and permitted lotteries) must not include advertising slogans of any kind or descriptions of the companies' commercial interest.

11. *Discrimination*

A sponsorship arrangement must not be seen to discriminate unreasonably against other advertisers and sponsors.

12. *Complaint Handling*

Stations should adopt appropriate procedures for the handling of written complaints about sponsored programming. Written records should be retained for a period of 12 months. Procedures shall include a requirement that members of the public who complain are properly informed that they may refer matters, if unresolved, to the Authority.

The Institute of Sports Sponsorship Code of Conduct

Reproduced with the kind permission of the ISS.

The Institute of Sports Sponsorship was established in 1985 to improve the links between sports organisers and commercial sponsors so that the needs and expectations of both parties to all sponsorship contracts might be met to the greatest possible extent. The ISS Code of Conduct is an expression of its determination to promote the highest standards of professional practice in the business of sports sponsorship. Adherence to its principles is not limited to members of the Institute, and the ISS hopes it will become the standard for all companies involved in sports sponsorship. Equally, the ISS hopes it will be used by sporting bodies and organisations as a guide to their expectations from a sponsor. Sport sponsorship is a partnership between business and sport in which both parties have rights and responsibilities. The Code of Conduct will help all parties to find their relationship from the outset and form a firm basis for long term co-operation to the mutual benefit of business and sport.

Members should at all times maintain and promote the highest ethical standards of conduct and professional integrity in their dealings with other organisations and individuals involved with sports sponsorship. In particular members should:

- **Deal** fairly and honestly with all other parties involved in sponsorship and ensure that the terms of their relationship are clearly agreed; unless requested, not involve themselves in the rules, regulations and governing structure of the sponsored sport.

- **Recognise** the risks to the image and long-term effectiveness of sponsorship as a result of over-commercialisation and act accordingly; ensure that the opinions of the legitimately interested parties—governing bodies, players, spectators, viewers and government—concerning acceptable levels of branding and associated advertising and promotion will be taken into consideration in the creation and development of sponsorship packages.

- **Avoid** any action that could give the impression of official sponsor status when such status has not been negotiated with the sponsored event or organising body.

- **Refrain** from undertaking programme sponsorship unless it has been first offered to the event sponsor by the television contractor.

- **Conduct** all sponsorship activities in accordance with the letter and spirit of all relevant legislation, voluntary agreements and codes of conduct and discourage all contrary practices by directors, employees and agents; disclose any actual or potential conflicts of interest, and respect the confidentiality of information supplied to them.

- **Encourage** training, skills development and understanding for the implementation of effective sports sponsorship programmes among their own staff and sporting partners.

- **Negotiate** clear and unambiguous sponsorship agreements that set out the obligations, responsibilities and benefits for each party, and recognise the need for a proper financial, commercial and legal structure; where minors are involved, ensure proper independent advice is made available.

- **Encourage** programme contractors to dedicate a proportion of the income from sponsored programming of sport to the long term benefit and development of the sport concerned.

- **Avoid** any arrangements that may endanger the health or safety of any participant or spectator of the sponsored event.

- **Promote** and encourage the highest standard of sporting achievement and personal behaviour among participants and spectators.

Sponsorship Notice 701/41/95 (VAT)

This notice replaces the February 1990 edition of VAT Leaflet 701/41, "Sponsorship". Major changes from the previous edition are marked by sidelining in the margin [not shown on this reproduction].

The information in this notice was accurate at the time of going to press (date on the front cover [July 1, 1995]). [Paragraph 8 was updated in January 1996 by Update 1.]

1. What is this notice about?

This notice explains how VAT applies to sponsorship whether this is in the form of money, goods or services.

If you are not already registered for VAT you should read Notice 700/1 "Should I be registered for VAT?" Even if your taxable turnover would otherwise be below the VAT registration limits, you may become liable to register because of your sponsorship income.

If you are a registered charity receiving sponsorship you should also read Notice 701/1, "Charities".

2. What is sponsorship?

Sponsorship is the term commonly used for financial or other support in the form of goods and services given by businesses or members of the public to sports, arts, education, charities, etc. The sponsor receives something in return, for example, advertising, free or reduced priced tickets, hospitality, etc.

You will be making supplies if there is a written or oral agreement or understanding that, in return for a sum of money, goods or other services, a sponsor will receive from you some publicity or any other form of benefit. It makes no difference if the sponsorship is called something else. What matters is the agreement or understanding between the parties.

3. What is a donation?

A donation is something which is freely given and which secures nothing in return. If you do not give or do anything in return for the sponsor's support, you are not making a taxable supply, and the sponsorship (whether of money, goods or services) can be treated as outside the scope of VAT (but see paragraph 4 which explains how donations of goods may give rise to VAT liability for the donor).

4. Is there a supply?

To be treated as outside the scope of VAT, the sponsor's support must be entirely voluntary and secure nothing whatever in return. A taxable supply will not be created by the simple acknowledgment of support such as:

— giving a flag, or sticker;

— inclusion in a list of supporters in a programme, or on a notice;

— naming a building or university chair after the donor;

— putting the donor's name on the back of a seat in a theatre.

If the sponsor's contribution is made on condition that the sponsor's trading logo is advertised or promoted or they receive some other type of benefit, then it is all consideration for a taxable supply and you must account for VAT on it. This applies regardless of whether you have a written sponsorship contract with the sponsor.

Examples of supplies commonly made are:

— naming of the event after the sponsor;

— display of the sponsor's company logo or trading name on shirts worn by a team;

— display of the sponsor's logo in programmes or at the venue;

— free or reduced price admission tickets;

— access to special events such as premieres or gala evenings;

— entertainment or hospitality facilities;

— exclusive or priority booking rights.

5. Accounting for VAT

You must normally account for VAT on everything you receive under a sponsorship agreement, including anything which is to be distributed as prizes or paid over as expenses to a third party. Where the agreement provides that the amount of money you will be paid depends, for example, on how successful you are, you must account for VAT on the actual amount you receive.

You must issue any VAT registered sponsors with a tax invoice for the amount on which you are accounting for VAT. The sponsor can then reclaim the VAT as input tax subject to the normal rules. If you agreed the amount without reference to VAT you must treat it as VAT inclusive.

6. Mixed sponsorship and donation

If you receive a donation in addition to sponsorship under a sponsorship agreement, you can exclude the donation from the amount on which you account for VAT provided that it is clear from any agreement that the donation is entirely separate from the sponsorship you receive.

If you provide benefits to your sponsor on condition that the sponsor gives you the donation, it is part of the consideration for your supply, and you must include it in the amount on which you account for VAT.

7. Donations of goods

True donations of money, or of services, are outside the scope of VAT. But if you receive a donation (or gift) of goods and the donor is registered for VAT, the donor must account for VAT at the appropriate rate on what it would have cost them to purchase the gift at the time it is donated. VAT incurred by you when using the gift for the purposes of your business may be reclaimed as your input tax subject to the normal rules. You will find out more about this in VAT Leaflet 700/35, "Business gifts." Information about the donation of goods to a charity for sale or export can be found in Notice 701/1, "Charities."

Goods given in return for services or other gifts are not "donated" but are consideration in a barter transaction (see paragraph 9).

8. Donations of prizes in newspapers and magazine competitions

If you publish a newspaper or a magazine in which you run a competition and goods are donated as prizes, there may be a general understanding that the donor will benefit from some publicity as a result. However, provided that you are under no specific contractual obligation to provide advertising or publicity in return for the donor agreeing to provide the prizes, you are not making a supply of advertising to the donor, and you need not account for VAT.

The donor is then making a free supply of goods to you and must account for tax on their current purchase price. There is an exception for small business gifts. Where gifts cost you £15 or less and were given away on or after November 29, 1995 (or cost you £10 or less and were given away on November 28, 1995 or earlier), there is no need to account for any tax unless the goods formed part of a series or succession of such gifts. These same rules apply for the onward supply of prizes by you to the winners.

However, if you have a clear contract under which the donor provides the prize on condition that you provide the advertising you are making a supply of advertising to the donor and you must account for VAT on this.

9. Donations of prizes other than goods—barter arrangements

The same principles apply as in paragraph 8 as to whether a supply of advertising exists.

Where there is no supply of advertising the donation of the prizes is free and outside the scope of VAT. However, where the donor provides a prize such as a weekend break or a day trip to a sporting event, the VAT incurred by the donor will not be deductible as input tax by the donor, by virtue of the business entertaining provisions.

Where there is a supply of advertising, a barter arrangement exists. Advertising is provided by the publisher to the donor in return for the provision of a holiday/day trip, etc. In these circumstances the publisher must charge VAT on the supply of advertising. The donor may have to charge output tax on the holiday/day trip depending on where the holiday takes place. Please refer to Notice 741, "Place of supply of services."

If the donor is accounting for VAT under the Tour Operators' Margin Scheme the donor will only be accounting for tax on the margin on the holiday/trip. However, the donor will not be allowed to reclaim the VAT on the direct costs of providing the holiday/trip as input tax. Under the Margin Scheme the donor will not be issuing a tax invoice and the publisher will not therefore be able to claim the margin VAT as input tax. The selling price of the holiday, for the purpose of the donor's Margin Scheme calculation, will be equal to the amount in money which the donor would normally expect to receive for the holiday. This will also be the value of the supply of advertising from the publisher to the donor.

If the donor is not using the Margin Scheme to account for VAT, the donor will be able to claim any VAT incurred in connection with the holiday/trip as input tax. However, the VAT charged by the donor to the publisher will not be deductible as input tax by virtue of the business entertaining provisions. For VAT purposes the value of the supply of the holiday/trip by the donor to the publisher will be equal to the amount in money which the donor would normally expect to receive for the holiday. This will also be the value of the supply of advertising from the publisher to the sponsor.

10. Sponsorship for non-business activities

If you are sponsored for something which is not in the course or furtherance of any business you carry on, for example, for a hobby, any services you supply in return may be treated as outside the scope of VAT, unless you supply these services on such a scale and with such regularity that they constitute a business in their own right. This will depend on the scale, frequency and regularity of your supplies to your sponsors. If you are in doubt about whether or not any of your activities are "business" for VAT purposes contact your local VAT office for advice.

If you are required to register for VAT only because of your sponsorship income, remember that the only VAT you can reclaim as input tax is the VAT you incur on expenses which relate to your services to the sponsor.

11. Agents

The VAT treatment of sponsorship is the same whether or not you or your sponsor employ an agent. An agent must account for VAT on any commission charged.

12. Sponsorship from overseas

If you make supplies of advertising services and publicity to overseas sponsors, your services may be outside the scope of U.K. VAT. If you receive supplies of advertising services and publicity from overseas, for example by sponsoring a non-U.K. sports personality to advertise your product, you may have to account for VAT using the reverse charge procedure. You will find out more about this in Notice 741, "Place of supply of services."

13. Sponsorship in association with fund-raising events

If you are making supplies to sponsors as part of a fund-raising event your supplies may be exempt. You will find out more about this in the Notice 701/1, "Charities".

14. Further help or advice

If you need further help or advice on any points covered by this notice, please ask your local VAT office. They are best placed to answer your queries because of their local knowledge. The address and telephone number are in the phone book under "Customs and Excise".

Notice 700/51, "VAT Enquiries Guide" gives information about making enquiries and the standard of service you can expect from Customs and Excise.

15. Comments

Customs and Excise would welcome any comments you have on this publication. Do you find it generally helpful? Are there any parts of it you do not undertstand? Can you suggest any ways in which it can be impoved?

Please send comments to:

VAT 1B
H.M. Customs and Excise
4th Floor West
New King's Beam House
22 Upper Ground
London
SE1 9PJ.

Legislation and Regulations Relevant to Sponsorship, Endorsement and Merchandising

Statutes amd Regulations

The following list of United Kingdom statutes and regulations are among those which may restrict, control or otherwise affect sponsorship, and should be particularly noted. The list is not exhaustive and the general law on matters such as contract and negligence should also be observed.

Arbitration Acts 1950 and 1996
Broadcasting Acts 1990 and 1996
Charities Acts 1992 and 1993
Companies Act 1985 (as amended)
Competition Acts 1980 and 1998 (1980 transitional only)
Consumer Protection Act 1987 and Regulations
Control of Misleading Advertisements Regulations 1988
Copyright, Designs and Patents Act 1988
Defamation Act 1952
Fair Trading Act 1973
Human Rights Bill
Income and Corporation Taxes Act 1988
Misrepresentation Act 1976
Olympic Symbol (Protection) Act 1985
Registered Designs Act 1949 (as amended)
Resale Prices Act 1976
Restrictive Trade Practices Act 1976 (transitional only)
Sale of Goods Act 1979
Sex Discrimination Acts 1975 and 1986
Supply of Goods and Services Act 1982
Trade Descriptions Act 1968
Trade Marks Act 1994
Unfair Contract Terms Act 1977
Value Added Taxes Act 1994

Codes of Practice

British Codes of Advertising and Sales Promotion
ITC Code of Programme Sponsorship

ITC Code of Advertising Standards and Practice
ITC Programme Code
ITC Rules on Advertising Breaks
Radio Authority Advertising and Sponsorship Code
Radio Authority Programme Code

Case Studies

This section contains examples of the issues that can arise in sponsorship. The case studies also demonstrate how successful sponsorship can be. In some cases the names and details have been changed to preserve confidentiality.

1. UNDER-FUNDING

1.1 The sponsor has not allocated sufficient budget over and above the buying price to exploit the opportunity properly

There can be two reasons for this:

- the sponsor is unaware of the necessity of additional funds being needed to fully exploit the opportunity.
- the sponsor had funds to buy the sponsorship, but not to exploit it.

The sponsor had a world-wide business. However, its name was not recognised globally since it had grown by acquisition and traded under different names in different countries.

The sponsored party wished to organise a worldwide event and thought that beneficial association could be gained by a global company. The sponsor was very interested in the proposition since it matched its desire to launch its brand globally.

Difficulties arose when it became clear that the project was underfunded. The sponsor took the decision to allocate additional sponsorship monies to ensure the success of the project; partly because it had already invested significant funds and did not wish to see these wasted, and partly because the potential to meet the sponsor's objectives had already shown itself to be valid.

Lessons learnt

The sponsor must satisfy itself that the budgetary requirements are realistic; a sole sponsor should require access to the sponsored parties' books of account. The sponsor must also consider whether its own budget will allow it to maximise the promotional opportunities available from the event. Failure to do so will be frustrating and ultimately lead to both parties being disillusioned, with the event either having to be cancelled or the sponsor having to provide considerable further funding, which may not be justified by the benefits received.

1.2 The sponsor has negotiated such a tough deal that the event organiser cannot afford to put on the event

The cheapest sponsorship deals are not always the best. In this example the sponsor negotiated an extremely tough deal with the organisers of a music festival. Unfortunately, the sponsor had tied the organisers down so much that they could not afford to put the event on and were forced to find other sponsors. This diminished the benefit received.

273

Whilst it is satisfying to negotiate a good sponsorship contract in terms of value for money, it is often not advantageous to pay the rights holder too little to enable the event to be a success. The resulting danger is that the image of the sponsor will suffer. An understanding of the value of the sponsorship needs to be coupled with experience of the cost of staging events.

In cases where the main sponsor accepts that secondary sponsors will also be involved, the main sponsor needs to be realistic about what it will do if the rights holder is unable to find such secondary sponsors. With a deficit of expected income will come the inability to deliver the "product". The main sponsor will then be faced with a decision as to whether additional funds are required in order to protect the original investment.

Sponsorship is a business partnership and parties must work together for a common cause. If objectives are not met relationships are seldom harmonious and mistrust can result.

2. BROADCAST SPONSORSHIP

2.1 Britannia Music and the Brit Awards

This example illustrates how broadcast sponsorship can be used to enhance an existing event sponsorship.

Britannia Music Company has sponsored the Brit Awards since 1987 and has achieved some notable success in terms of its marketing objectives. However, the name association between Britannia and the Brits—*The Brit Awards sponsored by Britannia Music*—has always presented a problem, especially in terms of media editorial usage.

In 1995, Britannia recognised the benefits of allocating additional funds to purchase the broadcast sponsorship. Not only did this decision ensure that Britannia was not overshadowed by another broadcast sponsor, its original event sponsorship was also enhanced through a guaranteed presence across the ITV network.

Britannia received opening/closing and break bumper credits. The company believed it important for viewing interest and recall that its sequences matched the tone and presentation for the event broadcast itself, with an animated award figure presenting the sponsor message. The creative treatment is used by Carlton TV today as an example to potential broadcast sponsors.

Independent research undertaken in February 1998 to establish sponsorship awareness revealed an impressive 38 per cent spontaneous awareness and total awareness of 55 per cent. The broadcast sponsorship is believed to be one of the major elements within the marketing programme that contributed to this result.

Although it required an additional investment, Britannia had proved that broadcast sponsorship of an event which it already sponsors can provide significant additional benefits.

2.2 BAFTA Sponsorship

A leading high street bank successfully sponsored the BAFTA awards for three years. The bank's sponsorship objectives were clearly identified from the outset and, of these, television coverage was fundamentally important.

Although previous television coverage figures were available, the bank took the view that it should protect itself against a possible fall in the length of broadcasts and thus, a drop in numbers of viewers. The direct relationship between the cost of the sponsorship and the levels of television coverage was unavoidable and, as a result, a formula was worked out which allowed the level of sponsorship fee to drop if the length of exposure fell from the expected levels.

Some rights holders would resist any correlation between the sponsorship fee and the amount of television coverage, especially if the latter is beyond their control. However, the stronger the rights holder, the more ability it has to negotiate a guaranteed amount of television coverage which should satisfy his sponsor.

3. CONFLICTING RIGHTS

3.1 Lucozade and the Football Association

In this example, the FA objected to Alan Shearer's appearance in a television commercial for the soft drink Lucozade on the basis that it implied an endorsement by the England team as a whole, in breach of the FA's exclusive contract with Coca-Cola.

Lucozade and Shearer argued that the advertisement was purely an individual endorsement by Shearer. England players can make individual product endorsements, but not as part of the England team.

Although he wore his England strip in the advertisement, and there were images of other players in the background, Lucozade argued that Shearer is not prevented by the FA contract from wearing an England shirt and that the background figures were not England players. Nevertheless, there was clearly a question over Lucozade's intention to imply a connection with the England team.

3.2 Umbro and McManaman

Umbro, the England football kit sponsor, sought a High Court injunction to prevent Liverpool player, Steve McManaman, from signing a sponsorship contract with a rival boot manufacturer, Nike. McManaman fought the action on the basis that he had not had any legal advice when he signed the initial agreement with Umbro and that his contract constituted an unreasonable restraint of trade and is therefore void and unenforceable.

Contractual Solutions

Almost all conflicts with other sponsors are avoidable through effective contracts.

Access

One of the most effective ways of controlling ambush marketing is by controlling the environment in and around the event. The event organiser has the ability to control and regulate its own event and the sponsor should make sure they use it.

The majority of events that may prove attractive to potential sponsors are staged in defined and controlled venues enabling event owners to control admission, photo and broadcasting opportunities, and souvenir stalls and hoardings in and around the venue. Where the event takes place in a public place it will be more difficult to control, but the event owner should at least be required to control key sites such as start and finish lines, control the angle of TV cameras so that the offending advertisements are not seen on TV, and co-operate with local authorities and the police to, for example, obtain an air exclusion zone over the venue. The contract should:

- require the sponsee to have a carefully structured enforcement plan in place
- require the sponsee to take legal and other action to defend the sponsor's rights
- include a right for the sponsor to take action itself if the sponsee fails to do so
- require the sponsee to control the billboards in and around the venue and prevent spectators from displaying unwanted advertising banners

Other Controls

In addition to controlling access the sponsor should require the sponsee:

- to control other sponsors or companies who have a connection with the event by placing them on notice in their contracts of the specific rights granted to the sponsor and making other contracts subordinate to the main sponsor's contract
- to include appropriate restrictions in players' contracts and other third party contracts
- to provide for a clear form of dispute resolution and require the sponsee to bear the costs
- provide through its broadcast contract preferential opportunities for the event sponsor to become sponsor of the broadcast and to have first option rights over TV advertising time surrounding and during the event broadcast
- prevent competitors obtaining official merchandise containing their branding by providing in its contract with official merchandisers that they cannot supply rivals of the official sponsors

4. Arts Sponsorship on the Internet

4.1 Mitsubishi Electric PC Division's Sponsorship of Ryuichi Sakamoto Concert

Mitsubishi Electric's PC Division sponsored Ryuichi Sakamoto's London concert at the Royal Festival Hall in July 1996. The sponsorship included television advertising and an extensive joint press campaign and was an extension of the relationship in Japan between the artist and Mitsubishi Electric, which included Sakamoto appearing in the company's television advertisements.

The sponsorship also profiled Mitsubishi Electric's state of the art computer technology as it facilitated the first live broadcast on the Internet of a classical concert in the United Kingdom.

Objectives of the Sponsorship

Mitsubishi sees Sakamoto as an artist who is wholly relevant to the company because of his interest in advanced technology. Through this sponsorship, Mitsubishi therefore aimed to demonstrate their Internet expertise, linking this with

Sakamoto's incorporation of technology in his compositions. At the same time, the sponsorship reflected Mitsubishi's Japanese roots and the global nature of its business. By sponsoring the concert. Mitsubishi reinforced its association with Sakamoto in Japan and introduced it in the United Kingdom.

Requirement from the Sponsor

Mitsubishi ran the live Internet broadcast, which had a worldwide audience of 38,000, from the Royal Festival Hall and was responsible for ensuring that the transmission was of high quality. The concert was broadcast over the Internet using Apricot PCs and servers and was linked to the Festival Hall's own sound system with a live ISDN link back to the Offices of Mitsubishi Electric's Internet Services Division and on to the world. The transmission was enhanced by digital photographs taken during the concert and scanned onto the Internet. The ISDN line now remains at the Royal Festival Hall for use by other concert promoters.

Mitsubishi helped to promote the concert as part of its advertising campaign. By including details of the event and the Internet broadcast in a television advertisement featuring Sakamoto, the concert was given a profile and reach which could not have been achieved without such a partnership.

Requirement from the Sponsored Party

Serious Ltd, International music producers, worked with the South Bank Centre to facilitate the live audio Internet broadcast. Serious also made it possible for Mitsubishi Electric to set up product displays in key areas around the Royal Festival Hall to heighten the public's awareness of the company's association with the concert.

Mitsubishi was given 50 complimentary top-price guest tickets and was offered extra tickets at a concessionary rate. Free copies of the concert programme were also made available to guests. The programme included a full page advertisement placed by Mitsubishi free of charge. The organisers ensured that the sponsor was credited prominently on all print items produced for the concert. This included 1,000 fly posters; 9,000 leaflets; 1,500 concert programmes; and advertisements in *Time Out, The Guardian* and *The Independent.*

A reception for Mitsubishi was organised by Serious in the Chelsfield Room at the Royal Festival Hall for key staff and their business contacts. Mitsubishi requested that the reception should follow a Japanese theme so Japanese caterers were used throughout the evening. To reinforce this, Mitsubishi also presented all female guests with a saki set. The organisers liaised with the U.K. agent for Sakamoto to attend a reception after the concert to meet key representatives from Mitsubishi, including the President of Mitsubishi Electric PC Division, as well as members of the arts and trade press.

Evidence of success and achievement

The event created considerable interest from the media and received coverage both in trade and arts press. During the concert itself the website was accessed by over 20,000 people subsequently increasing to in excess of 38,000 hits worldwide. These figures are in addition to a live concert audience of nearly 3,000.

Mitsubishi was delighted that its association with Sakamoto had been extended to a U.K. audience and a sold out concert hall but particularly that it had been able to obtain further exposure of such a partnership through the Internet. The global nature of this medium enhanced the sponsorship and its objectives.

INDEX

(All references are to paragraph number)

Trademark registration
merchandising
abandonment of, 6–47
Elvis Presley, 6–42
generally, 6–42—6–44
specially protected marks, 6–45
timetable, 6–46
sponsorship, 1–56
Trademarks
endorsement, 7–29—7–30
merchandising
generally, 6–40—6–41
licensing of, 6–22
registration of, 6–42—6–47
sponsorship
creation, 1–54
generally, 1–53
passing off, 1–57
protection, 1–55
registration, 1–56

Trophies, 4–29

Unauthorised endorsement
generally, 7–11, 7–16
Molschenbacher, 7–14
Olivia Newton-John & Maybelline,
7–15
Tom Waits & Frito-Lay, 7–12
*Vanna White & The Wheel of
Fortune,* 7–13
Undertakings, 9–34—9–35

"Virtual" advertising, 3–55
Voice-overs, 7–07—7–08

Warranties
generally, 9–36
sponsorship, 5–33